THE MEASURE OF THE AGES

CHARLES DICKENS AND EARLY VICTORIAN ENGLAND

Designed and produced by
ADPRINT LIMITED
LONDON

CHARLES DICKENS

AND EARLY VICTORIAN ENGLAND

R. J. CRUIKSHANK

with 64 illustrations in photogravure

37 text illustrations in line

and 14 Isotype charts

in colour

LONDON

SIR ISAAC PITMAN AND SONS, LTD.

FIRST PUBLISHED 1949

by Sir Isaac Pitman & Sons, Ltd.

SIR ISAAC PITMAN & SONS, LTD.
PITMAN HOUSE, PARKER STREET, KINGSWAY, LONDON, W.C.2
THE PITMAN PRESS, BATH
PITMAN HOUSE, LITTLE COLLINS STREET, MELBOURNE
27 BECKETTS BUILDINGS, PRESIDENT STREET, JOHANNESBURG

ASSOCIATED COMPANIES
PITMAN PUBLISHING CORPORATION
2 WEST 45TH STREET, NEW YORK
205 WEST MONROE STREET, CHICAGO
SIR ISAAC PITMAN & SONS (CANADA), LTD.
(INCORPORATING THE COMMERCIAL TEXT BOOK COMPANY)
PITMAN HOUSE, 381-383 CHURCH STREET, TORONTO

Printed in Great Britain by Love & Malcomson Ltd., Redhill
D9—(G. 314)

CONTENTS

ILLUSTRATIONS IN PHOTOGRAVURE

ILLUSTRATIONS IN LINE

ACKNOWLEDGMENTS

Plate 1 is reproduced by gracious permission of H.M. the King. The author is also grateful to the following for permission to reproduce plates: The Trustees of the British Museum (Pls. 2a, 18a, 18b, 19b); the Director of the Victoria and Albert Museum (Pls. 2b, 22a, 22b, 24b, 24c, 28b, 29a); the Library Committee of the Corporation of London (Pls. 5b, 19a); the Trustees of the National Portrait Gallery (Pls. 9a, 9b, 9c, 9d, 27, 28a); His Grace the Duke of Wellington (Pl. 11a); the City Art Gallery, Manchester (Pl. 11b); the Parker Gallery, London (Pls. 13a, 13b); Walker's Galleries, London (Pls. 14a, 14b); the Museum and Art Gallery Committee of the Corporation of Birmingham (Pl. 15a); the Trustees of the National Gallery (Pls. 15b, 20b, 23); the Trustees of the Tate Gallery (Pls. 20a, 21, 24a); Lady Anderson (Pl. 17a).

LINE ILLUSTRATIONS: The Director of the Victoria and Albert Museum (p. 2); the Trustees of the British Museum (pp. 5, 71, 197); the Proprietors of *Punch* (pp. 8, 102, 106, 117, 122, 129, 140); the Trustees of the National Portrait Gallery (p. 211).

The author would also like to thank the following for permission to quote copyright material: Messrs. Longmans, Green & Co., (*Lord Shaftesbury* by J. L. and Barbara Hammond; *British History in the Nineteenth Century* by G. M. Trevelyan); The Macmillan Company (*The Emergence of Modern America* by Allan Nevins); Messrs. Constable & Co. (*The History of the Chartist Movement* by Julius West); *The Police Chronicle* (*The English Police* by E. H. Glover); Messrs. John Murray (*Collections and Recollections* by G. W. E. Russell); Ernest Benn, Ltd. (*The Story of an African Farm* by Olive Schreiner); Messrs. Hodder and Stoughton (*A Bookman's Letters* by William Robertson Nicoll); H.M. Stationery Office (Statistical Abstract for the United Kingdom 1840-54, 1851-65 and 1863-77, published as Command Papers).

PICTORIAL CHARTS IN COLOUR

DESIGNED BY THE ISOTYPE INSTITUTE

following page 308

PART I

GREAT EXPECTATIONS

CHAPTER ONE

WAIF'S PROGRESS

What *was* the Age of Dickens? Charles Dickens was born in 1812, the year of the Retreat from Moscow—and of Britain's absent-minded war with the United States. He died in 1870, the year of the Franco-Prussian War. He was not an old man when he died, but, between these two dates, what a span of history! Look at the books on the shelves, student, and turn pale—rows on rows of them, commemorating great men and great happenings within that spread of years; and many of them very dull reading. The mind blurs, the heart falters, the back aches in sympathy, one groans compassionately, thinking of all the labouring professors, the devoted biographers, the faithful old eyes that have grown dim among the archives. It is a cruel, it is a killing period, with its great mounds of histories, and lives, and memoirs, its mountains of journals, newspapers, periodicals, State papers, memoranda, not to speak of its music, paintings, playbills; all its precious scraps and its indispensable rubbish. Truth, that shy Truth, that we run panting after through the halls of State and the drawing-rooms, often turns out to have secreted herself, after all, in an old trunk in the attic. One begins to suspect, too, that the real point about a number of mighty transactions of modern times has been lost through the early morning charwoman tipping out the wastepaper baskets of the eminent. Who knows what secrets have vanished for ever with the Princess Lieven's unsorted laundry bills?

Let me see, it was six thousand separate and individual scraps of Palmerston's papers—with the fading of ink increasing the terrors of the worst handwriting in Europe—that a distinguished historian told me he

CHARLES DICKENS AT THE AGE OF TWENTY-SIX
Pen drawing by George Cruikshank, 1838
Victoria and Albert Museum

had pored over during one green summer at Broadlands. Then there is that American scholar who has spent more than twenty years of his life in the study of Shelley's thirty years. And there is that other American who has been engaged, for I know not how many years, in brooding upon the old *Athenaeum*; I mean the literary review which James Silk Buckingham founded in 1828, not the great club in Pall Mall where the bishops' gaiters twinkle up and down the stairs. Where to start counting the pebbles on this beach? And who might hope to find a rainbow shell that these vigilant eyes have missed? Who could aspire to rival in learning and understanding the great French historian Elie Halévy? Who could bring a more humane passion to the industrial theme than the Hammonds? Who could comprehend the economic forces of the time better than Clapham or C. R. Fay? Who could be better informed than Woodward? Who could be more amusing than Lytton Strachey?

Luckily for this writer, the hero he has chosen was, as Santayana said of him, "a waif and utterly disinherited". That is a human condition which has its advantages. Waifs pursue their own ways through life, threading the solid world of statesmen, generals, bishops, bankers, philosophers and economists, twisting and slipping through that world like quicksilver. And the disinherited, while they are naturally hazy about dates, often possess a poetic sense of the inmost colour and secret rhythms of their time. "Perhaps, properly speaking, he had no *ideas* on any subject," Santayana went on: "what he had was a vast sympathetic participation in the daily life of mankind; and what he saw of ancient institutions made him hate them, as needless sources of oppression, misery, selfishness and rancour."

Could not one then, perhaps, take heart from this to make some kind of clearing in the choking undergrowth—and then follow the waif's progress through the Victorian wild woods? Could one not make a start with the hero himself at 1837? That was the year when the waif awakened to find himself famous, when the disinherited came into a title as grand as a duke's. For Charles Dickens the year of Pickwick was the beginning of the Age of Dickens. Before that he had certainly never dreamed of giving his name to an Age, nor of being a pillar of an Age, nor of having anything to do with an Age except to live in it as best he might. There are few things more touching among the oddities of authorship than his astonishment at finding *Sketches by Boz* listed under the heading "Literature" in a journal of the time. Wandering the streets in a delighted daze, he asked: Am I a writer, an *author*? Something of even greater moment in the world than a good Parliamentary reporter?

And, then—but see! Macaulay's schoolboy, that classic little prig, is making outraged signals to us down the corridors of time. "Eighteen thirty-seven", he pipes up, "is a memorable date in British history because . . . "

CHAPTER TWO

A PEAL OF BELLS

So here by our side stands Charles Greville, obliging and indiscreet. Creevey totters on his last legs. The inexhaustible Crabb Robinson is in the wings. All is prepared. We address ourselves to the page, and inscribe our theme—"Accession of Queen Victoria, 1837".

At once, a pleasant, old-fashioned mirage forms on the paper, a Christmas-card image of a kind out of favour in these times. It is a picture we have all seen at one time or another, in the coffee-rooms of country inns, and in the drawing-rooms of rectories in the green depths of Somerset. There she is—the slender young girl, a very young and touching figure, little more than a child; in her white night-wrap, looking a ghost in that early morning light; still half-asleep; in a trance, in a dream, as she stretches her hand out to receive the first kiss of homage as Queen of England. The circumstances are all romantic—the earliest sunshine of midsummer morning spreading over the gardens of Kensington Palace—the great personages who had driven in their landau from the old King's death-bed at Windsor to Kensington through the shortest night of the year—all that tugging of bells and stamping around in the yard to awaken the sleepy palace; and then Howley, the turkeycock Archbishop, gobbling with chagrin that doors will not fly open at once at the apparition of mighty Canterbury in his canonicals. And, in the end, his explosion when the pert little maid says that the Princess is "in a sweet sleep" and is not to be roused. Was there ever such a fairy-tale scene from the story-book of English history?

History would be a much more enjoyable occupation if it could be confined to calendar art, to the pictures that relate a graceful anecdote. But, truth to tell, most of the emotions, the chivalrous and romantic feelings, attaching to this particular scene have grown up around it since. It was a very tarnished crown that the fairy-tale Queen inherited. Her wicked uncles, particularly the wickedest and cleverest of them, George the Fourth, had made such heavy drafts upon the people's loyalty that there were, so to speak, but a few farthings left in the till for the child to set up her housekeeping. The great boors of the House of Hanover, the Dukes with their thick German accents, their dismal mistresses, and their unhidden distaste for the ways of the English, had exhausted the affections of the people for the Royal family. When Radical working-men met in the upper rooms of taverns to smoke a pipe and drink their ale, hard

DELAPORTE'S PRINT-SHOP IN THE BURLINGTON ARCADE
Pen drawing from Richard Doyle's Diary, 1840
British Museum

names were used, names that would not look well under that picture in the country rectory. The rosy-cheeked young Queen was called a parasite—her coronation would be the last of such mummery and flummery in the old Abbey—her court, with its stars, ribbons and toadies, would make a fine bonfire on the day of wrath. Old men, who remembered the terrors of 1792, repeated Burke's lament for the fair Queen of France and changed but one word of it: "But the age of chivalry is gone. That of sophisters, œconomists and calculators has succeeded; and the glory of England is extinguished for ever." She who was so young, pretty, innocent and gay must suffer for the heaped-up load of sins and follies of the Four Georges and the Fourth William.

The early years of her reign were to be full of troubles. The Chartist agitation began in the year of Victoria's accession, and its storms burst over the land in 1838. There were riots in Birmingham and in half a dozen other cities. On the other side of politics, loyal Tories murmured against the Queen because of the intrigue of the Whig Ladies of the Bedchamber which robbed Peel of office in 1839, and all charitable, decent, kindly people, of Blue politics or Buff politics, were scandalised by the Court's behaviour to Lady Flora Hastings. Upon Lady Flora, suffering from a fatal internal malady, had been visited the malice of patrician ladies who ran about the town sniggering that she was big with child. Was the Queen in any way to blame? The victim, in her dying hour, absolved her. But it was remarked that the Queen's absolution was, in turn, granted to the evil-speakers. That year (1839), at the Ascot races, a company of Tory peeresses, with a duchess at their head, hissed the Queen.

Philosophers, remembering Versailles, reflected that it is frivolity rather than cruel tyranny that, in the end, brings about revolutions; that a society is brought to despair of itself through the insensitiveness of the young, the proud, the light of heart. How strange a thing it is that Victoria, who stands in our history as the symbol of responsibility and obligation, clothed in the moral severity of her widow's weeds, could once have been thought a reincarnation of Marie Antoinette!

The ravens of doom were croaking in those opening years of Victoria's long reign. In politics, a sullen disillusion had set in after the brief ardours of the Reform Bill. The Whigs in office proved no more humane and enlightened, and something less efficient, than the Tories. The sprightly cynicism of Melbourne was less tolerable than the honest stupidity of Wellington. Statesmen were without ideals, the Church without vision, the Crown without honour, and the common people without hope. The discontents of the working classes were so great that it was not Engels alone who believed the country was bound to be engulfed in the bloodiest of revolutions. Thoughtful men shivered at the prospect before them. How could they dream, Tories or Whigs or Radicals or Chartists, that they were standing in a dawn, not in a dusk—that it was already *here*, that it had begun—the Victorian age, that renowned and preposterous glory? What an age it proved to be!—coming up out of all the ages with a noise of thunder, the Victorian Time with its driving pistons of physical energy, its rushing trains, its iron monsters floating on the water, its furnaces, forges, counting-houses and slums; its ripping of the belly of the earth to get coal and iron, the secret jewels that gave it power and dominion; its fertility in scientific discovery and inventions, its command of Nature; its piling-up of great possessions; with money, money, money pouring in as its commerce spread to all seas, all lands.

Who could have predicted such an explosion of vitality? How does such a release of energy come about? What combination of elements caused it? The creative forces of that age manifested themselves in nearly every sphere of human activity. Economic determinism may very well explain the iron-master and the prince of soap-boilers, but how account for the appearance of geniuses so various as Darwin, Newman, Disraeli, Faraday, Mill and Robert Browning? If one thinks only of the money-bags, the ships loading up in the harbours, the mines, the forges, the busy railways, and the children swarming in the rookeries, then all seems material, and mechanistic, and doomed. But a new vision comes when one thinks of the great writers, Dickens himself, Thackeray, Emily Brontë, Tennyson, Carlyle and Arnold—and one discovers no simple evolutionary theory that fits. Florence Nightingale, Lister, William Booth, Gladstone—somehow one has to find a framework that will accommodate *them*, as well as Stephenson, Brunel, Paxton, Armstrong. In that age there were triumphs for the spirit of man as grand as the defeats were sordid. One remembers the poets whose dreams bewitch us and inspire us yet. Theirs was an energy, shining and constant as a star's. But what of that other energy, the consuming passion of the age to spread around such ugliness as eye never before witnessed?—creating miles on miles of desolation; the building of cities in Gehenna; with never-ending rows of little houses bearing the mark of the plague upon them. Who can measure the power of that age to inflict suffering, or, through the agency of anaesthesia and the ministry of its healers, to relieve, as no other age did, the burden of the world's pain? Its intellectual curiosity, its moral obliquities, its economic anarchy, its political wisdom, its culture, its cruelty, its sensitiveness—all these were of a piece. But, beyond all things, its driving energy, so wide in its diffusion—its *daemonic* energy—cause us now to stand and gape at it.

In reading many of the life stories of men of mark born in the early years of the century, men who pursued employments as diverse, say, as politics and architecture, railway-building and novel-writing, one has a sense of their being possessed by a spirit that would never let them rest. The daemon on their backs beat them and drove them mercilessly. Success itself, when it came, came flourishing fresh whips and flails. The man of commerce who had built a splendid fortune worked with all the desperation of a bankrupt. The professional man renewed his boyhood's devouring ambitions, with the triumphs of his maturity. Men and women of all conditions behaved in those days as though they were under the compulsions of a new territory, frontiersmen, clearers of the wilderness, rather than as dwellers in a land of ancient renown. The daemon drove them savagely on and on until their burned-out bodies dropped by the side of the rushing road. This fierce concentration of physical and nervous energy—with the big guns of genius and talent going off on all sides—remains for me the prime mystery of the Age of Dickens. It staggers, it stuns. It fascinates. And no one has explained it to my satisfaction.

One word of warning. Let us at least do the men and women of the Age of Dickens the honour of not regarding them as solemn bores and humourless prigs. Passion was theirs, and fantasy—the dark awareness of sin, which, by contrast, heightens all the colours of life—and a glorious release of laughter and nonsense. There comes down the years the voice of Carlyle prophesying woe—but listen to that other voice, that equally authentic mid-Victorian voice, singing, "Far and few, far and few are the lands where the Jumblies live". There is a poet hymning, "One equal temper of heroic hearts", and another poet chanting, "So turn not pale, beloved snail, but come and join the dance"—and both are immortal. We can turn from George Eliot's Dorothea Casaubon, who had by heart whole passages of Jeremy Taylor and Pascal, to that sublimer figure, Mrs. Gamp, saying, "If I could afford to lay all my feller creeturs out for nothink, I would gladly do it; sich is the love I bear 'em". In dipping into the volumes of Hansard for the fifties we may quail at the four-hour orations on momentous nothings, but we can rejoice for ever in the dazzling wit of Disraeli.

"A master rum 'un" was Fletcher the fisherman's description of Edward FitzGerald. The age abounded in rum 'uns. Eccentrics were esteemed—the quirks and quiddities of odd characters treasured. Was there ever a House of Commons man less conventional than Charles Buller whom Peel rebuked for his incorrigible frivolity and who once invented and published an uproarious imaginary debate in the French Chamber of Deputies on the Queen of England's fancy-dress ball? Was there ever a more engaging original character than Monckton Milnes of the Heaven and Hell Amalgamation Society?

Above all things, a sketch of the period linked with the name of Dickens, however superficial it might be, could not very well leave out the elements of the grotesque, the Gothic and the phantasmagoric. Nightmares stalked "the cold wet shelterless midnight streets". What was the atmosphere which surrounded the most successful age in Britain's history? It was the fog that spreads through the pages of *Bleak House*, choking, blinding, befuddling. It was the dark crimes and prison stenches in *Oliver Twist, Little Dorrit* and *Great Expectations*. It was the opium hallucinations of Jasper. And all round about prosperous London lie the snaky coils of the sinister river that dominates *Our Mutual Friend*.

CHAPTER THREE

PICKWICK'S YEAR

The image on the page dissolves. The young fairy-tale princess standing in the early light of morning is replaced by another shape out of 1837, a portly angel in tights and gaiters, with twinkling spectacles, a virgin innocence of soul, and a power of giving dignity to the ridiculous and investing the cheap and vulgar with a certain sublimity. It was Pickwick's year as well as Victoria's year. Even in days when politics make a great stir all the people do not talk politics all the time. The private life mercifully flows on beneath the surface. Nobody knew then, nobody will ever know, if Pickwick were a Whig or a Tory, if he stood for the Reform Bill or against it, and there is no evidence that his Theory of Tittlebats was affected by a reading of Jeremy Bentham, Adam Smith, Tom Paine, William Godwin or William Cobbett, though the old fellow had inside him a strong fire against injustice, and held stern views on the roguery of the law. Pickwick's one excursion into politics showed a mugwumpery that any good party man must find shocking. It took place in the High Street of Eatanswill, during the by-election in that borough. The crowd filling the street was hot, sweating, primed with beer, hooting, cheering; yelling cries and counter-cries. On the balcony of the Town Arms Inn stood an orator, sawing the air, bawling, but inaudible. I suspect he was that character we all know so well, "the leather-lunged chap sent down by Headquarters to help the candidate out". It was the old-time election—the free and independent voters making their enlightened choice through bribery and corruption, rowdiness, strong drink and horseplay. Caught up by the excitement of the scene, Pickwick let out a "Hurrah", and then explained to his nervous companion, Snodgrass, that "it is always best to do on these occasions what the mob do". "But suppose there were two mobs?" inquired Snodgrass. "Shout with the loudest," recommended Pickwick.

To use such solemn terms as "social significance" or "political implication" about *The Pickwick Papers* seems a little humourless. Cannot we be content to be happy in the book's happiness, in the enjoyment of its gaiety and high spirits? Yet if we are to take Charles Dickens as our symbolic character, we cannot very well overlook one significant aspect of *Pickwick*: that it brought upon the stage—indeed full into the centre of the stage of life and letters—a great writer who had sprung from that mysterious, silent, almost unknown layer of society, the British lower middle class. How few books have come out of those back streets! Yet the lower middle class has given us two writers who have nothing in common except their radiant genius—John Keats and Charles Dickens. The back streets might well have reason to be proud, if they were capable of any collective pride, of such a novelist and such a poet. For this, the world owes the British lower middle class a salute. It is a class that has been overlooked by most political and social historians who, whether they are Marxist, Liberal or Conservative, are usually public-school and University fellows. Dickens was not a proletarian novelist. He was less a proletarian novelist than the Disraeli who wrote *Sybil.* He was certainly not an "upper class" novelist, as Thackeray was—Thackeray, who, as George Saintsbury remarked, was always conscious of the footman behind his chair. Dickens was incapable of competing with George Eliot in writing for the intellectual, Darwin-and-Mill middle class, or of competing with Trollope in depicting the squire-and-parson, riding-to-hounds class. He had a universe of his own to explore; a thousand nameless figures to christen, a host of silent types to make audible. From the point of view of lower-middle-class literary eugenics, Dickens was an almost perfect specimen. He was the grandson of a footman and a housemaid; he was the child of a feckless clerk and a shabby-genteel mother. He was acutely sensitive about his origin. That is understandable. For it was a snobbish age, and, like Pip, Dickens wanted to be thought a gentleman. He never forgave his mother for the wretchedness to which he was exposed in boyhood. To the end of his days he suffered torture when he remembered his early handicaps: the interrupted schooling; his father's imprisonment for debt; the "horrible nightmare" of his being put to work as a child in the blacking factory at Charing Cross. But is it hard-hearted to suggest that all this has been a little overdone by those whom Mr. Hesketh Pearson has called the Dickolators? It is true that his abandonment to misery and humiliation left wounds on his mind that never healed. But great art does not arise from the survival of the fittest. It is often the oyster's pearl—the glorious consequence of a private misery desperately working itself out on paper in order to keep this side of madness. Happy, well-cared-for, sun-bathed children seldom become great poets and novelists. It was the remembrance of the shame and the wretchedness that gave the world such magical pages as the eleventh chapter of *David Copperfield*. "When I tread the old ground, I do not wonder that I seem to see and pity, going on before me, an innocent romantic boy, making his imaginative world out of such strange experiences and sordid things." The fairies came to his christening. One said, "My gift is early hardship; as a child he shall know the ugliness of life." The second said, "My gift is his abandonment; he shall be a castaway." The third, "His school shall be the streets." The fourth, "I will give him a sensitive spirit, so that he may feel early pain sharply, and

MR. PICKWICK WAITING IN THE ATTORNEY'S OFFICE
Etching by Hablot K. Browne from the first edition of "Pickwick", 1837

remember it vividly all his life." The last fairy said, "I will give him genius. Out of the hardship shall come the power to live a hundred lives. The castaway shall have the freedom of the whole world of men and women. The education of the streets shall provide him with boundless treasures of comic and tragic invention. The humiliations of the child shall fertilise the imagination of the poet."

The shifts, subterfuges and hazards of his childhood—the bitter desertion—the knowledge of all sorts and conditions of men that he picked up as a boy clerk in a lawyer's office, and as a boy reporter dashing about the country on the heels of the great—the privilege of finding *Humphry Clinker* and *The Arabian Nights* for himself when a tiny child—was it not from all this that there came the charm, pathos, humour, terror and imaginative power of the novels? He was a waif in that dream world of the dragons and hippogriffs of the low life of the early nineteenth century! He was disinherited at a time when the old European society was breaking up, and the feudal oaks were being pulled up by their roots. What more could we ask for the making of our greatest novelist than that he should be brought up by hand by Life, the hard stepmother?

The writer who would seem to merit sympathy for his upbringing is the traditional rival of Dickens, Thackeray—well-bred Thackeray of the long, illustrious Anglo-Indian line, with his warm and sensitive heart, and his power of writing the most melodious familiar prose, with its lovely trailing cadences; but so limited in his range of observation, cribbed and confined in the narrow square mile of Clubland, knowing all the right people who, being dry and loveless, are always the wrong people for a poet or novelist, torturing himself by chopping up dreary snobs and mocking at footmen, all for lack of a wider range of subjects. The good fortune of Dickens was that his experiences gave him access to that wide world which lay between the proletariat and the commercial and professional middle classes. Its frontiers were not sharply drawn. Failures among the upper middle classes took quiet refuge among its shadows. The shabby-genteel and the decayed gentlewomen slipped down gently into its enfolding greyness. Artisans and working-class folk who had "improved themselves" moved up easily into it. It was Radical but it was not revolutionary. It had a strong sense of property. It was intensely respectable. I am afraid that, like the good people in Dickens, it often showed a "holier than thou" attitude. No matter how poor it became, it jealously cherished its pretensions of being a cut above the proletariat, whom it thought to be dirty, immoral, drunken, profane, comical and potentially murderous. The small shopkeepers, such as Snagsby and his neighbours in Cook's Court, the blacksmiths like Joe Gargery, the barbers like Poll Sweedlepipe, the solicitors' clerks like Guppy and like Wemmick, the little engineers like Daniel Doyce, the general factotums like Pancks, the undertakers like Mould, and all that swarming miscellany of shabby, sometimes seedy, types who would have been mortally offended at being confused with the working classes, were not likely to be found in a Chartist procession. Dickens, their spokesman in literature, shared with the writer of *Coriolanus* a strong dislike of "the mob". There is little sympathy with labouring men shown in the grim realism of the brick-kiln scenes in *Bleak House*—"Your master", said her husband, muttering an imprecation with slow emphasis, "will break your neck, if you meddle with wot don't concern you." Disraeli's account of the boy Devilsdust in *Sybil* contains a far deeper sympathy with the proletariat than is to be found even in *Hard Times*. Dickens's feeling for the poor and the under-dog crystallises around such a figure as the clerk, Bob Cratchit; and the pictures of the Cratchit family are among the best and most tenderly drawn studies of lower-middle-class life in all his books; but you would not have found the Cratchits on Kennington Common in 1848.

This was a class that often held the balance of power at general elections, but it never seemed to succeed in getting direct representation for itself in the House of Commons, for neither Victorian Liberals nor Tories would choose candidates from its ranks, and it never organised and made fast and hard its strength in trade unions. It thought of the aristocracy as being corrupt and sensual, of the Church of England as the preserve of the upper classes; it had a morbid fear of the Catholic Church; but it found atheists and agnostics shocking and disreputable. So it tended to be Nonconformist. It was pacifist, it was individualistic, it was ignorant, it was conventional. It preferred aspirations to systems of thought. Its political outlook might be defined—and this can be said with no intent to sneer—in Tiny Tim's prayer, "God bless us every one". Its education, before 1870, was obtained at little hedge schools, or it went without any. It was almost devoid of artistic sensibility. It admired crude pictures that "told a story", it liked the most ugly architectural styles, as is shown in its chapels. It had the Puritan suspicion that the sensuality of art is a snare of the Tempter; it was distressed by the representation of the nude, even in reproductions from the old masters; the only composers it found acceptable were Handel, Mendelssohn and Haydn (*The Creation*); and it was indifferent to philosophers and metaphysicians, and to mystics. Nothing pleased it more than to be complimented on its respectability—as politicians always did after it became enfranchised, though, whether they were of the Left or the Right, they preferred its votes to its company. It was a class that disapproved of the attitude towards sex of the classes above it and of the classes below it. Not for it the Dionysian ecstasy, not for it the Rabelaisian humours, not for it the pagan nor the Latin approach to the central mystery of mortal life. Most manifestations of the sex instinct gave it, indeed, embarrassment. It was a narrow class, it was honest, it was fast-rooted, it was mawkish; it threw up a number of eccentrics, fanciful characters and pathetic characters, queer stunted growths like those trees one sees on a cliff, torn and twisted by the sea-wind, and thwarted in their desire to put on their full regalia of leaves and blossoms. It was, above all, faithful to certain simple standards of conduct.

In the struggles for power of the Victorian times, this grey, amorphous class stood between the mercantile oligarchy and the mutinous proletariat, exercising an influence as the buffer state. Its recoiling from violence, its very mousiness, its indifference to political theory, prevented issues from ever being pushed to extremes. The novels of Dickens present this lower-middle-class world, bathed in the light of his own rare poetry, the tiresome oddities turned into fantasy and immortal humours, the obscure little lives enveloped in a haunting mystery and a wild romanticism. You may find the prejudices, the limitations and the virtues of this class displayed in Dickens as in no other great English writer.

Who is the most attractive and engaging hero in the novels of Charles Dickens? Certainly not the juvenile leads, the young gentlemen or the would-be young gentlemen, Pip, Martin Chuzzlewit, Eugene Wrayburn or even David Copperfield himself. It is the disreputable Dick Swiveller, the lower-middle-class young man, the attorney's clerk, greasy and shabby and drunken, that most attaches the sympathies. Dick Swiveller ranks with Micawber, Sam Weller, Mrs. Gamp and Pecksniff as a creation of the highest imaginative power. The character is drawn with such a god-like understanding that he not merely wins our affections, he contrives in some curious way to increase our respect for the generality of human kind, and, even in his cups, vindicates the dignity of man. Let us look at the shoddy material out of which Dickens created Dick Swiveller. In one of the weekly journals of the time, I came upon this account of the typical attorney's clerk:

> We have the smart young fellow about the East, attired in humble imitation of the swells in the West, in a fall-down black stock with a small pin, *said* to be a diamond, a ditto plain gold one, attached to a small chain, to prevent the diamond one from running away; also, the hat cocked on one side, with "aggrawating curls" pulled and pomatumed down the side of the face to conceal the absence of whiskers. In holiday times, a cigar and a black cane and tassel are indispensable accompaniments to the East-end beau.

This East-end beau was not a very winning figure in his ambitions, his escapades, his debaucheries; in his facetiousness, his horseplay, his amours; in the gatherings of his kind in "the cellars of harmony" to hear endless bawdy songs. Now look at what the genius of Dickens does with Dick Swiveller:

> Last night he had "the sun very strong in his eyes", by which expression he was understood to convey to his hearers in the most delicate manner possible, the information that he had been extremely drunk. "But what", said Mr. Swiveller with a sigh, "what is the odds so long as the fire of soul is kindled at the taper of conwiviality, and the wing of friendship never moults a feather? What is the odds so long as the spirit is expanded by means of rosy wine, and the present moment is the least happiest of our existence?"

He bursts upon the eyes of that Amazon, Sally Brass, "in full freshness as something new and hitherto undreamed of, lighting up the office with scraps of song and merriment, conjuring with inkstands and boxes of wafers, catching three oranges in one hand, balancing stools upon his chin and penknives on his nose, and constantly performing a hundred other feats with equal ingenuity".

Turn to the love story of Dick Swiveller and the Marchioness, that romance of the grubby clerk and the starved little kitchen slut which in its tenderness and compassionate imagination is the finest love story in Dickens, and, it may be argued, one of the half-dozen best love stories in the world.

Their first meeting—what a scene it is! with every stroke delicate, and telling, and restrained.

"Why, how thin you are! What do you mean by it?"
"It an't my fault."
"Could you eat any bread and meat? . . . Yes? Ah! I thought so. Did you ever taste beer?"
"I had a sip of it once," said the small servant.
"Here's a state of things!" cried Mr. Swiveller, raising his eyes to the ceiling. "She *never* tasted it—it can't be tasted in a sip! Why, how old are you?"
"I don't know."

He goes out, and comes back with a boy from the public house who bears in one hand a plate of bread and beef, and in the other a great pot of that aromatic and potent drink of the time called purl.

"There," says he. "First of all, clear that off, and then you'll see what's next."
The plate was soon empty. "Next," said Dick, handing the purl, "take a pull at that; but moderate your transports, you know, for you're not used to it. Well, is it good?"
"Oh! isn't it?"

Then he falls to teaching her cribbage, which she soon learnt tolerably well, for she was sharp-witted.

"Now," said Mr. Swiveller, putting two sixpences into a saucer, and trimming the wretched candle, when the cards had been cut and dealt, "those are the stakes. If you win, you get 'em all. If I win, I get 'em. To make it seem more real and pleasant, I shall call you the Marchioness, do you hear?"
The small servant nodded.
"Then, Marchioness," said Mr. Swiveller, "fire away."
The Marchioness, holding her cards very tight in both hands, considered which to play, and Mr. Swiveller, assuming the gay and fashionable air which such society required, took another pull at the tankard, and waited for her lead.

That is Dickens's lower-middle-class hero, as chivalrous as Edward Chester, and a hundred times more real.

One sees in Dickens a passionate absorption and saturation in his especial *scene*, his lower-middle-class scene, a power of discovering endless riches in ugly commonplaces. Above all, there is in him, as Santayana said, a vitality of friendship, that serves as substitute for religion, aesthetics, morals, economics and political theory. The whole of Dickens might be called the saga of those people who were, and are, the permanent non-governing class.

Pickwick was a celestial accident. There was this lively young Parliamentary reporter, who had displayed considerable spirit in writing magazine articles that hit off London characters, city clerks, vestrymen, landladies and the like. And there was at that time a fashion in books about the adventures of sportsmen, their jaunts and jollities, slangy, racy pages about Nimrods and Corinthians. What more likely than that the youth who had written *Sketches by Boz* should be asked to do—for "do" is surely the word that Chapman passed to Hall on this occasion—the letterpress to accompany a series of sporting plates by Robert Seymour? He was a master of his craft, Seymour, and commanded so strong a following of his own as to give him the right to reverse the usual relationship between sketchers and scribblers. Seymour proposed to draw the adventures of certain Cockney sportsmen, the Nimrod Club, by field and flood, and the Cockney youth might cudgel his wits to supply the connecting threads. Could there be a more dismal project for a writer? Yet the earliest masterpiece of the Victorian age was made that way. Out of that hopeless scheme came Pickwick and his travelling companions, the discovery of Sam Weller at the White Hart Inn, the inspired lunacies of Jingle, and the rest of the gallery; and it may be that poor Seymour going mad on reaching *The Stroller's Tale*, and shooting himself, was part of the fateful necessity.

Than *Pickwick* there is no other novel that has more in it of the secret dream of the lower middle classes, the unknown people. Romance comes not riding in like the lovely, bare-backed equestrienne, but tumbling in like a clown with chalked face and strawberry nose. But it is romance none the less. Beauty is there, sometimes turned upside down and seen as in distorting mirrors, but it is a beauty living and warm. It is an old dream of town-dwellers that finds fulfilment in *Pickwick*. It starts with the sun dancing on Easter morning and it flows into the long bright Easter of our liberated fancy. We have the notion of rising early on that cloudless morning of our vision to escape from the dingy town before the carts are stirring; to run away from the chimney-pots before they have begun smoking, and from the tongues of the tradesmen before they start clacking. Without passports, permits or licences, we shake ourselves free, and enjoy this visionary relish of reprieve from bills, landlords, neighbours, phobias and politics, we taste the sweetness of the air over April meadows and we travel mile upon mile, far away through that enchanted countryside of ours, that beloved England, which we have read about and have seen in pictures but which we have had so little chance of knowing—journeying in the first freshness of the day and of the year. That note of glad release sounds in many a fine English book from *The Canterbury Tales* to *The History of Mr. Polly*, but in none does it sound more clearly than in *Pickwick*. The members of the Pickwick Club, setting off in the Commodore Coach to make the golden journey to Rochester, were embodiments of these old yearnings to keep high days, and enjoy long holidays, bottled up inside their lower-middle-class countrymen. Snodgrass, Winkle, Tracy Tupman—*they* were not gentlemen by any Whig or Tory interpretation—or Radical or Chartist interpretation. They were *petits bourgeois*, most certainly—and if Flaubert had written the chronicles of the Pickwick Club, how he would have tortured himself, and four generations of his admirers, by the spectacle of their vulgarity, their banality! But Pickwick, the retired tradesman who could never be elected to Brooks's, was a Grand Mogul in the eyes of the lower middle class. He had money, he had leisure, he could seek adventures, he was a free man. Glorious demi-god! He was what every little ironmonger, corn-chandler, stationer, law clerk longed to be—a respectable merchant who had, as they say, "made his little pile" in the City, and was now free to go to Brighton or Leamington Spa or Boulogne or any wild, fantastic place he pleased, there see life, and eat and drink like a lord.

In looking at the Victorian period it is possible to pay too much attention to the big capitalists and not nearly enough to the little capitalists. The lower middle class was the class that was really romantic about money. They viewed it with a dewy innocence of eye. Some clever men of our age have interpreted the novels of Dickens, particularly *Great Expectations* and *Our Mutual Friend*, as parables of the vanity of riches. They see these great books heavy with the sickness, the madness, the feverish hallucinations of wealth. Yet I suspect that if anybody had talked to Dickens and the Dickens characters, and, indeed, to any representatives of the lower middle classes from which these characters sprang, about the corrupting power of money, he would have been met with a resounding chorus of "Fudge! Nonsense!" For Dickens, the Dickens characters and the lower middle classes all loved money—they had a great respect for money—their grievance was that they had not more of it. They would never have any trouble to know what to do with a fortune. The chief thing they would do would be to live happily ever after upon it. "When my ship comes home", was one of their favourite sentimental aspirations. That phrase carried no suggestion of the malaise of money. On the contrary it suggested a three-master, with all its wings spread, gliding into a quiet harbour, loaded with the riches of the East and promising unending delights. The most clear-eyed of all modern critics of Dickens, Mr. George Orwell, has drawn attention to the sensuous comfort, the spiritual exaltation his characters derived from the thought of hard cash. Hence the fairy-tale endings in Dickens, with virtue being rewarded by a handsome legacy or at least an agreeable competence. Dickens, like most of the politically conscious members of the lower middle class, was very fierce against Privilege; he was eager to tear down most old institutions, but he had a strong feeling about the sanctity of cash and private property. In those days one could be a burning revolutionary, hate kings, aristocrats, landlords and priests, but preserve a tender feeling for bankers, merchants and stock-jobbers. One could make money, and not be too scrupulous how one made it, nor care very much about the poverty of working men, and yet still rank as a Radical. That was an odd sort of legacy our Radicals got from the French Revolution.

Pickwick and his travelling companions entered our native folk-lore almost as soon as they were created. *The Posthumous Papers of the Pickwick Club* ran in monthly parts from April 1836 to November 1837, then the whole was brought out in book form. If you had been strolling through the streets of London in the summer of 1837, you would have observed how quickly the topical became the legendary. Wagons named *Sam Weller* rumbled along. The pastry-cooks made and baked Pickwicks, and the sentimental ate him. The Fat Boy was etherealised into sugar and spice. The faces of Tupman, Snodgrass and Winkle grinned from silver spoons. Wardle, most warm-hearted of hosts, was commemorated in silver tankards. Among the "haunts of harmony", the dives, the cider-kitchens, the back-kitchens devoted to beer, tobacco and song, where tradesmen and clerks gathered at night, a Pickwick club or two was founded, and portly men, with a passable likeness to the hero, were figged out in swallow-tails and tights and made presiding officers of the revels.

Pickwick and his friends were symbols of liberation. They had achieved their "competence", and they were free. They were fulfilments of that hope of the lower middle class, a life of leisure.

"Did it ever strike you, on such a morning as this, that drowning would be happiness and peace?" asked the Dismal Man on Rochester Bridge.

"God bless me, no!" said Pickwick, who had been contemplating the charms of nature and sharpening an appetite for breakfast.

"God bless me, no!" echoed the lower middle class, thinking how good a time they too would have when their ships came home.

CHAPTER FOUR

THE ORIGINS

There is another point about *The Pickwick Papers* well worth noting. Its writer went to some pains to make it clear that these adventures had taken place, not in 1836 or 1837, but in 1827, when he was a boy, and when George the Fourth was King. He was precise. "That punctual servant of all work, the sun, had risen and begun to strike a light on the morning of the thirteenth of May, one thousand eight hundred and twenty seven when Mr. Samuel Pickwick burst like another sun from his slumbers, threw open his chamber window, and looked out upon the world beneath."

The first Victorian classic was in truth a Georgian book, it was the book of a very young man remembering his boyhood, as young men of genius like to do. In one sense, the whole of that age was looking back. Old Mr. Weller, mottled of face, and wrapped round by waistcoats, shawls and capes, in layers on layers, like a big, redolent onion, might himself have been out of date, might have possessed the charm of an antique for the sprightly young noblemen who in 1837 drove the Brighton coach at a breakneck clip. But Mr. Weller's soul, transported to "that excellent public house near Shooter's Hill", which was part of that Paradise Dickens kept for his virtuous characters, most certainly went marching on through the Early Victorian years. So did a good many other stout Georgian souls. The curious interest of these first years of our Dickens Age comes from the meeting—perhaps one ought to put it, the colliding—of *two* ages of strongly marked character; the old time dying hard, fighting to keep what it owned; and the new time, unsure of itself, but stretching out its young, bony fingers to clutch its inheritance. Walter Besant decided that 1837 was the last year of the eighteenth century. In truth, the afterglow lasted longer—as we shall see later. The physical energy, the rude health of the Georgians animated Victorian life for many a year. I do not see how one can well comprehend the Age of Dickens without taking that into account. The year 1837 was like that time of day when a fine sunset lingers, but the street lamps are already shining, and the shops and houses have put up their lights. The sky and air, though, are still burning from the sunset, and the windows on the east side of the street are splashed with crimson. There is then a mixing of illuminations, and a confusion of shadows; a scenical transformation of houses and trees; the lamps turn a queer light as they are said to do, in old stories, when Mephistopheles appears; and men and women in the streets look larger than life, and twice as strange. The early novels of Dickens are drenched in that weird illumination.

The eighteenth century cannot be neatly tied up and labelled; its profusion is too various and splendid. But one may touch upon certain of its qualities that shone upon the surface or *under* the surface of Early Victorian times. There is apparent that quality of a lusty, glowing earthiness, the animal magnetism radiating from a healthy, well-fed creature who is never troubled by nervous *tics*, is contemptuous of aches, and acts on the notion that this is the only world we are likely to know. Such a character sees this world at its best as a good inn; a man would be a fool not to take pleasure in its roast beef and its easy beds, for the last morning comes soon enough. The eighteenth-century mind was formed upon a clear, hard sense of here-and-now gratifications; a globing of the hand around the red apple on the bough; a holding of the glass of wine up to the sun to see the ruby dancing in it. The eighteenth-century men were masters of the sensible prose of life; their arts were secular and manly; they were elegant, coarse-fibred, insolent, exquisite and metropolitan all together. They pulled a sour face, or most of them did, over poetry that was not rational poetry, was not topiary poetry, with the growing branches clipped into shapes at once formal and fanciful. The Muse whom they invoked was a plump, worldly young woman, with pearly skin, and with her ten toes planted squarely on the turf. They had a distaste for the translunary order of poetry. This they thought to be an imposture on the emotions, an hallucination. To them, the Romantic School of poetry was as plain a hoax as the Cock Lane ghost. What they called *enthusiasm* in religion was as nauseating to them as the cant of a wild naturalness in poetry. They were disgusted by the vulgar abandonments of those Bedlamites who, when they said they loved God, said so with a more than earthly passion, their faces transfigured, their voices choked, or who quaked in mortal terror, broke out in a ghastly sweat, and rolled on the earth at the thought of their sins and the imminence of damnation. The eighteenth-century fine gentleman felt for the "ecstasies" of the Methodists the distaste that a Roman gentleman of the first century felt for the rites of the early Christians. With their contentment in the world of solids, of orbs, planes, cones, bottles, nymphs, rounded prose, Roman oratory, handsome paintings, grand architecture—and what fine taste they had inside that frame!—with their contentment at the sight of all elegant, graspable possessions, these eighteenth-century beings would manifest a stoic habit in their distresses. Theirs was a temper in misfortune worthy of the old Romans. In the hours of grief, death and losses there came from them but little whining—few reproaches against the Universe that they should be so ill used. Of a piece with this was their indifference to the pains of others—beneath the elegance the brutality of the young and the callousness of the mature are nearly always visible.

PLATE I

QUEEN VICTORIA AND PRINCE ALBERT AT WINDSOR
Detail from the painting by Sir Edwin Landseer, 1840–43
By gracious permission of H.M. The King

PLATE 2

THE PLOUGHING MATCH
Water-colour by Frederick Tayler, *c.* 1860
British Museum

HEAVY TRAFFIC AT CHARING CROSS
Water-colour by Louis Eugène Lami, 1850
Victoria and Albert Museum

The lips that sang Gay's lilt, "The life of all mortals in kissing should pass—lip to lip when you're young, then the lip to the glass", were made for pleasure, they were not framed for gentleness and pity. Although it was the age of Uncle Toby, the tenderest-hearted of men, the eighteenth century was very cruel to the sick, the poor, to madmen and domestic animals. Men of cultured tastes of that period were often brutish in their sports and loutish in their humours. Some of those attitudes were carried into the Victorian period. One pictures big, oafish faces grinning over practical jokes whose victims were the old, the feeble and the half-wits. One thinks, too, of the holiday crowds laughing at the poor lunatics in Bedlam.

I have read somewhere that in her old age Queen Victoria, after telling a story that startled her ladies-in-waiting, retorted comically upon them, "Do not forget that I am a niece of George the Fourth." Of Dickens himself we can surely say that he was the heir of Henry Fielding and Smollett. His novels, and it is particularly true of the early ones, are filled with the bustle and the flashing colours of the full-blooded existence of the eighteenth century, and he never lost that sense of regarding life as though it were an exciting play, part melodrama, part comedy, which marks his literary uncles. He was born in Portsmouth, the city with the sea dazzle in its eyes and behind it the picaresque comedy of the twisting Hampshire roads.

The Industrial Revolution, with its benefits and miseries, was rooted in Georgian times. We may put its beginnings at around 1760, the year when George the Third became King. We have few means of knowing what life was like for the very poor and least regarded subjects of His Majesty in the early decades of the Industrial Revolution; how many miners a year lost their lives in the Scottish mines, for instance; how many infants perished from fevers and plagues in the cities. The Victorians, at least, had a conscience about such matters, even if they sometimes muffled that conscience when it began to cry out too loudly. The late eighteenth century had its "men of sensibility", men with moist palms and morbid refinements of affection, for ever trembling on the brink of tears. But one cannot find a novel with the pity for ill-used children of *Sybil* or *Mary Barton*, or a politician with Lord Ashley's sensitiveness to human suffering in the slums behind the great mansions. There were certainly no such reports brought out then as Dr. Kay's on the health of Manchester, or Chadwick's on sanitation.

The mill, factory, furnace and mining towns grew steadily, but their growth was spread over many years. At the time when Cobbett called it "the great wen", London was about a quarter of the size it is today. It took some time for the millions to be sucked into the great cities. It was in the farms and pasture lands, the orchard lands, villages, little market towns, the big parks and enclosures, the Palladian mansions, it was in squire's ways, parson's ways, in the farmer's and cottager's ways, that was to be found the dominant tone of English life in the late eighteenth century. That remained true, though it is easy enough to forget it, throughout the early years of Victorian times.

What misleads us is that the town is always articulate, and the country dumb; the city has a hundred voices of grievance and protest as against the country's one or two. One becomes hypnotised by the noise of the looms, the clatter of "The Rocket", the cry of a sick child from Tom-all-Alone's, and one almost forgets the fields of wheat and barley that were waving then, the thousand and one villages, the cows and the pigs, and that spectacle of fat, white sheep on sunny uplands, stretching for miles and miles, that used to delight Cobbett on a day's ride. In the late eighteenth century and early nineteenth, however grisly were the spectres flitting about the rookeries of the new industrial districts, there was no lack of robust types among the ordinary people. One may judge as much from the prints of street scenes, and by the physical descriptions in the old novels. Those brawny fellows and full-orbed women who appear in the sketches of common life—soldiers with fists like hams, porters with the shoulders of prize-fighters, footmen tall as lamp-posts, young butchers with the thews of Samson, chubby girls selling lavender, and cherubic apprentices taking down shutters—they were not reared on skilly and dry crusts in a dark slum. Consider Gillray's cartoon of "John Bull Happy". There sits a contented fellow if ever there was one, bulging fore and aft, a corpulent, chair-filling yeoman, nursing his ale-mug by the fire, while his plump, pretty children play round him. Or look at the solid, earthy figures in Rowlandson—did ever creatures more wholly belong to the world of the senses? No green sickness about *them*, nothing wan nor fey.

There was a great lustiness there, a coarseness if you like, but certainly stamina. Country juices flowed in the veins of the men and women who were being drawn into the towns by the Industrial Revolution. Their mothers had started them off in life with constitutions strong enough to withstand the siege of smoke, dirt, foul air, bad drains, fevers, poxes and strong drink. Gainsborough's fine ladies were far too ethereal for steak and porter; nourished on moonbeams and delicate airs, they melted away in a lovely silver and blue cloud on the canvas; they would "die of a rose in aromatic pain"; but the mothers of the race were far more akin to Joseph Andrews's Fanny who was "so plump she seemed bursting through her tight stays, nor did her hips want the assistance of a hoop to extend them. Her arms were a little reddened by her labour, her complexion's bloom a little injured by the sun, and the small-pox had left only one mark on her chin which was so large it might have been mistaken for a dimple."

On the foundation of animal health was based a manly spirit of independence, a sturdy standing on rights, a be-damned-to-you air on

"JOHN BULL HAPPY"
Cartoon from the series "John Bull's Progress", by James Gillray, 1793

being hauled up before one's masters. When such hearty characters sang, "Britons never, never, NEVER shall be slaves", they put such a feeling into the words as made the windows in Westminster rattle. The ordinary people were without votes, but in all the noisy political agitations, from the cry of "Wilkes and Liberty" onwards, by the show they made in the streets, by their storming around the coaches of the great, they made their will known and, on most occasions, those raucous voices were on the side of Freedom and Honour. The punishments for rebels in that age were very cruel, the merciless floggings, the irons, the starvings in black holes and the rest, but dread of them did not deter the English sailor in the eighteenth century from his mutinies. "Heart of oak are our ships, heart of oak are our men"; and those stout hearts could be cowed neither by a foreign enemy nor by my Lords of Admiralty. The bluejackets with their tarry pigtails who swarmed on Plymouth Hoe and Portsmouth Hard were not prone to say "God bless your honour", and give three cheers for the established order of things; but these were the men of Nelson's fleet.

It was not a docile, servile population that sustained the war with Napoleon through all those wearisome years.

I knew no harm of Bonaparte, and plenty of the Squire,
And for to fight the Frenchman I did not much desire;
But I did bash their baggonets because they came arrayed
To straighten out the crooked road an English drunkard made.

"Respect for one's betters" seems to have been far more widely observed in the eighteen-sixties than fifty years earlier, or than twenty years earlier. One thinks of the crowds that hurried through the West End of London, compelling the great houses to illuminate their windows to celebrate the triumph of some popular cause—the crowds that ran hurrahing after the chariot of that crazy, ill-used creature, Queen Caroline, and brought her to the balcony in South Audley Street, waving and smiling and weeping—the crowds that broke the great Duke's windows, and roared that they would stand no more nonsense during the wild "days of May" when it looked as though King William and the Duke had, between them, cheated Grey on Reform. When we turn back upon the period in which Charles Dickens was born, we often think how picturesque it must have been ; we see it as a ballet on the stage, with all the dancers keeping their places. They were, in truth, rough, disordered, rowdy, hard times. The radical protest was violent then, the revolutionary sentiment strong, and the events of the French Revolution still very fresh. There were many who, at the time of the Reform Bill, felt with Disraeli's Lady Marney "that a revolution was inevitable, that all property would be instantly confiscated, the poor, deluded King led to the block or sent over to Hanover at the best, and the whole of the nobility and principal gentry, and everyone who possessed anything, guillotined without remorse".

It was a powerful brew that the eighteenth century had concocted of liberty, equality, fraternity, rationalism, direct action and animal earthiness, and its children's heads grew dizzy. Milder beverages, that would cheer without inebriating, political temperance drinks, so to speak, were to be dispensed later by Peel, Russell, Gladstone and Disraeli. Some indwelling ordinariness, some instinct of dull common sense, some flair for bathos and anti-climax saved England, the country apparently most ripe for revolution in the eighteen-forties, from the bath of blood.

The change from Georgian morals to what the world came to call Victorian standards did not take place in a day. It is true that the morals and manners of provincial life were not those of the capital. At the time when the Prince Regent was setting the tone of London society, Mrs. General was driving "the Proprieties, four-in-hand, through her cathedral town".

Mrs. General was not to be told of anything shocking. Accidents, miseries and offences, were never to be mentioned before her. Passion was to go to sleep in the presence of Mrs. General, and blood was to change to milk and water.

> The little that was left in the world, when all these deductions were made, it was Mrs. General's province to varnish.

There is the canon of Victorianism as most of us think of it nowadays. But in the metropolitan society of the thirties and the forties the rakes walked unashamed. A disreputable private character was not a handicap to social success or to political advancement. No Minister forfeited his seals by acquiring the repute of the Marquis of Steyne. Palmerston's amours contributed, indeed, to his popularity, and, on the hustings, it did not put him out of countenance to be hailed by his friend the butcher of Tiverton as "Cupid". The Queen's first Prime Minister, Lord Melbourne, was, in Lytton Strachey's phrase, "the autumn rose of the eighteenth century": his gallantries and misadventures in love had provided the paragraphists and the street ballad-writers with many themes. The Puritans of the counting-house and the factory, the sons of Adam Smith and Jeremy Bentham, had to achieve their economic revolution before they could alter the tone of society by their moral reformation.

Down the years comes the faint thunder of an Archdeacon preaching on "The Home Life of our Beloved Queen". True it is, that the domestic virtues of Victoria and Albert set a pattern for the age, purified the Court, abashed the rakes (though without driving them out of the kingdom) and imposed a prudery of speech and writing. The process was a gradual one, and the severity of the Puritan Reformation was not felt until the sixties, after the Prince Consort died, and the Queen had withdrawn into the seclusion of her immoderate grief. There she dwelt like an Egyptian queen, in an impassioned absorption with the dead, and her name was invoked as sanction for all repressions of the natural man. Not man alone. I recall the old woman of whom my mother spoke (passing it on from *her* mother) who would not give her pet monkey water and food on a Sunday so that he, poor brute, should share in the general penance and be purified by a day's fasting and meditation on his sins. Vice did not take a holiday —it went underground, and there became more odious. No historian presents that midnight aspect of Victorian Puritanism so strikingly as Mr. Michael Sadlier in his novels.

It is constantly interesting to trace through English life, as indeed through American life, the conflict between our Puritan and Cavalier strains. It was, on the whole, the Cavalier qualities that lent their hues to the cultivated society of the eighteenth century. In the second half of the nineteenth, it was the Puritan strain that dominated. The civil war in our blood never comes to an end. You may at times perceive the struggle going on within a single person—the Roundheads capturing the citadel of his soul one day, while on the next day it hoists King Charles's flag. Through our history, one party is now on top, and now the other, but there is seldom any time when England is utterly subdued by either.

That completeness of conquest must be left to Calvin's Geneva—or to early Massachusetts. The Puritans who went out from our Fenlands to set up a theocratic state in New England had been unable to do as much at home under Cromwell. The contest for power between Puritan and Cavalier sways to and fro through our centuries; sometimes it is sharpened by economic struggles between groups; very often it crosses the lines dividing classes. The conflict within the individual soul may be just as frequent nowadays as it was in the seventeenth and nineteenth centuries, though the words are now quite changed, and in the place of the old religious names we use economic and political terms. In one mood, my friend takes after his father: he is possessed by a sad view of man's destiny, he works as one heavy with the thought that the night comes soon when man works no more, he perceives the final beauty to lie in abstinence, and is in no doubt that the rarest treasures of mind and the emotions reside beyond the longings of the flesh. Then he changes, in consequence of promptings in his blood from some remoter forebear, and suddenly he awakes again to the world of the rose and the nightingale, to the present virtues of wine and ale and good beef, to the fire in the stone, to the seduction of the passing moment, to melody, and to Aphrodite's yellow curls rising from the waves—he curses prudence and all long, bilious faces, and concludes that existence is, on the whole, a laughing matter, and that Providence is a gentleman. This double nature is to be observed in a number of great Victorians, Charles Dickens, Thackeray, Tennyson, even Arnold among them, and the internal war in them often brought, not so much in its victory, or defeat, as in its unresolved moments, a wry and strange beauty. The national genius seems to gain depth and colour from this dualism. Often when the conflict between the Roundheads and Cavaliers is at its sharpest—when it is dramatised in the outer world of code and custom as it was in Victorian times, when there is a powerful resurgence of one side or the other—our politics gain ardour from the clash, our religions rekindle their fervour, our literature glows at the heart, men speak with the eloquence of conviction, they are more passionate about what they know and believe, and there is little boredom with life. When the two temperaments are stirred up, the one reacts vigorously upon the other, and both throw off streams of sparks. The repressiveness of the Puritan rule over so wide a reach of family life and national conduct in Victorian times intensified emotions, as heath flowers give out their strongest scent when they are trampled on. It called out the defiance of the sensitive, the gay rebellions, the gallant songs that are as much a part of the Victorian heritage as the gloomy moralities.

CHAPTER FIVE

SPEED

The Industrial Revolution was rooted in Georgian times, so, too, was "our modern craze for speedy motion" that the moralists complain about.

Long before Dickens died, the railway locomotive had come to be thought of as the grand emblem of the Victorians. Belching flame and smoke as it charged across pastoral England, or roared into the cavities of the hills, the locomotive was seen as a sort of heraldic English dragon; it was worthy to appear on the coats of arms of the new nobility. This monster of metal, dashing at unimaginable speed along a shining track, devouring space through day and night, was as splendid a symbol of Victorian Progress, of the exhilarating momentum of mechanical Progress—everybody going faster and further, and getting richer all the time—as could be dreamed of. Yet when we set out on our travels in 1837, we find the horse triumphant. The horse, indeed, galloping madly; the brave music of the hooves on the frosty road. "Proputty-proputty-proputty—that's what I hear them saäy." It was as though the eighteenth century were putting out a valiant effort to prove that *it* had achieved the acme of Progress, the height of Speed—and had made its argument conclusive by taste and elegance. Never before were the roads so crowded, never so gay. They have been more crowded since; they have never been so gay. Through the land sounded that typical eighteenth-century note, the impudent, happy coaching horn.

It was as early as 1825 that Mr. Creevey, chosen as member of a Parliamentary Committee to consider the Bill of the Liverpool and Manchester Company, did his best to choke the little railway dragon at birth. "This infernal nuisance," he grumbled to Miss Ord on March 16th, "the locomotive Monster, carrying *eighty* tons of goods, and navigated by a tail of smoke and sulphur, coming through every man's grounds . . ." Stanleys and Cavendishes were appalled at the prospect, for they had great possessions. The Parliamentary contest was not an easy one. There were, said Creevey, "Scotchmen" on the Committee, who were infatuated by notions of Progress—and there were "perfidious Whigs" to overcome. In particular, there was one "insane Ferguson who frothed with rage at the mouth", not, as might be supposed, *against* the new horror, but on behalf of it. It took from March to June to overcome this combination of lunacy, perfidy and Scottish infatuation. One hears the gentle sigh of Creevey as he reports at last to Miss Ord, "Well—this devil of a railway is strangled at last." Despite the speculative booms, and the great laying-down of tracks that had taken place since this first struggle with the dragon, there was but one terminal station in London in 1837—Euston. At the start of Victoria's reign, elegance, fashion, youth—even civilisation itself—seemed to be pounding off to Kingdom Come on horseback, or at least went rolling that way behind the bays and the roans. Preachers lamented, as preachers have done since the launching of the Ark, the sick hurry, the mad rush of the times. That moral alarm had vibrated in Pickwick's throat when he set out on his own immortal journey; he recognised it involved danger as well as the promise of glory. "Travelling", he reported, "was in a troubled state, and the minds of coachmen were unsettled. Let them look abroad and contemplate the scenes that were enacting round them. Stage-coaches were upsetting in all directions, horses were bolting . . ." The perils of the roads were much greater in 1837 than they had been in 1827, for everyone was going faster, very much faster. De Quincey's *The English Mail Coach* is still no piece for reading late at night when the house is still—and the wind outside is whining. His coach carries you off through the scenery of a nightmare; there is choking fear, bolting terror in it. Here, surely, one would say, is a moralist's parable of a speed-intoxicated world tearing down the smooth high road to perdition. No account of a collision in the stratosphere could outdo it in the power to strike imaginative terror.

Those last years of the coaching times, when everything was brought to a perfection together, horses, coaches, drivers, road surfaces, presented a continuous light-hearted pageantry, sparkling with cheerful colours and high spirits, showy and modish, effervescent, raffish. When the London to Southampton railway started up, Harry Littler, the renowned coachman of the Southampton *Telegraph*, spoke these words of farewell, "Hang my old whip over the fireplace, I shan't want it never no more", and the spark went out of the old man, and he died. "Never no more." It was the passing bell of an age. But to most who watched the animation of the roads in the thirties, it was not probable that this quick-pulsed and arrogant life could ever wither away before the breath of the dragon. Horses were bred for fleetness, fined down and etherealised like Gainsborough ladies; they were become all fire, dash and quivering sensibility; one might have thought their very bones had been aerated; the lumbering, clumsy old Dobbins and Margerys had been put out to grass. Mr. Weller and his cronies, old Dobbins too, had also been put to grass. "We get to Brighton from Charing Cross in five and a quarter hours nowadays", said the stylish young men who had picked up the whips of the Littlers. "It took near enough ten hours to do that twenty-five years ago." They now changed horses every ten miles. See the horses clattering into the post-inn yard, their hearts almost bursting, clouds of steam rising from their hides,

A STAGE COACH
Wood engraving from Pierce Egan's "Book of Sports", 1832

and a yellow froth dribbling down their straining chests, the stable boys running out, the whole yard in a cheerful tumult. See the coach arriving out of the rime of winter darkness, the leaders tossing the snow from their manes, the flashing to and fro of lanterns, the breath of man and beast going up like puffs of smoke, the coughing and cursing, the rhythmic beating of arms across chests, the stamping around in the yard to requicken the blood, the groans over the wretchedness of travel on a polar night in England, and the joys promised by the rosy windows of the inn. Those scenes had rawness, solidity, harsh density; they were not thought of as Christmas-card scenes until they had passed away. They are more attractive as pictures hanging on the wall than as experiences endured. While the engineers, Stephenson, Brunel and other imps of darkness were already spreading their railway tracks over the country, the coach-makers in a fine and final frenzy were constructing the airiest shells on wheels, they were rarefying woodwork and leather to a fanciful spideriness. The middle-eighteenth-century squires, happy only when they could be in the saddle all day long, had seemed to aspire to the condition of the centaur; of man half-horse, of horse half-man. Their sons discovered a passion for wheels as well as an enthusiasm for horses. They raced in their flimsy curricles, spinning along Macadam's new surface that had turned the broken old roads of Tony Lumpkin's day into polished tabletops. They took to driving the public coaches for the sport and the fun of it. The wheezy hippopotamus coachman of the old tradition, spreading around him a spicy aroma of brandy-and-water, an autocrat of the road, renowned for his sarcasms, had given place to sporting young baronets in white capes, and sprightly heirs to earldoms, just as the rumbling old coaches had been replaced by the *Comets* and *Royal Yorks*, built for lightness and speed. *Noblesse oblige!* The noble drivers weren't too proud to pocket a tip at the run's end. One catches the voice of Great-great-grand-aunt Louisa floating across the gulf of the years: "It was a most adventurous run, my dear, and at such a speed. They said we had broken the record but I felt no alarm. I had the utmost confidence in the *very agreeable* and *clever* young man who was driving. What *do* you suppose, my dear?—he proved to be the son of the Earl of Towers, the *third* son, I believe. Wasn't that a very romantic circumstance? Could anything be more distinguished? There is no doubt about it, that birth, blood and breeding all *tell*, particularly in their influence over horses. But I must confess, I was in some confusion at the thought of offering him a florin, even if he were the *youngest* son of an Earl. In my position, what would you have proposed, Georgiana?"

My time tables for 1837 show a hundred and fifty coaches or so starting from London, and that was half the number running in the whole country. What attractive names most of them had, as pleasant to roll on the tongue as calling over a tally of ships, or racehorses, names such as *Defiance*, *True Blue*, *Wonder*, *Tantivy*, *Star of Brunswick*, *Isis*, *Irresistible*, *Tally Ho*, *Rocket*, *Zephyr*, *Ariel*, *Emerald*, *Flower of Kent*, *Mazeppa*! The new coaches had a swagger as they rattled out of the yard of the Golden Cross or the Red Lion, leaving behind "the crowd of nondescripts outside the coach office who seem to consider, Heaven knows why, that it is quite impossible any man can mount a coach without requiring at least six pennyworth of oranges, a penknife, a pocket-book, a last year's annual, a pencil case, a piece of sponge, and a small series of caricatures" (*Sketches by Boz*). The smart coach, the crack coach, rolled out in a glitter of new paint; there were scrolls on its sides carrying in golden letters the names of famous cities—that handsome, grave lettering of the period which makes even JNO. JONES, POULTERER TO THE NOBILITY AND GENTRY look like the beginning of an ode, or the inscription of a military victory. The brasses were so beautifully polished that they flashed like looking glasses, the ornaments on the harness rippled and tinkled, and there were coloured ribbons and streamers floating out, as though every day was from now on to be proclaimed a holiday. The coachman was young and cocky, perking his head at the thought of what a fine fellow he was. The saucy horn let out its cock-a-doodle-do. And *now* they were off in a flurry of dust, everybody scurrying out of their road, for it was a sad matter how many persons were knocked down by these mad coaches in a year. London was still a small city, by contrast with today's unending sprawl, and they would soon be out in the country, skimming along a macadamised main road with an exhilarating fluency of motion; the lilt of the horses making a music for the ear and a running poetry for the eye—and all the chances were that inside the coach one would be jolted and bumped amid the nasty, smelly straw for five or six hours or more, in the company of the most infernal bores in Christendom. (Let us ask the most devoted lover of Victorian literature how many of its characters *he* would choose to share with him the discomforts of a long coach journey!)

There comes back to one, almost like the memory of one's own physical discomfort, the travels of young David Copperfield.

> The night was not so pleasant as the evening, for it got chilly; and being put between two gentlemen (the rough-faced one and another) to prevent my tumbling off the coach, I was nearly smothered by their falling asleep, and completely blocking me up. They squeezed me so hard sometimes that I could not help crying out, "Oh, if you please!"—which they didn't like at all, because it woke them. Opposite me was an elderly lady in a great fur cloak, who looked in the dark more like a haystack than a lady, she was wrapped up to such a degree. This lady had a basket with her, and she hadn't known what to do with it, for a long time, until she found that, on account of my legs being short, it could go underneath me. It cramped and hurt me so that it made me perfectly miserable; but if I moved in the least, and made a glass that was in the basket rattle against something else (as it was sure to do) she gave me the cruellest poke with her foot and said, "Come don't *you* fidget. *Your* bones are young enough, *I'm* sure."

For centuries on centuries man had used the horse to carry him around. Now that was to change. The railway dragon could not be throttled. It would soon rampage over the whole land. A revolution of such a kind, such a size, makes its influence felt beyond the material level. Such a triumph for a mechanical force affects politics in their deepest courses, sets the economists running off on fresh tracks and changes the long-held rules of society. New theories are spun, new laws inferred. Most of all, the machine alters the way private men look at the world and their own lives—not only the world of bread and bricks, but the world of thoughts—and the inner purpose of their lives and the work they do. The railway dragon was, in his way, a great philosopher. He preached a philosophy of change and flux, but it was a cheerful philosophy. All change was change for the better. Progress was inevitable. So the faster you went the happier you became. The dragon was the friend of man. Through his aid, man would subdue his environment. The dragon was such a popular and convincing preacher that he set up a whole school of optimistic philosophers, politicians, writers and parsons. Before his cheerful snorts and genial puffs, the spirit of the eighteenth century, that was so loth to die, quailed, flickered, and at last faded away.

Mr. Tommy Twiddlewhip
playing at being a Coachman.

PART 2

HARD TIMES

CHAPTER ONE

THE QUEST

To most of us, worried about today's bread or the rent at the end of the week, history, even the history of our grandfathers' times, comes in the end to resemble a series of mural paintings in a long, royal corridor along which fog is slowly gathering. The figures on the wall remain gorgeous but grow steadily dimmer with the years. As our eye wanders along the vista, it is caught every now and again by some remembered flare of crimson, by the fading representation of a violent action, by an enigmatic face that starts out of the canvas. There were, we remember, *dates*—oh yes! dates. There were, we recall, movements and causes. There were great men and parties now dead and gone. But let a new crop of schoolboys commit *them* to memory, and then sit miserably for their examinations. For our part—we being old, weary and having many cares—let us be content with the dogmatic inexactitude of our recollections and a rosy haze of early impressions. 1832, Reform; 1846, Repeal of the Corn Laws; 1854, the Crimean War; 1868, Gladstone; 1870, the Education Act; and so on. What are these points in Time to us now? The accounts are closed, aren't they? The issues are settled. The eminent statesmen have long been frozen up inside their marble statues, and their impetuous spirits are buried for ever under those unreadable three-volume biographies that Victorian piety erected. All history is vanity, we decide.

But the past is always alive. Its elements endure in us, and around us. We are subject to its impulses in our daily life. The thoughts, the ideas, the passions that moved masses of men and women, the forces that created parties and found their incarnation in leaders, stir in our blood today. The struggle of political philosophies goes on, though the names change. The evolution of ideas and emotions is continuous. It is not simply the nostalgia of a child for a lost garden where the flowers were brilliant, the sunshine eternal, and the Punch and Judy show very amusing, that leads us back to the Victorian times. *There lie our origins.* That is the womb of present times. Our human condition was decided there. Apart from this natural interest in our parents, I fancy it is still useful to us, after two world wars and a social revolution, to see how the tides and currents were moving in those days. A broad "stream of tendency" towards freedom, liberal institutions, social democracy, set in something like a hundred years ago. Sometimes its flow was sluggish, sometimes arrested, but it always resumed, and today our Tories, Liberals and Socialists alike have set sail upon it.

I remember with clearness the effect on myself of the talk of old men and women that I listened to as a child. Some had been reared in the country, some had spent their lives in the big towns, some were well born, or had done well in trade; others had been born poor, and were always to be poor. But with their varying fortunes, their different stations in life, all of them, as I see now, contributed to my impression that the nineteenth century had been not only a period of emancipation, but was one long fluctuating struggle to define the frontiers of freedom. The names used and the issues were different, but the underlying principles were identical with those joined in conflict today on the field of politics.

The Age of Dickens was a Liberal Age. It is interesting to us today to follow its own successive interpretations of Liberalism, and to observe the struggle of ideas within the framework of a proud and assured Liberal State. Proud and assured, I said, but never utterly complacent. For from beginning to end it vibrated with the fierce, continuing debate on the theme—*what is human freedom*?

Liberty! To strive consciously from generation to generation to extend its borders, to enrich its meanings, to widen its applications until no member of the living community should be enslaved in mind or body—that was the aspiration of the best men and women of the Victorian time. In pursuit of their ideal, they were often led into the slough of despond by will o' the wisps. They retreated, and blundered, and were sometimes untrue to themselves. Sometimes they willed the good, but achieved only cruelty and the infliction of suffering upon the innocents. They were many times defeated by the blind rages and stampedes of public opinion; by the greed and stupidity of the compact majority; by their own buccaneers and pirates; by the crafty, smiling men who from age to age always use the language of freedom, justice and reform in defence of privilege and abuses. Morley said there were two hundred definitions of freedom; most of them were enunciated with vigour during the Victorian age; and most of them look now like recipes for extracting sunshine from cucumbers. But always the faith sustained the devoted minority, that their world *could* be set free, set free in the ultimate sense of freedom, that is by the freeing of the highest faculties of all the members of the community.

At one time they thought happiness might be reached through the overthrow of an aristocratic caste that had outlived its usefulness and by the destruction of worm-eaten institutions. At another, through the freeing of trade from its fetters. At another, through science—a fond and recurring delusion of the human race. They were cocksure often—and often events cheated them, and often history made fools of them. The meaner ambitions of their fellows were granted, and their own rarer hopes denied. But they had faith, and they strove. It was their aspirations and their strivings which created in the end the inner nobility of the Victorian age, and gave to it an enduring vitality, making it so real a thing that its voices are all about us still, and its ghosts still haunt us. These men and women might not have found the right answers, but they knew the right questions to put to their times and their fellows—and to themselves.

CHAPTER TWO

MAN WAS BORN FREE?

Suppose that you or I had been living a hundred and twenty years ago, had been young, impressionable, and in revolt against our fathers' old-fashioned conservatism, as a great many young men were. How thrilling then the stir and ferment of political ideas! How delightful the variety of novel theories presenting themselves to the awakening mind! How easy to believe that any of them might hold the secret of human happiness! We might, for example, have been captured by the idealism of those who believed that men were by nature good, kind and just, but were the victims of evil systems of government. These visionaries saw the divine mind of man as bound in chains by tyrannous kings, by corrupt ministers, by superstitious religions. Shatter the chains! they cried—and Man, the captive, would rise in beauty and majesty, and move towards that perfection which was his true destiny. He would expel evil out of his own soul, and out of the universe. Nothing was beyond the reach of man's unfettered will, no delights, no truths, no triumphs. War and want, cruelty, intolerance and injustice, were the consequences of the old absolute governments. Once these despotisms, and the wicked systems of thoughts that sustained them, were broken, the world's great age would begin anew and the golden years return.

> Heaven smiles, and faiths and empires gleam
> Like wrecks of a dissolving dream.

The fright caused in Britain in 1792 by the Terror in France had brought about a persecution of liberal minds as well as cranks and avowed revolutionaries, but even Pitt and John Scott, the Attorney-General (afterwards Lord Eldon), were unable to quench the generous enthusiasm of those who had caught fire from the Declaration of the Rights of Man. How, too, could a passion of such celestial flame as Shelley's be easily extinguished? How could any public prosecutor silence such persuasive voices as Rousseau's and Tom Paine's? It was against the law to own a copy of Paine's *The Rights of Man*, but, banned, the book enjoyed a circulation exceeding the most popular of the Waverley Novels.

In human affairs, a negative, defensive, repressive policy must always be at a disadvantage when it comes into conflict with a creative, positive, warm-hearted enthusiasm, though the first possesses all the guns, most of the votes, and all the instruments of power on its side, and the second is

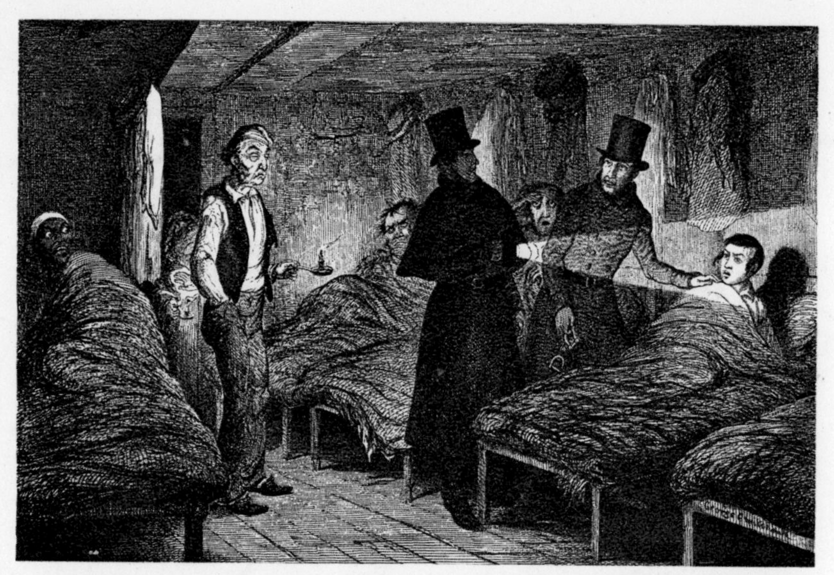

POLICEMEN MAKING AN ARREST IN A LONDON LODGING-HOUSE
Lithograph by George Cruikshank from "The Drunkard's Children", 1848

A SOUP KITCHEN IN RATCLIFF HIGHWAY
Wood engraving, 1861
From Henry Mayhew's "London Labour and the London Poor"

PLATE 4

HARDWARE ON THE BIRMINGHAM STALL AT THE GREAT EXHIBITION

Lithograph after H. C. Pidgeon

From "Recollections of the Great Exhibition"

shared by isolated men and women, lonely, often freakish, always unpopular. This affirmation of natural rights and civil freedoms was to prove of the highest political value in the Victorian evolution, but the real *strength* of these idealists derived from their sense of the natural dignity and majesty of man. They were lifted above themselves by such a vision of his greatness as *Prometheus Unbound* unfolded:

> To suffer woes which Hope thinks infinite;
> To forgive wrongs darker than death or night;
> To defy Power, which seems omnipotent;
> To love, and bear; to hope till Hope creates
> From its own wreck the thing it contemplates;
> Neither to change, nor falter, nor repent;
> This, like thy glory, Titan, is to be
> Good, great and joyous, beautiful and free;
> This is alone Life, Joy, Empire, and Victory.

Man, even when flung in chains into the pit, and suffering the extremes of misery, humiliation and despair, was still a god. He was not "a species of ape afflicted by megalomania"; most certainly not an economic unit.

The doctrines of natural rights, of the inherent goodness of man, of the "social contract" came under heavy bombardment from Jeremy Bentham and the Utilitarians as well as from the staunch Conservatives in State and Church. But politicians and philosophers are often profoundly, if subconsciously, affected by the doctrines they themselves have most vigorously combated. Bentham's reasoning brought him before he died to a position not very far from that of the believers in natural rights whom he had ridiculed, and, as the century advanced, more and more respectable middle-class Britons came to speak of Liberty, and to reprobate foreign despotisms, in language that would almost have brought the charge of Jacobinism in Pitt's time. Mary Shelley, in the preface of the 1839 edition of her husband's poems, wrote: "He died, and the world showed no outward sign. But his influence over mankind, though slow in growth, is fast augmenting; and, in the ameliorations that have taken place in the political state of his country, we may trace in part the operation of his arduous struggles." The increasing acceptance of human values was to be perceived as the century unfolded. The philosophies of the early nineteenth-century idealists have crumbled, their self-delusions have been exposed, but they exercised a lasting influence even over their enemies and scorners. Most of them were Deists, some of them were defiantly Atheists, but their contribution was, in truth, a religious one, made at a time when the Established Church was sunk in materialism and sloth. They vindicated that great central principle of the Christian belief, the supreme value of the human personality, the dignity and worth of man. They saw man standing in the white radiance of eternity.

The opening years of the nineteenth century were years of "great events and little men". Poor Spencer Perceval, the dull little Prime Minister, who was murdered in the lobby of the House of Commons in the year that Dickens was born, was typical of the dwarfs who followed the giants of the eighteenth century. Perceval; the Duke of Portland, "the stupidest Duke in England"; Jenkinson (Lord Liverpool) who ruled for fourteen years—what a crew! How on earth did such characters manage to bring the war with Napoleon to a successful conclusion? After the deaths of Pitt and Fox, "that period of public languor which intervenes between the breaking up of parties and the formation of factions now succeeded", said Disraeli. There was "an exhausted sensualist on the throne [George IV] who only demanded from his Ministers repose, a voluptuous aristocracy, and a listless people". But beneath the lethargy of exhaustion there was the deep smoulder of unrest. In the eighteen months after Waterloo, riots and civil disturbances took place in twenty cities and a dozen shires. The Corn Law of 1815 made bread dear at a time when wages were falling, and there was much misery and want in both the industrial and rural areas. The Luddites, taking their name from the crazy youth Ned Ludd, broke up the machines which were replacing the traditional handcrafts. In the year that Dickens was born, the newspapers reported machine-wrecking in the Midlands and North, and the meeting of alarmed magistrates to put down the frenzy. The men in power, the Jenkinsons, Sidmouths, Eldons and the like, were men of narrow and unillumined minds and they were easily thrown into a fright. Repression was their one remedy for discontent. The Six Acts of 1819 brought Britain as near to the Police State as she has ever been in modern history. These statutes forbidding freedom of assembly and speech stifled the voice of protest—who now could sing "Britons never shall be slaves"? In the same year the "Massacre of Peterloo" took place. A crowd had peacefully gathered in St. Peter's Fields, Manchester, for a demonstration in favour of Parliamentary Reform. They were broken up by a charge of cavalry and yeomanry, eleven persons were killed, and some six hundred injured.

The French Declaration of the Rights of Man in 1789 did not concern itself with what we call nowadays economic rights. Nor, for that matter, did the American Declaration of Independence (1776)—"We hold these truths to be self-evident: that all men are created equal, that they are endowed by their Creator with certain inalienable rights, that among these are life, liberty and the pursuit of happiness". But if you or I had been living in the early decades of the nineteenth century and had belonged to the middle class, we should have found it hard not to have been caught up in a very brisk debate on economic freedom, or, at least, one conception of it. We should have found that a great many progressive characters, enemies of the old order, children of the light as they thought themselves, conceived of economic freedom as a freedom from all Government restraints. They asked—how could a mouldy, rickety system of government, which had changed little since Elizabeth's reign, hope to direct and control the uprushing forces of the Industrial Revolution?

It was in 1776, the year in which the American Colonies revolted, that Adam Smith, who had won great renown as Professor of Moral Philosophy at Glasgow University, brought out *The Wealth of Nations*. That eighteenth-century testament of free enterprise had a profound influence upon the nineteenth century and it certainly remains today a living influence in the British Commonwealth and the United States. It gave the rising commercial and industrial classes an awareness of their own virtues. There are few experiences in life more agreeable than to find oneself, after working hard for one's private gain, saluted as a public benefactor. Adam Smith presented the independent, self-reliant merchant or manufacturer as a national hero. In pursuing his self-interest, he advanced the general interest. The benevolent individualist, who sought to enrich the community by enriching himself, was placed in vivid opposition to a parasitic bureaucracy, to the Tite-Barnacles, to my lords of the Circumlocution Office.

The political parts of *Little Dorrit* are, in a sense, a brilliant dramatisation of Adam Smith. No member of the Society of Individualists ever put the case against officialdom with such energy as Meagles when he came roaring out of the Circumlocution Office, dragging little Daniel Doyce, the inventor, by the collar. Meagles, it will be recalled, wheeled on Arthur Clennam:

"Mr. Clennam, will you do me the favour to look at this man? . . . You wouldn't suppose this man to be a notorious rascal; would you?"—"No."—"But he *is*. He is a public offender. What has he been guilty of? Murder, manslaughter, arson, forgery, swindling, housebreaking, highway robbery, larceny, conspiracy, fraud? Which should you say, now?"

"I should say," returned Arthur Clennam, observing a faint smile in Daniel Doyce's face, "not one of them."

"You are right," said Mr. Meagles. "But he has been ingenious, and he has been trying to turn his ingenuity to his country's service. That makes him a public offender directly, sir."

"This Doyce," said Mr. Meagles, "is a smith and engineer. He is not in a large way, but he is well known as a very ingenious man. A dozen years ago, he perfects an invention (involving a very curious secret process) of great importance to his country and his fellow-creatures. I won't say how many years of his life he had been about it, but he brought it to perfection a dozen years ago. Wasn't it a dozen?" said Mr. Meagles, addressing Doyce. "He is the most exasperating man in the world; he never complains!"

"Yes. Rather better than twelve years ago."

"Rather better?" said Mr. Meagles. "You mean rather worse. Well, Mr. Clennam. He addresses himself to the Government. The moment he addresses himself to the Government, he becomes a public offender! Sir," said Mr. Meagles, in danger of making himself excessively hot again, "he ceases to be an innocent citizen, and becomes a culprit. He is treated from that instant as a man who had done some infernal action. He is a man to be shirked, put off, browbeaten, sneered at, handed over by this highly-connected young or old gentleman to that highly-connected young or old gentleman, and dodged back again; he is a man with no rights in his own time, or his own property; a mere outlaw, whom it is justifiable to get rid of anyhow; a man to be worn out by all possible means."

The solemn old Barnacle who "wound and wound folds of white cravat round his neck, as he wound and wound folds of tape and paper round the neck of the country", and the airy young Barnacle who said, "You had better take a lot of forms away with you. Give him a lot of forms!" were to Dickens and his middle-class readers embodiments of that crusted Conservatism which was in their eyes the curse of England, and which the young, the hopeful and the radical were in league to destroy.

It is one of the charms of English history that in the end it reconciles nearly all opposites. Sooner or later one hears the Liberal arguments of one generation repeated by the Conservatives of another, and a loyal Socialist of 1949, rising to support his party, will advance a theory akin to that of a loyal Tory of the long ago defending the trade policies of Lord Liverpool. In politics we should be tolerant of any argument of an opponent. We never know when we may need it ourselves. The student of history turns aside from the clamour of a century ago, a little deafened by the outcry of those early Victorian business men against the dead hand of Government. He seeks a respite in his own age. What does he find? A deafening outcry by business men against the dead hand of Government. There is this difference. That in the bygone time the commercial classes complained that their enterprise and vigour were cramped by an antiquated Toryism. Nowadays, they complain that these qualities are repressed by a doctrinaire Socialism. Those who were acquainted with the United States during the years of President Franklin Roosevelt's Presidency will recall with what vigour the Conservative Republicans denounced the New Deal for its crippling interferences with private enterprise. "Set the people free!" In one period it is the call of the Liberal, in another of the Conservative.

Laissez-faire has served as a term of contempt and abuse for a very long time. But it is just to recall that *laissez-faire* was once a cry of freedom, and that it had its real part in the evolution of the idea of freedom. The mercantile policy of the old Conservatism, the "restrictive practices" imposed by the Navigation Acts, the Corn Law of 1815, convinced liberal-minded men in those days that Government interference with trade and commerce represented the negation of liberty. Dickens's anger against the Circumlocution Office was the anger of the new Liberalism against the old Toryism. In those days the bureaucracy and aristocracy often seemed indistinguishable. The control of trade by my lords of the Circumlocution Office seemed to represent privilege at its most insolent and indefensible.

The ideas of Adam Smith, the moral philosopher of the middle classes, proved irresistible, for the middle classes were themselves irresistibly marching to power. And, to do them and Adam Smith justice, they believed they were advancing the cause of humanity and ensuring a happier life for all classes. Even before the Reform Bill, William Huskisson, one of the ablest of the Conservative Ministers, had begun the process of freeing commerce from its shackles and, so late as 1887, one finds Charles Wood, Mrs. Henry Wood's son, writing of Huskisson as one who had betrayed the true principles of Conservatism. Peel was to complete what Huskisson began. Economic determinism? Undoubtedly. Yes, but it would be wrong to underrate the power of moral indignation and remonstrance, and the very real idealism that lay behind the Free Trade movement. If Free Trade had been no more than a material doctrine, no more than a system of exchanging tin trays for cheap food, it would never have commanded the fealty of so many good, humane, idealistic men and women for so long. Political change in Dickens's Britain could be brought about only when an economic interest was allied to a moral passion.

CHAPTER THREE

THE DREAM OF FREE TRADE

During the lifetime of Charles Dickens there were two great popular agitations which drew their strength from a wide coalition among the classes, Radicals, Socialists, young Tories, old Whigs, new Liberals, working men, manufacturers, farm labourers, Nonconformists. The first was the movement which culminated in the Reform Act of 1832. The second was the movement which brought the Repeal of the Corn Laws in 1846. Dickens was rather cynical about the first. He was an enthusiast about the second, and in his devotion to that cause he undertook the arduous enterprise (made much against the grain) of starting a Liberal newspaper, *The Daily News* (1846). His sympathies were touched by the sufferings of the hungry workmen in the cities and the pinched labourers on the farms. "Oh God, that bread should be so dear and flesh and blood so cheap!" summed up his politics at that time. Repeal would bring the cheap, abundant food to fill those hollow bellies, and would provide an expanding prosperity in which all might share. To Dickens and the Liberals of his time, Free Trade was a policy of emancipation. It would set Mr. Rouncewell, the benevolent manufacturer, free from thraldom to the stupid Sir Leicester Dedlock; it would be a keg of powder under the Circumlocution Office. To Victorian Liberalism, tariffs and the protective system were instruments of absolutism; they represented an unhallowed alliance between the old despotism and the new technology. They were instruments used to oppress the people, to maintain outworn privilege, to stifle the fresh energies thrusting up from the middle classes, and to thwart the development of a world society. Free Trade was an international ideal. The Liberals of that period believed that an unrestricted exchange of goods between the world's peoples would lead to universal prosperity and universal peace; and most of the Conservatives of that period came in time to think the same. If each nation were free to sell its neighbours its own fruits and buy from them in return what it lacked, then a natural harmony and order would arise in human affairs. Each would profit from the other's well-being, and, as those ties of family dependence strengthened, the threat of war would vanish. For what was war but a product of feudalism, of the old absolute forms of government now fast decaying? In the year of the Repeal of the Corn Laws, the Liberal Free Traders were greatly pleased by news from the United States that the Senate—by a close vote, it is true—had reduced the

PAPIER-MÂCHÉ ARMCHAIR BY JENNENS AND BETTRIDGE, 1851
Engraving from the official catalogue of the Great Exhibition

American tariff. Hurrah! The great Republic of the West was on our side. The propaganda of the Cobdenites, started in 1838 by the Eight Men of Manchester, had captured Britain in eight years. Was there not reason now to hope that this grand movement of liberation might, within a decade, sweep round the whole globe? Why, look! from Rome, from the most august ruler on earth, there came a cheering signal. A new Pope, a *Liberal* Pope, as he was called, had been elected, and he had marked his accession by cutting down the tariffs of the Papal States. Temporal Power was on the side of the Protestant angels. Lancashire and Yorkshire were gratified to observe that His Holiness had diminished the duties on imported textiles. In this same year, hopes were entertained that even autocratic Russia might reduce her protective tariff—the Tsar smiled but to deceive. When in 1860 Richard Cobden went to Paris to negotiate a commercial treaty with the Ministers of Napoleon III, he was inspired by the prospect of establishing an everlasting peace between traditional enemies. What rivers of blood had divided them! And in the fifties, how fragile was the peace between them; what ugly faces Frenchmen and Britons were pulling at one another across the Channel; how insulting the cartoons; how fierce the leading articles! When Lord Raglan was in command against the Russians at the Crimea, and the French were fighting with us, the old bemused general would wave his sword at the enemy trenches and address them as "those damned Frenchies". Of all the vulgar performances of a great writer none are worse than Thackeray's pieces about the French from the *Paris Sketch Book* onwards; as cheap and nasty as any of the cartoons about "the Froggies". Cobden's eagerness to end the ancient feud with France was a decent and honourable sentiment, and his manner of going about it was in the temper of our present times. Today, almost a century later, the broken hopes of European unity are being picked up again at Strasbourg.

By the middle of the century, the Conservative Party, as well as the Whig-Liberals, had accepted Free Trade as the national policy, and it went unchallenged until that erratic genius, Joseph Chamberlain, early in the twentieth century, let loose his "raging, tearing" propaganda for Tariff Reform. All that was best in that tradition, as well as much that was bad, and even preposterous, found its expression in the Great Exhibition of 1851. Sensitive characters (the young William Morris, for example) recoiled from its insolent ugliness, its parade of engines, machines and inventions, its assumption that through mechanical progress man would attain happiness. But a faith, a missionary faith was there made manifest. Paxton's strange building of glass and iron was its temple.

Matthew Arnold's fastidious spirit might mock the Philistines, might torture itself with the spectacle of their outrageous vulgarities, but those barbarians of Arnold's had virtues that look half-heroic to a later age. Their conception of democracy, it is true, was stunted and partial. There is a general agreement on that among Tories, Liberals and Socialists of today. They had no sense of industrial democracy, we say. Their idea of Freedom was inadequate because it ignored economic freedoms. Yet they were conscious that theirs was a marching kind of democracy—that it was a positive, aggressive fighting Freedom. They were never on the defensive. They had an evangelistic belief in the mission of the British people. And what was that mission? To bring about the reign of peace and the rule of order in the world: through the force of example, exhortation and persuasion, through propaganda, through commerce, through financial arrangements. Leadership? There was never any debate among these mid-Victorians as to whether Britain should give a lead. There was something at once comical and sublime in their assumption that they were the acknowledged captains of the world's destinies. They had a faith that never faltered in the inherent power of their ideas to transform and rule the world. Sometimes they were exceedingly naïve and boyish in their enthusiasms, as in the belief that if every nation from China to Peru provided itself with a House of Commons and a House of Lords, with H.M. Government neatly arrayed on one side and H.M. Opposition on the other, manna would automatically start falling. But, oh, the tremendous strength and happiness of certainty! What does it matter who laughs if one has assurance? What is the mild martyrdom of ridicule to a believer? "Do foreigners talk of hypocrisy, of cant? Do they say that Pecksniff is the incarnation of Victorian Britain? Let them talk. But let them get a faith as creative, a leadership as confident, a mission as inspired, a hope as radiant, and we will listen to them."

To the men and women who gathered under Paxton's crystal dome in the pleasant summer weather of 1851, the nobility of the ideal was as evident as the pomp of the occasion. Britannia had invited the nations, "Gaul and German, Russ and Turk, each with his native handiwork", to demonstrate the astonishing variety of the world's riches and the manifold skills of its children, not as native princes yielding tribute to a paramount monarch, but as allies in an exhilarating enterprise. The rubrics on the walls of the Palace of Crystal, the boom of the orators, the jubilant music of Handel, all proclaimed peace on earth through men of good will, enterprise and self-reliance. Saint Cecilia was at the organ, the Hallelujah Chorus thundered through the naves, and Saint Michael and Saint George sat on the clouds above Hyde Park. Labour, invention, science, industry, the free exchange of ideas and of goods would bring a universal harmony. Was it an illusion? If time has proved it so, it was, at least, not a mean illusion.

Yet with all that was so powerful and splendid in the outward manifestation, there was an inner weakness apparent to those who looked below the flashing surface. The Industrial Revolution had developed so rapidly that it not only burst through the old political frames, but was likely to overwhelm the popular new philosophies. It brought with it a frightening accumulation of problems of human wretchedness and degradation, of child slaves and of women reduced to the condition of animals. "Hell is a city much like London." So, for that matter, were Manchester, Birmingham, Sheffield and the other great towns. It was even more true in 1850 than in 1820. As industry and trade expanded, as Britain became the world's forge and smithy, so Britain's slums increased in size and deepened in squalor. Was this the new civilisation promised by the machines and by the liberation of the repressed energies of the mercantile classes? To a workman's family, huddling at night on the wet straw in a stinking cellar in Ancoats, the benevolent proposals of Adam Smith and Jeremy Bentham might well seem more cruel than the ordinances of the old tyrants. The Conservatives asked, "Was it for this that you destroyed traditional England?"

Britain might have come to the end of this nightmare of the Industrial Revolution earlier if the defenders of the system had all been bad men, selfish, greedy men; if the forces of good had been ranged on one side and the forces of evil on the other. But the advocates of *laissez-faire* were not by any means a union of Scrooges and Bounderbys. In their ranks were men of humane instincts, of deep religious impulses, of profound attachment to the idea of Liberty, of high sense of public duty; men inspired, as we have seen, by the ideal of universal peace; and, like many good men before them (and since) they were capable of endless self-deception. They were so absorbed by the beauty of their theory that they were blind to its worst consequences. They believed that they had laid hold upon a great truth, upon a new revelation of Freedom and Justice, and that its application must inevitably bring "the greatest happiness of the greatest number". There were times when it seemed as if Britain was a volcano that must blow its head off. The political ideas and the moral sense of the nation seemed to be lagging hopelessly behind mechanical and technological progress.

Changes were taking place at such a pace that men and women could not keep up with them. It is odd to think now that the first steam locomotive employed to carry coal away from the mines was called a "Whimsy", because it looked such a ridiculous monster. To the tenants of Horseback Hall, to Sam Weller, Senior, driving his coach along the Portsmouth Road, and to the man at the plough this was a dragon escaped from a Drury Lane pantomime. It was not to be thought that Whimsy could alter their lives, could bring them grief or losses, or anything but laughter. There was an allegory of the Industrial Revolution in Huskisson's death at the opening of the Liverpool and Manchester railway in 1830. "Take care, sir, for God's sake take care!" cried the Duke of Wellington. But Huskisson did not take care, he ventured too near, and was mangled by the wheels of that hideous child of whimsy. The new machines, the loom, the locomotive and the rest were not taken seriously enough until it was nearly too late. They created wealth; they devoured men.

The glare of doom lay over town and countryside. As early as 1826, William Cobbett was writing from the Valley of the Avon:

> This is, I verily believe it, the worst-used labouring people upon the face of the earth. Dogs and hogs and horses are treated with more civility; and as to food and lodging, how gladly would the labourers change with them! This state of things never can continue many years! By some means or other there must be an end to it; and my firm belief is that that end will be dreadful. In the meanwhile I see, and I see it with pleasure, that the common people know that they are ill used; and that they cordially, most cordially, hate those who ill-treat them.

Nearly twenty years later (1844) Frederick Engels ended his study of the working classes in Manchester with these words:

> It is too late for a peaceful solution. The classes are divided more and more sharply, the spirit of resistance penetrates the workers, the bitterness intensifies,

> the guerilla skirmishes become concentrated in more important battles, and soon a slight impulse will suffice to set the avalanche in motion. Then, indeed, will the war cry resound through the land: "War to the palaces, peace to the cottages!"—but then it will be too late for the rich to beware.

In 1831 John Stuart Mill reflected, with the detachment of a man who is sure his own throat will not be cut, on the certainty of revolution if the Reform Bill was lost. "Until the whole of the existing institutions of society are levelled with the ground, there will be nothing for a wise man to do which the most pig-headed fool cannot do better than he. A Turgot even could not do in the present state of England what Turgot himself failed to do in France—mend the old system." So late as 1848, when the Chartists gathered for their last rally on Kennington Common, Ministers were sending notes to one another that the violent end so long expected was at last upon them. They sat like the gods in Valhalla waiting for the flames to consume them.

Surely the design of historical necessity was written plain across the face of Britain. The middle classes had overthrown the aristocracy, and had consummated their revolution in two stages, through the Reform Bill and through the Repeal of the Corn Laws. They had brought into being a capitalist society of unparalleled size and might. Now all was ripe for the final development. A brutalised proletariat, more formidable in size and more concentrated than any in the world, suffering unimaginable miseries and humiliations and goaded to despair, would rise against its masters and seize power. The revolution begun in 1832 would be a continuing revolution. So thought the authors of the Communist Manifesto of 1848.

Yet the most remarkable thing about the Age of Dickens was that no general uprising did take place. During that great year of the revolution, 1848, when all Europe was convulsed, and crown went tumbling after crown, there was no revolt in Victoria's realm. Indeed, by a paradox, the demonstration on Kennington Common on April 10, 1848, marked the end of the Chartist Agitation, a great movement flickering out in the bathos of a chill London rain, and Feargus O'Connor shaking hands with the police, and a damp, respectable deputation driving to the House of Commons in a cab, as though they had been going there with a petition about drains from the Southwark Vestry. Fatalism had not conquered. The inherent political genius of the British people refused to accept the notion that the Industrial Revolution had let loose forces too powerful for it to master. And the silent, unrepresented lower middle classes had once more provided a useful buffer.

Was this our new environment? Then we must dominate it. A change came over the Victorian conception of Liberalism, and, let it be said in all honesty, it was a change to which two illustrious Conservatives materially contributed, Disraeli and Shaftesbury. There had been a day when the pressure of Liberal opinion had forced the abolition of the Income Tax because it encroached on the freedom of the individual (1815). There had been a day when every attempt to regulate hours and conditions in factories was resisted as an invasion of private rights. Now the climate was changing. Slowly, hesitatingly, more and more men of power and influence became converted to the view that they had a collective responsibility for protecting the weak from cruel exploitations, for safeguarding children, for redressing injustices and ending abuses. The State, they felt, should do more than "hold the ring" for the lusty young heroes of free enterprise. This effort to organise the will and conscience of the nation was the saving grace of the Victorians. So remarkable a change in the habits of thought could not be brought about in a day. It was not easy to persuade such vigorous, dogmatic characters as the Victorians that they had ever erred in believing that unregulated enterprise would bring happiness and prosperity to the human race. Those sturdy beings who had devoted their energies to breaking the chains of State, and had often been inspired in so doing by a religious ardour, needed some little time to adjust themselves to the new idea of the State as the collective conscience, as the embodied will of the people. The process of conversion was slow. It was the tardy, painful, grand spiritual adventure of the Victorian age.

CHAPTER FOUR

THE ACCURSED HILL

Pleasure is the highest good. We all seek it. Pain is horrible. We all run away from it. What more rational a principle of Government than that? The purpose of the wise Governor is to assure the greatest happiness of the greatest number. That philosophy, liberal, humane and enlightened, as it seemed, captivated a great many of our forebears. Jeremy Bentham was a good man, indeed a great man, but he suffered from spiritual pride. He was what simple folk call a "know-all". He rendered sterling services to his age as a reformer of institutions. He was like the man from Missouri who refuses to take anything for granted, but says "I want to be shown!". Nothing escaped his critical faculty except, alack, his own positive theories. The reforms he achieved in the domain of Law and in the treatment of criminals, and his services to education entitle him to an everlasting respect. And it was largely because he was so devoted, high-minded and benevolent a servant of the public that he was able to impose upon his contemporaries some notions that are as frightening as Swift's "modest proposal for eating little children".

On a railway journey one falls into conversation with a rosy, bright-eyed old gentleman in the corner seat. How knowledgeable he is! How well he talks! How logical and full of good sense he is! How piercing his criticisms of shams and follies! He is a radical without intolerance, he is a reformer without spite. Ah! one says, if only there were more such characters alive, combining sweet reasonableness with encyclopaedic wisdom, this would be a far happier world. Then, as one nods assent to the old gentleman's admirable series of propositions for rescuing the human race from its plight, one notices that the gentle voice is growing a little shrill, the clear eyes are beginning to blaze. Yet there is no break in the linked logic; one proposition flows into the next. What is he saying? Can one believe one's ears? Is it possible that he really believes he has constructed an exquisite pair of scales, so finely balanced that he can not only weigh the soul when he has extracted it from a human body, but can measure the proportions of joy and grief in it, of success and failure? Yes, he says, with his sweet smile, he has often dissected a man's faculties in his laboratory, has made a chemical analysis of his hopes, dreams and terrors, and, by an ingenious rearrangement of his salts and elements, has made quite a new and sensible fellow of him. But wasn't he dead by then? Sir, here is my card. Do pray call at my laboratory. I have much of interest to show you, and I am certain I could be of great service to you personally. Kindly take note of the name. Bentham—Jeremy Bentham. . . . So the old fellow's mad! But he is so sanely and persuasively mad that a great many honest folk will be taken in by him.

Coiled around all the excellent good sense of the father of Utilitarianism lay this shining vein of lunacy. When a poet like William Blake goes mad, one knows it is the madness of a God-intoxicated man, the madness of a man with too much poetry fermenting in his brain. When Bentham runs wild, we suspect that he has been driven insane by the pressure of a terrible logic and by the swarming assault of the ant-like battalions of facts. His dementia is, indeed, a wild excess of reason. Blake was haunted by angels, Bentham by theories. Blake would see God and the prophets on Hampstead Heath; and his nightmares were visited by the Ghost of a Flea, a monstrous but not ignoble object, prowling in mailed panoply, steeped in an infernal light among subterranean corridors of steel. The Benthamite nightmares were filled with algebraical formulae and economists' symbols writhing in the equations of the damned. A poet who—to use a high poetic phrase—goes off his head may give us something as thrilling as Blake's "Rose, thou art sick", but a political economist who takes leave of his senses is quite likely to do what Bentham did, that is design Panopticons (model prisons) and model workhouses for his fellows. The soul then becomes filled with a black despair at the vision of the Universe as the ultimate Panopticon, the perfect prison so designed that God, sitting at the centre of it, can keep His eye on every prisoner's every movement and thoughts at every moment of the day and night. Bentham's geometry of Calvinism clutches the heart in an icy grip.

Who was to slay this monster of benevolence, the philanthropic eater of men? Who would destroy the philosophical Radical? Not the Whig; not the Tory; for their arms were weak and their honour sullied. The *unphilosophical* Radical alone could slay the dragon.

The inspired leader of the unphilosophical Radicals of the nineteenth century was William Cobbett. The unphilosophical Radical has been at once a very great nuisance to authority and a saving grace in British and American politics during the past hundred years. Whatever form of government is set over the people, he usually finds himself, sooner or later, pitted against it. In one age, we find him in revolt against kings and landlords; in another against Parliament, or Public Corporations, or Boards of Directors. If he is the enemy of privilege, he is also the foe of theory. He is suspicious of nearly all political philosophers. He is always discovering that new Presbyter is old Priest writ large. He is on the side of every heresy until it is accepted as the true faith, and itself begins persecuting. The flame in his belly is the old Promethean flame. He is that chief guarantor of the survival of democratic institutions, the perpetual dissenter.

HOMELESS WOMEN AND CHILDREN SLEEPING OUT-OF-DOORS
Steel engraving from Gustave Doré's "London", 1872

The philosophical Radical is filled with a passion for humanity in the abstract. To his unphilosophical brother, this seems a morbid passion, as though a man were to fall in love with the local Gas Works. The philosophical Radical is capable of cruel and inhuman conduct in pursuit of the greatest good of the greatest number. The unphilosophical Radical loves only what he knows and fights for what he loves. His blood is up, and his sword is out, in defence of poor Tom when he's a-cold, of Naboth when the Ahab Construction, General Utility and State Viniculture Corporation is about to dispossess him of his vineyard; and of Tib and Joan, and Dick and Harry, when they are ill-treated either by despots or by philanthropists.

Through his *Political Register* and his *Rural Rides* Cobbett communicates to a modern reader the immediate anger of the unphilosophical Radical of the early part of the nineteenth century. Cobbett was born in 1762, a farm labourer's son, at a time when the Industrial Revolution itself was being born, and he died in 1835 when its most distressing effects were being exhibited through the country. Inside the House of Commons, he cut rather an absurd figure. Outside the House, he served as the natural leader of His Majesty's loyal, unrepresented Opposition, the English yeoman, small farmer and peasant, and their brothers in the cities, the mechanic and artisan. For one half of his life, Cobbett was an old-fashioned Tory, for the other half an old-fashioned Radical. That made him the most effective political voice the lower middle classes have ever had. Both Tory and Radical strains were mixed up in him to the end, and they made an explosive combination. He was God's angriest saint. His fury was not that of a man whose private ambitions are thwarted, it was the cloudburst of a disinterested rage; and in this world a disinterested rage is very often stronger than armies. Cobbett was the type of all brave, honest men who, seeing cruelty done under the most elegant auspices, under the most distinguished patronage, under such fine names as progress, civilisation and efficiency, roar out their protest to the heavens.

In reading Cobbett—no! nobody can simply *read* him. Reading is too quiet a word to describe our experiences with that Man of Joyous Wrath. One doesn't read Cobbett, one hears him. His stormings of rage, and his loud, angry laughter still shake the earth. How the wind whistles when you open his pages! The blackthorns are bent double. And what a flight of dead leaves comes spinning and tumbling along in that high wind! Bits of paper, too—lots of them—leaves from parsons' sermons, shreds of Acts of Parliament, lawyers' writs, landlords' and bailiffs' notices. Now look!—there he is, the old warrior himself—outlined against the bare sky on the upheaved shoulder of the Sussex Downs. He is tramping along with the wind, and going as fast as the wind, and cursing and roaring with a voice louder than the wind. Now he is marching upon that pleasant country town, and the singing wind goes with him, thrashing the trees, and whisking off old gentlemen's wigs. He is twirling his big stick around his head with the joy of a drum-major. He is rehearsing for the drummings and poundings he is about to deal out. As he goes past it, he glares at the great, white, colonnaded mansion whose lovely park, with its high walls, is as empty of signs of human life as the gardens of the Sleeping Beauty. Hear him growl his maledictions. "That is Lord A's place. His family began as robbers of the monasteries and go on as robbers still . . ." "Plundering and murderous sons of corruption . . ." "Maggots that inhabit the public carcase . . ." "Reptiles that would transport the poor to save themselves food." Thwack! crack!

Here he comes, the oldest of Tories, the youngest of Radicals, laying about him in imaginary conflict—ready to take on a dozen powerful foes at one set-to—in imagination driving in front of him the respectable rabble, the belted rogues, the moneyed scamps of his age, the tax-gatherers, the attorneys, the "loan-mongers", the fat vicars and the lean economists, all of whom alike he abominated with a generous and equal abomination. In that great heart there was room for a thousand splendid

CHILDREN IN A GIN SHOP AT NIGHT
Lithograph by George Cruikshank

THE LICENSED VICTUALLERS' DINNER AT HACKNEY, 1846
Coloured aquatint by George Hunt after E. F. Lambert (detail)

A LONDON SLUM

Detail from steel engraving by Gustave Doré

From his "London", published 1872

hates. There was nothing that was established, privileged and honoured that he feared to attack—no abuse, consecrated by long reverence; no cruelty, sanctified by convention. He loved England, he loved this dear land. He loved its good country stocks and their virtues. He loved them so much that he was beside himself at the sight of the ruin that was overtaking them.

Oh, listen to the joyous thwack—crack—thwack of Cobbett's stick as he brings it down on the backs of the new aristocracy of Pitt's creation, that lay like a blight along the old rural Britain.

> The baseness, the foul, the stinking, the carrion baseness of the fellows that call themselves "country gentlemen" is that the wretches, while railing against the poor and the poor-rates; while affecting to believe that the poor are wicked and lazy; while complaining that the poor, the working people are too numerous, and that the country villages are too populous; the carrion baseness of these wretches is that, while they are thus *bold* with regard to the working and poor people, they never even whisper a word against pensioners, placemen, soldiers, parsons, fund-holders, tax-gatherers or tax-eaters! They say not a word against the prolific dead-weight to whom they give a premium for breeding, while they want to check the population of labourers! . . . Oh! they are the most cowardly, the very basest, the most scandalously base reptiles that were ever warmed into life by the rays of the sun!

And, now, a hammering for the politicians: "May that man perish for ever and ever who, having the powers, neglects to bring to justice the perjured, the suborning, the insolent and perfidious miscreants who openly sell their country's rights and their own souls." And now comes a great battering upon cobwebbed college doors. Recalling that he had got his own education by the simple and unorthodox method of "rolling down a sandhill", Cobbett roars out:

> If I had been brought up a milksop, with a nursery-maid everlastingly at my heels, I should have been at this day as great a fool, as inefficient a mortal, as any of those frivolous idiots that are turned out from Winchester and Westminster School, or from any of those dens of dunces called Colleges and Universities. It is impossible to say how much I owe to that sandhill; and I went to return it my thanks for the ability which it probably gave me to be one of the greatest terrors to one of the greatest and most powerful bodies of knaves and fools that ever were permitted to afflict this or any other country.

He was a rowdy, vulgar, chivalrous, brutal, sensitive, rationalist, mystical, egocentric old Radical-Tory curmudgeon; often wrongheaded, nearly always true-hearted; tough of fibre as an oak, but full of the most womanly tenderness for children and the weak; a pacifist-patriot with a deep feeling for the beauty of his native land. He thought not with his headpiece alone but with his whole sturdy body. In his writings, Cobbett uses the fist and shoulder muscles of a Tom Cribb. The poor, the dispossessed and the frightened-to-speak-for-themselves worshipped him as their Saint George. As an example of his prophetic powers, and as a sort of charcoal drawing of England at this time, let us choose this passage, with its symbolic value, its sense of a bad dream lingering on in the clear sunshine of the landscape:

> I resolved to ride over this Accursed Hill. As I was going up a field towards it, I met a man going home from work. I asked how he got on. He said, very badly. I asked him what was the cause of it. He said the hard times. "What times", said I, "was there ever a finer summer, a finer harvest, and is there not an old wheat rick in every farm-yard?" "Ah!" said he, "they make it bad for poor people, for all that." "*They*?" said I, "who is *they*?" He was silent. "Oh, no, no! my friend," said I, "it is not *they*; it is that Accursed Hill that has robbed you of the supper that you ought to find smoking on the table when you get home." I gave him the price of a pot of beer, and on I went, leaving the poor dejected assemblage of skin and bone to wonder at my words.

They? "Who is *they*?" The ineluctable, remote, ineffable *They*. Their mystery weighs upon us still. The people of England are always listening for the thunder of these unknown gods among the hills, and waiting for their thunderbolt to strike.

To us today Cobbett stands for the divine anarchy of love which is at odds with all political systems. He was an enemy of the new Tories because he was himself so old a Tory that his sympathies were grounded in the life of the land as it was before the Reformation. And he was so modern a Radical that he revolted against the cruelties wrought in the names of Liberalism and Reform by the Utilitarians, and by those he so heartily damned as Scots "feelosophers". It was a black sin for Tory and Whig landlords to treat their villagers less kindly than their cattle. But it was equally dark a crime for Benthamite politicians to treat them as figures on a class-room blackboard. Cobbett could see at a glance that the rosy old gentleman in the corner seat of the compartment, who spoke so sweetly and so reasonably, had a streak of homicidal lunacy in him. So he raged against the new Poor Law and the model workhouses of the Benthamites as he had raged against the Enclosures.

William Cobbett rides the Accursed Hill no more. But whoever fights for the individual againt any soulless institution will always have Cobbett's manly spirit on his side. During the century and more that has gone by since he died, his influence, diffused, humble, often uncredited, has inspired later men to resist the tyranny of organisations, even benevolent and patriarchal ones, and to strive to bridle "the never-ending audacity of elected persons". Cobbett's revolt against reformers as well as reactionaries had its effect on so great an American statesman as Lincoln and on so great a poet of democracy as Whitman. There is a great deal of Cobbett in the author of *Hard Times*, *Bleak House* and *Little Dorrit*. His very ghost is more solid than the bodies of many living men of mark. Into the night of storm that ghost marches on, whirling its blackthorn stick and cursing; and crying courage to us down the night.

CHAPTER FIVE

THE NAMELESS WOULD NOT DISAPPEAR

To the growth of sensibility and the development of a conviction that man was in some part his brother's keeper, no finer contribution was made than that of a highly diversified group of writers, among them Disraeli, Thomas Carlyle, Dickens, Elizabeth Gaskell, Charles Kingsley, Tom Hood, Elizabeth Barrett, and a host of almost forgotten journalists, such as Douglas Jerrold and Albert Mayhew; writers who get less than their due from history. Politicians, as one comes to know them in the mass, are usually jealous, possessive creatures. They do not like to concede that the vast tides of human affairs may be moved by any lunar influences beyond their own. They are often contemptuous of novelists as mere drawing-room entertainers, weavers of profitable dreams; and of political journalists as impudent fellows who set themselves up to be both censors and rivals of Parliament. So it has come about that the writers "of social significance" of the early Victorian times have seldom been given full credit for the part they played in changing the political outlook of the middle classes and in remedying the worst abuses of the period.

It is at least arguable that the young Disraeli who wrote *Sybil, or The Two Nations*—the young man who was half a drawing-room daisy and half a seer, and wholly a genius—rendered as lasting a service to his country as the old Disraeli who, as Prime Minister, crowned his Queen Empress of India. The writers I have named were notable enlighteners and educators of public opinion during a period when the ignorance of the comfortable classes appeared invincible and might well have proved ruinous to the nation. The well-to-do had little conception of the depraved and wretched condition of the masses in the great cities. In the middle decades of the century nearly everybody worked hard, often far too hard for the good of their souls, for they did not give themselves sufficient time to consider where they were going. The making of money brought a moral glow. Personal gain and the public welfare appeared indistinguishable. Those who lived Puritan lives, with a mind fixed upon success on earth and assured of a leasehold in the skies, had scant thought to give to the lot of the slaves in the mills and mines. Disraeli goes to see Lancashire and then, in the preface to *Sybil*, writes like a traveller returned from far-off lands who barely expects civilised society to credit his tales of the anthropophagi, the dwarfs who carry their heads under their arms and eat their fellow men. He admits that, while he "hopes he has alleged nothing which is not true, he has found the absolute necessity of suppressing much that is genuine. For so little do we know of the state of our country that the air of improbability which the whole truth would inevitably throw over these pages might deter some from their perusal".

Macaulay might toss aside Dickens's *Hard Times*, with a pout for its "sullen Socialism" and its author's ignorant failure to understand the principles of the Manchester school. Mrs. Gaskell might suffer social ostracism for reporting what her serene, clear eyes had beheld in the slums of Manchester. The Rev. Charles Kingsley might forfeit his hopes of becoming a Bishop by publishing *Alton Locke* (1850), a novel that espoused the cause of the working people in a manner that was at once chivalrous and patronising. Christian Socialism was *not* the path to preferment in the days when Lord John Russell was Prime Minister. Yet these writers, and a score of minor novelists and journalists who survive only in the British Museum Library, brought a change in feeling among their compatriots more revolutionary than that achieved by any political party. It was the major novelists and the minor poets and forgotten hacks who quickened the public's sensibilities in a harsh money-getting age. They were the indispensable allies and auxiliars of those few, but how noble, characters in politics who strove desperately to enlighten the darkness of the House of Commons—such men as Michael Sadler of Aldborough, Fielden, the Liberal cotton-spinner, and Ashley (afterwards Lord Shaftesbury), the Tory Evangelical.

When Shaftesbury, the tender-hearted, the single-minded Shaftesbury, was going about the country, seeking to stir up a public emotion to rescue little children from slavery, he was saddened by the indifference of the clergy of his own Church and the Ministers of other faiths. They passed by on the other side of the road. The Churches were more slow to wrath over the serfdom of babies in mills and mines than they had shown themselves towards the enslaving of the African Negroes in the times of Wilberforce and Clarkson. We can sympathise with the emotions which prompted the "alien patriot" Disraeli to dart his sharp gibes at the Society for the Propagation of the Gospel in Foreign Parts, or impelled the lower-middle-class waif Dickens to draw his caricature of Mrs. Jellyby, neglecting her children for the sake of the natives of Borrioboola-Gha.

Yet if the trumpet of the Church gave out an uncertain sound, there were eloquent tongues in our great secular cathedral of English literature to discourse upon the text, "But the greatest of these is Charity", and to move the hearts of men and women to compassion. The ill-requited profession of letters may always reflect with pride that in an age when there was much cruelty and much indifference to human suffering, a group of writers, some still renowned, others forgotten, kindled a conscience among the self-complacent. In the history of the Victorian times, the books and the politics are interwoven. The politics cannot be comprehended without reference to the novelists. It was the function of the leading writers of the Victorian period to keep the springs of sympathy from drying up in that hard winter of materialism; and to preserve the vital sparks of pity and imagination, both in those who were grown drowsy from a surfeit of bread and meat, and those whose stomachs were aching with hunger.

The dominant classes in the nation had become rich and were in a hurry to grow richer and stronger. One recalls the bitter irony of that description in the Hammonds' *Life of Shaftesbury* of the array of noble lords and rich manufacturers in the House of Commons who felt it their duty to vindicate the painful truths of political economy. "They always win who have no leak into tenderness." It was apparent that there now were others beside the aristocrats to trample upon the weak. The French Marquis whose coach knocked the child down, and then drove on, was once upon a time the embodiment of cruel oppression. Now the tyrant might be one who himself had started life in grimmest poverty and had attained power by his own exertions, according to the principles approved by Adam Smith and Jeremy Bentham. Mr. Bounderby in *Hard Times*, for example.

> He was a rich man: banker, merchant, manufacturer, and what not. A big, loud man, with a stare, and a metallic laugh. A man made out of a coarse material, which seemed to have been stretched to make so much of him. A man with a great puffed head and forehead, swelled veins in his temples, and such a strained skin to his face that it seemed to hold his eyes open, and lift his eyebrows up. A man with a pervading appearance on him of being inflated like a balloon, and ready to start. A man who could never sufficiently vaunt himself a self-made man. A man who was always proclaiming, through that brassy speaking-trumpet of his, his old ignorance and poverty. A man who was the Bully of humility.

The application of science to industry provided the lamp of the Djinn. Rub it and wish—and all your wishes would be granted. But the proletariat in the new cities of the Industrial Revolution knew that they had been sold into the captivity of the lamp. They were lost souls, their present condition desperate, their future without hope. Mrs. Gaskell wrote of the Manchester workpeople in 1848, "At present they seem to me to be left in a state wherein lamentations and tears are thrown aside as useless, but in which the lips are compressed for curses, and the hands clenched and ready to smite".

As we look back now upon that desolate scene, we perceive that the humanitarian impulse in Victorian literature did a great deal to prevent a civil war between Disraeli's two nations. Humanitarian? One is not easy about that word. It suggests a flabby and diffused sentimentality; it calls up the ghosts of stout ladies in black bombasine passing resolutions at Exeter Hall, or it brings to mind the nasty shape of Mr. Honeythunder in *Edwin Drood*, Dickens's philanthropic thug, the prize-fighter of organised morality, boring and bruising his man to the ropes, but lacking the decent manly virtues of the Ring. It was certainly no thin gruel of sentiment that the Victorian writers dispensed.

Listen to the harsh angry voice of Carlyle, like the voice of John from the pit cursing Herod:

> British industrial existence seems fast becoming one huge poison-swamp of reeking pestilence physical and moral; a hideous *living* Golgotha of souls and bodies buried alive; such a Curtius' gulf communicating with the Nether Deeps, as the Sun never saw till now. . . . Thirty-thousand outcast Needlewomen working themselves swiftly to death; three million Paupers rotting in forced idleness, *helping* said Needlewomen to die: these are but items in the sad ledger of despair.
>
> Thirty-thousand wretched women, sunk in that putrefying well of abominations; they have oozed-in upon London, from the universal Stygian quagmire of British industrial life; are accumulated in the well of the concern, to that extent. British charity is smitten to the heart, at the laying-bare of such a scene; passionately undertakes, by enormous subscription of money, or by other enormous effort, to redress that individual horror; as I, and all men, hope it may be. But, alas, what next? This general well and cesspool once baled clean today will begin before night to fill itself anew.

Or this again, from *Past and Present*:

> At Stockport Assizes . . . a Mother and Father are arraigned and found guilty of poisoning three of their children, to defraud a "burial-society" of some £3 8*s*. due on the death of each child: they are arraigned, found guilty; and the official authorities, it is whispered, hint that perhaps the case is not solitary, that perhaps you had better not probe farther into that department of things . . . The Stockport Mother and Father think and hint; Our poor little starveling Tom, who cries all day for victuals, who will see only evil and not good in this world: if he were out of misery at once; he well dead, and the rest of us perhaps kept alive? It is thought, and hinted; at last it is done. And now Tom being killed, and all spent and eaten, is it poor little starveling Jack that must go, or poor little starveling Will?—What a committee of ways and means! In starved sieged cities, in the uttermost doomed ruin of old Jerusalem fallen under the wrath of God, it was prophesied and said, "The hands of the pitiful women have sodden their own children." The stern Hebrew imagination could conceive no blacker gulf or ultimatum of degraded god-punished man. And we here, in modern England, exuberant with supply of all kinds, besieged by nothing if it be not by invisible Enchantments, are we reaching that? How come these things?

Sentimental Victorians? What resemblance was there between Elizabeth Gaskell and the *Keepsake* beauty, soft and lush, the Victorian lady of conventional refinement; mixing pot-pourri; pressing a violet between the covers of Mrs. Hemans's poems; embroidering a little; strumming a little; making pale watercolour sketches of Fairlight Glen; taking refuge in an elegant headache; shielded, cossetted, cocooned? Let this passage from the introduction to *Mary Barton*, describing Manchester in the eighteen-forties, provide an answer:

The cottages are old, dirty, and of the smallest sort, the streets uneven, fallen into ruts, and in parts without drains or pavement; masses of refuse, offal, and sickening filth lie among standing pools in all directions; the atmosphere is poisoned by the effluvia from these, and laden and darkened by the smoke of a dozen tall factory chimneys. A horde of ragged women and children swarm about here, as filthy as the swine that thrive upon the garbage heaps and in the puddles. In short, the whole rookery furnishes such a hateful and repulsive spectacle as can hardly be equalled in the worst courts on the Irk. The race that lives in these ruinous cottages, behind broken windows, mended with oilskin, spring doors, and rotten door-posts, or in dark, wet cellars, in measureless filth and stench, in this atmosphere penned in as if with a purpose, this race must really have reached the lowest stage of humanity. This is the impression and the line of thought which the exterior of this district forces upon the beholder. But what must one think when he hears that in each of these pens, containing at most two rooms, a garret, and perhaps a cellar, on the average twenty human beings live; that in the whole region, for each one hundred and twenty persons, one usually inaccessible privy is provided; and that in spite of all the preachings of the physicians, in spite of the excitement into which the cholera epidemic plunged the sanitary police by reason of the condition of Little Ireland, in spite of everything, in this year of grace 1844, it is in almost the same state as in 1831! Dr. Kay asserts that not only the cellars but the first floors of all the houses in this district are damp; that a number of cellars once filled up with earth have not been emptied and are occupied once more by the Irish people; that in one cellar the water constantly wells up through a hole stopped with clay, the cellar lying below the river level, so that its occupant, a handloom weaver, had to bale out the water from his dwelling every morning and pour it into the street!

Elizabeth Gaskell, the wife of a Unitarian minister, this grave, gentle, sensitive woman, had the courage to look at the world around her, and the courage (and the skill) to tell what she had seen. In doing so, she was greatly abused, and one of her novels was cut off in its serial publication because it offended the taste of the magazine's subscribers. When we think of Victorian women, when we think of prunes and prisms, when we recall the mock modesty, the pantalettes, the simpering affectations, the velvet curtains drawn against the tragic face of night, it is well to remember that this courageous Elizabeth Gaskell was also a Victorian woman.

Now let us take an illustrative page from a very different character, but one who also never in his whole strange life lacked that first virtue of humanity, courage. This concrete image from Benjamin Disraeli's *Sybil*, the sketch of the youth known as Devilsdust, this tortured affirmation of any poor devil's power to survive, has always appeared to one reader, at least, to sum up the consequences of the Industrial Revolution more effectively than a hundred dissertations on economics.

"Well, Devilsdust, how are you?"

This was the familiar appellation of a young gentleman, who really had no other, baptismal or patrimonial. About a fortnight after his mother had introduced him into the world, she returned to her factory, and put her infant out to nurse—that is to say, paid threepence a week to an old woman, who takes charge of these new-born babes for the day, and gives them back at night to their mothers, as they hurriedly return from the scene of their labour to the dungeon or the den, which is still by courtesy called "home". The expense is not great: laudanum and treacle, administered in the shape of some popular elixir, affords these innocents a brief taste of the sweets of existence, and, keeping them quiet, prepares them for the silence of their impending grave. Infanticide is practised as extensively and as legally in England, as it is on the banks of the Ganges; a circumstance which has apparently not yet engaged the attention of the Society for the Propagation of the Gospel in Foreign Parts. But the vital principle is an impulse from an immortal artist, and sometimes baffles, even in its tenderest phases, the machinations of society for its extinction. There are infants that will defy even starvation and poison, unnatural mothers and demon nurses. Such was the nameless one of whom we speak. We cannot say he thrived; but he would not die. So, at two years of age, his mother being lost sight of, and the weekly payment having ceased, he was sent out in the street to "play", in order to be run over. Even this expedient failed. The youngest and feeblest of the band of victims, Juggernaut spared him to Moloch. All his companions were disposed of. Three months' "play" in the streets got rid of this tender company—shoeless, half-naked, and uncombed—whose age varied from two to five years. Some were crushed, some were lost, some caught fevers and cold, crept back to their garret or cellars, were dosed with Godfrey's cordial, and died in peace. *The nameless one would not disappear*. He always got out of the way of the carts and horses and never lost his own. They gave him no food: he foraged for himself, and shared with the dogs the garbage of the streets. But he still lived; stunted and pale, he defied even the fatal fever which was the only habitant of his cellar that never quitted it. And, slumbering at night on the bed of mouldering straw, his only protection against the plashy surface of his den, with a dungheap at his head, and a cesspool at his feet, he still clung to the only roof which shielded him from the tempest.

At length, when the nameless one had completed his fifth year, the pest which never quitted the nest of cellars of which he was a citizen, raged in the quarter with such intensity, that the extinction of its swarming population was menaced. The haunt of this child was peculiarly visited. All the children gradually sickened except himself; and one night, when he returned home, he found the old woman herself dead, and surrounded only by corpses. The child, before this, had slept on the same bed of straw with a corpse, but then there were also breathing beings for his companions. A night passed only with corpses seemed to him in itself a kind of death. He stole out of the cellar, quitted the quarter of pestilence, and after much wandering lay down near the door of a factory. Fortune had guided him. Soon after the break of day, he was awakened by the sound of the factory bell, and found assembled a crowd of men, women, and children. The door opened, they entered, the child accompanied them. The roll was called; his unauthorised appearance noticed; he was questioned; his acuteness excited attention. A child was wanted in the Wadding Hole, a place for the manufacture of waste and damaged cotton, the refuse of the mills, which is here worked up into counterpanes and coverlets, the nameless was preferred to the vacant post, received even a salary, more than that, a name; for as he had none, he was christened on the spot—*Devilsdust.*

That is surely, by all the gods, a moving piece of writing. Certain sentences in it toll in the ears—"*We cannot say he thrived; but he would not die*"—and that other phrase "*The nameless one would not disappear*". It is an odd circumstance, much to be remarked in the political history of this era, that some of its warmest Radical writing came from its most eminent

Conservative. There is, in fact, as much high explosive in Disraeli, the novelist, as in Dickens, or Mrs. Gaskell, or Charles Kingsley, or Tom Hood. There is no English writer of equal power who has been more scurvily treated by fame and fashion than Benjamin Disraeli. The political snobs felt that his novels were indiscretions which loyalty should veil or, at least, minimise. Commentaries on Homer or translations of Propertius were dignified occupations for a statesman, but novels! and such novels!—no, no! On the other hand, the literary crew, jealous of outsiders, contemptuous of politics, and irritated by the spectacle of a rival with talents sufficient to achieve fame in two careers, have always talked him down. At his worse, in his descriptions of ducal breakfasts, and in his accounts of "fair forms bending over embroidery frames", Disraeli is comically like Ouida, but at his best he is by far the finest political novelist Britain has produced, and when he is most true to himself his combination of wit and social understanding is unrivalled.

It is worth comparing that sketch of Devilsdust with a passage from the report of Michael Sadler's Committee:

> A worsted spinner of Huddersfield, Joseph Hebergam, aged seventeen, described his day's work at the age of seven. His hours were from five in the morning to eight at night, with one solitary break of thirty minutes at noon. All other meals had to be taken in snatches, without any interruption of work. "Did you not become very drowsy and sleepy towards the end of the day and feel much fatigued?" "Yes; that began about three o'clock; and grew worse and worse, and it came to be very bad towards six and seven." "What means were taken to keep you at your work so long?" "There were three overlookers; there was one a head overlooker, and there was one man kept to grease the machines, and there was one kept on purpose to strap." His brother, who worked in the same mill, died at sixteen from spinal affection, due to his work, and he himself began to grow deformed after six months of it. "How far do you live from the mill?" "A good mile." "Was it very painful for you to move?" "Yes, in the morning I could scarcely walk, and my brother and sister used, out of kindness, to take me under each arm, and run with me to the mill, and my legs dragged on the ground; in consequence of the pain I could not walk."
>
> (See J. L. and Barbara Hammond's *Lord Shaftesbury*.)

We must not suppose that these horrors betokened a double dose of original sin in the Victorian British. Wherever the Industrial Revolution spread, it carried these evils. In the period of expansion after the Civil War, the big cities of the United States displayed similar spectacles to these that disfigured Manchester and Birmingham. Some vivid lines from Allan Nevins's *The Emergence of Modern America* (1865–68) (The Macmillan Company, New York, 1927) may serve to illustrate:

> It is a singular fact that the organised protection of children was in a large degree an outgrowth of the protection of dumb animals. In 1874, a little girl of nine, beaten, gashed and starved by her foster-mother in a New York tenement, was brought into court as an animal—for the law sanctioned no interference between parent and child—on the complaint of the Society for the Prevention of Cruelty to Animals. Jacob Riis has described the scene on that

bitter winter day when the unclothed mite was brought into the court room, "carried in a horse blanket, at the sight of which men wept aloud. I saw it laid at the feet of the judge who turned his face away, and in the stillness of that court room I heard a voice raised claiming for that child the protection men had denied it, in the name of the homeless cur on the streets." In the dingy court room was born the New York Society for the Prevention of Cruelty to Children . . . other cities adopted the idea. Children had been trained to beg and steal; they had been whipped into hazardous occupations; they had been exposed to surroundings of vice and obscenity. All these abuses together with physical cruelty to minors were attacked. Like its predecessor the new society was criticised for officiousness but it quickly made itself respected.

To quote Nevins again, writing on the period of the sixties:

The slums, recently a mere name, had become a firmly rooted American institution. New York City had one hundred thousand slum dwellers sheltered in twenty thousand tenement houses, many of which were the foulest of rookeries. The cellar population alone, the troglodytes, approached nearly twenty thousand people. In some districts there was a congestion that has never been equalled in any other great city of Christendom. The tenements erected by grasping speculative builders were crowded together in solid blocks with rear houses jammed in behind those facing the streets. They were unheated and most of the houses had no connection with a sewer. In such an immense and notorious rabbit-warren as Gotham Court on Cherry Street, each home consisted of two rooms and housed an average of some five to seven people. In Boston where the slum districts are smaller than in New York but hardly less repellent, the construction of tenements after the war amazed all observers. By the time of the Panic more than one-fifth of the whole population of about sixty thousand people dwelt in the two thousand eight hundred registered tenement houses. What tenement life sometimes meant in human misery can best be suggested by a brief extract from an official report describing a tenement home not half an hour from the Boston City Hall. "The room was unspeakably filthy; the furniture two or three old chairs and an old dirty table. No fire, and the room was damp, dark and cold. It was the only room the family occupied except a little dark box in the corner with no window in it—a part of the room itself partitioned off for a bedroom. And such a bed! The two oldest children were dirty and ragged and leaning against the window on the side of the room. The youngest was about worn out and apparently half starved. Its only clothing was an undershirt scarcely reaching to the waist and the child's body, face, hands, and hair were reeking with the vilest filth and the child was pinched with the cold!" Many mill towns of Massachusetts, and other eastern cities, were just as shockingly overcrowded. Fall River, a conspicuous example, reported tenements where a dozen people dwelt in three rooms or fifteen in four. Throughout the slums of the cities so few were the sanitary precautions death stalked almost unchecked. In the congested parts of New York, typhoid, smallpox, scarlet fever and, above all, typhus fever were never idle. A wretched building in East 17th Street, a stone's throw from the Mayor's House, sent thirty-five typhoid patients to the city fever hospital in a single year while nearly a hundred more were treated at home. Garbage was allowed to collect in many streets until they became almost impassable.

As under Victoria, so under President Grant. The new Republic of the West, founded to assure men and women life, liberty and the pursuit of happiness, had not escaped the contagion and the stains.

The complacent assumption that Victorian Britain had attained a shining plateau of civilisation, where all might gather the fruits of plenty, could not be long sustained in the face of the reports of Chadwick on Sanitation or of such studies as those of Dr. Kay on health in Manchester. The bumptiousness that Macaulay exhibited in the thirties when surveying the expansion of British commerce, the progress of industry and the increase of wealth, was not the mood of thoughtful men and women in the fifties. What is this wealth of yours? Carlyle had asked—it brings the nation nothing but misery and shame. The cry of the children, once it was heard, set men and women questioning their political faiths. Adam Smith's fine theory that the common interest was best served through the self-reliant individual pursuing his private ends became as dubious to the new generations of Liberals as to the sprigs of the old nobility who formed the Tories of "Young England". John Stuart Mill was reared, so to speak, on the steps of the altar in the high temple of the Utilitarians. His father, James Mill, was the most eminent figure in the movement after Bentham himself. But what a difference there was between the world of the son and the world of the father! Mill's *Autobiography* is a saddening book, though it is quite without self-pity. Victorian literature is rich in the testimonies of imprisoned souls, and this is one of the most touching. The terror and the grisly grandeur of the Victorian daemon lie all about that book. Almost as pathetic as the children in the factories is the spectacle of that unhappy mite of five having Latin and Greek, the Holy Writ, English poetry, mathematics, hammered and pounded into him until it was a miracle the child did not go blind or that his little brain did not crack. In the infinite mercy of God, it was a fine humanist and not a great monster, who emerged from this forcing process. The Infant Phenomenon in Vincent Crummles's stage company who was reared on gin to stunt her growth had a happier life than the infant Mill. Yet the heart in him did not wither away. The hunger for affection and for the gentle intimacies of companionship is manifest through all the priggishness and the precocious erudition of that killing education. The love story, when it came, wry, baffled and less than half-articulate, is one of the most affecting to be found among Victorian memoirs. One may think of it as a parable of Victorianism.

Mill was called by Gladstone "a saint of rationalism". The broodings and explorations of his spirit carried him to a point far beyond the Liberalism of Bright and Cobden. It is said that Mill *developed* Utilitarianism into a humanist faith, but that is rather like saying that the pumpkin in *Cinderella* was developed into a coach and four. Mill's was a transforming mind. After his work was done there were few intelligent men and women in Britain who believed that a just society could be created by allowing each individual to pursue his own unbridled instincts. The consequence of that conception of Freedom had been to produce the horrors of Little Ireland and the massacre of the innocents. Wider definitions of Liberty had to be found than the classic ones of freedom of speech, of assembly, of religion and of trade. No matter how one juggled with terms, a free civilisation could not be based on a slave caste. The liberty of each individual in the community must be subject to the condition that it could never be bought at the expense of the essential liberties of his fellows. It was cardinal to Mill's interpretation of Freedom that workmen should enjoy the right to combine to bargain for better wages, hours and conditions of labour.

Mill was certainly anything but a warm, romantic writer. His pen is never dipped in earthquake and eclipse. His political economy is never touched by the gorgeous visions of man's destiny that Shelley saw amid the wrecks of the sunset. Never could he say, " on the brink of the night and the morning, my coursers are wont to respire". Not for him the glow and fury, like the bellows blowing on the coals, that one gets in John Ruskin nor the passion for beauty which, later in the century, suffused William Morris's highly individual Socialism. Mill's writings are cool, logical, sweetly reasoned; the subleties expressed in a prose that is without heat, but sheds a white, steady light upon its theme. He is like a great judge, serene, dry and deeply wise, finding in some little local dispute inspired by hate and greed an occasion not merely to assert some eternal principle of justice, but to give a fresh and subtle interpretation of the Law which will govern men's conduct long after the squalid disputants and the judge himself are dead. As with the great judges, so with Mill—he leaves the ordinary sensual man of honest intentions, but inadequate staying power, overawed, and hopeless of long sustaining himself in so rarefied an air. For Mill asked a great deal from his fallible contemporaries, and he asks a great deal from us today. He dreamed of the good society in which all the faculties, and gifts, and skills, of its various members would be liberated for the common good. His notion of individualism was very different from the concept of the enterprising freebooter pursuing his private gain, with benefit to the whole community being, so to speak, his by-product. Mill urged that the powers of the State should be used to set free and to protect the latent capacities of the weak and the despised. But he saw that this could only be achieved by a community whose members were enlightened enough to impose disciplines and restraints upon their predatory instincts, and to forgo some part of their individual sovereignty for the sake of an ideal that could not be realised for several generations. This was a severe demand to make upon the disciples of Adam Smith.

Yet when one thinks how powerful was the combination of religious orthodoxy, economic dogma, political theory, private interest and demonstrable success that buttressed the bad old days, it is astonishing that changes for good came steadily and without the use of dynamite and the shedding of much blood. The emotional appeal of the writers of fiction and the intellectual explorations of Mill did not fail in their effect. There was a wide gulf fixed between the average Whig gentleman who supported Melbourne in 1841 and the average Liberal who followed Gladstone in the elections of 1868. A chasm at least as wide separated the Wellington Tories of 1830 from the Disraeli Tories of 1874. It was foolish of the Liberals to jeer at Disraeli's "policy of Drains and Sewers". It was equally foolish of the Tories to dismiss Gladstone and Bright as demagogues. Better drains and an awakening of Demos to his own condition were both needed. The truth is that after the two great Administrations (Gladstone's of 1868–74 and Disraeli's of 1874–80) there could never again be any question of the use of the social organisation to redress abuses, to care for the weak, to protect the right of working-men to combine, to educate the people, and to safeguard their health. The disputes of home politics would subsequently revolve over the speed and extent of reforms, not over the necessity for them. There were times when wars and the raising of constitutional issues, such as Home Rule for Ireland, deflected politics from the steady evolution of social reform. But the "Condition of the People" question always returned to challenge the political leaders, and the philosophy of our parties increasingly showed its influence. Mr. R. A. Butler expounding the Conservative Party's Industrial Charter stands in a line of direct political descent from Mr. Richard Cross, Disraeli's enlightened Home Secretary, while British Socialism as well as modern British Liberalism honours Mill as one of its founding fathers. Just as the mechanical processes begun by the Industrial Revolution are still developing—and we see no end to them, the wheels spinning faster, atomic energy following on the internal combustion engine, on electric power, on steam—so the revolt of the heart and the natural instincts against the domination of the machine goes on, taking new forms.

There is a fine passage that ends the Hammonds' *Lord Shaftesbury*:

> The devil, with sad and sober sense on his grey face, tells the rulers of the world that the misery which disfigures the life of great societies is beyond the reach of human remedy. A voice is raised from time to time in answer: a challenge in the name of the mercy of God, or the justice of nature, or the dignity of man. Shaftesbury was such a voice. To the law of indifference and drift, taught by philosophers and accepted by politicians, he opposed the simple revelation of his Christian conscience. This was his service to England; not the service of a statesman with wide plan and commanding will, but the service of a prophet speaking truth to power in its selfishness and sloth. When silence falls on such a voice, some everlasting echo still haunts the world, to break its sleep of habit or despair.

Might not those noble phrases serve as an epitaph for all the Victorian prophets who, in the name of God or man, denied that the misery of their great society was beyond the reach of human remedy?

CHAPTER SIX

PHYSICAL PAIN

The growth of sensibility to pain, to the pain suffered by others, coincided with certain beneficent discoveries in medicine. Whatever cruelties were inflicted during the Victorian age, whatever wrongs were suffered, that age must be accorded the glorious credit of signally diminishing the sum of human pain. One needs a strong stomach to read the accounts of surgical operations in the eighteenth century—the victim first made blind drunk or roaring drunk—then strapped down to a table—the surgeon in a dirty apron cutting and hacking like a butcher—no anaesthetics—no antiseptics. Can one dare imagine what the amputation of the poisoned leg of a child must have been like in those days? I have read somewhere in De Quincey that if the brain could comprehend in the flash of a second the weight of the world's anguish, it would crack in madness. We are saved by our protective callousness. The reading of past history would be insupportable to an imaginative mind if it were not for this merciful law of insensibility; and we comfort ourselves with the hope that what is true of our own immediate experience of pain—that, when it becomes unendurable, stupor sets in, and there is a dead nothingness—may be true of all the bygone centuries of torture.

The most cheering pages in *The Annual Register* for the year 1846 are those that describe the coming of anaesthetics into general use. W. T. G. Morton, a dentist in Boston, had made a stir in the world by administering sulphuric ether to a patient at an operation in the Massachusetts General Hospital. The surgeon, who had been sceptical of Morton, operated for a tumour in the neck on a man sent to sleep by ether, then he turned to the watchers and made his recantation. "Gentlemen," said he, "this is no humbug." One who saw that demonstration wrote to a fellow-American in London, Dr. Francis Boott. On December 19th, 1846, Boott administered ether to a woman for the extraction of a tooth. Two days later, Liston, the surgeon, used the merciful gas in University College Hospital, in cutting off a man's leg at the thigh. Had the grand pundits of the medical profession paid heed in their season to such inventive Britons as Joseph Priestley, Humphry Davy, Henry Hill Hickman and Michael Faraday, anaesthesia would have been in use a good many years before 1846, and a great deal of pain and misery saved to the world.

Jeremy Bentham's theories do not seem to have been readily accepted by the medical and clerical professions in the early nineteenth century.

James Young Simpson, of Edinburgh, who discovered the anaesthetic property of chloroform and applied it to women in childbirth, met with obloquy. The text, long used to justify the enforcement of pain upon women in child-bed, "In sorrow thou shalt bring forth children", was hurled at him from the pulpits. "Simpson, however, was a good match for the ecclesiastics, and he pointed out that the Hebrew word for sorrow did not mean physical pain, but the muscular effort involved in labour. He also quoted the Book of Genesis, chapter 2, verse 21, showing that God was the first anaesthetist, for he threw Adam into a deep sleep, and removed a rib from his side, and made Eve." (Quoted from the Cantor Lectures on "Recent Advances in Anaesthesia" by Frankis T. Evans, M.B., *Journal of the Royal Society of Arts*, 8th October, 1948.)

History, that ironic Muse, likes to tell us of the cruelties of the good and likes to exhibit the unhappiness which men of principle inflict. It is curious that men who were not only virtuous but intelligent should insist that pain must be endured to the last dreadful spasm. To the devout, it was the fulfilment of God's will that His children should suffer. Through the torturings of the flesh the soul was purified. To the secular believers in the ministry of suffering, pain had the sanction of "a natural process"—it was a character-builder, it disciplined the body, it aroused its fighting resistance. These, like so many other speculations of philosophers, were admirable in every way except that they bore no relation to observation and experience. The great healers of the age, the Simpsons and the Listers, knew that pain is a dragon that devours everything; it destroys beauty, it shrivels up the faculties of man, it centres the waking moments of the body so completely upon itself that there is nothing to spare for the affections and interests. In this monstrous egotism of pain, the knife-blade turning in the heart or the aching of a limb shuts out the generous and tender thoughts. The wife looks at the husband with the eyes of an unhappy stranger. The friend, the familiar, has no more power to please.

There was one sorry sequel to the use of anaesthetics. Operations which before then would have been out of the question because they were too difficult and complex were now performed; the wards were filled; but the number of patients who died from gangrene after an operation were many. The poisoned bodies of the poor made the hospitals places of horror. Those hospitals were very dirty places. No care was taken against infection. The surgeons wore their old, blood-splashed coats day after day in the operating-room; there was no sterilising of instruments. Lister, the patient searcher, devoted himself to finding a remedy for the horrors of septic poisoning. His first attempt in providing a cure was to paint fractures with carbolic acid. Then Pasteur's theory of germs came to his notice. It is pleasant to turn aside from the mid-Victorian *Punch* cartoons of the French, from the dreary diplomatic notes, and from the spitting venom of deputies in the Chamber to contemplate the marriage of minds between

Lister and Pasteur. That union of discovery and research—of two minds selflessly dedicated to the service of man—brought a new victory over death. Antiseptic surgery must be recorded as one of the triumphs of the Victorian age, and Lister as one of the lasting benefactors of the human race.

Who, dealing with such matters, can ever leave out the name of Florence Nightingale? Many pretty, sentimental pictures have been drawn of her, but there was nothing soft or flocculent about Miss Nightingale. She was a realist; she was endowed with much hard practical sense; and she had that sleepless energy and sense of divine destiny which marked the great Victorians. The nation was immeasurably shocked by the callous carelessness and inefficiency of the arrangements for its wounded soldiers in the Crimean War. Of all the blunders of the unhappy campaign this was the worst, the least forgivable. Letters home, and the despatches of the war correspondents, described ghastly conditions in the hospital at Scutari, with the wounded dying in hundreds uncared for. Miss Nightingale had trained herself for this moment. Contemptuous of the methods of nursing in her country, she had spent years abroad, absorbing the wisdom and experience of foreign hospitals. She was sent out to the Crimea with a staff of thirty-seven in time to take care of the wounded from Balaclava. The story of her transformation of a grisly scene has been told a hundred times. Miss Nightingale's heroic labours at Scutari are linked to our theme in more ways than one. Her example and her teaching, presented on the stage of war where the whole world could see both, changed the treatment of the sick. Her lamp was lighted in many a dark, dreary hospital. But apart from this, Florence Nightingale, by merely being what she was, by doing what she did, gave a spur to the movement for women's emancipation such as it had not known since Mary Shelley died. It was plainly impossible to think of her as a clinging vine, as a specimen of the weaker sex, for she had shown in the fever-ridden hospitals a strength and endurance beyond that of most men. Her signal competence and her power to organise were in marked contrast to the bungling of the generals and the fecklessness of the politicians. A few aristocratic and middle-class women were beginning to stir up the issue of women's rights. Miss Nightingale was in herself their best argument.

PLATE 7

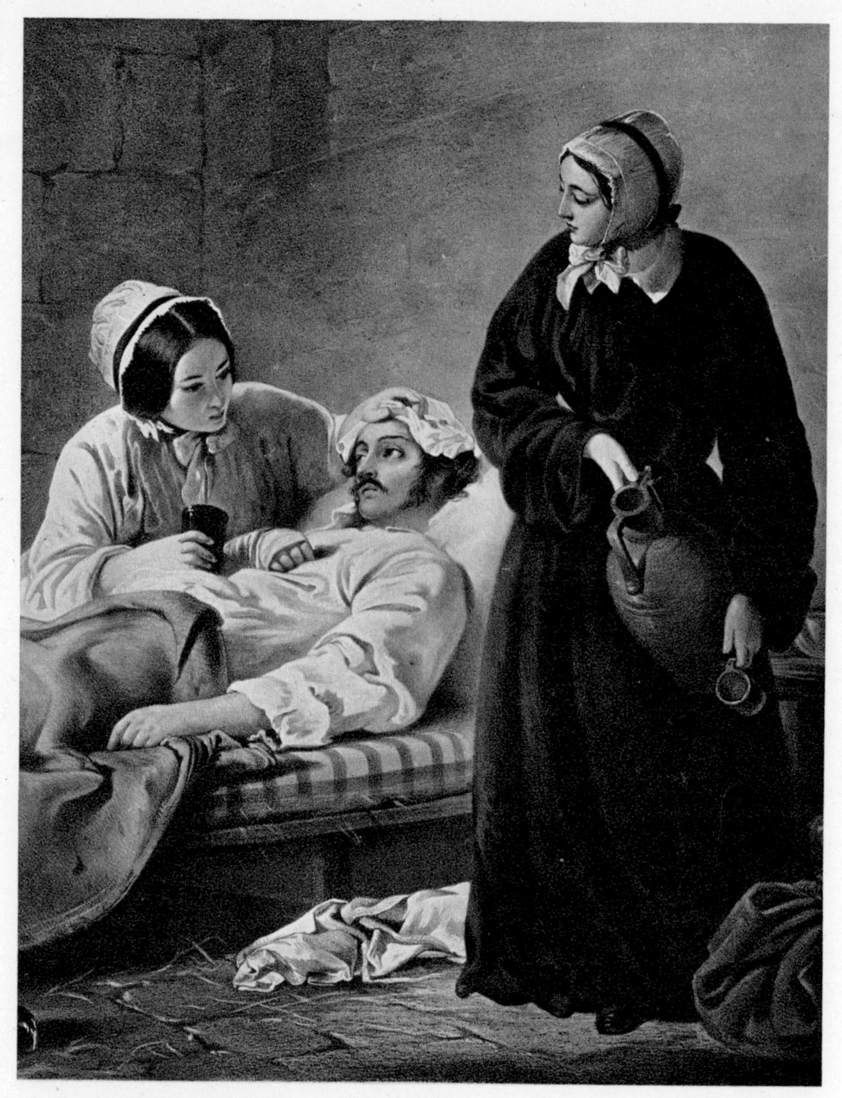

FLORENCE NIGHTINGALE NURSING THE WOUNDED AT SCUTARI
Lithograph by J. A. Vinter after Henry Barraud, 1855 (detail)

BETTY HARRIS, AGED THIRTY-SEVEN, DRAWER IN A COAL PIT

"... The belt and the chain is worse when we are in the family way ..."

AGNES MOFFAT

"It is no uncommon thing for women to drop their burthen and fall off the ladder"

TWO WOMEN WORKING A WINDLASS

The Royal Commission regarded this as "a decided improvement", though they had to admit that the work was hard

CHAPTER SEVEN

THE GENIUS OF BRITAIN

Lovers of Dickens have been greatly touched at hearing from time to time that no people entertain a warmer regard for his genius than the Russians. It was reported during the late war that his novels were included in the training course of staff officers of the Red Army. That, in turn, called up the story of the taking of the trenches in the Crimea, and the astonishment of the British infantry at finding there among the abandoned treasures of an army in headlong flight copies of *The Pickwick Papers*. One remembered, too, that Tolstoy had placed Dickens among the few, the very few, writers chosen of God to speak with His voice. There was Gogol. And there was Dostoievsky. Both of them, great originals that they were, were not ashamed to acknowledge themselves pupils of the Master. It was gratifying beyond measure to find among the Russians this perception of a genius we had cherished as part of our inner lives, as part of the private English monologue, but who also, we insisted, had universal quality. This was a road of understanding that drove straight into the heart of the mysterious Slav. The pleasure was a little tempered, however, when it was made clear that our novelist's pictures of life in Britain a century ago were presented to the heroes of the Red Army as guides to British life today. In particular, the Eatanswill election was strongly recommended to military students of the workings of the British Parliamentary system. In January 1947 the voice of the Moscow radio was to be heard saying that it knew all about Britain's boasted democracy. It had read *Pickwick*!

There are several lessons to be drawn from this. The one that concerns us most on this occasion is the enduring force that inheres in a caricature drawn by a great comic artist. Its dazzle blots out the conscientious lines, the half-tones and the careful reservations of the sober historical painter. Dickens entertained a steady affection for the last of the great Whig leaders, Lord John Russell. He could work well with such men as Milner Gibson, and there was even an occasion when he was tempted to accept an invitation to become a Liberal Parliamentary candidate. But Dickens did not like politicians. It is even possible that he was a little jealous of them. How odious a crew are the politicians in his novels, from the crooked M.P., Gregsbury, whom Nicholas Nickleby served as secretary, down to that flashy Veneering in *Our Mutual Friend*! Dickens was less than fair to the tribe. Politicians are not as bad, they never were quite as bad, as all that. Dickens had as sharp a pair of eyes as ever were set in a writer's head, and he saw many things with a very cruel clearness. I suppose that any man who has looked at politics from the disillusioning wings of the stage, who has moved about in the draughts and the dust behind the showy back-drops and behind the spouting actors, any man who has ever been a mere scene-shifter or call-boy for politicians, must always grin and smack his chops with relish over the chapter in *Little Dorrit* which described how Lord Decimus and Merdle were brought together for that precious five minutes of bargaining. Birth, Privilege, Divine Right look steadily at the Bounder with Cash, and then say cajolingly, "We shouldn't fight, we two, we have too much in common, we are really on the same side of the fence. Might I see the colour of your money—there, on the counter?" (Bar submitted in a low voice across the table to Bishop, "that it was a kind of analogical illustration of those physical laws, in virtue of which Like flies to Like. He regarded this power of attraction in wealth to draw wealth to it, as something remarkably interesting and curious—something indefinably allied to the loadstone and gravitation.")

All the fine, amusing humbug of political high life is in that scene. Lord Decimus brings the awful frozen splendours of his patronage to the counter; Merdle has his money, ever so much money. So the deal is done—and young, brainless Edmund Sparkler becomes a Lord of the Treasury—or was it the Circumlocution Office? "This admirable appointment was to be hailed as a graceful and gracious mark of homage, rendered by the graceful and gracious Decimus to that commercial interest which must ever, in a great commercial country—and all the rest of it, with blast of trumpet." Some part, some intrinsic and enduring element in the history of our political parties is in that scene, but—let us take care, or we will get things wrong—only a *part*, not the whole.

The atmosphere in which this transaction is bathed, the drawing of the characters who pirouette around the two central figures, betoken a wicked understanding of one side of politics. It is the politics of Whips' rooms, of week-ends in country houses, of colloquies in low tones in a cosy corner at the Megatherium Club, of voices whispering at a time when a new Government is in the making, "Joe will land him, you watch! But something must be done for poor old Jim. And we daren't leave George out. As for our friend 'Hoity-Toity' settling down with 'Long Misery', well, the Old Man will just have to address his team-spirit appeal to both of them—close the ranks, loyalty and so on, and don't give the other side a chance to laugh. And if Bill is too difficult, he'll just have to be *told* to take a peerage. No nonsense from Bill."

I know things have changed out of all recognition since Melbourne's Parliament, and Peel's, but I still seem to see around us some old stagers very like those who were at Merdle's dinner-party all those long years ago. Why, how recently is it that I saw Bar, the political attorney, in the

LORD JOHN RUSSELL AND BENJAMIN DISRAELI
Drawing by Richard Doyle
British Museum

Club? After two world wars, and a social revolution, Bar is still on the winning side—Bar, with his jury droop—"Bar, with his light-comedy laugh for special jurymen; which was a very different thing from his low-comedy laugh for comic tradesmen on common juries". Supple, wily, clever fellow that Bar is, it really astonished nobody that he became Attorney-General, *Mr.* Attorney, so quickly. Was it true, though, that what clinched preferment was the exquisite tact and discernment he showed in listening to the Prime Minister's little joke, his one and only little joke, about pears at Eton and Parliamentary pairs? Not a shade missed! On Bar's part there were no premature giggles nor a vulgar blurt of guffawing, but a kind of sustained sacred rhapsody of the senses, a transfigured face, veiled eyes, and seraphic nose, absorbing the heavenly bouquet of that vintage joke. Bar, now, would never have been capable of the howling blunder of Wig, who lost the Woolsack itself in one Government reshuffle, through his folly in trying to cap the Prime Minister's joke by one of his own dull ones about Parliamentary trains. The conceited ass! Yes, it still goes on—the divine farce in which the flatterer and perfect listener is often wafted by his own delicate puffs and zephyrs to the heights of power. Everything changes; but still the great decisions as between man and man are often governed by the most feather-light reasons.

That buttoned-up Tite Barnacle!—we can recognise him in the world of Attlee as in the world of Palmerston. He never dies. At any given time you will find him installed on the Treasury Bench, no matter whether Buff, Blue or Red is the prevailing colour there. There he sits, blinking like Minerva's owl, expressing in his solemn phiz the wisdom of the oracle who is always about to utter, but never *does* completely utter; and when he rises and says "Mr. Speaker, sir", that much-harangued Speaker will be aware only that a thick, gnomic silence has somehow been made palpable, and that an all-enveloping verbal fog is being spread over the battlefield. "All buttoned-up men are weighty. All buttoned-up men are believed in. Whether or no the reserved and never-exercised power of unbuttoning fascinates mankind; whether or no wisdom is supposed to condense and augment when buttoned up, and to evaporate when unbuttoned; it is certain that the man to whom importance is accorded is the buttoned-up man." Be you Conservative, Labour man or Liberal, you can surely put a contemporary name to that character as readily as I can.

And Ferdinand, that sprightly, glossy creature, Private Secretary to Lord Decimus—we certainly know *him*. He skips and frolics through Whitehall today like Robin Goodfellow. It is the Ferdinands, the breed of P.S's and P.P.S's, who are the pilots of Parliamentary government, manœuvring those vast, unwieldy hulks, their Ministers, through the narrow channels, turning them about skilfully to avoid colliding with one another, saving them from running ashore and sticking fast in the mud-flats. Lively Ferdinand will in due season win his just reward. When he grows middle-aged and pursy, he will be made Ambassador to Madrid, or Chancellor of the Duchy of Lancaster with a seat in the Lords, and then another glossy and vivacious young man of a later generation will appear, fresh from New College, and be attached to Ferdinand, to navigate *his* august bulk safely into and out of harbour.

That brilliant chapter of *Little Dorrit* entitled "In Which A Great Patriotic Conference Is Holden" is true to the mechanical business of politics. It is all very fine—so far as it goes. But there was a great deal more in Victorian politics, as in our modern politics, than the Tite Barnacles and Stiltstalkings, than the jockeyings for place between the Coodle and Buffy factions, than Boots and Brewer taking cabs and madly dashing about. If it had not been so; if the pillars had been as rotten and worm-eaten as they look in *Bleak House*, then the whole glittering dome of Victorian life and society must have fallen in with a tremendous crash some time about the middle of the century; say, around the year 1854.

For it is hard to see how such a ramshackle structure could have survived the Crimean War. That was the first war the nation had known since Napoleon toppled at Waterloo nearly half a century before. The War Office naturally conducted the campaign on the lines of the Peninsular; doddering old generals became confused when they saw the

Russians and thought they were fighting the French again; nothing that bone-headed incompetence in high places could do to lose the war was left undone, and only the inextinguishable courage of the serving soldier, officer and man, outmatched and outdid in the end the indomitable resolution of the Command to ruin the cause. While the crowds at home were cheering for the war, their sons and brothers in the line were starving because the Quartermaster-General was such a poor student of logistics. The issue of the war—when all was simplified—was to check the spread of Russian aggression. (That phrase has a very familiar ring.) Britain had some odd allies in that struggle, the Sultan of Turkey and the French Emperor Napoleon III—neither of whom could well be called, even by the most fawning sycophant, a friend of Freedom.

One of the platitudes of history is that a government confronted with misery and a mounting discontent among its people seeks the diversion of war. A second platitude of history is that nothing brings down a corrupt and rotten regime more quickly than military reverses. Given the desperately wretched condition of the urban population and the crisis of faith in government brought about by a mismanaged war, then if the fabric of society was as decayed as it looked to Dickens and Carlyle, it must have collapsed under the strains, and mid-Victorian Britain would have suffered a revolution even bloodier than that foretold by Engels. There could conceivably have been civil wars between town and country, dictatorships, red terrors, blue terrors, buff terrors and—in view of the primitive sanitation—black plagues as well. Lord knows what horrors our mutton-chop-whiskered grandfathers and crinolined grandmothers would have seen before they perished in the final flames!

Great writers are not always sound guides in politics. The truth is that Dickens, like Mr. Shaw in our age, was magnificent in drawing cartoons of politicians—consummate in hitting off the "light externals"—cartoons that very often have a fierce life about them that make photographs look pallid and unreal. But Peel and Gladstone, Disraeli and Bright were very considerable pieces of the Creator's handiwork conceived in three dimensions, and with a soul inside them. They caught up and expressed in themselves strong currents of thought and emotion in the nation, and it now seems, looking back, that Disraeli and Gladstone, at least—with little in common but their genius—both possessed an intuitive sense of forces that ran deeper than the conscious aspirations of their times. Those leaders were more—and how much more!—than the Coodles or the Buffys. How different too, from Gradgrind and the Coketown politicians was Eugene Fielden, that wealthy cotton-spinner and Member of Parliament who strove hard to diminish the cruel stretch of hours worked in the mills. And how different from the fictional Honeythunder was the real Shaftesbury.

It was sometimes put about in Victorian times that Peel served as model for Pecksniff, the incarnation of British hypocrisy. He snuffled sentiment, said his enemies. He used fine words to hide a cold heart and the pursuit of a selfish ambition. Yet how hard it is for us now to see Peel as he was. There are certain characters of this period, Palmerston and Disraeli for example, who seem to move like favourites of the theatre on a well-lighted stage. The meaning of every gesture, the point of every glance, the spring of every action are obvious in the stream of illumination. By a hundred strokes the well-graced actor conveys to us, his breathless audience, the idea of a personality, rich, various, exciting and spectacular. As the curtain falls we applaud, and say: "That was a fine part—and that was a very fine actor." There are other figures of this period, and Peel and Gladstone are notable among them, who, by some caprice of destiny, appear to walk in shadows. They have been even more unfortunate in their admirers than in their detractors. The complexity of their characters, the extraordinary mixture they presented of the conventional and the unpredictable, have never made them suitable subjects for a crude black-and-white treatment. But black-and-white is usually the treatment they have received.

To outward view, Peel was icy, haughty, pompous and platitudinous; in modern lingo, a stuffed shirt. He lacked the grace and familiar ease of the aristocrat. He was the son of a member of that class of *nouveaux riches* whom the Younger Pitt drew into the Conservative Party and made a counterweight to the Whig nobility. Pitt had said that he did not see why any man worth £10,000 a year should not be made a peer of the realm, but it was easier to become a baron or a baronet than to acquire the negligent assurance and the elegant informalities of breeding. The casual reader of Victorian memoirs is familiar with a twice-told tale of Peel's awkwardness. Majesty must not be astonished to find Majesty's first Minister a little gauche—a *leetle* provincial. The awful truth is Sir Robert *does not know what to do with his hands*. They wave about—they carve the air—they are capable of flourishing alarmingly under a royal nose—they claw at lapels—they fidget with ornaments on the mantelshelf—they flutter disconnectedly. Majesty coolly observes, "Why doesn't Sir Robert try putting them in his pockets?" This piece of advice was attributed both to William IV and Queen Victoria, so perhaps it is true.

There was, however, one employment of those hands that received inadequate attention from the Early Victorian recorders of gossip and serve to illuminate a character. They were hands diligent in stealthy acts of kindness. Who can read the account of Peel's succour to the families of those two poor devils, painter and poet, Benjamin Haydon and Tom Hood, in their worst distress, without warming to him? Peel's conduct in these affairs was marked by a most sensitive delicacy of feeling and his generous acts were performed on occasions when he himself was loaded with cares. Thackeray's tribute to the man of whom Daniel

O'Connell said, "He has all the qualities of a poker except its occasional warmth", and again, "His smile is like the gleam of the silver plate on a coffin", is the response of a nature that understood chivalry and fineness of spirit. Thackeray is writing of Tom Hood's death and he says, "How noble Peel's figure is, standing by that sick bed! how generous his words, how dignified and sincere his compassion!"

Peel had a singular hidden attaching power, an *adhesiveness*, that prevailed over those who were ever drawn into any close association with him. That was true of the Queen and of the great Duke; and it was true of that gifted group of politicians who afterwards were known as Peelites —Gladstone, Sidney Herbert, Graham, Cardwell and the rest. They perceived in this frigid, stilted figure, with his arrogant nose and his fatuous, smooth expanse of cheek, his dry and cutting manner, his ungraciousness and his self-righteousness, a Roman nobility of character and buried treasures of the heart. There is no solution of the conundrum of Peel to be found in his biographies, nor in his autobiographical papers, nor in that four-volume edition of his speeches published by George Routledge in 1853—a Gobi desert of Parliamentary polemics over which are strewn the bones of prehistoric monsters. Burnet wrote of Shaftesbury, "His strength lay in his knowledge of England". Disraeli, quoting that phrase said, "Now that is exactly the kind of knowledge which the Duke of Wellington never possessed". But it *was* exactly the kind of knowledge which Peel did possess. It may be that when he started out on a campaign he had no clear idea of how it would finish. But inside that formal, buttoned-up figure there were to be found intuitions about his countrymen which were of a piece with the delicacy of his private sentiments. Mark him in his conduct of his Administration of 1841–46. He often reminds one of a man walking through rough country on a dark night, with no lamp to guide him, and not the glimmer of a cow-track ahead. Yet he manifests a sense of location that preserves him from falling in the bog, or breaking his neck in the gravel pit, and it brings him safely home at last.

This bump of locality that Peel possessed enabled the country to make the perilous passage from the High Tory age of George the Fourth to the Liberal age of Victoria. He had in particular an instinctive understanding of the movements of opinion among the mercantile middle class who had become the country's new masters. He was accused of inconsistency, of opportunism, of betraying the causes he was chosen to serve, and of being the thieving magpie of other men's ideas. Yet it was fortunate for our Victorian ancestors that Peel's conservatism was pragmatic and empirical. The Conservatives of nineteenth-century France, the Ministers, in turn, of Charles the Tenth and Louis Philippe and Napoleon the Third, were only too eager to make concessions to the liberal spirit of the age *after* their clock had struck midnight. Sir Robert yielded, over Catholic Emancipation and the Corn Laws, for example, at the moment when the historian, as a producer setting the stage, and blessed with all the wisdom of hindsight, would say "This and this only is the moment when he could act". Peel's sense of timing was remarkably good. And in politics, as in the theatre, timing is more than half the victory.

Morley thought Peel lacked courage. He complained that Peel never marched ahead of the people. He watched and waited while the forces of popular opinion gathered momentum. But he did respond, and he did act according to his own sense of timing. If he delayed action until he was assured that he not only expressed the will of a majority, but carried with him that general consent of the country (which is very different from a mechanical Parliamentary majority), was he not performing the highest function of a statesman in an Anglo-Saxon democracy? A greater spirit than Peel—Lincoln—and a cleverer political leader than Peel—Franklin Roosevelt—were both in their day aspersed for lack of courage in their leadership, but each of them achieved their goals by methods as cautious and as sure as Peel's.

Peel merits consideration as a representative figure in the Age of Dickens, not only because he built a bridge between the half-feudal Britain of the early century and the new democracy of the middle classes and the lower middle classes, but because he is an exemplar of the principle of public office as a public trust. One of the finest of Victorian traditions is that of public service. In the weathering of many storms that have beaten upon this island in the past century, Britain has owed much to men and women who have given themselves with single-mindedness to the service of the community. The absorption of the faculties which in other lands was devoted to the Church or to the arts was in nineteenth-century Britain enlisted by national affairs. Peel was a perfect example of that order of Briton, unimaginative, frozen, but everlastingly trustworthy, who discovers in himself a bent and vocation for politics and affairs that can no more be denied than the call to poetry or music; a fierce, possessive certainty. Peel was a wealthy man, he was a very sensitive man, he was a shy, tangled-up man; happy only in domestic intimacies; secure only *there*, and in the shelter of his library. In the settled atmosphere of the early nineteenth century to be a rich Englishman was to have at call every comfort, every pleasure the civilised world could provide. It was fortunate for the country that during the testing Victorian times so great a part of the old Puritan strain of duty and obligation remained, that the sons of the first millionaires of the Industrial Revolution did not become aesthetes or sybarites. Without Peel and his like it is hard to see how the frightening social dilemmas of the Age of Dickens could ever have been resolved.

Peel was a paragon of administration. His industry was unbelievable. He had an intimate acquaintance with the workings of every Department of State, and could have answered with equal ease, and without notice, a question about the Ecclesiastical Commissioners, the staff of the British

Consul in Naples, the latest crime figures in the Metropolis, or the state of the jute trade. He was the last Prime Minister to possess an intimate command of all departmental business.

A better clue to the secret of Britain's power and place in the nineteenth century is to be found in Peel—and in his most renowned disciple, Gladstone, who stamped the Peelite virtues on our higher Civil Service—than in Palmerston and Disraeli. Those four hulking volumes of Sir Robert's speeches would not make such amusing reading (in translation) for the Russian cadets as the Eatanswill election pages in *Pickwick*. Many a Muscovite student would groan, as this writer has groaned, over the great man's four-hour oration on the Bullion resolutions. But above the fog of words, above the dusty clouds of those dreary old party struggles, there shows fitfully, apprehended rather than perceived, the authentic gleam of a patron, a stern-faced Miltonic goddess, half-Roman and half-Puritan—the political and Parliamentary genius of Britain.

CHAPTER EIGHT

AFTER CHARTISM

There was a furious bubbling and foaming of political ideas among working men and the lower middle classes throughout the Age of Dickens. Misery, Want and Discontent were hard schoolmasters, but at least they gave their pupils a grounding in political theory. Julius West in his *History of the Chartist Movement* (Constable, 1920), a good book, too little known, wrote that within the space of a few years there was forced upon the attention of working men

> the pros and cons of trade unionism, industrial unionism, syndicalism, communism, socialism, co-operative ownership of land, land nationalisation, co-operative distribution, co-operative production, co-operative ownership of credit, franchise reform, electoral reform, woman suffrage, factory legislation, poor law reform, municipal reform, free trade, freedom of the press, freedom of thought, the nationalist idea, industrial insurance, building societies and many other ideas. The purpose of the People's Charter was to effect joint action between the rival schools of reformers; but its result was to bring more new ideas on to the platform, before a larger and keener audience.

A modern reader may find it difficult to comprehend how the demands of the Charter could have so alarmed sensible citizens in the forties. One man, one vote; annual elections; payment of M.P.s; electoral districts of equal size, and the rest—were these prefigurings of ruin? The Charter was moderate, but the Chartists were violent. They paraded the symbols of the French Revolution. They flourished the red cap of Liberty, stuck on a pole, under the windows of magistrates and manufacturers. Most of them (though not all) were anti-religious. The priest was as mortal an enemy of the people as the King. Many of the articles in their weekly journals were written in an angry rhetoric whose images were those of 1789. The Goddess of Reason was invoked and the memories of Marat and Robespierre honoured. The chants of tyrannicide were sung again. The demonstrations on the moors, with the wild shadows and the waving torches, the hurrying multitudes, rising mysteriously like trolls out of the underworld, were spectacles to frighten respectable burghers. Gammage, the old Chartist, has left some picturesque accounts of them in his books, as witness the following:

> In the autumn of 1838 the meetings began to assume a formidable character. It was inconvenient to hold repeated assemblages of the people by day. Their means of living were too circumscribed to admit of their voluntarily subjecting themselves to loss of time. Now and again it might be very well for them to

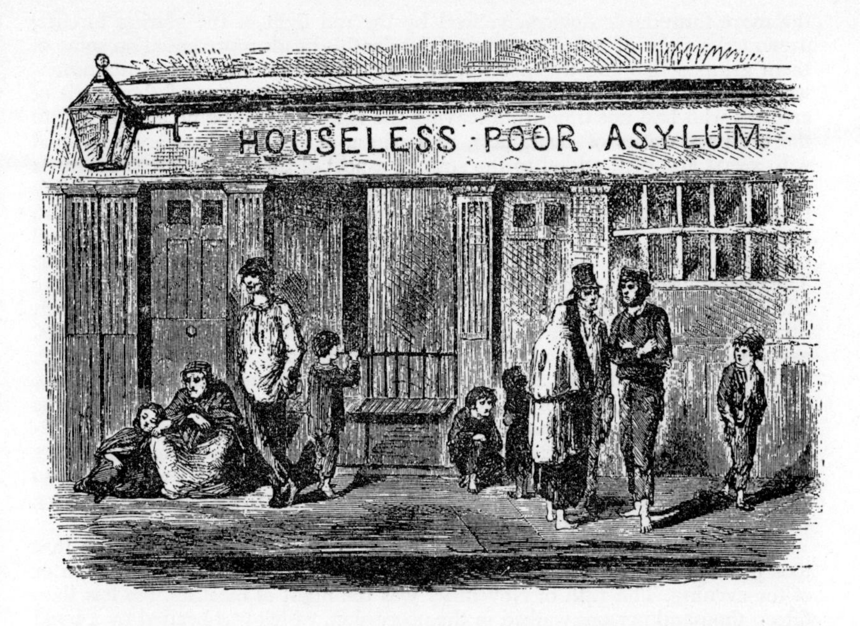

ASYLUM FOR THE HOUSELESS POOR, CRIPPLEGATE
Wood engraving from Henry Mayhew's "London Labour and the London Poor", 1862

assemble in their myriads, as at Kersall Moor; but it was an experiment which would not often bear repetition. There were no rooms to be obtained capable of holding the dense crowds who were every day more anxious to express their hatred of the existing system, and the Town Halls were almost always refused. There is a way out of every difficulty, and a project speedily suggested itself to the minds of the leading men which would make them independent of all halls and places for indoor meetings. They suggested the holding of meetings by torch-light, as being better suited to the people's convenience, both as regards time and expense. The expedient was but little sooner suggested than adopted, and for a short period the factory districts presented a series of such imposing popular demonstrations, as were perhaps never witnessed in any previous agitation. Bolton, Stockport, Ashton, Hyde, Stalybridge, Leigh, and various other places, large and small, were the scenes of these magnificent gatherings. At the whole of them, the working people met in their thousands and tens of thousands to swear devotion to the common cause. It is almost impossible to imagine the excitement caused by these manifestations. To form an adequate idea of the public feeling, it was necessary to be an eye witness of the proceedings. The people did not go singly to the place of meeting but met in a body at a starting point, from whence, at a given time, they issued in huge numbers, formed into procession, traversing the principal streets, making the heavens echo with the thunder of their cheers on recognising the idols of their worship in the men who were to address them, and sending forth volleys of the most hideous groans on passing the office of some hostile newspaper, or the house of some obnoxious magistrate or employer. The banners containing

> the more formidable devices, viewed by the red light of the glaring torches, presented a scene of awful grandeur. The death's heads represented on some of them grinned like ghostly spectres, and served to remind many a mammon-worshipper of his expected doom. The uncouth appearance of thousands of artizans who had not time from leaving the factory to go home and attend to the ordinary duties of cleanliness, and whose faces were therefore begrimed with sweat and dirt, added to the strange aspect of the scene. The processions were frequently of immense length, sometimes containing as many as fifty thousand people; and along the whole line there blazed a stream of light, illuminating the lofty sky, like the reflection from a large city in a general conflagration. The meetings themselves were of a still more terrific character. The very appearance of such a vast number of blazing torches only seemed more effectually to inflame the minds alike of speaker and hearers. O'Connor, Stephens, and M'Dougall, were frequent attendants at the torch-light meetings, and their language was almost unrestrained by any motives of prudence. Incitements to the use of arms formed the staple of the speeches of the two latter gentlemen. O'Connor, in nearly every speech, went so far as to name the day when the Charter was to become law, and usually finished up by a declaration that if it were not granted by the 29th of September, the Legislature should have Michaelmas goose on the 30th. Stephens did not hesitate to declare that the ruling class were nothing better than a gang of murderers, whose blood was required to satisfy the demands of public justice.
>
> Among other torch-light meetings held about this time, there was one that took place in the town of Hyde, at which the Rev. Mr. Stephens was the orator of the evening. The 14th of November was the night of meeting. No less than fifteen thousand persons walked in the procession, which was headed by a band of music, and a large number of banners were to be seen in the blazing light. One of these was Stephens' favourite device, "For children and wife, we'll war to the knife!"
>
> On another, the scriptural quotation, "He that hath no sword, let him sell his garment and buy one". A third bore the inscription, "Ashton demands universal suffrage or universal vengeance!" Another banner showed the words, "Remember the bloody deeds of Peterloo!" While a fifth bore the ominous inscription, "Tyrants, believe and tremble!" There were a large number of red caps of liberty carried upon poles, and, at intervals, the loud reports from pistols announced the fact that persons in the meeting were armed.

The glare of the torches has long since vanished from those lofty skies, but Chartism touched off trains of political thought and passion that blazed, and flickered out, then blazed up again for a century and beyond. Chartism was, in Julius West's words, "the basis of the first working-class agitation on a national scale". It opened men's minds. The intelligent mechanic or artisan became conscious of the large world of political ideas; he became a citizen of it; he grew familiar with a variety of systems and schemes, of home or foreign growth, the visionary and the practical all mixed in together; and there was laid upon him the responsibility of choice. He learned to debate. There was a wealth of new theories as well as concrete wrongs to argue about with his mates at the bench, or on Sunday afternoon walks on the common, or in the upper rooms of taverns where tobacco, ale and argument alike had more body in them than they possess today. The winds of controversy blew him first this way, then that.

Some of his fellows were all for striking hard against masters and institutions, stroke after calculated stroke, to get their dues. Others, like Devilsdust, favoured biding their time, waiting until that time was ripened by events, until the price of the loaf soared to so much, or until the Iron Duke had driven his middle-class supporters into sullen revolt, or until Lord John was at the end of his tether.

There was always among the Victorians a serious leaven with an unquenchable curiosity about ideas, political, social, economic, religious and artistic. Their descendants in the middle years of the twentieth century owe a great deal to that ceaseless mental activity. The heaviest debt, it may be, is due to those working men who, amid lives of arduous toil, forced themselves against the natural weariness of the flesh to devote their little leisure to study, and became acquainted in some part with the Universe of Discourse.

Arguments sharpened the wits of disputants and gave them flexibility of mind and readiness of tongue. The meetings in public houses or on commons, the endless pamphlets, the polemical writings that appeared in the swarm of Radical sheets formed a school of politicians who could compete in vigour, analogy and statistics with the members of the House of Commons or the quidnuncs in the Pall Mall clubs. The men trained in that school were the Parliamentarians of the street-corners, the forerunners of several generations of highly articulate working men, who, disputing, protesting, shooting out awkward questions, gesticulating against enthroned pomposity, humorously deflating the platitudinous, have up to now stood firm against the excesses of reaction and revolution. As the dusk settles on the damp London parks in November evenings, and the melancholy lamps are lighted, one hears an eternal hoarse cockney voice, amiable but insistent, demanding, "That's what *I* want to know".

If we take the view that debate is the moving air that keeps our politics fresh, and our institutions healthy, then we must acknowledge the value of the Chartists and Radicals of the early nineteenth century in setting men thinking freely and talking freely. The debates begun in dingy mechanics' institutes were in the end continued in the House of Commons. That had the effect of notably broadening the scope of Parliamentary discussion, of bringing a wind from the street corner into the cloisters. Throughout the nineteenth century, the representatives of Buff and Blue were too narrowly chosen, they were usually the sons of privilege, either gentlemen by birth or gentlemen by the patent of wealth, and, had it not been for that prolonged clamour outside, they might have engaged too greatly in the mimic battles of faction for place, and squabbles over constitutional niceties, until the barbarians were upon them. Sydney Smith cruelly parodied the Parliamentary style of his day in *Noodle's Oration*: "The hon. gentleman has taxed me with illiberality, sir. I deny the charge. I hate innovation; but I love improvement. I am an enemy to the corruption of Government, but I defend its influence. I dread Reform; but I dread it only when it is intemperate. I consider the liberty of the Press as the great Palladium of the Constitution; but at the same time I hold the licentiousness of the Press in the greatest abhorrence." Fresh ideas, even scandalous and lunatic notions, were needed to stir these stagnant pools. The acquired skill of disputation was taken up and developed further in the growth of the Union movement. I have sometimes heard in recent years master manufacturers regret that in negotiations over wages and hours, the representatives on their own side proved less fluent dialecticians than the union men, and so let themselves be out-argued.

They were not all village Hampdens, these spokesmen of the working man. The demagogue, the professional exploiter of the unhappy, was depicted long ago in *Hard Times*.

> "Oh my friends, the downtrodden operatives of Coketown! Oh my friends and fellow-countrymen, the slaves of an iron-handed and a grinding despotism! Oh my friends and fellow-sufferers, and fellow-workmen, and fellow-men! I tell you that the hour is come, when we must rally round one another as one united power, and crumble into dust the oppressors that too long have battened upon the plunder of our families, upon the sweat of our brows, upon the labour of our hands, upon the strength of our sinews, upon the God-created glorious rights of Humanity, and upon the holy and eternal privileges of Brotherhood."
>
> As he stood there, trying to quench his fiery face with his drink of water, the comparison between the orator and the crowd of attentive faces turned towards him, was extremely to his disadvantage. Judging him by Nature's evidence, he was above the mass in very little but the stage on which he stood. In many respects he was essentially below them. He was not so honest, he was not so manly, he was not so good-humoured; he substituted cunning for their simplicity, and passion for their safe solid sense.... Strange as it always is to consider any assembly in the act of submissively resigning itself to the dreariness of some complacent person, lord or commoner, whom three-fourths of it could, by no human means, raise out of the slough of inanity to their own intellectual level, it was particularly strange, and it was even particularly affecting, to see this crowd of earnest faces, whose honesty in the main no competent observer free from bias could doubt, so agitated by such a leader.

There were other impulses besides social grievances animating the working people.

"And yet, steeped in sentiment as she lies, spreading her gardens to the moonlight, and whispering from her towers the last enchantments of the Middle Age, who will deny that Oxford, by her ineffable charm, keeps ever calling us nearer to the true goal of all of us, to the ideal, to perfection—to beauty, in a word, which is only truth seen from another side?—nearer, perhaps, than all the science of Tubingen." That passage of Arnold's—hackneyed as it is, but always seducing to the ear—came into my head as I thought of all those obscure searchers for whom Oxford was but a far-off mysterious name like Samarkand or Heliopolis. In the darkest streets, in the ugliest and dirtiest parts of the industrial towns, there were always men and women who sought after intellectual beauty with a pure and unwearying passion. Amid the degradation of the pit, there were sons and daughters of the captivity who were crowned with stars. Certain human beings are born with an instinct for beauty that nothing can kill, neither a childhood of squalor, nor debased surroundings, nor the blinding toil of slaves. In reading some of the confessions and memoirs of old Chartists or the later trade unionists, the heart is lifted by a sombre pride at this miracle of survival. There steals back into the circle of the lamplight the skinny phantom of a young boy who, between labour at the mill and a wretched home, has somehow managed to teach himself to read, and at nine years of age has got by heart many of the loveliest lines of English poetry. Among the grimy, rain-dark streets of Bolton or Oldham there spring up the cloud-capped towers and gorgeous palaces of Shakespeare, his visionary city of Italian skies and everlasting sunshine, filled with the smell of April, and peopled with half-divine beings whose very speech is music. Into that city strays an urchin, peak-faced, spindle-shanked, pigeon-chested, stunted; blinking at the radiance, confused by the splendours, enraptured by the music even though often missing its meaning. But it is his city. Its glory is for ever his. He holds the freedom of it. Nothing can ever take it away from him.

If e er education was a reality it was to the poor who battled for it under such desperately hard conditions. If ever the true values of civilisation meant anything to men, it was to those who gained them at so great an expense of body and spirit. There were prodigies of scholarship achieved by peaky students whose names were never entered upon any rolls. Can we not still see, in a backward look, the diligent heads bent in the candle-light in the cold, dismal room, the clocks outside striking midnight, the eyes half-blind with tiredness as they pore over the lexicon. And there upon the page, in the miserable taper-light, suddenly flashes "the multitudinous laughter of the sea", the Grecian sea, the sea of Ulysses and the sirens. An ancient magic works its spell amid the degradations of Coketown as among the dreaming towers of Arnold's Oxford.

I think now of her, a tiny girl in a labourer's cottage, in the years when *David Copperfield* was coming out, catching the infection of reading from a favourite uncle, a sailor, who had a shelf of ragged favourites, *Tristram Shandy* and *Joseph Andrews* among them, and *Humphry Clinker*, and *The Fortunes of Nigel*, and *Ivanhoe*, and *Nicholas Nickleby*. To teach oneself to read; to spell out the hard words with the stub of the finger—that was but the start of the fight. The forces of society, of religion and parental authority were in a confederacy against the mite. To Parson, novel-reading was a snare of the Old One. To Squire, it was a wicked idleness of the undeserving poor. The little creature was beaten for a sin as scarlet as lying or thieving, but she kept her faith, and she hid her treasures, and prayed for her friend to come home from the sea and give her new courage.

We can only dimly guess now, through the broken memories of the very old, how stern such persecutions of a young imagination could be. Puritan moralists, Manchester economists and ignorant parents between them should have been strong enough to crush for ever the thin little tendrils, stretching out towards romance and wonder. But in that sunless underground of Victorian poverty, the values of English civilisation somehow miraculously survived. Jude the Obscure, gazing at the distant lights of Christminster, is a tragic figure, but perhaps he most represents the projection of a sensitive, middle-class mind brooding upon inequality, and finding images for its own personal despair among the disinherited. In an access of sentiment over injustices that we have not suffered or wrongs that we perceive from the outside, it is easy to suppose the victims to be always weak and helpless. There were many such, without doubt: many poor shadows like Jude. But the characters of that age to whom one pays everlasting honour and respect are those who would not acknowledge defeat so long as the breath of life held out in them. These were the men and women who lacked everything, who had been exiled from the sun, who had been thrown into the pit, but yet proudly said, "We are indeed the disinherited. The legacy of knowledge and beauty was bequeathed to us and denied us. But we do not despair. We fight for our inheritance." When this writer was a child, he frequented the gallery of the Old Vic in the Waterloo Road, and there learned, by keeping his ears open, how like a persecuted religious sect were the devout believers in salvation through Shakespeare, for they had to contend against the hostility of their own kind as well as the pressures of organised society. But they had the obstinacy and the tough cheerfulness of persecuted sectaries; they were proud, and they were sure of salvation. They had no self-pity, and they would not relish *your* pitying their condition. "The lines of beauty are not softly wrought", and those who wrested their joy out of the rock were not dilettanti; they had a fierce pride in their secret, and in all that they had so hardly won.

This is a side of Victorian life which would repay a deeper exploration; it might throw new lights upon that enigmatic people, the British. It is far removed from the bright and shining gardens of Oxford culture that have been described so well and so often by those who moved in them with such ease. There on the enamelled lawn, among the rose-trees, as the afternoon lengthens, Arnold dispenses "sweetness and light" and meditates the sentimentalities of *Obermann*. But that other world—how far it is beyond the ken of Arnold, and Leslie Stephen, and W. K. Clifford and Benjamin Jowett and the Metaphysical Society! It is the world of the penny reprints of the classics in ruby type, and the penny readings, and the free libraries and the working men's colleges.

What has all this to do with political evolution? Well, for one thing it meant that the growing Radical revolt of the century was not a purely materialist movement. It was tempered by religious feeling and by the influences of that small but passionate minority among the very poor to whom beauty was a necessity of life.

CHAPTER NINE

SEALED EYES

It is more than a hundred years since Carlyle wrote the superb passage in *Chartism* on Education. When one reads it today the air about one appears to be still vibrating with the voice of the furious prophet.

> Were it not a cruel thing to see, in any province of an empire, the inhabitants living all mutilated in their limbs, each strong man with his right arm lamed? How much crueller to find the strong soul with its eyes still sealed—its eyes extinct, so that it sees not! Light has come into the world; but to this poor peasant it has come in vain. For six thousand years the sons of Adam, in sleepless effort, have been devising, doing, discovering; in mysterious, infinite, indissoluble communion, warring, a little band of brothers against the black empire of necessity and night; they have accomplished such a conquest and conquests; and to this man it is all as if it had not been. The four-and-twenty letters of the alphabet are still runic enigmas to him. He passes by on the other side; and that great spiritual kingdom, the toil-won conquest of his own brothers, all that his brothers have conquered, is a thing not extant for him. An invisible empire; he knows it not—suspects it not. And is not this his withal; the conquest of his own brothers, the lawfully acquired possession of all men? Baleful enchantment lies over him, from generation to generation; he knows not that such an empire is his—that such an empire is his at all. . . . Heavier wrong is not done under the sun. It lasts from year to year, from century to century; the blinded sire slaves himself out and leaves a blinded son; and men, made in the image of God, continue as two-legged beasts of labour; and in the largest empire of the world it is a debate whether a small fraction of the revenue of one day shall, after thirteen centuries, be laid out on it, or not laid out on it. Have we governors? Have we teachers? Have we had a Church these thirteen hundred years?

It is no wonder that many a reader of that page caught fire from it, and became primed for eager action. The life of such a man as James Kay-Shuttleworth (1804–77), the true father of the modern British system of educating the people, attests the influence of Carlyle's magnificent rhetoric. We first meet Kay in history as the medical officer of the Ancoats and Ardwick Dispensary and secretary to the Board of Health at Manchester during the cholera plague of 1832. In that year he wrote *The Moral and Physical Condition of the Working Classes employed in the Cotton Manufacture in Manchester*. Kay (he became Kay-Shuttleworth when he married the heiress Janet Shuttleworth in 1842) was brought into the field of popular education through his work in the training of pauper children. National education began with the appointment in 1839 of a committee of the Privy Council to administer the grants for teaching voted yearly by

IN THE CLOISTERS OF RUGBY SCHOOL
Wood engraving by Arthur Hughes from "Tom Brown's School Days", 1869

the House of Commons. The figures at the end of this book show how meagre were these grants compared with the sum Britain spends upon education today. Kay-Shuttleworth was the first secretary of this committee of the Privy Council. He had the capacity for fanatical absorption which marked alike Victorian buccaneers and Victorian idealists. Whenever those fellows caught the gleam, whether it came from heaven or from Tophet, there was no stopping them. Kay-Shuttleworth came near killing himself through his day-and-night labours. In 1840 he and Carleton Tufnell started at Battersea, with their own money, the first training college for teachers. The original class there was composed of pupil-teachers from the pauper school at Norwood. The principles on which the British system of public education was built up derived from Kay-Shuttleworth—the training of teachers, the employment of pupil-teachers, the method of inspection, the blending of local and central control through finance, the instruction in scripture. "When at last the system of that education comes to stand full and fairly formed, Kay-Shuttleworth will have a statue", said Matthew Arnold.

It was through the devoted exertions of such a man that the successors of Jo, "sometimes called Toughey" the crossing-sweeper, were rescued from the total darkness of ignorance.

> "Here he is, very muddy, very hoarse, very ragged. Now boy!—— But stop a minute. Caution. This boy must be put through a few preliminary paces. . . . Name, Jo. Nothing else that he knows on. Don't know that everybody has two names. Never heard of sich a think. Don't know that Jo is short for a longer name. Thinks it long enough for *him*. He don't find no fault with it. Spell it? No. *He* can't spell it. No father, no mother, no friends. Never been to school. What's home? Knows a broom's a broom, and knows it's wicked to tell a lie. Don't recollect who told him about the broom, or about the lie, but knows both."

In his splendid outburst Carlyle was a little less than fair to the Church. Matthew Arnold, who could hardly be described as a clerical apologist, paid the parsons this tribute: "If there is a class in English society whose record in regard to popular education is honourable, it is the clergy." It is not easy to lay one's hands upon the statistics, and it requires a test of quality rather than of quantity, to measure the contribution of the Church. The quarrel over religious teaching in the schools was an everlasting nuisance; it engaged honest men on both sides in intemperate sectarian struggles when they might have united their energies against the curse of darkness.

Of 130,000 couples married in 1844, one-third of the bridegrooms, and pretty near a half of the brides, were unable to sign their names in the register. That shocked our liberal ancestors. By 1870 the proportions were noticeably smaller: only one-fifth of the men and rather more than one-quarter of the women were unable to sign their names. In Scotland the situation was much better. Does it shock us today? Are we not in fact a little surprised that the proportion of illiterates was not higher? Did we not have a vague idea that before the Act of 1870 the overwhelming mass of our people could neither read nor write? For the churches, for the Nonconformist chapels, for all the admirable groups and societies, for the single-minded individuals who laboured to bring some scraps of learning to the children of the labouring classes before 1870 let there be some remembrance. That these labours were not wholly disinterested does not rob them of their uncovenanted virtue. The parson and the squire's lady who busied themselves with the village school were doubtless concerned to instruct the young in "the principles of sound morality", reverence for the established order in Church and State, respect for one's betters. The little boys were to be taught to tug their forelocks to the lord of the manor as well as to do their sums, and the little girls were to be shown how to curtsey in clean pinafores to the rectory ladies. They must be taught to name the lesser and the greater lights. The starry universe provided a model for human society. Planets and satellites moved in their unalterable orbits; and the children of men must be happy in the stations to which God had, at their births, appointed them. Lady Lufton in *Framley*

"THE RAGGED AND THE REFORMATORY SCHOOL"
Wood engraving from George Cruikshank's "System of General Education", 1869

Parsonage had no doubt of the social structure she wished to preserve. The Nonconformists, who created a distinct culture of their own based on the granite rocks of Milton, Bunyan and Defoe, were equally concerned to preserve their tradition of intellectual mutiny, and the infants whom they gathered into their schools were likely to retain through life a firm view of the profligacy of kings, the tyranny of bishops and the wickedness of privilege. Nor would it belie that remarkable man, Francis Place the tailor, to suggest that in his persistent sapping-and-mining efforts for popular education he was thinking of producing a generation of little Radicals. Gradgrind, too, had a propaganda purpose in opening his school at Coketown. It was to produce willing little slaves for the factories and workshops. But even at Gradgrind's school the infant helots were taught to read; and once a boy or girl can read he or she possesses the master key which, if he chooses to use it, will open almost any door. The Churchman has to face the risk that the child will one day grow up to throw Keble and Magnall's Questions out of the window and take Haeckel's *Riddle of the Universe* as his Bible. The child of Nonconformity, coming across some persuasive pages of Newman, may be led to a belief in miracles, transubstantiation, sacerdotalism and Lord knows what. Similarly, a pupil of Gradgrind is just as likely as not to arrange Gradgrind's facts according to a very different pattern from that of the master after he has read William Morris or Marx.

During the first half of the century, intelligent men and women of the middle classes who thought about the future of their country were worried at the prospect of an uneducated proletariate taking over political power. It was the fear of Caliban. The widening of the franchise could not be resisted, but what perils might it not bring if the new voters were sunk in ignorance? We must educate our masters, said the serious fellows among the upper middle classes. In the year that Dickens died, the Education Act of W. E. Forster, the Quaker, put elementary education on a national footing. The debates in the House and the leading articles in the newspapers on the Bill make melancholy reading. The disputation over religious teaching—whether a child should be taught that the God of Church or the God of Chapel was the true God—made men forget Carlyle's strong souls with sealed eyes, incapable of comprehending the existence of any God. Under Forster's Act, the new schools gave religious instruction without any sectarian colouring. But the old schools, in which the Church catechism was taught, received the blessing and the money of the State. This put a great strain upon the loyalty of the Dissenters to the Liberal Party. To be compelled to send their children to a Church school because no other kind of school was accessible was bad enough, but that this grievance should be perpetuated by the State, and the Dissenters forced to pay taxes to keep it going—this was insupportable. There were some dismal struggles between Church and Chapel folk in rural areas; sectarian rancour was to hamper all progress in education up to our own days. A people that showed itself so mature in the arts of political compromise was unable in the nineteenth century to reach a decent settlement of its religious differences.

PART III

STEAM AND SMOKE

CHAPTER ONE

RAILWAYS

The Victorians dominate us through their memorials. They have left none more impressive than the British railway system. Standing between the barbaric pillars of Euston, or looking up at the arch of Paddington, one can say, "If you seek their monument, look around you". Our grandfathers saw those great stations as temples of civilisation and those shining rails as mysterious symbols in the world of ideas.

By the middle forties, after the early hostility to them had died away, the railways were generally regarded as the missionaries of Progress, the agents of the dominant philosophy of the age. The railways spread the beneficence of commerce. They increased the national wealth. They opened up the sleepy countryside to new ideas as well as to trade. They hurried the London newspapers through the night so that a hundred thousand remote breakfast tables might know what mischief Palmerston and Russell, "the old ringleaders", had been up to in the House of Commons at midnight. They unified the sentiment of the country, so that Cockneys and Mancunians, Newcastle Geordies, Suffolk yellow-bellies and Hampshire hogs were all mixed up together and might take their simultaneous cue in cheering for Progress and the Queen, for Rule Britannia and Free Trade.

Before the locomotive was used, railway wagons had been drawn by horses. This was a familiar sight in the coalfields throughout the eighteenth century. The first of all the swarm of Railway Acts that cluttered up Parliament during the century was passed in 1800; it sanctioned the Surrey Iron Railway, which ran for 9½ miles from Wandsworth through

EARLY MORNING IN A THIRD-CLASS RAILWAY COMPARTMENT
Wood engraving by William M'Connell from "Twice Round the Clock"
by George Augustus Sala, 1859

Mitcham to Croydon and had a double line of plate rails of four feet gauge. The horse-drawn Stockton to Darlington line, opened in 1825, was the first on which locomotives were employed and it was the first that was granted Parliamentary powers to carry passengers. In 1833 the horses were taken off, and steam engines took their places. The Baltimore and Ohio railway in the United States was opened in 1829.

Walter Besant used to say he thought a taste for statistics morbid, but he recognised there were occasions when he must pander to it. These figures, then, may be quoted to show the expansion of the railways in Victorian times: in 1825 there were 27 miles of railway in the country, in 1840 there were 1,857; in 1845, 2,235; in 1850, 6,621; in 1860, 10,433; and in 1880, 15,563. This statistical story is told in pictorial form in diagram number XI at the end of this book.

There are pages in Dickens, particularly in *Dombey and Son,* in which one is made aware of the monstrous terror of the railways, as a sensitive child might feel it, watching from his bedroom window the fiery devils dash past at night over the viaduct, screeching, glaring, tossing behind a trail of red cinders. Dickens, as we have seen, was a child of the coaching days, and in *Dombey* one can catch something of the horrid mystery in which the first steam trains were invested. To imaginative eyes they seemed to reflect a glare from Gehenna. If you would comprehend the pride and exhilaration that the Middle Victorians found in contemplating their railways, it is necessary to read, not Dickens nor Thackeray, who were both nostalgic souls, but Samuel Smiles—the old philosopher of *Self Help*. The thought of a locomotive made Smiles write like a young man in love. One beholds him standing among the smoke-wreaths, among the rushing crowds, the shouting porters at Paddington, watching the express trains rattling in and out, his honest face shining with the rapture and wonder of the revelation. One hears the ecstatic note rising in his voice as he chants of the miracles:

> And now see the enormous magnitude to which railway passenger-traffic has grown. In the year 1873, 401,465,086 passengers were carried by day tickets in Great Britain alone. *But this was not all!* For in that year 257,470 periodical tickets were issued by the different railways; and assuming half of them to be annual, one-fourth half yearly, and the remainder quarterly tickets, and that their holders made only five journeys each way weekly, this would give an additional number of 47,024,000 journeys, or a total of 448,489,086 passengers carried in Great Britain in one year.

There! says Smiles—doesn't that stagger you? But the gentle fanatic is resolved you shall not simply nod and smile, and turn aside. He presses on in his eager, detaining way,

> It is difficult to grasp the idea of the enormous number of persons represented by these figures. The mind is merely bewildered by them, and can form no adequate notion of their magnitude. *To reckon them singly would occupy twenty-five years, counting at the rate of one a second for twelve hours every day.*

Who but Smiles, the infatuated fellow, would have worked out that last calculation? (These passages are quoted from the introduction Smiles wrote to the 1874 edition of his *Lives of the Engineers George and Robert Stephenson*, first published in 1857; a book as full of moral gusto and didactic fervour as *The Fairchild Family*.)

What a difference it makes to a man to have a passion for *something*, even if it be but for the old London, Chatham and Dover line! I confess I find such an enthusiasm infectious, although I am one of those poor mortals who cannot count with much conviction beyond ten. The rapt innocence, the holy joy of Samuel Smiles reciting his mileages, his freight loadings, his passenger tallies—these come near giving statistics the excitements of the novel and the stage. He recalls, for example, that Mr. Porter, in his *Progress of the Nation*, had estimated that thirty millions of passengers, or about eighty-two thousand a day, travelled by coaches in Great Britain in 1834, an average distance of twelve miles each, at an average cost of five shillings a passenger, at the rate of fivepence a mile. Poor Porter!—he lived in the world before the Flood. His wretched little posy of statistics draws from Smiles a triumphant whoop on behalf of the crowning glory of the seventies—"About 448 millions are *NOW* carried by railway an average distance of eight-and-a-half miles each, at an average cost of one shilling and three-halfpence per passenger, or about three-halfpence per mile, in considerably less than one-fourth of the time." Smiles was not the man to let us forget that as well as the carrying of these tribes of passengers the railway transported so many tons of minerals, merchandise, mails, cattle, parcels and other solids.

The hypnotic eye fixes us; Smiles grasps our lapel; now his voice is soaring into a paean:

> To perform this service, there were in 1873, 11,255 locomotives at work in the United Kingdom, consuming about four million tons of coal and coke, and flashing into the air every minute some forty tons of water in the form of steam in a high state of elasticity. There were also 24,644 passenger carriages, 9,128 vans and breaks attached to passenger-trains, and 329,163 trucks, wagons and other vehicles appropriated to merchandise.

Now comes Samuel's final leap to Dionysian joy:

> *Buckled together, buffer to buffer, the locomotives and tenders would extend from London to Peterborough; while the carrying vehicles, joined together, would form two trains occupying a double line of railway extending from London beyond Inverness.*

Steam in a high state of elasticity indeed! There is no withstanding such enthusiasm "flashing into the air". Hurrah for Mr. Bazley, M.P., who stated "at a late public meeting in Manchester that it would probably require ten millions of horses to carry by road the merchandise which is now annually carried by trains". Three cheers for the far-sighted Post Office which had recognised the value of the railways as mail-carriers as far back as 1830, when the Liverpool and Manchester Line was opened. (The last of the old four-horse mail coaches was taken off in 1858; it was the *Derby Dilly* which ran between Manchester and Derby.) Bravo for Rowland Hill and the Penny Post, that triumph of liberal enlightenment —but without the railways how could the Post Office have coped with the avalanche of mail that cheap postage brought down? Statistical Smiles informs us that in 1839 "the number of chargeable letters carried was only 76 millions and of newspapers 44½ millions; whereas, in 1865, the numbers of letters had increased to 720 millions, and in 1867 to 775 millions, or more than ten-fold, while the number of newspapers, books, samples and patterns (a new branch of postal business began in 1864) had increased, in 1865, to 98½ millions".

Do we laugh, and think it very vulgar and naïve to write in this way about these ugly new toys? Where, in this, is the dignity of man's spirit? But the Victorians remembered what life was like in the days before the mechanical revolution. To them the railways were emancipators. When, at the opening of the Stockton and Darlington line, George Stephenson prophesied that a day would come when working men would ride about the land in his chariots, and when such lordly travel would cost them less than their expense in leather, he spoke as a conscious liberator and radical egalitarian. When Smiles was contemplating the heavenly length of locomotives buckled together, buffer to buffer, from London to Peterborough, he was not merely anticipating the peculiar intellectual curiosity of *Tit-Bits* and *Answers* later in the century. He was thinking of the enhancement of human faculty which those railways brought—of the freedom of human movement—of the breaking of the primal tyrannies of time and place. It was exhilarating to Smiles and his friends to see the barriers that confine men go crashing down, to behold Squire Hardcastle and Parson Trulliber put to rout just like the old sheep that stampeded for their lives when they heard the whistle of the locomotive in the valley. Prometheus was unbound when he could buy a railway ticket.

A greater man than Smiles, Arnold of Rugby, regarded the opening of the London to Birmingham line as a notable advance in the march of civilisation through the ages. Think of Arnold standing on the railway bridge and solemnly watching the Birmingham train shooting and rattling past underneath him, following it until its tail vanishes among the flowering hedges, then saying with all the force of his moral authority, "*I rejoice to see it, and to think that Feudality is gone forever. It is so great a blessing to think that one evil is gone forever.*" That is one of the supreme Victorian perceptions, and from it sprang the whole new cult of the machine.

One gathers from their unthumbed look that the volumes of the *Collected Poems of Ebenezer Elliott*, the Corn-Law rhymer (1781–1849), in the London Library are not greatly read nowadays. I confess I find them worth plodding through; for every now and then there rises from those soggy pages, like a muffled voice at a spiritualist seance, the true, old-fashioned note of Radical rhapsody over the Iron Horse.

> Engine of Watt! unrivalled is thy sway,
> Compared with thine, what is the tyrant's power?
> *His* might destroys while *thine* creates and saves.
> Thy triumphs live and grow, like fruit and flower
> But his are writ in blood and reared on graves.

One thinks of the 9.15 steaming out of Mugby Junction today with the sober insignia of British Railways painted upon it. Is it possible that once the sight of such a chuffing locomotive with its string of clattering coaches could have made despots tremble, and the sons of Freedom rejoice? Yes, indeed, replies the shade of Ebenezer Elliott:

> This metal god that yet shall chase
> The tyrant idols of remotest lands
> Preach science to the desert, and efface
> The barren curse from every pathless place.

Is that innocence of faith not to be envied? Who today can feel any such lift of spirit in watching a flight of jet-propelled planes? The Victorians, lucky as they were in many things, had this advantage over us that most of our drab commonplaces were shining apparitions to them. To live at the beginning of the age of mechanical invention was to inhabit a fairy-tale world of perpetual wonders. To comprehend the happiness of the Victorians, we must think ourselves back into a time when it really seemed a mad fantasy that a string of wagons could be dragged along a metal track by a steam locomotive at a speed faster than Mazeppa's wild horse. The parson of Redruth who saw William Murdoch's experimental engine whistling and flaring along the country road at night genuinely believed that he had met Beelzebub himself. It was exhilarating to live in a world in which one could still believe demons were abroad.

To a young Radical, the young master of the machine took on heroic strength and graces.

> The hope of futurity—the engineer,
> The far-praised, self-taught, matchless engineer.

The great marble statue of Robert Stephenson at Euston Station expresses this hero-worship. He is hewn to look like a god. There is no other image of Victorian eminence cast in such an heroic mould. I have heard that simple savages from Africa, arriving at this station have trembled and prostrated themselves before it. It is so plainly the white man's god, carved from the whitest marble on view in London, a majestic, remote, ineffable, frightening figure of Power.

In the thirties, as we saw from Creevey, conservative people raised a great cry against the railways. The noblemen in the great country houses, the cathedral clergy, the dons, the lovers of pastoral England and of the beauty of historic cities joined the agitation against "the infernal engines". The alarm was spread that the monster would set villages and forests ablaze, would destroy pheasants with its poisoned breath, would, indeed, drive all bird life from the country and would kill the sheep and cattle with fright. Wordsworth, in his sonnet "On a proposal to Carry a Line from Kendal to Windermere", a sonnet which contains strange echoes of his glorious invocation to Toussaint L'Ouverture, asked:

> Is there no nook of English ground secure
> From rash assaults? . . .
> Plead for thy peace, thou beautiful romance
> Of nature; and, if human hearts be dead,
> Speak passing winds, ye torrents with your strong
> And constant voice, protest against the wrong.

Cynics have since liked to point out that the venerable Poet Laureate, while leaving the winds and torrents to conduct their protest meetings, himself prudently invested in railway stock. But Wordsworth did no more than fall in with the national compromise. Poets must eat.

The British aristocracy and the clergy showed that graceful capacity to adapt themselves to changed circumstances which has often saved the country from bloodshed. How different from the attitude of Creevey's Duke of Devonshire in the thirties was that of the Marquis of Bristol in the forties. Speaking at a public meeting called to support the proposal of a direct line from London to Norwich, the Marquis declared, in a burst of sacrificial zeal, that "if necessary they might make a tunnel beneath his very drawing room rather than be defeated in their undertaking". The audience at a railway rally at Banbury was delighted by the whimsical confession of a Reverend Mr. Litchfield who said that "he had laid down for himself a limit to his approbation of railways—at least of such as approached the neighbourhood with which he was connected—and that limit was, that he did not wish them to approach any nearer to him than *to run through his bedroom, with the bedposts for a station*". One hears again the affectionate laughter, the genial cheers that greeted that ecclesiastical whimsy.

A few craggy men of principle continued to resist. A yeoman farmer in the neighbourhood of Carlisle, dying in 1868, bequeathed the bulk of his estate to a relative on condition that he should not at any time travel upon the Carlisle and Silloth Railway. But that will was regarded as being, like the thumbscrew and rack, an illustration of the barbarism of the past. Even Colonel Sibthorpe, the eccentric Conservative M.P. for Lincoln, who had once said "I hate these infernal railways as I hate the Devil", bought a railway ticket and compounded happily with Satan before he died.

There is a delightful passage in Disraeli's *Sybil* which exhibits the graceful yielding of the aristocracy to the monster:

> "You came by the railroad?" inquired Lord de Mowbray mournfully, of Lady Marney.
>
> "From Marham; about ten miles from us," replied her ladyship.
>
> "A great revolution!"
>
> "Isn't it?"
>
> "I fear it has a very dangerous tendency to equality," said his lordship, shaking his head; "I suppose Lord Marney gives them all the opposition in his power."
>
> "There is nobody so violent against railroads as George," said Lady Marney; "I cannot tell you what he does not do! He organised the whole of our division against the Marham line!"
>
> "I rather counted on him," said Lord de Mowbray, "to assist me in resisting this joint branch here; but I was surprised to learn he had consented."
>
> "Not until the compensation was settled," innocently remarked Lady Marney; "George never opposes them after that. He gave up all opposition to the Marham line when they agreed to his terms."
>
> "And yet," said Lord de Mowbray, "I think if Lord Marney would take a different view of the case and look to the moral consequences, he would hesitate. Equality, Lady Marney, equality is not our métier. If we nobles do not make a stand against the levelling spirit of the age, I am at a loss to know who will

fight the battle. You may depend upon it that these railroads are very dangerous things."

"I have no doubt of it. I suppose you have heard of Lady Vanilla's trip from Birmingham? Have you not, indeed! She came up with Lady Laura, and two of the most gentlemanlike men sitting opposite her; never met, she says, two more intelligent men. She begged one of them at Wolverhampton to change seats with her, and he was most politely willing to comply with her wishes, only it was necessary that his companion should move at the same time, for they were chained together! Two gentlemen, sent to town for picking a pocket at Shrewsbury races."

"A countess and a felon! So much for public conveyances," said Lord Mowbray, "But Lady Vanilla is one of those who will talk with everybody."

Morality and aesthetics both proved accommodating when it was found that the London and Birmingham, the Liverpool and Manchester and the York and North Midland Companies were paying ten per cent. and the Stockton and Darlington Company fifteen. Where the City bankers led, rank, fashion, statecraft, the Church and academic thought followed. There was a burst of speculation in 1836 which brought a number of new lines into being. But this was a small matter compared with the great Railway Mania of 1845–46. Nothing like that had been seen since the madness of the South Sea Bubble. A gambling hysteria seized the town.

That, said later moralists, particularly those of them who lost their money, was not an agreeable sight. You and I, they agreed, can always find an admirable moral justification for our trying to make a little money by a flutter—for the bottom drawer is stuffed with bills, and we dread the postman's face at the door, and it is intolerable that the odious Evanses next door should be able to entertain at dinner three nights a week. We are so plainly people who merit a winning number in the grand lottery. But how revolting a spectacle is the stampede of those other people to the counter to snatch at the prizes. Their faces are twisted by the beastliest passions—greed, money-lust, cruelty, avarice, envy, treachery, malice. There was a good deal of writing in this vein when the Railway Mania reached its disastrous end. By 1845 the country had become intoxicated by the very notion of railways. Hundreds of lines were projected, hundreds of companies formed. Most of them might as well have been projects for railways in the moon. Two or three scamps would rent an office, buy a county map, pick at hazard from Debrett a brace of noble names, inscribe them (without permission) on a prospectus, advertise in the newspapers—and then wait for the money to tumble in. Now was the time for such as Montague Tigg, the sponger, to transform himself into Tigg Montague Esqr., the City magnate, to lay aside his seedy old coat and set up as a fine gentleman at the subscribers' expense. According to Frederick S. Williams (*Our Iron Roads*, a book published in Nottingham in mid-Victorian times), "One line was declared to enjoy the patronage of gentlemen who had been dead for several months; and ten others had no knowledge of the existence of the scheme till they saw it paraded before the public, avowedly under their own sanction. In another case, the three leading projectors of a very costly railway were notoriously living by their wits and could not have raised a hundred pounds among them except by fraud."

The *Manchester Guardian* file for 1845 records that during one week 89 new schemes had been announced in three newspapers, the capital required for which was estimated at more than 84 millions; while in the space of a month 357 railway projects were advertised in the same journals, having an aggregate capital of 332 millions sterling. In the Parliamentary return of railway shareholders for 1846 there were 900 lawyers, 364 bankers, 257 clergymen and 157 M.P.s. The lists were gemmed with the names of great noblemen and great ladies, but there were also to be found there representatives of every other class in the community—clerks, potboys, tradesmen, labourers of all kinds, college scouts, domestic servants, fishwives, sewing women, boarding-house landladies, and, inevitably, those foredoomed victims of every fraud, the widows and maiden ladies living on a small income. It was a carnival for "stags" in low life, for those who sold scrip for which they had not paid. Lord Clanricarde told the House of Lords of a clerk named Guernsey earning twelve shillings a week, his mother being a charwoman, who had his name down as a subscriber for shares in the London and York line for £52,000. Butlers and footmen were leading figures in the Railway boom. Jeames Yellowplush would write from Belgravia on his master's coroneted letter-paper, take up a large subscription to the West Diddlesex Railway, pay a very modest sum on account, and then dispose of the scrip at a splendid profit. A butler told his mistress that he was retiring from her service on a fortune he had made from his shares. How did he manage it? "Why, ma'am," said he, "I applies for the shares, and gives a reference here; and as I opens the door myself, and answers the reference, I always give myself the wery highest character for property and all that, and so I gets the shares and sells them."

George Cruikshank wrote at this time, "Every man of the present day is a holder of shares in a railway; that is, he has got some pieces of paper called scrip, entitling him to a certain proportionate part of a blue, red or yellow line drawn across a map and designated a railway". The bloating of the bubble may be judged from the calculations of the painstaking Williams:

> We find that in November 1845, the enormous number of 1,428 lines were either made, or announced to the public and registered. . . . The 47 lines completed from 1823 to the end of 1844 cost £70,680,877. The number of railways then in progress was 118, their aggregate mileage 3,543 and their estimated cost was £67,359,325. By adding, therefore, to the actual cost of all the completed lines the estimated cost of all lines then in progress, we arrive at the aggregate capital of the railway undertakings of the country as it then stood, amounting to £138,040,202. Of the projected lines there were 1,428

with an estimated capital of £701,243,208 and a deposit of £49,592,816. On one scheme £40,000,000 was to be expended.

"We know no spectacle so ridiculous as the British public in one of its periodical fits of morality," said Macaulay. Such a fit seized the British public when this bubble burst. The head on which its anger was chiefly visited was that of George Hudson, the Railway King, a creature of daemonic power who was something more than a greedy speculator. To a greater degree than any other man of his time, Hudson saw the railways in a true relation to the economic and social life of the nation.

CHAPTER TWO

GEORGE HUDSON

One pictures the old man at the end of his days, ruined, sick, living on the bounty of friends, but still sanguine and unashamed, still believing in himself, saying to some young journalist or politician who had come to see him in his seedy obscurity: "Sydney Smith, sir, the Reverend Sydney Smith, the great wit, first called me the Railway King. And I remember very well that he made a very pretty speech about it, saying that while some monarchs had won their title to fame by bloodshed, and by the misery they inflicted on their fellow creatures, I had come to my throne by my own peaceful exertions, and by a course of probity and enterprise." (Quoted from F. S. Williams.) Probity is not the word we should nowadays apply to the chairman of the Eastern Counties line who paid dividends out of capital. But as for enterprise, oh! certainly, he was the embodiment of it. In 1848 Hudson controlled 1,450 of the 5,000 miles of railways that then stretched across Britain, and he "superintended the practical working of half a dozen lines separated a hundred miles or more from each other". He was chairman of four companies: the Midland; the York and North Midland; the York, Newcastle and Berwick; and the Eastern Counties line. In his prime he straddled England, north, centre, east.

The prices of railway stocks fell heavily through 1848. The revolutions that swept Europe during that year affected British trade, and railway earnings suffered. Hudson's mighty schemes were threatened by disaster. Through '48 and '49 he covered his retreat by rearguard actions. He twisted and turned, he bullied and bluffed, he shamelessly cooked his accounts, he tricked his partners, he swindled his stockholders. With desperate hardihood, he even staged a counter-thrust as late as 1850 when he opened the fine new docks that he had built for Sunderland. But he could not fend off ruin. Company Law was in so primitive a state a century ago that Hudson was never prosecuted. His creditors once succeeded in locking him up in York gaol, but that was a political trick to keep him from running for the House of Commons, and in the end he fled to the Continent to escape their importunities.

A conspiracy of silence was drawn around his name after his fall. He could never be forgotten, but the fashionable world that had so willingly eaten his magnificent dinners affected not to see him. It was an uneasy ostracism—sidelong glances were cast at the pariah, for he was supposed to have some awkward secrets in his owning. He could blast some fine

H

ANNOUNCEMENT OF A DIVIDEND OF TWOPENCE HALFPENNY
AT A RAILWAY SHAREHOLDERS' MEETING
Cartoon by Richard Doyle from "Punch", 1849

respectable reputations if he opened his mouth. But Hudson never opened his mouth, and never received his deserts. In our times his balance sheets would have earned him penal servitude. Yet, all the same, crook or genius that he was, he merits hanging up in the portrait gallery of eminent Victorians. Hang him there on the wall, then, by the side of the Queen, Gladstone, Disraeli, Bright and Palmerston; with Dickens, Thackeray, Browning and Tennyson; with Darwin, Arnold, Mill and Miss Nightingale. Gladstone would agree, I think, no matter who among the others growled. Gladstone had fought a great duel of words with him over the Railway Bill of 1844, but he was always most generous in his estimation of Hudson's virtues. After Hudson's fall, Gladstone said of him, "He was no mere speculator, but a projector of great discernment, courage and rich enterprise . . . a very bold, and not at all an unwise projector".

The portrait is of a thick, broad-shouldered fellow, with sharp, shrewd little eyes and a Yorkshire obstinacy written on his face, an intelligent headpiece on him, no neck at all, and a paunch of prodigious rotundity that excited envious comment among the workers on his railways. Hudson should be hanging in that gallery as a representative Victorian industrialist. He was a representative man in his tearing energy, his hurry of spirit, his daring, his gambles, his taking of risks, in his general harshness to his workpeople mitigated by flashes of kindness to individuals among them who caught his eye. He was representative, too, in believing that he was an instrument of the Divine purpose. He was ruthless, he was fraudulent, and he talked of "the great moral effect of railways on the human race"—but there was no doubt of his sincerity. Hudson was partly, but not wholly, an Adam Smith hero. This uncouth illiterate linen-draper from York, who after inheriting a small fortune turned to financing railways, was, on the face of things, a good example of the man who adds to the wealth of the community by pursuing his own gain. Unlike most of the Adam Smith heroes, however, Hudson was not an economic anarchist. He was a Tory at a time when the commercial community was overwhelmingly Liberal. To be a Liberal in that age of Liberalism's triumph was to be an individualist. But a Tory in the night of Toryism's decline could be almost anything—a feudalist, a monopolist, an old-fashioned mercantile restrictionist, even a State planner. Lord George Bentinck invited Hudson to the Front Opposition Bench to show that at least one successful man of business supported the agricultural interest. The Conservative Front Bench has never presented a more remarkable spectacle than in those months after the Repeal of the Corn Laws when its ornaments were such dissimilar characters as honest, stupid Lord George, the squire of broad acres, Disraeli, who had been both a Radical and a dandy, and was the author of that revolutionary novel *Sybil*, and Hudson, the vulgarian business man, who looked and spoke like a *Punch* caricature of a magnate, but had ideas far in advance of his time and his kind.

Hudson's virtue was that he saw the railways as a function of the nation's growth. He had a vision of a regulated development of traffic between the industrial North and Midlands and the rural South; he wanted, in the modern phrase, to rationalise the system. By bullying, by persuasion, by cajolery, often by cheating, he strove to impose order upon swarming confusion. The little railways and the big railways were running madly in all directions. To build a line at all was in itself Progress. What mattered where it ran, who wanted it, what purpose it served? Who dared call competition chaos? Hudson was a dangerous man, said the advocates of unrestricted free enterprise, a monopolist, his hands greedily reaching out to grasp all the lines in the country and so to transform free Britain into Hudsonia, a slave State.

Nothing is new, and Government ownership of the railways was originally debated a century and more ago. Gladstone's Railway Act of 1844 contained a clause making any new line liable to State purchase or control after a period of 21 years, provided it had yielded a dividend of ten per cent for three successive years. One gathers that Hudson would have been willing to accept some measure of Government control if the main lines could have been amalgamated under his chairmanship. He was far-seeing; the grouping of the lines ordained by Government after the First World War was not very different from the plans he had laid. Had he lived in our day, Hudson would have been a member of the Transport Commission—if he could have kept out of gaol.

Hudson also holds a considerable place in the social comedy of English life. The method applied by Society to such a character, to a Caliban who acquires power through wealth or political success, is known as "taking up a quaint and original creature". Hostesses say, "He is such an *amusing* monster, and he says such absurd things, that I know you will adore him. He is so refreshingly different from the stupid people of our own kind one has to meet every day." They never confess they court him because he is powerful and has patronage to dispense. A bargain is struck between social influence and the money power, or political power, but it is never avowed in so many terms. So it comes about that one day Society discovers treasures of charm and wit in some dull dog who has made a great deal of money, or some tedious politician of second rank who, because he commands a strategical position or belongs to a group that holds the balance of power, has become a Minister in a party crisis. This is part of that endless process of absorption which began in the late eighteenth century when, to offset the power of the Whigs, the Tory Party made nobles of merchants and bankers. The winning over of wealthy tradesmen and "captains of industry" was the continuing manœuvre on the part of a class that was determined to retain power.

The writers on the early period of the railways, Samuel Smiles, Frederick Williams and the rest, have given us accounts of the flattery which the fashionable world poured upon Hudson. His most celebrated appearance in high life was made at Lord Northampton's reception in Carlton Terrace to the members of the Royal Society. The description of that day as given by the admiring Williams is a page from social history worth reading as a companion piece to the account in *Little Dorrit* of Merdle's dinner-party.

> England's greatest painters, greatest authors, greatest sculptors, greatest inventors, greatest philanthropists, greatest statesmen, greatest physicians, greatest engineers, greatest captains jostled each other in the crowded rooms. Amid the constellation of celebrities, there were two men round whom the crowds circled, let them turn which way they would—bright particular stars each with revolving satellites, and both receiving the deference of the great and noble as their right. One was the late Prince Consort, the other was Geo. Hudson. They looked rival monarchs, each with his obsequious courtiers round him, and divided pretty equally the honours of the evening.

The supreme moment came when a buzz ran round the room—"His Royal Highness has asked to be introduced to Mr. Hudson". Before such a dazzling conjunction, the illustrious crew lowered their heads. Within

LORD PALMERSTON, AGED EIGHTEEN
Water-colour by Thomas Heaphy
National Portrait Gallery

LORD PALMERSTON, AGED SIXTY-TWO
Oil painting by John Partridge
National Portrait Gallery

SIR ROBERT PEEL
Oil painting by Robert Linnell, 1838
National Portrait Gallery

JEREMY BENTHAM
Oil painting by H. W. Pickersgill
National Portrait Gallery

ROAD VERSUS RAIL
Coloured aquatint after C. C. Henderson, 1845

PRIMROSE HILL TUNNEL
Aquatint after E. T. Dolby, *c.* 1850

the circle drawn by their gentlemen-in-waiting the two Great Personages conversed—affably, it was noted. Then on a sudden, all that was eminent in the arts and sciences, in statecraft and in war, was astonished to hear a burst of laughter coming from the Prince Consort's lips. Albert seldom laughed in public—or in private.

It is painful to explain any jest, but this one does require a certain scaffolding to be understood after all these years. There was at this time a powerful competitor to the steam locomotive—the atmospheric railway. The method of applying the power in the atmospheric railway was through a pipe laid between the rails, a piston in the tube being linked by a shaft to the under-framework of the carriage. The propulsive force was supplied by the ordinary pressure of the atmosphere acting against the piston in the tube on one side, a vacuum being created in the tube on the other side of the piston by the working of a stationary engine. So great an engineer as Isambard Brunel had staked his faith on it, and large sums of capital had been pledged to it. The Prince, always curious about science and invention, asked Hudson what he thought of these atmospheric railways—would they replace steam locomotion. Was this the *new* thing? Then came the colossal retort which set the Prince roaring—"It's all 'oombug, your Royal 'Ighness". And it *was* humbug.

Much fun was poked at the vulgar display of Mr. and Mrs. Hudson by those who ate with delight the inordinate dinners they gave in that great house at Albert Gate which is now the French Embassy. Those who hung with rapt solicitude on Hudson's lips to pick up a tip for the stock market lunched out for a week afterwards on their amusing stories of his frightful blunders of speech. The best people swallowed his delicacies, often brought by packet and express train from France, consumed his exquisite wines, profited by tapping his shrewd speculative instinct, and made him the laughing-stock of the town. Poor Mrs. Hudson was a considerable butt, for, like Mrs. Disraeli, she could never be sure whether it was the Greeks or Romans "who came first". But I like best that story of the Duke of Wellington coming to Hudson to seek help for his sister who had been brought near to ruin by railway speculation. The King of Hudsonia kindly rigs the market for her ladyship's benefit—starts the whispers on their rounds—sets the traps for other innocents—advises the lady when to sell—and so her fortune is won back. The Duke comes back to Hudson, full of gratitude. "Is there anything I can do for you in return?" King Hudson reflects. No!—nothing! Then, as the Duke is going out of the door, Hudson detains him—blurts out his secret sorrow. He has a daughter. She is at a seminary for young ladies. She is unhappy; she is an ugly duckling. The daughters of gentlemen peck at her, and tease her, and make her life wretched on account of her vulgar origin. To be a linen-draper's daughter among young gentlewomen was an awful fate. Her father may be the richest and powerfullest man in England, but he's no gentleman, say the young ladies. Will the Duke do Hudson a favour? Will he call at the seminary for young ladies and ask to see his girl? Wellington acts as Wellington would. He buys a fine bouquet and gallops off on his horse to the seminary. "The Duke of Wellington, ma'am, with his compliments, to see Miss Hudson." Profound sensation in the seminary. Fluttering curtseys of mistresses, their hands pressed over their agitated hearts. Scatterings and congealings of excited girls, squealings, pushings, swoonings at the sight of England's hero.

The god descends. He presents his flowers. He bows low. He treats the little ugly duckling with the ceremonial courtesy he would pay a princess. He chats of Papa, his friend. The Duke had heard so much of her that he insisted on making her acquaintance.

It was finely done, as he alone could do it. He caught up the ugly duckling in his glory, and the seminary perceived what a beautiful and graceful silver swan it possessed.

This makes a pleasant page in the Book of Snobs.

CHAPTER THREE

THE CITY OF THE REAL

The railways, then, gave their tone to the age. They were the spectacular representation of that spirit of mechanical progress before which men and women abased themselves. Tennyson provided the age with its motto:—"Faster let the great world spin down the ringing grooves of change!" The railways gave release to the fierce, daemonic energies which possessed Britain. Those freight trains that enchanted Samuel Smiles as they thundered past him were loaded with coal and iron and manufactured goods of every kind. "Let the country but make the railroads and the railroads will make the country," Edward Pease, the Quaker pioneer of railways, had said. They did. In the backward glance of history, it is startling to observe this ancient and settled land, conservative, steeped in tradition, suddenly becoming seized by all the qualities of a pioneer community: hustle, bustle, improvisation, vulgarity, hasty cruelty, sudden generosity, irreverence. Get rid of the Woolsack! cried George Stephenson—the Lord Chancellor should now sit on a sack of coals to mark the change. Was that not very much in the mood of the Connecticut Yankee at the Court of King Arthur? Everything that is said by fastidious critics against American values could be said—and, indeed, *was* said—against the pioneering society of the Victorians. In that society the emphasis was laid on material ends. The figures most greatly admired were those who had made fortunes by exploiting natural resources. Tradition was a dead hand. Privilege was effete. A manufacturer believed that he had proved the virtues of Radicalism by becoming rich. Equality of opportunity was exalted above equal justice. Freedom of enterprise was the new morality. New York today, in its mental climate, is very like the City of London in 1850. Manchester was the mid-Victorians' Chicago, Birmingham their Philadelphia. The Chamberlains were Republicans in the seventies very much for the reason that American plutocrats were Republicans, because "this King business" was a ridiculous anachronism that yielded no dividends to its shareholders. Ebenezer Elliott, the old Chartist, dedicated his poem "Steam at Sheffield" to Charles Hindley, M.P., "one of our creators of national wealth—who while they enrich themselves, subtly reproach the splendid drones of society, by increasing the productive capital of the State".

Such men as Paxton, Stephenson and Hudson worked—as the old woman said—as though Old Nick were after them. Paxton, as his granddaughter Miss Violet Markham has described in her book on him, dashed ceaselessly about the country, as though he were himself an iron locomotive; whirling from one project to another; hurtling from Board meeting to committee; scribbling his correspondence on the platform of Mugby Junction at two o'clock on a frosty morning. Hudson would be in his office all day, giving staccato interviews to fifty callers, juggling accounts, projecting tremendous schemes, outwitting the pack that was on his trail, in the evening preside over a monstrous big banquet at Albert Gate, then go down to the House of Commons and take part in an exciting division, then at two or three o'clock in the morning call his carriage and bowl off to the station for the early morning train for York. Weeks, months and years, life went on like that. What possessed these fellows? What were they tearing after? What were they running *from?*

John Forster in his *Life of Dickens* has a penetrating passage on the relation of his hero to his world which would stand good for many eminent Victorians:

> Not his genius only, but his whole nature, was too exclusively made up of sympathy for, and with, the real in its most intense form, to be sufficiently provided against failure in the realities around him. There was for him no "city of the mind" against outward ills for inner consolation and shelter. . . . By his very attempts to escape the world, he was driven back into the thick of it. But what he would have sought there, it supplies to none; and to get the infinite out of anything so finite has broken many a stout heart.

George Gissing's comment on this in his *Charles Dickens* (1898) is an interesting one:

> We see the type of nineteenth-century Englishman; the breed of men who established a commercial supremacy which is (or very lately was) the wonder, the envy and the jest of the outer world. You cannot create Lancashire and Yorkshire if at the same time you have to guard a "city of the mind"; much too embarrassing would be the multitude of uneasy questions rushing in at every new step. This typical Englishman has no "detachment". In work or play, he must press onwards by the world's high-road.

This feverish energy was not confined to a class. The gangs of navvies who moved about the country in those early years building the railways undertook prodigious feats of strength and energy. These Homeric fellows were at once the admiration and despair of the moralists of the time. They were paragons of hard work—no moralist of the Manchester School could hope to see men work harder—but the respectable lamented that their manners were savage, their appetites coarse and their pleasures pagan. Drawn from all parts of the country—and not a few of them coming from Ireland—these lawless and indispensable characters formed a community of nomadic frontiersmen inside the ordered peace of the old-fashioned rural life. They were as picturesque and theatrical in appearance as the forty-niners of the Californian gold rush, and they seemed as greatly out of place in the sleepy villages. Their dress set them apart from the village hind and the tradesman—the corduroy breeches, the square-cut velveteen coat, the flaring waistcoat of scarlet plush with a dazzle of black dots, and the hat of white felt. Smiles recorded, "Their powers of endurance were extraordinary. In times of emergency they would work for twelve and even sixteen hours, with only short intervals for meals. The quantity of flesh-meat which they consumed was something enormous; but it was to their bones and muscles what coke is to the locomotive—the means of keeping up the steam." Keeping up the steam! That simile is racy of the period, and it is in the true vein of Pecksniff and Chadband. "They displayed great pluck", said Smiles, "and seemed to disregard peril. Indeed, the most dangerous sort of labour—such as working horse-barrow runs, in which accidents are of constant occurrence —has always been most in request amongst them, the danger seeming to be one of its chief recommendations." When the British navvies crossed the Channel to tear up the earth for the Continental railways they staggered the natives by their feats of endurance and caused mutinies among the weedy French labourers. I would draw no general conclusion from the manly virtues of our own forty-niners. I would do no more than record that an empire was built upon the sinews and animal vigour of these lowly, unregarded, coarse, common but tremendous fellows. They built the Victorian pyramids—and they were not slaves. That their virtues and their faults were entwined should not be forgotten by modern moralists, politicians and economists.

"In no age or nation of the earth, I believe, has matter ever been better handled or utilised," wrote a Frenchman who came to Britain in the fifties. "Enter London by water, and you will see an accumulation of toil and work which has no equal on this planet." In looking at the records and pictures of these times, there are moments when one has a feeling of wandering among the subterranean races of Northern legend—trolls and gnomes and insatiable dwarfs. One hears Wagner's question: Which is the race that lives under the earth? A voice answers: They are the grimy, half-naked little men, their chests narrowed and thighs twisted by the toil of hacking away at treasure in the underground caves and corridors, sometimes lying on their backs, clawing at the roof of their caverns, now crouching and hunched like frogs in excavating their loot, sweat blinding them, dust choking them. What is this treasure they seek? It is the treasure of the ages, Coal. It is more precious than the gold of the Incas, it gives its owner more power than the ring of the Nibelungs. It is a guess that 20,000,000 tons of coal were dug in 1830. In 1854, the first year for which officialdom rendered statistics, the amount was 64,661,401 tons. In 1870, it was 110,431,112.

Then there are the gnomes who live among the rocks above the earth:

they stoke the furnaces that must never die down and grow cold. They are forging not the sword of conquest but the peaceful and benevolent domination of iron. The production of pig iron in 1830—again a guess—was 677,000 tons; in 1854 it was 3,069,838 tons; in 1870 5,963,515 tons.

What the port of London looked like in the sixties we may judge from Taine's description:

> The Thames is a mile broad, and is but a populous street of vessels, a winding work-yard. Steamboats, sailing vessels, ascend and descend, come to anchor in groups of two, three, ten, then in long files, then in dense rows; there are five or six thousand of them at anchor. On the right, the docks, like so many intricate, maritime streets, disgorge or store up the vessels. If you get on a height, you see vessels in the distance by hundreds and thousands, fixed as if on the land; their masts in a line, their slender rigging, make a spider-web which girdles the horizon. Yet on the river itself, to the west, we see an inextricable forest of masts, yards, and cables; the ships are unloading, fastened to one another, mingled with chimneys, among the pulleys of the storehouses, cranes, capstans, and all the implements of the vast and ceaseless toil. A foggy smoke, penetrated by the sun, wraps them in its russet veil; it is the heavy and smoky air of a great hot-house; soil and man, light and air, all is transformed by work. If you enter one of these docks, the impression will be yet more overwhelming: each resembles a town; always ships, still more ships, in a line, showing their heads; their hollowed sides, their copper chests, like monstrous fishes under the breastplate of scales. When we descend below, we see that this breastplate is fifty feet high; many are of three thousand or four thousand tons. Long clippers of three hundred feet are on the point of sailing for Australia, Ceylon, America.

Long clippers! That brings to mind how late the lovely empire of the sails endured. Steamboats had been on the waters since 1811, and in 1842 the S.S. *Great Western* made the trip from New York to Bristol in twelve and a half days. Yet so late as 1880 the Royal Navy was, according to Admiral Wester Wemyss, "still in a state of transition from dependency upon wind to reliance upon steam for its motive power". In spite of every ship being fitted with a propeller, "sail power was still in the ascendancy". In the Age of Dickens, the approaches and the harbours of Britain were filled with the glory of those winged victories, the old sailing ships. These apparitions of beauty were part of the poetry of the race. It was possible in those days for a romantic spirit to ask, "Whither, O splendid ship, thy white sails crowding, leaning across the bosom of the urgent West?"

Those vessels had an infinite grace; they gave unending pleasure to the eye; they attested a high order of craftsmanship; those who manned them were craftsmen brought up in a hard school and subdued to old loyalties of their race. The ships sailed from Britain's ports to carry to the ends of the earth all that British ingenuity and skill could contrive, and, venturing the farthest span, brought home again the rarities of the East, the tea, the silks, the spices. Those straining wings, daring the twelve winds of heaven, represented, as nothing could better represent, the confident adventuring of the Victorians. They would sail all seas, all weathers, carrying their cargoes to all lands. "The earth was made for Dombey and Son to trade in, and the sun and moon were made to give them light. Rivers and seas were formed to float their ships; rainbows gave them promise of fair weather; winds blew for or against their enterprises; stars and planets circled in their orbits, to preserve inviolate a system of which they were the centre."

It will be recalled that just around the corner from the house of Dombey and Son "stood the rich East India House, teeming with suggestions of precious stuffs and stones, tigers, elephants, howdahs, hookahs, umbrellas, palm trees, palanquins and gorgeous princes of a brown complexion sitting on carpets, with their slippers very much turned up at the toes". These ancestors seem to us nowadays a mysterious people of an old mythology, obsessed by their treasure, labouring in a dark frenzy, and, like the Nibelungs, working out a distant fate.

The tables of industrial development which appear on pages 284–99 show how fierce was the drive towards material triumph and commercial victory. They indicate, too, how striking was the amassing of wealth during those decades. Was the doom of these Victorian Nibelungs sounded in 1914? Was the final word said in 1940? In the two great wars of the twentieth century the piled-up riches were prodigally spent. The investments made by the Victorians from China to Peru were dissipated—they were sold that the grandchildren might live at all. What would have astounded the Dombeys most of all was the thought that the beggarly and bankrupt United States of their time, whose development had owed so much to British capital and was the City of London's troublesome debtor—just a shade less dubious then than Brazil—should become in the lapse of time the grand creditor. How queer a nightmare for the Dombeys that this impoverished Jonathan, skinny, dyspeptic, ruined, living on saleratus bread, coated with the dust of the prairies, sick with swamp fever, should become the master of the western world, should hold the mortgage on John Bull's estate!

The Puritan doctrine of hard work, of the moral obligation laid on a man to make money, prevailed among the mercantile classes throughout our period. Religious belief and economic theory reinforced each other. Time was money; amusements were sinful. Most of our mid-Victorian manufacturers and tradesmen would have been appalled at the idea of the long week-end; of taking a sunny afternoon off on the golf links; of buying a little place in Northamptonshire in order to ride to hounds. The aristocracy, who were half-despised, half-envied, might waste their substance and imperil their immortal souls by indulging in all unhallowed pleasures. The turf was theirs, the sport of kings; and the hunting field. Let the ungodly pursue such vanities. For the Puritan business man the joy of life was—business. The competitive system provided him with an exhilaration beyond that of the chase. To outwit and to under-cut rivals, to capture new markets, to make fresh combinations of capital—these should satisfy all the primitive instincts of man. The mass of working people rendered homage to these same idols, even when they themselves were sacrificed upon the altars. They prostrated themselves before Baal while their children were being devoured by his fiery jaws.

The relaxing of these austere standards came slowly. The sons of the self-made men did not in those days go to the Universities; they were usually taken from school at the age of fifteen or sixteen to enter their fathers' counting-houses and to work twelve hours a day. But the *sons* of the sons—the third generation—they showed a hankering after a more easy and graceful life. The softening influences of the old aristocratic traditions began to be felt. Many fortunes had been accumulated by then; the satiety of wealth had begun to manifest itself; there was a longing for a more subtle and elegant display of the rich man's pride than that supplied by the great, gross eight-course dinners in Belgravia. The story of the first half of the nineteenth century is the story of the wresting of power from the aristocracy by the mercantile middle classes. And, then, when the victory was complete, the victors began to absorb the manners, the virtues and the frailties of the vanquished. The plutocracy of the Industrial Revolution began to aspire after the condition of the landed gentry. It began, once again, to be thought that success and wealth were most impressively demonstrated by the power to achieve a distinguished leisure. To become a country gentleman, to be at ease with the Longs in Wiltshire or the Digbys in Dorset, set the final seal upon a family that had been founded by a shipping agent in Liverpool or a mill-owner in Rochdale. In the end, the heirs of Mr. Rouncewell almost certainly inherited Sir Leicester Dedlock's place in Lincolnshire, and one feels confident that the third generation was magnificently represented by a Sir Leicester Rouncewell, M.P. for the county, a great gentleman of the old school who was adored by his tenantry, and whose speeches, deploring the revolutionary sentiments of Mr. Gladstone, delivered in the unstrung voice of the true aristocrat, recalled to elderly members the primeval Conservatism of Colonel Sibthorpe of Lincoln.

If one reads any book about the British people written in the last fifty years, one is certain to find a great deal in it about the influence of sports on the national character. The terminology of sport is liberally used in our politics, in commercial affairs and in the ordinary exchanges of daily life. A good man struggling with adversity—the tragic hero of the Greeks—is sympathetically described as one "batting on a sticky wicket". Almost the worst thing that can be said about a politician is that he is "a poor sportsman". I remember the outraged look on a recent Prime Minister's face in repudiating the notion that "he would ever fish with dirty bait".

THE DUKE OF WELLINGTON WITH HIS GRANDCHILDREN
Miniature by Robert Thorburn, 1852
By courtesy of the Duke of Wellington

THE FACTORY GIRLS' DINNER HOUR, WIGAN
Oil painting by Eyre Crowe
City Art Gallery, Manchester

A LONDON DUSTMAN
Wood engraving, 1861
From Henry Mayhew's "London Labour and the London Poor"

NICHOLAS FELIX,
THE CRICKETER
Coloured lithograph
after W. Drummond, 1849

ALFRED MYNN
First of the round-arm fast bowlers
Coloured lithograph
after John C. Anderson, 1852

A POINTSMAN ON THE
GREAT EASTERN RAILWAY
Wood engraving by John Gilbert,
1867

Glancing at the newspaper just now, I noted a Liberal orator scornfully accusing the Tories of not "observing the Queensberry rules". We have all heard at political meetings a little man in a cap shout at the platform speaker, "Why don't you *try* to play the game?" In a hot debate, one side is almost certain to accuse the other of "hitting below the belt". If Mr. Papyrus of Throgmorton Street feels that he has been deceived over the arrangements for fusing Gadgets Incorporated with Widgets Unlimited, he accuses his fellow financier, Mr. Winkelstein, of not playing with a straight bat.

All this would have been incomprehensible to the mid-Victorians. Their awareness of the influence of sport on the national character was limited to the recognition that Waterloo had been won on the playing fields of Eton. A century ago cricket belonged largely to the Dingley Dells of the country. It was a rural pastime, played on village greens by fellows in tall beaver hats, and shirts of bright hues, or—as Pickwick saw them—by players in straw hats and flannel jackets. There was no talk of amateurs and professionals, of players and gentlemen in those days; nor of gate money. There was, indeed, an easy mixing of the classes on the village green. An eleven would, in Meredith's phrase, be drawn from muscle and science without regard to rank. It would include squire's son and gamekeeper's son, the young farm labourer and the young peer from the Palladian mansion on the hill. It was not until the seventies that cricket became a subject of national interest. The Australians paid us their first visit in 1878.

At the opening of the nineteenth century football was thought of as a mediaeval custom, of the same order of quaint survivals as beating the bounds of the parish by bumping a choirboy. Tennis, regarded as an arrangement of quaint Tudor figures in a faded tapestry, was not revived until 1874, when a Major Wingfield designed a portable court of hour-glass design which he called Sphairistike. This was the improbable fore-runner of the Wimbledon courts. Golf remained a custom of the barbaric Scots until little more than fifty years ago, and there are many persons alive who will remember the appearance of golf clubs being hooted on the streets. It was not until the end of the century that the Puritan suspicion of games was overcome among the commercial middle class, and the lower middle class retained its prejudice much longer.

CHAPTER FOUR

THE VOICE OF POWER

A drive towards power so strong as that of the Victorian mercantile class, an energy so fierce, will plainly demand its own especial political expression—it will select one voice to speak for it in the outer world. How paradoxically the choice fell!

It has been said that the Victorian age began when Macaulay knocked for the first time at the door of Holland House. It may be said with equal truth that the eighteenth century did not die until Lord Palmerston died in 1865. It is an oddity of the period that the statesman who became the idol of the Victorian industrial and commercial middle classes was a character from another age, an aristocrat formed in the Georgian mould, whose philosophy, morals and manners were entirely different from theirs.

But the British seem to love paradox in their political leadership. It is as though there were some mysterious law which ordained that the Buffs must always be led by a Blue. Gladstone, the High Churchman, became in the end the Leader of Liberal Nonconformists, squired by Morley, the atheist, who spelt God with a small "g", and by Acton, the Roman Catholic. Disraeli, the Radical Jew, and the dandy of letters, was the leader of the English country gentlemen. Palmerston, who sat for years in the House as a Tory at a time when to be a Tory was to be a troglodyte, was one of the creators of British Liberalism.

The Podsnaps cheered themselves hoarse when Palmerston made a speech. He was the man to whom the country instinctively turned when the mismanagement of the Crimean War by the half-hearted Lord Aberdeen humbled the national pride. His whiskers were dyed, his manners were rakish and jaunty, his amours were notorious, he had a sublime sense of the superiority of Britain to other nations, he had the ineffable insolence of the English Milor' making the Grand Tour, he had an aristocratic contempt for the Court and enjoyed baiting that foreign prig, Prince Albert—and yet the solemn, sober, mercantile Evangelical middle classes adored him. During a General Election campaign, when Palmerston was already a venerable figure, Taper and Tadpole brought to Disraeli, his Conservative rival, a scandalous story of the Prime Minister's wooing of a clergyman's wife. "Don't repeat that story," cried Dizzy in mock horror. "If it is spread about we shall be ruined, for it will make him so popular he will carry all the constituencies."

Palmerston appealed to a mixed emotion among the middle classes, part of it base, part of it fine; half of it the truculence of a man who knows that he has become the cock of the walk, half of it the generous passion for liberty. In his most famous speech, Palmerston gave expression to the pride the middle class took in its own particular conception of freedom at home and its firm conviction that this was the ideal that must be spread abroad:

> We have shown that liberty is compatible with order; that individual freedom is reconcilable with obedience to the law. We have shown the example of a nation, in which every class of society accepts with cheerfulness the lot which Providence has assigned to it; while at the same time every individual of each class is constantly striving to raise himself in the social scale—not by injustice and wrong, not by violence and illegality—but by persevering good conduct, and by the steady and energetic exertion of the moral and intellectual faculties with which his Creator has endowed him.

Palmerston's diplomacy has been much censured by modern writers. It is true that his conduct of the matter of the Spanish royal marriages was clumsy and stupid. He was reckless, he was a jingo. He behaved like a bully in the schoolground, say his critics; though in fairness they should add that he usually struck his bullying attitudes in protecting smaller boys from having their arms twisted. Some of Palmerston's censors belong to that school of criticism which would make Tom Brown the villain of *Tom Brown's Schooldays*. In the celebrated affair of Don Pacifico, much fun has been poked at Palmerston for calling in the might of Her Majesty's fleet against Greece to enforce the claims of an unpleasant character of Portuguese-Jewish ancestry, born in Malta and living in Athens. The affair was a farce which ended in a rattle of gunfire. The people of Athens had been in the habit of celebrating Easter by burning an effigy of Judas Iscariot. In the year 1847 the Greek Government suspended the custom "out of compliment", we are told, to Baron Rothschild, then staying in the city—the Baron may have reflected that it was an odd sort of compliment. The mob, angry at the suspension of the folk festival, avenged itself by burning down the house of Don Pacifico—an act which I heard a diplomatist once describe as understandable in its exuberance but beside the point. The Don put in a bill for £26,618 for this bonfire, an excessive amount in the view of most good judges. Other British subjects had at this time claims outstanding against the Greek Government, among them Finlay the historian of Greece, but it was Don Pacifico's demands that lent colour and extravagance to the affair. The Greek Government was dilatory in offering compensation, and Palmerston sent the Fleet to the Piraeus to round up all the Greek and foreign shipping in the harbour. There were many in Britain who felt that this action, like Don Pacifico's bill, was immoderate; more particularly as, through that baleful magic of diplomacy by which molehills suddenly become mountains, it led us into a sharp quarrel and threat of war with France—one more irrelevance.

The division list in the four-night debate of 1850 on "the Affairs of Greece" shows a combination of Peel, Disraeli, Gladstone, Bright, Cobden, Sir William Molesworth and Cardwell among the forces ranged against Palmerston—Tories, Peelites and Radicals leagued against him. The Minister won a majority of 46 at four o'clock in the morning. The challenge brought from him his most renowned speech, the *Civis Romanus Sum* oration which enthralled the country and cannot but quicken the pulse of a reader today. The closing words of that speech! To inscribe them brings back the savour of those times: the pride of Britain; the broodings upon power and destiny; the hot, excited, crowded House of Commons in the early morning hours; the famous figures and the illustrious names; the feeling of manifest *greatness*; the mysterious sense that Rome was born again in Britain at the middle of the century.

> I therefore fearlessly challenge the verdict which this House, as representing a political, a commercial, a constitutional country, is to give on the question now brought before it; whether the principles on which the foreign policy of Her Majesty's Government has been conducted, and the sense of duty which has led us to think ourselves bound to afford protection to our fellow subjects abroad, are proper and fitting guides for those who are charged with the Government of England; and whether, as the Roman, in days of old, held himself free from indignity, when he could say *Civis Romanus Sum*; so also a British subject, in whatever land he may be, shall feel confident that the watchful eye and the strong arm of England will protect him against injustice and wrong.

Is it any wonder that after that speech almost any patriotic publican who opened an inn would hang outside it the sign of the Lord Palmerston—an orange-whiskered, dilapidated, raddled Saint George, with an unquenchable spark in his eye—jumping out of the paint to speak for England? Palmerston was an old-fashioned aristocrat who certainly did not believe that all men are born equal, but who had an instinctive understanding of the essential democratic notion that the test of a principle is its application to highly undeserving cases. Suppose, for example, one of the more brilliant and dashing of young Victorian dukes had become involved with the police at Trieste or Naples, then Parliament, the Press and the nation would have cheered the Fleet on its punitive way with the resounding cry *Civis Romanus Sum*; and there would have been no division on a vote of censure in either House. But the principle was much more vividly illustrated and vindicated by its application to a Maltese Jew of dubious reputation and unattractive manners. In this respect it may be said that it is always poor cases that make good law.

In many modern eyes, Palmerston appears as Giant Blunderbuss. But to most of his contemporaries he was Jack the Giant-Killer. They admired the intrepid courage with which he flouted the Court, and all its royal ramifications through Europe, and the coolness with which he turned upside down the conventions of the Foreign Office. The average Briton took pleasure in hearing that Palmerston had snubbed a despot, and had received at the Foreign Office Continental exiles and revolutionaries. A detestation of tyranny was a generous emotion that bound the classes together in those days. The brewers' men who threatened to lynch General Haynau, the Austrian, when he came to London, had more in common with the duchesses who espoused the cause of Garibaldi and Italian freedom than brewers' men and duchesses have had since. It is all very well to say, as clever modern men have said, that it was easy for the Victorians, being rich and strong, to take the side of the victims of foreign despotisms, as though this were some extravagant indulgence on their part, like cultivating orchids at Highbury. The remarkable thing about the mid-Victorians is that despite all the corruptions which wealth and power bring, despite all their reverence for material good, they were capable of a romantic attachment to liberty. The tale of History assures us that a society grown rich is usually indifferent to freedom, indeed comes to fear and hate freedom. If they had run true to historical form, the mid-Victorians, having made Britain the most powerful nation in the world, should have become aggressive in their designs and authoritarian in their instincts. Their hearts should have throbbed in sympathy with every foreign tyrant. Instead, they cheered Garibaldi; they fêted Kossuth. The Victorians in their full vigour at the middle of the century were idealists. It was not until the dismal end of the century that the Victorians put their money-bags and power first and became imperialists.

CHAPTER FIVE

LOST HERITAGE

The railway civilisation, built up with such fierce concentration of energy, was a lop-sided one. It was too greatly concerned with urban and industrial values for the island's health, happiness or even safety. The effects of this ill-balanced economy did not become apparent, though, for a good many years. The landed interests had foretold that the repeal of the Corn Laws would bring the speedy ruin of agriculture. Instead of that happening the farmer, as well as the industrialist, was caught up on the broad tide of prosperity that rolled in at the end of the forties. The free-trade system fulfilled the most sanguine expectations of its advocates. Trade was buoyant; the city labourers could now afford to pay for their daily bread; and the farmers went on getting good prices. In 1849 gold was found in California; and the new Eldorado was able to buy more goods from Britain. A set of happy accidents had consummated the triumph of a theory. Whenever events and theories are in alliance, it is naturally the theory that is given the credit of the victory.

"My own recollections date back to 1855—a Golden Age of agriculture for squires and farmers, when the land not only supplied bread to 17,000,000, and meat to the whole of the existing population, but employed nearly 1,100,000 rural workers." That was said in *The Times* in 1932 by Lord Ernle, once upon a time Minister of Agriculture, now more likely to be remembered as R. E. Prothero, whose book *The Psalms in Human Life* is still read in devout homes. The period of which Lord Ernle wrote was, be it noted, nine years after Repeal. And Taine, observing Britain in the dawn of the sixties, remarked:

> The country is a great kitchen-garden—a manufactory of grass and meat. Nothing is left to nature and chance; all is calculated, regulated, arranged to produce and to bring in profits. If you look at the peasants, you find no more genuine peasants; nothing like French peasants, a variety of fellahs, akin to the soil, mistrustful and uncultivated, separated by a gulf from the citizens. The countryman here is like an artisan; and, in fact, a field is a manufactory, with a farmer for a foreman. Proprietors and farmers, they lavish capital, like great contractors. They have drained; they have a rotation of crops; they have produced a cattle, the richest in returns of any in the world; they have introduced steam-engines into cultivation, and into the breeding of cattle; they perfect already perfect stables. . . . Under this universal effort, the products of agriculture have doubled in fifty years. The English acre receives eight or ten times more manure than the French hectare; though it is of inferior quality, they have made it produce double. Thirty persons are enough for this work, when in France forty would be required for half thereof. You come upon a farm,

> even a small one, say of a hundred acres; you find respectable, worthy, well-clad men, who express themselves clearly and sensibly; a large, wholesome, comfortable dwelling—often a little porch with climbing plants—a well-kept garden, ornamental trees, the inner walls white-washed yearly, the floors washed weekly—an almost Dutch cleanness; therewith plenty of books—travels, treatises on agriculture, a few volumes of religion or history; first of all, the great family Bible. Even in the poorest cottages we find a few objects of comfort and recreation: a large cast-iron stove, a carpet, nearly always a paper on the walls, one or two moral novels, and always the Bible. The cottage is clean; the habits are orderly; the plates, with their blue pattern, regularly arranged, look well above the shining dresser; the red floor-tiles have been swept; there are no broken or dirty panes; no doors off hinges, shutters unhung, stagnant pools, straggling dunghills, as amongst the French villagers; the little garden is kept free from weeds; frequently roses and honeysuckle round the door; and on Sunday we can see the father, the mother, seated by a well-scrubbed table, with tea and butter, enjoy their *home*, and the order they have established there. In France, the peasant on Sunday leaves his hut to visit his *land*: what he aspires to is possession: what Englishmen love is comfort.

This is very like the sentimental idylls on the calendars of our childhood; the rose-wreathed cottages, the fields white with harvest, the apple-cheeked village children singing "All things bright and beautiful". It brings back the smells of the world stored up in childhood recollections, the smell of cottage breakfasts—the fragrance of the bread dominating all, and challenging in fresh and poignant sweetness the breath of the garden lilacs. How sharp has become the contrast with the accounts of starving villagers during the peasants' revolt of the eighteen-thirties or during the potato famine of the black forties. It helps us to understand why the opposition to Free Trade dissolved so quickly in 1846, and why Protection remained a sleeping issue in British politics for more than half a century. Lord Ernle in the article from which I have quoted, observed that between the bad harvest of 1931 and the rotting crops of 1879 stretched fifty years of agricultural decay. "The arable area gradually fell by more than 4,000,000 acres and upwards of 500,000 workers left the land." This slow dying of the land falls outside the frame of our period, though the seeds of decay were sown during it.

Taine in his day was deeply impressed by the skill and expertness of British agriculture. His comparison between a farm and a well-run manufactory was a shrewd one. In many parts of the country agriculture was carried on with an efficiency, and a willingness to experiment, that won the admiration of Europe. The influence of such men as the celebrated Coke of Norfolk, first Earl of Leicester, had spread far beyond his own county. Husbandry became an exact science. In the eighteenth century, and in the early years of the nineteenth, the national genius for the practical was largely applied to the rotation of crops and to the breeding of cattle, as in later decades it was bent almost exclusively upon perfecting industrial machines. In the economy of a number of the great noblemen's estates, an inspired rule of thumb and a native wisdom of the soil anticipated the discoveries of later biologists and eugenists. Agricultural England was pulsing with life in those days; there was no drawing away of energies to concentrate them in London and Manchester; the blood moved freely among the members. Disraeli's abused "Whig oligarchy"—such a house, for example, as the Bedfords—showed the best that was in them in the running of their estates. They lived like little kings inside their model kingdoms. They were enlightened, progressive, scientific farm managers; they would seize upon any idea, no matter who put it forward, and put it to a free test; they had no reluctance to experiment. Few of them had much respect for the paramount monarch in London. They folded themselves in a scornful and comfortable isolation from the Court. They were secularists of the eighteenth-century breed. At their banquets they toasted Liberty; in their libraries they read Voltaire. The tutelary genius of Georgian agriculture, Coke of Norfolk, was a Whig so implacable that he said to his grandson, "My boy, whatever you do in life, never trust a Tory. I never have myself, and, by God, I never will."

All accounts of the high development of agriculture in Georgian times —and it was high—should always be read a second time in the light of that wild torch which William Cobbett held up to discern the shadows on the face of truth. The cruelties of the enclosures and the loss of independence to the peasant were the other side of the story. Simple villagers, whose methods of husbandry had changed little since the days of the Plantagenet kings, were no match for a great lord who was as proud as a French marquis and more efficient than a Manchester cotton-spinner, a highly practical aristocrat who had read a paper on wheat-growing to the Royal Society of Agriculture, and had corresponded with Arthur Young on both roots and religions. During the wars with Napoleon, there came a life-and-death call to the shires to grow more food. The nation's necessity, the pride of the landlords, and the progress of science were all on the same side. What could a poor hind do against so powerful a coalition? Britain in Georgian times produced its own version of collective farms; its managers were dukes and marquises. The efficient crushed the free.

The argument over the enclosures that still goes on among our historians is really one part of the everlasting argument between planners and libertarians. Is a man happier when a wise shepherd drives him by day into green pastures where he grows sleek and fat, and by night into the fold where the wolf cannot grab him, or is he happier when he is let to go his own way to perdition, rambling with Tom o' Bedlam over the hills and through the bogs, hungry and dirty, but free, always free? The old village system was broken up, and the peasants were brought into the big new estates while their brothers in the city were drafted into the fine new factories. These movements were approved by patriots as augmenting the nation's strength, and by economists as increasing the national wealth and raising the status of the common people. It was only a cantankerous fellow like Cobbett who challenged the goodness and mercy of these changes—who spoke for those who could not speak for themselves. Inhumanity is usually poor policy. It might well have turned out that had the great lords been kinder to humble flesh and blood they would have kept their own state and power longer. Had there been any union of hearts between the proprietors and the peasantry, Corn Law Repeal could not have won so speedy a success. The opposition of the landlords was eaten away from within by the discontents of the villagers. The Anti-Corn-Law League took joy in exhibiting upon their platforms farm labourers who had been driven to mutiny by their accumulated wrongs, and had been instructed in a rude eloquence by their going to Methodist meetings. The voice of Lucy Simpson crying through the villages, "If we be purtected we staarve", disturbed the slumbers of the Dorset squirearchy, like the voice of conscience itself.

In the prospect of the abundant prosperity that smiled upon the land in the years after Repeal, it was not easy for the broken ranks of the Country Party to discover any weapons sharp enough to use against the dominant philosophy of the nation. Who would put up with a Cassandra in the house when the looms were roaring, and the furnaces blazed all night, when the price of corn ruled high, and the clouds dropped fatness?

The Middle Victorians are nowadays cursed by their unhappy grandsons for not looking ten, thirty, fifty, a hundred years ahead—for not seeing that other countries, then in a pastoral state, would become industrialised, that they would build up their own manufactures, and would protect them by tariffs against Britain's goods. They are blamed for not divining the growth of the United States after the Civil War—for not guessing the ultimate wheat yields of Canada, of the Argentine, of Australia. That is a true charge—but which of us today is laying his plans to meet the acute and peculiar crisis of the year 2000? What generation, in fact, has ever seen beyond its own nose?

It has been fashionable in late years to present Disraeli as the man of prophetic soul who did look into the seeds of time, and perceived the coming doom. But Disraeli's fame is not best served by those who praise him for his rearguard defence of Protection in 1846. He won the leadership of the Country Party by his immoderate assaults on Peel; but, in the end, he revived Conservatism by accepting Peel's policy. On the issue of Protection and the Land, Disraeli, as much as Peel, Russell, Gladstone, Palmerston and the rest of them, was subdued to the necessity of history. Nothing could have stopped Britain declaring for Free Trade in the middle of the century. When the majority of the nation was converted to this course of action, when the symbolic figures, the sibyls, the totems, were ranged on that side—the Queen and the Duke of Wellington—when the Methodist chapels and the Stock Exchange were at one, when the stern call of the moral law reinforced economic interest, when the most pathetic pleas of the humane were joined with the importunings of the cashier, there was nothing that the most wilful genius in politics could do but submit. And Disraeli submitted. The gifts that had been used in 1846 to rally the country gentlemen to resist Free Trade were employed two or three years later to induce Stanley to accept it.

In the year that Dickens died, 1870, the panorama of the countryside was more sunny and more smiling than in the year that he was born. The economic consequences of the decay of the land were long concealed by the general prosperity. The strategic perils never made themselves apparent until the submarine blockade of 1917 brought the country within six weeks of starvation.

CHAPTER SIX

TO THE SEA

There was one great benefit the railways brought to the lower middle classes and to working people that ought to go down in the same account with the industrial and mercantile effects. They made holidays possible "for the likes of us". A century ago the mass of those who lived in cities had never seen the sea. The stage-coach fares of fivepence or sixpence a mile were too dear for humble folk. Even when the horse-drawn omnibuses were started in London, clerks and artisans whose homes were some way off from their work would tot up the difference between the cost of the ride and the wear of shoe leather in the walk. It was hard for the poor to escape from the place of their toil, even for a day or two's change. Many of them lived, married, begat children and died in the boroughs, in the streets, in the very houses where they were born. Some experiences of my own make me think that you may even yet find such characters among old men and women in the back streets of Southwark or Camberwell.

The pleasures of the seaside had been discovered by the aristocracy in the eighteenth century. Doctors recommended the ocean for constitutions undermined by the excesses of town life, but there was for some time a dispute as to whether an exhausted dandy should swallow sea-water or bathe in it. What a crew it was that followed the fat Prince Regent to Brighton ("Though Ireland starve, great George weighs twenty stone")—a feathered mob, with flying ribands, sparkling gems, a mob of scented ladies, rouged old dukes and white-faced young bucks, tearing down to the coast in their spidery curricles. How many sniffs of that keen, sweet air, how very few dips in the cold sea do you suppose sufficed the royal voluptuary? He would shut himself up among the crawling Chinese dragons and the big, over-blown lotus flowers of his great fairy-tale Pavilion and he would seal up the windows against the fresh breath of the sea—he would pile up the coal in the grates until the rooms were so hot that everybody was bathed in sweat—he would loll for hours over dinner, gormandising his eight courses, and drinking wine until he was dizzy—and meanwhile a noisy German band in the long saloon was blaring *Rule Britannia.*

When Britain first, at heaven's command
Arose from out the azure main,
This was the charter of the land,
And Guardian angels sung this strain:
"Rule Britannia, rule the waves;
Britons never will be slaves."

"AT THE SEASIDE"
Cartoon by Richard Doyle from his "Bird's Eye View of Society", 1864

Beyond the Chinese Pavilion, its swooning heat, its glaring lights, its regal din, its reeking perfumes, its animal smells, the tide was roaring over the shingle in the blackness of the night, and at some distance off in the Channel the lamps of the fishing boats floated tranquilly on those waves from which the goddess had risen.

Late in the evening great George would rise from the table to conduct the band and sing the airs of Handel in a surprisingly loud, firm, round voice. He was a gross creature—but he was an artist. "What are you thinking, Duke?" asked the Princess Lieven of Wellington at one of these entertainments. "I am thinking, ma'am, that I find myself in damned queer company."

The fishermen of the old village of Brighthelmstone sometimes caught a glimpse of the puffy white face of royal George at the windows. There he would stand, goggling at them like the queerest of queer fish in an aquarium, his eyes haunted by a universal distrust, a fat royal fish cut off from the world of men by more than a sheet of glass, breathing through pallid gills—swimming to and fro in his own dense element.

Yet there he stands for ever at the window, staring sullenly at the crowd—becoming, in despite of himself, the eternal royal patron of that most democratic institution, the British summer holiday. How he would have shuddered at the thought of the excursion trains, packed with East End children singing their tousled heads off; the whelk and jellied-eel stalls on the front, the naphthaline flares at night, the beach minstrels that Phil May drew so well, the bath-chair men, the hoarse voice bawling "All aboard for the Skylark", the band at the end of the pier playing, "I *do* like to be beside the seaside", the mashers in straw hats whistling after the girls; the flashy, noisy hotels, and the seedy boarding-houses along Marine Parade, with the sand-streaked bathing-suits hung out to dry from second-floor windows, the mingled reek of cabbages and haddock, and parboiled infants tumbling down the front steps. Yet it is indeed a just fate that the Prince Regent should be honoured upon the posters of British Railways and nowhere else nowadays. He is the presiding genius of the beach bungalows and the bathing-huts, of Brighton Rock and the pierrots and Punch and Judy—he whose taste in architecture, painting, music and novels was so truly patrician.

In going to the seaside the aristocracy and the landed gentry aped the Prince; then the middle classes aped the aristocracy. *Punch*'s Fat Contributor (he was Thackeray), writing from Brighton in 1847, found that

> the crowd, sir, on the Cliff was perfectly frightful. It is my belief nobody goes abroad any more. Everybody is at Brighton. I met three hundred at least of our acquaintances in the course of a quarter of an hour, and before we could reach Brunswick Square, I met dandies, City men, Members of Parliament. I met my tailor walking with his wife, with a geranium blooming in his wretched button hole, as if money wasn't tight in the City and everybody had paid him everything everybody owed him. I turned and sickened at the sight of that man.

The Fat Contributor fled to the Pier. In vain.

> Who do you think approached us? Were you not at one of his parties last season? I have polkaed in his saloons, I have nestled under the mahogany of his dining room, at least one hundred and twenty thousand times. It was Mr. Goldmore, the East India Director, with Mrs. G. on his arm and—oh Heavens! —Florence and Violet Goldmore, with pink parasols, walking behind their parents.

Then, too, you may recall that in those Early Victorian times Mrs. Caudle nagged Caudle all one hot July night to go to the seaside. Caudle, the drowsy fellow, full of ale, proposed Gravesend, because it was handy for business. "Gravesend! You might as well empty a salt-cellar in the New River, and call *that* the seaside", cried Mrs. Caudle. She insisted on Margate, although it was expensive. "What will I do at Margate? Why, isn't there bathing, and picking up shells; and aren't there the packets, with the donkeys; and the last new novel, whatever it is, to read? —for the only place where I really relish a book is the seaside . . . The ocean always seems to me to open the mind," reflected Mrs. Caudle. "Sometimes at the seaside—especially when the tide's down—I feel so happy; quite as if I could cry."

In the train of the middle classes came the lower middle classes; and then, tardily trailing after them, the working people. The speckled shell held to the ear brings back the roar of the sea. It brings back, too, the cries of happy children on the first morning of the holidays, racing down the sands to meet the waves. One imagines, besides, a certain transposition of the senses, that with that endless chime of the sea, heard in the shell's ear, one catches in a ghostly way the smell which has no match in all life afterwards, in all the world, the scent of the sea—the first time one caught it as a child—a fragrance so bright and keen that not all the flowers of Paradise, the asphodel, the moly, the amaranth and the rest could make it sweeter. The summer holiday—and even a Bethnal Green family's half-day outing to Southend was graced by that name—became the great folk festival of the British people. In the North of England the "Wakes weeks" presented the spectacle of big towns almost emptied of their working population—Oldham or Burnley or Bolton pouring into Blackpool or the Isle of Man or the North Wales resorts. A great many Victorian homes cherished lovingly souvenirs of the annual hegira. Among the prosperous middle classes there would be Miss Letty's pale water-colours of the opal mists at Ryde on August mornings, or of the Chines at Bournemouth, with the gorse in bloom, and, above the ramparts of gorse, the dim azure of the most Italian bay outside Italy melting into an Italian sky. Or there might be preserved in a brown leather album Uncle Harry's unrivalled collection of seaweeds, dried and pressed, the streaming pennons, the delicate tendrils, the floating hair of mermaids, that once looked so pretty in the clear water of the rock pools, now black and dusty, with the outlandish Latin names inscribed under them in a boy's sprawling hand. Or there might be a musical box encrusted with tiny pink and silver shells, collected with infinite patience in summer holidays through the years by Miss Scholtz, the German governess.

On another level of society the parlour overmantel would be cluttered up with forty mugs and jugs engraved with such legends as "A Present from Whitstable" or "For a Good Child from Gorleston"; so that an old wife at the end of her days could review the history in china of all the family's excursions, calling back memories of the old chain pier at Brighton that was swept away in the great storm; the donkey rides for the children at Ramsgate, the gentlest of ambles on the most docile of donkeys; the ruined July at Hastings when the family smudged its noses all day long on the dripping panes of a bedroom on the second floor back; the expedition to Fairlight Glen when little George was nearly stolen by the gipsies; the sunny afternoons of so many beaches, so many years, all melting into one another, and seeming in the end to be not much longer than one afternoon; the children growing up so quickly and going away; the beach left deserted, and the cold tide coming in to wash away the sandcastles.

PART IV

THE BATTLE OF LIFE

CHAPTER ONE

GRANDEES

In the year that *Pickwick* came out London had two million people, if you counted in the outer rings that, so early as this, were spoken of as Greater London. The streets ran for six miles from east to west, and three miles from north to south. Looking one way from the roof of a house in the Strand, you would see the brick labyrinths, with their smoking chimneys, ending at Edgware Road. Looking another way, you would see the fields beginning at Sloane Square. But the houses did not leave off all at once. They were strung out along the roads leading from the city, stretching farther and farther until they linked together little towns that had lived quiet lives of their own ever since their names were set down in Domesday Book—and had no desire to be linked together; market towns, village greens, genteel little spas, each with its own style and flavour, and with its pride in not being like its neighbours. Nowadays this process is called ribbon development. But such a flimsy name as that falls far short of describing those beetling domestic cliffs built by the merchants, bankers and lawyers of the City. No, those were not mere ribbons—not those baronial halls in stucco, and the huge rambling villas that needed at least twenty servants, indoors and outdoors, to take care of them. The rich merchants had long since given up the old romantic and poky tradition of "living over the shop"—a way of living that was once followed by the very grandest of trade grandees, the Greshams, the Dick Whittingtons and the Alderman Warrens. Some of these families lived happily enough in the cosy dignity of Bloomsbury squares or in Portland Place (near Mr. Dombey), or in stately Clerkenwell, but the movement of the early century was towards those haunts of still unravished quietness—Norwood, Clapham, Peckham, Camberwell, Highgate, Hammersmith, Parson's Green, Ealing, or even—daring thought!—to the wild remoteness of Mitcham or Pinner.

The Nabob of the early nineteenth century, exhausted by bills of lading or by the ardours of the discount market, sought a leafy fastness within carriage trot of the Mansion House where fresh zephyrs might bring a colour to his tallowy cheek. His wife and daughters approved Papa's decision. Had they not long pressed him so to choose? They yearned to be caught up into glory with the landed gentry. Fashion, and snobbery, and the medical profession all pointed outwards. Did Mr. Midas suffer from a cough and night sweats after a day in Lombard Street? Then Battersea, with its soft, relaxing river airs, its sheltered warmth, fostering half-tropical shrubs and palms, was the place for him. Did Mr. Croesus, the poor fellow, need bracing? Were his nerves jangled by jobbers and speculators? Why then, the tonic gusts of the heights of Muswell Hill were the very thing. Dr. Tooting! Dr. Hornsey! How many a master of the pepper and spice markets, how many a great captain of the jute or hemp trade, has owed his renewed vigour to your kindly ministrations. Acton! through your revivifying airs, you were a stepping-stone to the alderman's baronetcy. Gipsy Hill!—from your peak the corn-chandler's family first sighted the delectable prospect of the House of Lords. It was that very sage woman, Mrs. Caudle, who made the discovery that, when people get on in trade, London air always disagrees with them. She laid down the celebrated law of medicine, which has since brought great profit to Harley Street, that "delicate health comes with money". When Mrs. Caudle was plaguing her husband, the doll merchant, to leave the smoke of the city, she thought first of the sylvan peace of Brixton—"So select!" said she. "*There* nobody visits nobody, unless they're somebody. To say nothing of the delightful pews that make the churches so respectable!"

Mrs. Caudle! all your comedy of pretensions and amiable humbug is now a century and more dead. The squirearchy of Peckham Rye and Goose Green has gone for ever. What Caudle coarsely called "the aristocracy of fat", meaning the wholesale tallow business, has now moved far beyond Penge. Brixton no more has its local nobility drawn from the "wholesale, retail and for exportation" trade. The explorer must seek to trace the names of these families on the stone urns of half-forgotten suburban churches. They had their day, they made a noise and now nobody remembers them.

London grew into a very gross, obese monster during the nineteenth century. And when one says London, one means as well Manchester, Birmingham, Liverpool, Glasgow and the other cities. The bricks and mortar, the yellow streets of little houses glued together in rows, the small shops, the corrugated iron tabernacles, the post offices, the police

"THE BILL-STICKERS' EXHIBITION"
Cartoon by William Newman from "Punch", 1847

stations with the blue lamps outside them—they all sprawled out over those fields and gardens that once surrounded the ugly big mansions of the early Victorian merchants; and the big ugliness of the mansions became embedded in a mean ugliness—they were left stuck in the mud, like the philosophy of their first owners. Many of these houses were broken up in late Victorian days, and in King Edward VII's time, and in later years. I think of a small boy who used to play among the ruins of some of those mansions when they were derelict and left lying naked, squalidly naked, to the pickaxes and shovels of the house-wreckers. They were not romantic ruins, even by moonlight, even to a boy. Poetry and poetic mystery were not to be found hiding in the black caves that once had been kitchens, among the rusty wrecks of ovens—three or four big, hulking ovens there would be in a row—with not the faintest redolent whiff left there from all the juicy roasts that once used to sizzle for dinner (and *what* dinners they were!). Nor was even the pathos of broken and despoiled beauty to be found among the cracked tiles of sunflower and codfish-head designs, the bits of tawdry yellow glass fallen from the conservatory dome, the flight of broken stairs going up to the roofless top of the mansion—these had now become stairs to the moon. Bygone generations of maids had once panted up them carrying scuttles of coal and pails of water to the twelve or fourteen bedrooms—and then, at last, when their watch was done at the long day's end, had carried their own weary legs up to the very topmost top, to sleep in the attics.

If there were any ghosts there, among those dreary ruins, they were uninteresting ghosts: Papa, in mutton-chop whiskers, and in a rare tantrum over Mr. Gladstone and the Consols; Mama, in a turban, harrying and badgering the spectral, squeaking parlour-maids; and a brood of little masters and mistresses, maybe a dozen or more of them, all taught to know their place, to sit up straight, to hold their tongues and to practise deceit if they were to know any private joys at all. It was in the gardens of these broken-down mansions, gardens all run to seed, choked with burdocks and nettles as they were, that the real, the waking joy of discovery was found, for they stood for a living thought that had outlasted a crumbled tradition. Through a gap in the wall, made by the house-wrecker's men, the boy I have in mind would sometimes come upon a very large and rambling garden, lying all bewitched in the summer moonlight and filled with the wailing of the owls—the last lords of these suburban forests. The croquet lawn, where curates had once demurely frolicked, was overgrown with thistles; in the ruins of the summer-house spiders and beetles kept their long holiday. The pergola, once thought to be as beautiful "as anything in Italy", but now laughed at by the know-all young architectural gentlemen from the London County Council as a wonderful bit of gimcrack—this pergola was falling down, and its graceful wistaria had run wild. On the broad terrace there was a statue of Hope which had been shown (it was said with pride) at the Great Exhibition of 1851. On that terrace, three peacocks used to strut, according to the tradesmen; they would flaunt the jewels of their plumage and would scare the owls in the beeches by their mad shriekings in the night. There was a legend in the neighbourhood that there had once been a white peacock there, bought because a Miss Amy, or a Miss Agnes, in the house had fallen in love with Tennyson's lovely line—"Now droops the milkwhite peacock like a ghost"—and the milkwhite ghost of the peacock, said local legend, was to be seen drooping in the patches of moonlight (could there be any doubt of it if you stayed out late there on bright summer nights of the full moon?), the one phantom of lost loveliness surviving out of all those years.

The shrieking of peacocks was heard no more, and soot and ashes had wrought a mocking crown for the brows of Hope. The tears of many rains had discoloured her round cheeks. Her flanks, once so sleek and white, were now soiled by yellow lichen; and her nose was chipped, poor girl. And look! one hand was gone. Her business hand, so to speak, for it was the hand that had pointed the thoughts of three well-fed generations to the skies—a kindly though fussy gesture, the complacent Victorians thought. Why should they, who owned such comfortable mansions here on earth, concern themselves too soon with celestial mansions? Heaven for them was a thought like the summer holidays. Renting one's final home beside God's smiling ocean could be thought about when the time came round, when the city streets were baking, and eyes had grown weary of the dust and the heat.

A mean and dingy estate, fallen in ruins—what is there in it to make us lose a beat of the heart, to make us feel any twinge of compassion? Let Boffin, the Golden Dustman, take it for his own. Yet there was one piece of redeeming beauty here. The trees!—that was it!—they were glorious! There were oaks of timeless age, broad beeches and umbrella chestnuts—and there was a row of shimmering poplars, those thin princesses of the world of trees, at the far end of the garden, screening the railway cutting which, by the way, had driven the first family in the house (they were aristocrats of the India trade) to move away to Dollis Hill where—to their displeasure—Mr. Gladstone also came. In the sixties they felt about the railways as the Cavendishes and Stanleys had felt in the thirties.

Those Victorian grandees had a notion of passing their own, but far gentler, "Enclosure Acts" when they built their new mansions in the suburbs. In their defence let it be said they did at least keep fresh the green look of the places where they built their homes. And they *did* hold back the tide of jerry-building, so long as they lived there. They liked leafiness. Even if their sprawling gardens, the lawns and thickets, the prospects and artful tangles, laid out in imitation of a duke's park in Derbyshire, and the ramparts of trees behind which they hid themselves, with ogreish warnings at the lodge gates—"Beware! Fierce Dogs at Large!"—even if all this was an affectation of Vanity, what matter if it kept London greener? And greener for so much longer? Suppose they did dream themselves to be little Marquesses of Norwood, or bantam Earls of Beulah Hill, keeping suburban state in comic imitation of Clumber or Chatsworth—what then? In such vanity there were uncovenanted benefits for the neighbourhood, for the whole town—even for the unregarded poor, for the workmen's families in the Regency cottages at the back. Trees wave their banners above high walls, they refresh and delight far more people than their masters who own them, and the chestnut blossom casts its fragrance far when May has come. The knocking-down of the mansions was no great loss to the eye, not to the eye of sensibility, not to the eye of taste. But the chopping-down of the old trees, some of them of great age, in those parts of London where there was no longer fashion nor money nor snobbery to protect their beauty (as in high Hampstead or Kensington), meant that the kingdom of dinginess and dust had spread its sway over ever so many more miles and miles. This was a ruthless, robber kingdom, which swallowed up great tracts of greenery and smiling beauty in the nineteenth and twentieth centuries.

"The retired Wholesales never visit the retired Retails at Clapham," said Caudle, giving his wicked Radical laugh, when Mrs. Caudle dangled the prospects of that pretty, pastoral retreat before him. That was in 1845. Today the wholesale tallow-merchant and the retail tallow-chandler are at one—and at peace—in the churchyard, or in the equal bliss of the vast nameless London huddle, with nobody, rich or poor, caring very much about anything or anybody, other than to make a living out of the place.

Farewell Holly Lodge, the Cedar Grange, and Ilex Villas and Yew Tree Towers! Farewell The Pines! Good-bye The Laurels! The dry rustle of the wind in the last euonymus, or in the dusty rhododendron on the new housing estate, is your requiem. You were, without doubt, absurd monstrosities, but I loved you better, I think, and I will remember you longer than Mon Repos, or We Twa, or Tedjane, or that dizzy red-brick cliff of flats—Plantagenet Mansions, S.W., I think it is called—which have taken your place, and looks by starlight, when the street lamps are out, like one of John Martin's engravings of Babylon.

The surviving families of the wealthy merchants of early Victorian times have long since become absorbed in the aristocracy. In *Sybil* Disraeli wrote:

> In a commercial country like England, every half century develops some new and vast source of public wealth which brings into material notice a new and powerful class. A couple of centuries ago, a Turkey merchant was the great creator of wealth; the West India Planter followed him. In the middle of the last century appeared the Nabob. These characters in their zenith in turn merged in the land, and became English aristocrats; while, the Levant decaying, the West Indies exhausted and Hindostan plundered, the breeds died away, and now exist only in our English comedies from Wycherley and Congreve to Cumberland and Morton. The expenditure of the revolutionary war produced the Loanmonger who succeeded the Nabob, and the application of science to industry developed the Manufacturer who, in turn, aspires to be "large acred", and always will, so long as we have a territorial constitution; a better security for the preponderance of the landed interest than any Corn Law, fixed or fluctuating.

The architectural legacy of the Victorians is prodigious, and I would not offer a word in behalf of the hideous sprawl of their cities. That was a sin against the light in more senses than one. But I have found much to interest and entertain me, and to stir the imagination, in the profuse variety and mixtures of Victorian styles. Whatever their crimes, the Victorians were not niggardly, they were not exclusive; they ransacked the centuries, and then piled up their loot in confusion, like happy barbarians. I saw a Victorian villa in South-East London the other day which had Tudor chimneys and mullioned windows, and Norman pillars at the front door, and a fine Gothic spire. You may see similar magnificent hybrids in most of the older suburbs.

I enjoy looking at such buildings as the mock-classic piles of stucco that Cubitt reared in the squares of Belgravia and Tyburnia (as they used to call Bayswater)—I always gape like a yokel at the Corinthian capitals in Sussex Square in South Paddington. I also enjoy the sight of that palace for an Italian prince which Sir Charles Barry built in Pall Mall, but which by some piece of sharp practice was seized by the Liberal Party before the Italian family had time to move in; and was then called *The Reform Club* when, plainly, in every line it proclaims the glorious insolence

THE CLIPPER SHIP "ETHIOPIAN"
Coloured lithograph by T. G. Dutton, 1865

H.M. WAR STEAM FRIGATE "TERRIBLE"
Coloured lithograph after W. Knell, 1847

THOMAS WILLIAM COKE, ESQ., M.P. FOR NORFOLK
With the Holkham shepherds and his Southdown sheep
Coloured mezzotint after Thomas Weaver, 1808

LORD SPENCER WITH TWO OF HIS STEWARDS AND HIS HERDSMAN
The bull is his famous champion "Wiseton"
Coloured lithograph after Richard Ansdell, 1844

of Roman privilege, with racks and thumbscrews provided in the cellars for any reformers that turned up. And how may I adequately express my reverence and admiration for that most impressive of all Victorian architectural achievements, the New Houses of Parliament, finished in 1860? No building could more fittingly be the home of Parliament, for it is in itself the most astonishing example on record of the British art of compromise. It is the joint work of Barry and Pugin. Barry, the romantic fellow, his head stuffed with notions of the Renaissance, conceived a classic building, a council chamber for Venetian senators, as it might be, an order of building which called for a Doge rather than a Prime Minister—a Paolo Veronese background for legislators who would wear velvet and ruffs, instead of striped trousers and frock coats. If Barry's fancy had been given rein, our Cabinet would surely have become the Council of Six, the Lord Chancellor would have inherited a poisoned ring, and the Borgia family would have had a prescriptive right to the chairmanship of the Kitchen Committee of the House of Commons. But Barry's partner, Augustus Welby Pugin, was in every atom of his being a man of the Middle Ages. He was monastic, he was fanatical, he was a pilgrim of the Absolute, and, in the end, he killed himself by the excesses of his converting zeal. To Pugin, the Gothic style was not an archaic quaintness whose revival would amuse the fashionable world—to him it presented the meaning of life—it symbolised the dedication of man to his Maker. Pugin was a cathedral architect of the Middle Ages who had been reincarnated in the civilisation of George Hudson and Lord Palmerston. He built not for the comfort of man but for the glory of God. His spires were prayers and adorations. I suppose that if Pugin's dreams had been fully realised, our new Houses of Parliament would have become the shrine of a theocracy. A new Thomas à Becket would have come to Downing Street. Tonsured heads would have bent late over the Treasury files, and monkish cowls would have flitted to and fro in the windows of the Privy Council Offices. The swish of long black cassocks would have filled the Home Office corridors, and St. Thomas Aquinas would have taken the place of John Locke in our political theorisings. How ever did it come about that the worldly Barry and the otherworldly Pugin made a match of it?—that the sacred and profane could be joined together in so lasting a union as that represented by the Parliament buildings? Who wins in that marriage? Which character dominates? Let the reader put that to himself the next time he crosses Westminster Bridge. By all the rules, the Houses of Parliament should have turned out to be a hideous piece of mongrel architecture, a mule, a monster. I will not argue that it is the best building in London. But I do know that it is the most endearing. I have on various occasions lived as an exile from my country, and I know *what* façade is imprinted upon the inner retina of exiles. The recollection of that building, so absurdly conceived, stands as home to us, it is our pride when the spirits are low, it is a habitation for our affections, our youth and our bygone happiness. Five thousand miles away we exiles hear ni the middle of the night the musical, melancholy thunder of Big Ben striking across the hubbub of the traffic, and subduing it with his kingly strokes—we catch the feeling of the great clock, gathering his strength and hurling his melodious thunderbolts across the city—then in imagination we look up at the lighted face, still dim in the river haze, and, with the noise of foreign waters in our ears, and the fireflies on the banks dancing around us, and the smell of foreign parts in our nostrils, we say, "Twelve of the clock and all's well—all's well with England, our home." This, of course, is grotesquely sentimental, but it is an effect that Barry and Pugin, through the most successful and happy misalliance in history, have contrived.

The period spanned by this book saw the grand Gothic revival. John Ruskin, through the exercise of his priestly authority, made the employment of Gothic a moral and mystical concern. The other modes of architecture were base, degenerate; Gothic expressed the sublimest aspirations of man. Ruskin's influence was responsible for many of the ugliest heirlooms in the Victorian bequest, but he gave an *excitement* to architecture. He stirred up the dull and sleepy. Even if he sent them all wildly galloping off in the wrong direction, causing some of them to break their aesthetic necks, at least they *were* kept awake and galloping. The best-known example of Victorian Gothic is G. E. Street's Law Courts in the Strand, London, begun in 1868. It has been an object of derision for at least sixty years. Since the first day that I saw it—I being then a tiny boy clutching my father's hand in fright at the tumult of the Strand—it has belonged to the private phantasmagoria. At that first infantine look it appeared to me to be a castle in one of Grimm's fairy tales, the castle of an ogre whose favourite lunch dish was a roasted small boy served piping hot, with two vegetables. One's eyes become staled in going up and down the Strand and Fleet Street, so that one misses seeing nowadays, as one saw in childhood, how wildly improbable a building is the Law Courts. It bears no relationship to anything for miles around it, and the only kind of Law such architecture should be concerned with are ordeals by fire and water, trials of witches and necromancers, suits between friars and gnomes, and punishments by slow torture. But once its splendid unsuitability for its purpose is recognised, what a place it is! See it by moonlight, or in the break of day, as I often did as a youth going home from the night's stint, and it will set your mind off on a train of agreeable nonsense: sorcerers' vaults under the Strand and a broth of baboon's blood, walking skeletons, and the apparitions of Helen, alchemists brewing love philtres, blue fire streaming from old warlocks' fingers, the Rosicrucian mysteries that the German playwrights of a century and a half ago revelled in, the stories of E. T. A. Hoffmann and "The March to the

Scaffold" in Berlioz' *Fantastic Symphony.* It is not a bad thing that a building in which lawyers wrangle over company taxes and patents should suggest a world of necromancy.

In their years of expansion, the Victorians built so much that they flooded over the marks of all the previous centuries; and most of our cities and towns today are dominated by them; public buildings, commercial buildings, monuments, homes; the Victorians hem us in. It is in the suburbs of London and the provincial cities that one has the most powerful sense that the mid-Victorians are still among us. Their flesh and bones have now become changed into stucco, stone and brick. Some baleful enchantment has rooted them to the ground—they cannot move a hand, but their eyes are watching—their ardent life and individualities persist. Strange was the fate of some of these earthbound creatures as I witnessed it during the years of the late war. I used to walk home from my employment in a Government office through the empty squares and terraces of Bayswater, looking with awe at the vast ruined houses that the merchants of the easy, fat Victorian times had built for their greater glory. This part of London suffered very heavy losses from the German raiders. The light of summer evening, as it slowly faded, spread over those Victorian fronts an unearthly lost look. The habitation of a full-blooded, well-upholstered, warm age was now turned to the poetry of ruins. The suety heaviness was fined away into broken columns, stairways suspended in air, and crumbled walls. The houses were desolate, the windows black sockets, the streets silent. The effects of blast on a deserted terrace was to create the illusion that these ruins had been dug out by an archaeological expedition from Canberra hunting for the remains of the lost civilisation of the ancestors. So Baalbec, so the Valley of the Kings! Here was the scrap of a tiled pavement such as one had seen at Pompeii; there were strewn some mementoes of domestic life—a playing-card, a child's toy, a broken cup—that would surely be sent tomorrow to the local museum, or sold for a fabulous price to the American millionaire whose yacht was anchored in the bay. Indeed it was in truth, so far as we were concerned, the disinterring of a long-lost way of life. These fallen roofs, the stone balustrades hanging over nothingness, and the hearths swimming with rainwater spoke to us of a city as far away from our present perplexities as Caerleon or Bruges the Dead. The witching light was long in dying on those summer evenings, and it touched those pathetic wrecks with the tenderness of memory itself. Then before the glow was quite gone, before the spell snapped, the trailing whine of the air-raid siren would weave in and out and around the broken houses, spinning around them a kind of grey spider's web of sound.

Out of the riches that trade had brought them from the ends of the earth, the Victorian Nabobs built those cream-coloured squares and streets of tall houses which looked like illustrations to the stories of Edgar Allan

Poe when seen in the mad lighting of raid nights. There were certain Bayswater mansions that reared up like mountains in those demented nights. Bizarre shapes, with pillars shooting up as high as the beeches in Hyde Park and crowned with mops of Corinthian curls—here an acre of peeling wall—there a row of long windows hinting at rooms large as public halls—conservatories jutting out in unlikely places at implausible angles—domed balconies where a dozen old ladies once could take the sun together—crumbling stone wedding-cakes and urns with cupids—underneath, basements black as Bluebeard's vaults—and then, the eye sweeping again, high aloft, iron-barred windows made to prevent lunatic nursemaids from dashing down to the pavement the seven young daughters of a Mincing Lane grandee. Such buildings could be possible only to men who possessed self-confidence in the highest degree and who had that courage which is prepared to back its fancy in the most public way.

Yet it was apparent that the proud men who had put up these monuments to their pride had been quite wrong in their guesses about the world they lived in and the world that would come after them. Their mansions represented the pathetic illusion of the Victorian age—which is also the illusion of other ages, including our own—that security, iron-clad security, can be achieved by wishing and working. They left out of account the element of the incalculable in the Universe, the unpredictable in history. They forgot the wisdom of the ancients that no man is ever safe, and that he is least secure when he believes he has found security. As one could see by that El Greco light in which the dropping flares of the German bombers bathed the street, the palaces of stucco had been pure fantasy-building. They were the pinnacles, turrets and domes of a dream life.

But is not that perhaps the fascination of so many Victorian buildings of diverse styles?—the divorce of the object from its purpose?—the wilful caprices of the unrestrained fancy? There are houses at Norwood and at Wimbledon, for example, that are Gothic grotesques in the same highly personal way in which Quilp in *The Old Curiosity Shop* and Wackford Squeers in *Nicholas Nickleby* are Victorian Gothic grotesques. Some of these houses in their impassioned ugliness might fairly be said to be one entire and writhing gargoyle. I cannot remember observing in any of the mansions or villas of the period any riotous excrescences of fun—there are no architectural counterparts of Pickwick or Sam Weller. But all shades of the grim, the crawling, the mysterious, the cruel—these are expressed in Victorian domestic architecture. A reader of Wilkie Collins, or Charles Reade, or Mrs. Henry Wood, even more than a reader of Charles Dickens, might be expected to appreciate these queer savours. That solid mansion (what are the epithets—"commodious and well-appointed"?) lying in wait, like a monster among its own dense evergreens, evokes a creeping terror such as no Norman ruins, gently romantic, could inspire. Those blackened windows under the Florentine cornice suggest the mad wife locked up by Mr. Rochester. It is the intimation of the sinister *inside the respectable* that yields the real thrill of modern terror. Many of the houses built for the wealthy merchant class have an air of undisclosed domestic crime, drownings in the bath of unwanted children, and poisonings of detested husbands that never came to light. Their solemn, ominous fronts hint at the intimacies of smothered sin. One can extract a great deal of pleasure from Victorian buildings if one forgets modern conventions of architecture and family ease. Those eccentric villas, with the evil eyeholes between the gables, are in truth frozen bits of Victorian melodrama. And, never let us forget, that Victorian melodrama possessed the intense gusto and vitality that derives from a Calvinist faith. When these buildings are ugly, they have the fierce, undying ugliness of sin itself. But, handsome or ugly, they have the impact of human personality. They arouse anger, they create laughter, but they are always interesting and entangling. That is more than can be said for the impersonal functional style.

The people of that time used a striking phrase about a man being "beside himself". If we keep it in our heads that most Victorian architects were "beside themselves", we shall better understand the weird hieroglyphics of our cities. When those architects built Town Halls they were not thinking of the Mayor, the Town Clerk, the Borough Rate collection and the Main Drainage Committee, but of Lorenzo the Magnificent and the brutal splendours of old Florence. Or they had been carried away by Victor Hugo's *Notre Dame* and were dreaming of Quasimodo instead of Alderman Higgs. Victorian architecture is in large part absent-minded architecture. Even the most self-satisfied men of that age longed every now and again to break through its frame of material and utilitarian values. They thought of architecture, particularly domestic and ceremonial architecture, as a way of showing that they had a soul—that they could rise above the world of the four per cents. Many a stout, red-faced builder, with mutton-chop whiskers, shared the boyish romanticism of Tennyson:

> By Bagdat's shrines of fretted gold,
> High-walled gardens green and old;
> True Mussulman was I and sworn,
> For it was in the golden prime
> Of good Haroun Alraschid.

A less convincing defence might be made on behalf of the fantastications of the furniture and household appliances of the time. The three-volume catalogue of the Great Exhibition of 1851 shows what craftsmen can do when they let loose all the curling snakes, all the freaks, all the goblins that inhabit mankind's universal sub-conscious, and when they are not ignobly frightened by the prospect of ridicule or the bogies of good taste. Bad art is often an act of liberation. The vulgar rich of 1851 were so splendidly vulgar and so rich that they caught up into themselves the absurdities of all times, all climes. There were bedsteads on view at the Great Exhibition which were designed for the repose of provincial aldermen and their wives but could only with propriety be used by the Fairy Queen in a pantomime. There were cabinets built like the Taj Mahal—sofas that would have been more in keeping in the harem of the Sultan of Morocco than in the drawing-room of a churchwarden at Eccleshall—and gorgeous whatnots that naturally belonged to Scheherazade rather than to a Nottingham lace manufacturer.

Let me quote from my Exhibition catalogue an account of an easy chair called "The Day Dreamer", designed by a Mr. H. Fitz-Cook, and manufactured, we are assured, in papier mâché:

> The chair is decorated at the top with two winged thoughts—the one with bird-like pinions, and crowned with roses, representing happy and joyous dreams; the other with leathern bat-like wings—unpleasant and troublesome ones. Behind is displayed Hope, under the figure of the rising sun. The twisted supports of the back are ornamented with the poppy, hearts-ease, convolvulus and snow-drop, all emblematic of the subject. In front of the seat is a shell, containing the head of a cherub, and on either side of it, pleasant and troubled dreams are represented by figures. At the side is seen a figure of Puck, lying asleep in a labyrinth of foliage, and holding a branch of poppies in his hand. The style of the ornament is Italian.

It is clear, I think, that it was a happy man who created that chair. Fitz-Cook was gloriously fancy-free. And do we not all wish that we could follow our noses as freely as Fitz-Cook?

It was a utilitarian age, but yet the mutiny against utility marked the whole field of applied design. Hardly anything was functional. Even such practical articles as pen-knives and corkscrews were treated as absurd sprouts of the imagination. The day-dreamers who fashioned them saw them as clusters of metal flowers, as the ornaments on wedding-cakes, as the feathers on a Red Indian's head, as anything other than mere pen-knives or corkscrews. I suppose there was in this a feeling that everybody had become so grand and remarkable that the ordinary commonplaces of domestic life were mean and unworthy. These wonders, however, may be more readily appreciated in pictorial reproduction than through verbal description, and the illustrations on pages 43 and 48 display the endless horrid fascination of mid-Victorian industrial design.

In a modern sales room pictures that our great-grandfathers thought to be masterpieces are knocked down for a few guineas. The Victorians' habit of thinking of one thing when they were doing another has made it hard for their descendants to understand what they were really about when they took up brush and palette. Strictly speaking, the pictures of that period should be handed over to the literary critics for appraisal. The Victorians loved stories so much that they sought them in paint as well as in prose and rhyme. They liked to see on their walls delineations of the fancies of Shakespeare or Keats or Tennyson, or favourite scenes from Sterne or Thackeray. They were blessed with an unrivalled group of novelists, poets, miscellanists and journalists, but that was not enough for them; they insisted on the literary arts spilling over into the field of paint. Some of the best Victorian journalism, for example, is to be found in the canvases of Frith. His pictures of Epsom Heath on Derby Day and Paddington Station are descriptive reports of admirable quality, as lively as on the day they were painted, and filled with engrossing detail.

One of the most characteristic expressions of Victorianism were the Pre-Raphaelites who were for so long mistakenly regarded as rebels against it. The Pre-Raphaelites represented the visible world with the most scrupulous eye to detail, with a loving brooding over every blade of grass. They painted both the dreams of poets and the drawing-rooms of their friends, country fields and city streets with the same minute particularity, and with a joy in colour that charms the eye, especially so when one comes across one of their pictures in a provincial art gallery on a rainy Sunday afternoon. The Pre-Raphaelites were "literary gents"—indeed, the most celebrated figure in the Brotherhood, Dante Gabriel Rossetti, was as fine a poet as he was painter, and some of the minor figures of the movement wrote exceedingly well. The pictures of the Pre-Raphaelites remind one of the novels of the realist and naturalist schools, except that the accumulation and arrangements of detail on canvas is much more attractive than on the printed page.

The most popular artist of the Victorian period, J. E. Millais, began as a Pre-Raphaelite. He was a man of very considerable talent. Many have thought that he prostituted that talent to the commercialism of his age. Was it not pathetic, they ask, that the gifted boy who at nineteen painted the picture of "Christ in the House of His Parents" should become the successful man of business who turned out such almanac covers and calendar pictures as "Bubbles"? Millais is possibly a better painter, a finer colourist, a cleverer fellow in composition, than modern taste allows. He has been damned through his addiction to anecdotes on canvas. Significant form, abstract design and the purely pictorial values are not to be found in the Victorian galleries. Painting in the nineteenth century was the servant-girl of literature—often the drudge of journalism. Now in this fact, which is usually regarded as the final condemnation of Victorian art, is to be found its greatest glory. For the Victorians were superb illustrators of books and magazines. There are some artists of that period who were wretched daubers but were first-class men at woodcut and engraving. The true vigour of the Victorian genius is to be found in its sketch-books and periodical literature. That could be demonstrated triumphantly by an exhibition of the illustrations of Leech, Keene, Tenniel, Doyle, Caldecott, Sambourne, Millais—even Luke Fildes—and half a dozen others. In this regard, as in others, we shall only comprehend the Victorians if we ask what it was they were trying to do, and not apply to them the test of what we think they should have done. It may be, too, that before this century is out fashion will have turned back to pictures that tell a story. There is much to be said for them.

CHAPTER TWO

SOME WOMEN

In 1837, our starting-point, and indeed, in 1870, our ending-point, when the city grandees were wooing health and a quiet mind amid the humming of the bees on Clapham Common, inner London was not all sulphur fumes and grime. We may discount Mrs. Caudle's sniffs, and the pouts of the aldermen's wives who wanted to be countesses at Tooting Bec instead of comfortable tradesmen's ladies in Leadenhall Street. In the early years of the Queen's reign, London still kept some flavours of a market town, some fresh smells and sights of the country; they even crept into its hard, dusty heart.

There was one very pleasant sight, a symbolic kind of sight, to be seen on early summer mornings at this time. There would come into Bond Street and Oxford Street long Indian files of young girls carrying baskets of strawberries on their heads. Hundreds of these girls were to be seen on a summer's day. Their walk, the proud and easy way they carried themselves, brought goatish stares and gapes, and also decent, honest admiration. Their baskets were large, their load heavy. The girls balanced their baskets with peerless grace—hands on their hips, shoulders straight, eyes front, heads up and motionless—soldierly as the Guardsmen on the barrack square; but without stiffness, the body swaying very slightly, very gently. They had been trained, these girls, to poise heavy baskets on their heads ever since they were tiny things, when they were first set by their mothers to picking strawberries in the fields. Their every look spoke health; they took the stones and cobbles as though they were treading the elastic turf. These strawberry-carriers walked through the streets as to music; not to a jig, but to one of those slow country dances that the fiddlers in Mellstock played. They made pictures wherever they moved, pictures that were not to be matched for a fine pride—all unaware of itself—at the play, or at the drawing-room of the Queen. One sees them coming into the town in their hundreds and hundreds in the first mistiness of a summer morning before the shutters were down, and while the sleepy shop-boys in Bond Street were sprinkling the dust in front of the shops with watering-cans. They came, as it were, swimming out of the early heat-haze, in which the stucco fronts looked golden and Venetian—apparitions of beauty that were then regarded as a mere commonplace of the season. Country beauties they were, sturdy girls, their skins coarsened and their hair bleached by the sun. These strawberry-carriers wore simple, plain dresses of dark colours, woollen stockings, stout shoes—for they often had large, serviceable feet as well as big red hands—and they would wear a white or coloured handkerchief knotted at their sunburned throats.

Mr. Turveydrop and the dancing-masters nodded their heads at the deportment of the girls, while deploring their coarse, vulgar health. Were not they, the Turveydrops, instilling grace and ease in the young ladies' seminaries by saying to their pale young lilies, "Walk one—two—three—gently, now *gently*, ladies"—the girls balancing copies of *The Keepsake* or Harvey's *Meditations Among the Tombs* on their heads? Deportment, yes—but what is Deportment without refinement and an interesting pallor? The town rakes, staring hard at the girls, lamented their Decorum.

Where did they come from, these girls? One would have said from the look of them that they had been carried on a flight of magic carpets from the strawberry fields of the seaboard of far-away Hampshire. In truth, most of them had walked four miles or so from the fields of Hammersmith and Fulham. The Bishop of London from his palace windows looked over miles of these plantations. The girls would sometimes make the journey three times before dusk fell, so that they might not lose the profit of that long summer day and their brief harvest. Other girls would come in from the fields of Hackney in the north-east, or from Camberwell across the river. One of the happy, lost secrets of London, buried under its mounds of dismal masonry, under its Jubilee Crescents and Town Halls, is that it possesses, or at least it did possess in those days, a soil and weather friendly to the growing of this, the best of berries; as, indeed, it was friendly to all kinds of garden fruits. In those days, a Londoner might savour the true, the pure brightness of the berry. The girls carried their pottle baskets so steadily that there was never any bruising or staling of the fruit; the strawberries could be eaten with the morning dews upon them, and the cream that went with them came fresh then from the dairies of Kennington.

There would be as many as four thousand of these strawberry girls around London during the fair fruit season. They came to the city out of the heart of the country for the strawberry-picking season, journeying by carriers' carts from a dozen counties, near or distant, some of them from as far as the Welsh border. They would sleep in tents in the fields, and they came in flocks from their villages, keeping, amid the perils of Babylon, their village companionship. Regency morals and Early Victorian morals had not greatly changed that dim, green, little-known other England, the English countryside, and the easy manners of the Lady Jersey and Lady Conyham of that time, or of Lord Melbourne and Lord Palmerston, were not those of their rustic fathers and mothers. The strawberry girls would earn a few pounds in a season, five or ten pounds perhaps, and then go back to their faraway homes. Ten gold sovereigns or guineas was a fine prize to hug in a Northamptonshire or Dorset village in those days. The

KATE HAMILTON'S "NIGHT HOUSE"
Wood engraving from Henry Mayhew's "London Labour and the London Poor", 1862

girls went their ways, they had won their dowry, they married, and they brought forth their sturdy, red-cheeked boys and girls to renew the old stock while the feverish town burnt itself out.

It was a pleasant idyll, that of the strawberry nymphs, a London pastoral. It has an emblematic and token meaning, which is the only reason why it should find a place here. It was the other England breaking through the screens of urban life.

There is a companion picture which should hang by the side of this city pastoral.

The Cyprian band—it is as they glide between the pillars of the colonnades of Regent Street and Piccadilly, the freshly painted stucco pillars with their Corinthian capitals, that we catch our first glimpse of them. Between those creamy pillars, those curly-headed capitals—the elegant Regency setting—they moved as on a stage. Between the columns they would flutter, long scarves of Indian silk, of red or blue, floating behind them; cashmere shawls billowing, ribbons streaming out.

Green eyes of respectability watched them from the long windows of Regent Street. Look at the feathers, look at the diamonds! said respectability. Foamy plumes of ostrich ruffling above the beautiful, empty, silly little faces, the faces of beautiful monkeys—Lord A's diamonds, Lord B's diamonds, sparkling on bosoms usually as hard as the sparkling stones.

We think nowadays of Mrs. Caudle and Mrs. General as quintessentially Victorian, in the way we have been taught to think of Victorianism—that is of coal-scuttle bonnets, three layers of petticoats, and of a hiding of chair legs by frilled pantalettes—but these ladies were also Victorians. They kept the mock-Greek look that marked the Regent's time, the high-bosomed gowns, the feathered helmets, the hyacinth curls. These were the pagan slaves of the Christian era of Archbishop Manners-Sutton and Archbishop Howley.

Cyprians—the name has long since gone out of use. Sooty were the London pigeons, flying in and out of the piazza arches, cooing as they settled—the soiled doves of a stucco Aphrodite. These girls would come out to take the air on a summer afternoon at five o'clock, stealing out of genteel, thick-curtained houses in the streets off St. James's and Piccadilly. They would take a turn, not furtively but with a military flourish of their ostrich plumes and a rippling of their diamonds; pleased with themselves; showing themselves off, as the Roman *hetaerae* long ago would show themselves off behind their galloping ponies on the Appian Way. Mrs. General, Mrs. Caudle and Mrs. Grundy, if they were passing through the west end of the town, or looking down from those long windows, would start, jerk up their heads, dart out one glance, and turn their eyes to the other side of the street. Vulgar, lower-middle-class males on the sidewalk would wink and nudge one another; they might utter a bray, but they kept their distances. These lovely Cyprians lived in a world as high as the moon above "the young man of the name of Guppy". They were the *hetaerae* of noble and right honourable gentlemen who could endlessly invoke the endless felicities of Horace, in Parliament and out of it, and to whom these were the Lalages, Lydes, Myrtales and Phrynes of their idolatry. On the lips of these lovers was the prayer of their old poet, "Give me the beauty that is not too coy".

It is astonishing to find how much of the naked truth about living men and women could be put into print then. In raffish journals, such as *The Town*, whose issues I was turning over the other day, wondering what judgments His Majesty's Judges and any King's Bench jury would give against the editor nowadays, there are accounts of these women, their careers and their patrons, which are comically close to those biographies of actresses that tell how Miss Letty progressed from playing a child's part in a farce at the Theatre Royal, Bristol, to Ophelia at Drury Lane. In that period no rising statesman, no lord lieutenant, lording it over his county, was hurt by it being set down in scurrilous print that he was the protector of adorable Lalage or was a constant friend of the family to kindly, good, benevolent Madame Sycorax, whose establishment in St. James's was the resort of fashion and wit, beauty, intelligence, fame and everything except virtue.

The stories of the Cyprians bear a monotonous likeness. There are a few hours of sunshine and a long, cold night. Georgiana or Charlotte is the daughter of a small tradesman, a baker, or a butcher, or a cobbler in a little country town. She has a pretty face, a trim shape, and a look and air out of the common; a changeling look, by contrast with the honest, pudding-and-pie faces of her dowdy companions. There are not many brains in that pretty head; it is a head easily turned. She is vain, silly, selfish, greedy and dazzling. At fifteen or sixteen, she makes up her mind that she was formed for a life more silky and well-cushioned, a life far more amusing than that offered to a cobbler's wife or a farmer's wife, in Suffolk or Hertfordshire. Day of days for her, when young master on holiday, the sprig of gentility at the Hall, coming down with a dash in the white coat with the double cape, such as all the bucks in town are wearing, takes notice of her, sucks his teeth, and throws out a line or two from *Don Juan*, making her blush with pleasure, though the pretty fool does not understand the allusion. Then he says, slapping his thigh, that by God! it is a sin that so lovely a creature should be walled up like a nun in that dead town. To think that she, of all unearthly beings, should be spoiling her hands by the washing of greasy dishes and darning of old socks. By God! he, who can tell the points of a woman with as quick an eye as he can tell the points of a horse, sees well enough that she was born to shine as bright as the Countess of Jersey at town routs and assemblies. She is Haidee, she is Phryne, she is Delia, she is the evening star. Her eyes brim with tears at finding her beauty and her sensibility so tenderly valued by the first good judge she has ever met, the young man with the pimply red face, the smart white cape, the breeding and the aura of fashionable London. The disgust she feels for her own coarse, stupid kindred becomes too strong to be longer endured.

The summer of the Cyprians was brief. The Horatian and Byronic lover could not long suffer the sight of wrinkles around the lustrous eyes, he could not abide the sight of the rose fading nor the rose over-blown; the comical vulgarity, either lean or fat (equally absurd one way or the other), of an ageing Psyche. "His loves were like most other loves—a little glow; a little shiver." There was small kindness or mercy, less even than hard justice, for the race of Cyprians when their one charm against the dark—their youthful looks—was lost. No tenderness, no shared remembrance of past happiness, no loyalties. There endured for a season the dry, burning fever, the tortures, sufferings and extravagant jealousies —and then the brutality of contempt and boredom. In her lover's eyes, the lovely Lalage very quickly became changed into hideous Canidia, the cackling witch, grubbing for foul loot among the tombstones in the glare of a blood-red moon, drawing out of the earth by her incantations the serpents and hounds of the nether world. Tenderness for women was not in the Horatian, not in the Byronic, not in the early Victorian canon. These Cyprians, taking the air beneath the Regency arches, had a mortal

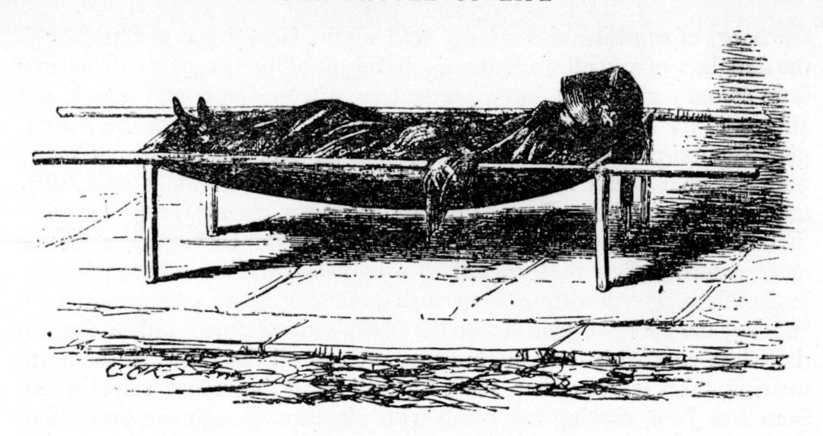

"GIN KILLED HER"
Wood engraving by George Cruikshank from his "Glass and the New Crystal Palace", 1853

dread of Time and truthful daylight; their looking-glass came to be their most spiteful enemy. Some there were, the brightest of the Cyprian band, rare ones with the wits of Becky Sharp, who saved themselves from damnation here on earth by brushing up their French and crossing the Channel at the right, the ripe moment. The fine gentlemen on the other side had no more heart or conscience about women than the English fine gentlemen, but the French, not being an incorrigibly boyish race, could detect and cherish a charm in women of thirty or forty years or more. It was possible for some of the Cyprians effortlessly to pass out of the pages of *The Town*, and so for ever out of reach of my lord's caprices, into the world of Balzac and the Princesse de Cadignan, and live there for a long time in the mellow light of a gentle, hardly perceptible decline.

But for the most part the motions of their fall were speedy: from St. James's, say, to the Edgware Road, from there again to Soho, from there to Islington or Cursitor Street. From my lord to his solicitor, from him to the fat tradesman or alderman, from him to the valet—and, after that, who can guess what humiliations? In their decline most of these characters took to tippling gin, the elixir of the disreputable Victorians, and though the Devil was in the bottle, he never gave them back the rose of youth for the buying of their souls.

The last scenes of the Morality Play were commonly played out on a dark, dreary stage.

There's a lamentable old crone dying in a rookery behind Short's Gardens, Drury Lane. There's the end to the banquet, to the face like April and the new moon, to the jewels and coaches, and my lord's favours. Now there's no more of Phryne or Lyde than a heap of old bones fallen on a pile of rags. The room is lighted by a candle stuck in a bottle—the last bottle from which she, poor wretch, was likely to draw any glow. By this dismal wick that spreads shadows rather than illumination you may see a pitiful old beak moving feebly; there are the straggling wisps of an old woman's hair in the place of the globed curls that were once painted by Sir Thomas Lawrence. The eyes see no more. There's all about her the stench of the slum. Brats are fighting on the landing outside the dying woman's door. The harridan from County Derry, who keeps this house, puts her long, potato face round the door—"An' she a'n't dead yet, bad cess to her". In the last fever, now upon her, the old woman is fumbling in her bosom for a locket or a jewel, a great sapphire, she says, that she can't now find. She falls to muttering about the blue riband and the Star of the Garter worn by my lord—and how that he looked as grand as a statue when he was dressed in all his finery—and what a clever, bold jest he made once upon the *honi soit qui mal y pense* of his Garter Order to make her laugh!—and she tries now to remember how it went, but her memory fails her. Then the old woman begins gabbling high-sounding names, but it is no matter, for the soot of history lies thick upon those names, and who in that wretched place, if he put an ear to the keyhole, would ever know what it was she was talking about?

George Gissing, writing just over fifty years ago, said that Dickens had never been popular with women readers. They resented the unrivalled gallery of shrews and termagants which his novels display. If all we knew of women was derived from reading Dickens, we should imagine that the sex was composed almost entirely of such idiots as Dora and Flora Finching; viragoes like Mrs. Gargery, who looked as if "she washed herself with a nutmeg-grater", Mrs. Varden, who was "of a temper tolerably certain to make everybody more or less uncomfortable", and Mrs. Wilfer, with her metaphysical toothache; these, and the impossible angel-women, too good for human nature's daily food, Little Nell, Little Dorrit and Agnes Wickfield, who reminded David of a stained-glass window ("Oh Agnes, Oh my soul . . . so may I still find thee near me, pointing upward"). It is not until we come to the last novels that we meet heroines we can fall in love with.

Are the women in Dickens unreal? Gissing, the master of the "new naturalism", certainly thought the shrews were real. To him, they were as true as reflections in a mirror. There are few grimmer pages in Victorian writing than those in which Gissing at the very end of the period reflects upon the terrible tyranny of the women in the mean streets through which he made his life's pilgrimage. In these pages, the windows are open on hot nights in stuffy, smelly courts: out of them come the shrill voices of the nagging wives, the streaming abuse of the sour landladies, the harangue of the domestic despot whose final note is the whine of self-pity. "Rumour, always flying bat-like about Cook's Court, and skimming in and out at everybody's windows, does say that Mrs. Snagsby is jealous and inquisitive, and that Mr. Snagsby is sometimes worried out of house and home, and that if he had the spirit of a mouse, he wouldn't stand it."

One assumes that the shrews, vixens and harridans of the Age of Dickens represented the price man had to pay for the subjection of women. Looking back over our history, one is astonished that the agitation for the emancipation and education of women was not led by angry manhood. For women, when they were boxed up and bottled up, took a terrible revenge. When they were treated either as exquisite dolls or as serfs, it obviously meant that a great deal of the milk of human kindness was soured inside them, and their pent energies turned to bitterness and mischief. That was especially true of the lower-middle-class *milieu* which Dickens and then, later, Gissing knew so well. In the social conditions of the times it was inevitable that the movement for women's rights should be largely a movement of upper-middle-class women. The daughters of the well-to-do came to resent the privileges of their brothers. A day dawned when Georgiana Podsnap, who had peeped above the apron of the phaeton, while driving in the Park, "like a dejected young person sitting up in bed to take a startled look at things in general, and very strongly desiring to get her head under the counterpane again", jumped straight out of the phaeton. But after that great leap of emergent evolution the poor dear could hardly be expected to spring out of her class as well. The opening of Queen's College in 1848 gave the Georgiana Podsnaps the hope that the women educated there would set up public schools for their sex to challenge Eton and Harrow, Winchester and Arnold's Rugby. Who can complain that Miss Buss, who started the London Collegiate School in 1850, and Miss Beale, who became Principal of Cheltenham Ladies' College in 1858, were so intent and so hard-pressed in their own upper-middle-class revolution that they had little thought to spare for poor, half-witted Maggy sheltering under the Adelphi Arches or Mrs. Plornish in Bleeding Heart Yard?

Among the saddest of all the figures that move across the crowded Victorian stage are the governess and the companion. Few there were who, like Jane Eyre, married the master. Some lived out happy lives in families that absorbed them and made them their own; some, like Robert Louis Stevenson's beloved "Cummy", were household deities of formidable power. But for so many of them, what was there in existence except frustration and humiliation? They belonged to the shabby-genteel order——they were the unmarried daughters of clergymen or soldiers who had died poor—they were very ladylike, they had the pretensions and standards of their class without the means to sustain them—and that laid them open to persecution both by mistresses and servants. Dickens had an instinctive sympathy with these victims of domesticity's upper and nether

"TO BRIGHTON AND BACK FOR THREE AND SIXPENCE"
Oil painting by Charles Rossiter, 1859
City Art Gallery, Birmingham

PEGWELL BAY, KENT
Oil painting by William Dyce, 1858 (detail)
Tate Gallery, London

ST. PANCRAS STATION, LONDON: THE MIDLAND HOTEL
Built by Sir Gilbert Scott, 1865; originally designed for Whitehall

ORNAMENTAL DRINKING FOUNTAIN IN VICTORIA PARK, EAST END OF LONDON
Ceremonial opening by Lady Burdett-Coutts
Water-colour by Edmund Walker, 1864
Bethnal Green Public Library

millstones. His account of Ruth Pinch's experiences in the home of the well-to-do brass and copper founder at Camberwell, where she was tyrannised by the odious child and the hateful parents, is a disclosure of the torture chambers that existed behind those spacious double fronts. Then there comes into mind the tragic face of Rosa Dartle, companion of Mrs. Steerforth, with her hungry black eyes, her smouldering passion and incessant questioning. "I concluded in my own mind that she was about thirty years of age and that she wished to be married. It appeared to me that she never said anything she wanted to say outright; but hinted it, and made a great deal more of it by this practice."

The Victorians, who tackled many big problems successfully, made a fearful hash of the problem of woman. Their moral dualism, their besetting weakness of dreaming of one thing and doing another, might be amusing in architecture or painting, but it involved endless cruelty towards flesh and blood. Woman in the abstract was as radiant as an angel, as dainty as a fairy—she was a picture on the wall, a statue in a temple, a being whose physical processes were an inscrutable mystery. She was wrapped by the Victorians in folds on folds, and layers on layers of clothes, as though she were a Hindu idol. She was hidden in the mysteries of petticoats; her natural lines were hidden behind a barricade of hoops and stays; her dress throughout the century emphasised her divorce from reality. She was a daughter of the gods divinely fair and most divinely tall; she was queen rose of the rose-bud garden of girls; she was Helen, Beatrice, the Blessed Damozel, the Lady of Shalott. A romanticism as feverish as that could only bring unhappiness to its objects. Dickens, who had a sensitive understanding of women he was never likely to fall in love with—tortured Miss Wade who had a grievance against the human race, Rosa Dartle consumed with her hopeless love for the youth who had disfigured her—exhibited the cruelty of the idealist in his treatment of the women he *had* fallen in love with. The romantic Victorian sometimes wreaked a fearful revenge upon his idols. The young Dickens was once deeply in love with a beautiful girl named Maria Beadnell; she married someone else; and years afterwards he met her again—and his anger, despair and disillusion at the changes Time had made provoked him to draw her as Flora Finching in *Little Dorrit*, the stout, red-faced, appallingly garrulous widow. Yet even through that avenging caricature, brilliant and heartless as it is, there comes some emanation from the original woman. We feel that Flora Finching was kind, warm-hearted, generous, even though a chatterbox, and that these are qualities to be treasured in a hard world. The crime of this Maria-Flora was that she had once been the beloved, and a nimbus had once shone around her head, and the air had miraculously glowed where she walked; but now she was a middle-aged party, portly, ridiculous. In short, she had become human, and that was unforgivable.

No envenomed misogynist could have visited such cruel humiliations upon the hated sex as the Victorians who toasted Lovely Woman as a combination of Venus, Juno and Minerva. Some dark necessity of the soul compelled these idolaters to tear down the goddess from her pedestal. Venus became the little drudge in the basement, Dick Swiveller's Marchioness; Juno was sent early to the mills; and Minerva, because of her remarkable intellectual attainments, became a governess at Leamington Spa.

Yet here, as in other spheres, it is a folly to let an inviting generalisation run away with one. No graphs or charts can record for us the number of nameless happy partnerships between men and women in all walks of life. Some of them we know about because they are inscribed in the lives of the eminent. There was the union of Disraeli and his wife, at once comic and sublime—such an odd, absurd old woman and such a sophisticated genius—and, linking them, a love stronger than death. There was, on the other side of politics, the perfect relationship of the Gladstones, transfiguring the solemnest great man in all the solemn mumbo-jumbo of State affairs: and when they were quite old he and she would link hands, and dance together when no one was looking, singing nonsensical, happy songs, like a boy and girl who are just married. Then there were Browning and Elizabeth Barrett, and Tennyson and his wife—"when I married her, the peace of God came into my life". These were famous unions—but their happiness was not rare, not confined to the eminent.

CHAPTER THREE

CONSPICUOUS CONSUMPTION

They ate well in those days—those who could afford to do so. Morality approved high feeding. The sternest Puritans felt no sense of guilt in enjoying the pleasures of the table. Pecksniff ate as one consciously performing a public duty. Chadband exuded a rich animal unction, like buttered toast. The analogy of the locomotive stoked up with coal was highly approved. To eat well was a utilitarian function; and it was a patriotic duty. The continuing power and glory of Britain depended upon hundreds of thousands of stout middle-class locomotives being able to keep up a great head of steam. They must "stoke up" in order that they might dash along the ringing grooves of change at a faster speed, carrying a heavier load, than Frenchmen, Austrians, Italians—or than those new rivals, the Americans.

Nor was it accounted shameful to take a *sensuous* satisfaction in meat and drink. Joe, the fat boy in *Pickwick*, was a very sympathetic character. " 'Now make haste,' said Mr. Wardle; for the fat boy was hanging fondly over a capon, which he seemed wholly unable to part with. The boy sighed deeply, and bestowing an ardent gaze upon its plumpness unwillingly consigned it to his master."

The old vicar's wife in *Framley Parsonage* spoke most honestly in saying to the Bishop of Barchester's lady, "When we are hungry, Mrs. Proudie, we do all have sensual propensities."

"It would be much better, Mrs. Athill, if the world would provide for all that at home," Mrs. Proudie had rapidly replied.

The world, indeed, did. The recipes preserved among a great-aunt's papers, and the menu of an eight-course dinner in the cookery books of the period, are alarming to a modern digestion. That popular book, *The Cook's Oracle*, embodying "the result of actual experiments instituted in the kitchen of William Kitchiner M.D.," declares that "every man who is not perfectly imbecile and void of understanding, is an *Epicure* in his own way—the Epicures in boiling of Potatoes are innumerable—the perfection of all enjoyment depends on the perfection of the faculties of the Mind and Body, therefore—*the Temperate Man is the greatest* Epicure—and the only *true Voluptuary*". The stomach is every man's master, wrote Dr. Kitchiner, inscribing the sacred organ in italic capitals—*STOMACH*. With a missionary earnestness he continued, "The Stomach is the mainspring of our System—if it be not sufficiently wound up to warm the Heart and support the Circulation—the whole business of Life will, in proportion, be ineffectively performed, we can neither *Think* with precision—*Walk* with vigour—*Sit down* with comfort—nor *Sleep* with tranquillity". Dr. Kitchiner's hero was "the great English moralist", Samuel Johnson, who ate with a rapt, religious, silent devotion, and magisterially said, "For my part, I mind my belly very studiously and very carefully, and I look upon it that he who does not mind his belly, will hardly mind anything else." Kitchiner approved that description by Smale of Johnson's habits given in his *Journey Into Wales*: "His favourite dainties were a leg of Pork boiled till it dropped from the bone, a veal-pie with plums and sugar, or the outside cut of a salt buttock of beef. With regard to *Drink*, his liking was for the strongest, as it was not the *Flavour*, but the *Effect* that he desired."

Mrs. Glasse's cookery book, remembered now chiefly—and inaccurately—for the phrase, "First catch your hare", was published in 1747, and that eighteenth-century tradition of generous eating and drinking stamped the early Victorian age. Francatelli (his first edition came in 1846) was a veritable Bourbon whose menus for a small family are like baroque pavilions encrusted with spun sugar and nougat, garnished with scallops of larks and little jellied wheatears, and whose banquets are heavy with the Roman corruptions of the Regency.

There is a Gillray drawing—one of his finest prints—of "the royal voluptuary", the Prince of Wales, digesting his enormous lonely lunch, satiated, revolting, but with a dreamy look of ebbing ecstasy on his face, the gnawed bones and the empty bottles spread about him like the relics in an ogre's cave. That amorist had a passion for food more constant than his love of women. One remembers Thackeray's ghostly banquet at Dessein's, "in the moonlight, in the midnight, in the silence"—with Brummell's fat phantom in a dressing-gown mumbling, "I remember Alvanley eating three suppers once at Carlton House . . . Never saw a fellow with such an appetite except Wales in his *good* time. But he destroyed the finest digestion a man ever had with maraschino, by Jove—always at it."

Maraschino? Other authorities have held other views. The Cardinal in *Lothair*, for example, said with a sweet smile, "King George IV believed that he was at the battle of Waterloo and indeed commanded there; and his friends were at one time a little alarmed; but Knighton, who was a sensible man, said 'His Majesty has only to leave off curaçoa and rest assured he will gain no more victories.' " Somewhere else I have read that he found Nirvana by tippling cherry brandy and reading Miss Austen's novels. That is History—it never knows the difference between maraschino and curaçoa.

Prinny's delights were taken a little before our chosen times, but his pagan religion of food, the blending of the carnal and the aesthetic, the combination of the big goggle eyes and the fine discrimination in sauces,

THE WASSAIL BOWL
Etching by Robert Seymour from "A Book of Christmas" by Thomas Hervey, 1837

endured so long as the afterglow of the Regency lingered upon Victorian façades. It was as late as 1865 that Speaker Denison recorded this remarkable feat of Palmerston:

> Dined with the Prime Minister who was upwards of eighty years of age. He ate for dinner two plates of turtle soup; he was then served very amply to a plate of cod and oyster sauce; he then took a paté; afterwards he was helped to two very greasy-looking entrées; he then despatched a plate of roast mutton; there then appeared before him the largest, and to my mind, the hardest, slice of ham that ever figured on the table of a nobleman, yet it disappeared, just in time to answer the inquiry of his butler, "Snipe, my Lord, or pheasant?" He instantly replied "Pheasant" thus completing his ninth dish of meat at that meal.
>
> (Monypenny and Buckle's *Disraeli.*)

Thackeray's "Memorials of Gormandising" and the grand meals in Dickens are of a kind to draw tears of sensibility to the eyes of John Bull in these starveling years. Was it gross? Was it vulgar, that love of eating? Yes, of course it was, but it had an earthy naturalness. And do we not take more kindly to the vice of gormandising nowadays when we cannot indulge it?

The joys of food were not merely aristocratic joys, not even joys of the well-endowed middle classes: they were sometimes shared by poor, disinherited wanderers. One calls back that moment—one of the numberless fine, heart-warming moments in the great Dickens panorama—when Codlin, trudging through a wet evening, came to the door of *The Jolly Sandboys*. The landlord was leaning against the door-post, looking lazily at the rain. "All alone?" said Codlin, putting down his burden, and wiping his forehead. "All alone as yet," rejoined the landlord glancing at the sky, "but we shall have more company tonight, I expect." Inside *The Jolly Sandboys*

> there was a deep, ruddy blush upon the room, and when the landlord stirred the fire, sending the flames leaping and skipping up—when he took off the lid of the iron pot and there rushed out a savoury smell, while the bubbling sound grew deeper and more rich, and an unctuous steam came floating out, handing in a delicious mist above their heads—when he did this, Mr. Codlin's heart was touched. . .
>
> Mr. Codlin drew his sleeve across his lips, and said in a murmuring voice, "What is it?"
>
> "It's a stew of tripe," said the landlord, smacking his lips, "and cow-heel," smacking them again, "and bacon," smacking them once more, "and steak," smacking them for the fourth time, "and peas, cauliflowers, new potatoes and sparrow grass, all working up together in one delicious gravy." Having come to the climax, he smacking his lips a great many time, and taking a long hearty sniff of the fragrance that was hovering about, put on the cover again with the air of one whose toils on earth were over.
>
> "At what time will it be ready?" asked Mr. Codlin faintly.
>
> "It'll be done to a turn," said the landlord looking up to the clock—and the very clock had a colour in its fat white face, and looked a clock for Jolly Sandboys to consult—"it'll be done to a turn at twenty-two minutes before eleven."
>
> "Then", said Mr. Codlin, "fetch me a pint of warm ale, and don't let nobody bring into the room even so much as a biscuit till the time arrives."

Be you Calvinist or Jansenist, or of the sternest order of vegetarians, can you read that warm, tender, kindly, humorous, poetical page without emotion? The iron pot's odoriferous steam floats around us still.

One opens the pages of *The Cook's Oracle* and Francatelli and then the gaslight of that age becomes a painter of the Dutch School as it plays upon the still-life, the infinite variety of the still-life, unfolded in the kitchens, pantries and still-rooms of the large houses in Berkeley Square, Bedford Square, Portman Place, in Belgravia and Tyburnia. It produces a gallery of Jan Steens and Van Ostades. You can see the rich, slow brush moving with unction across the canvas, caressing the portliness of the silver salmon on a silver dish, all garlanded in parsley; and lingering with affectionate regard on the huge baron of beef, wreathed in sumptuous yellow fat, dropping fatness from his sides like an Old Testament sacrifice,

A CHEAP EATING-HOUSE
Etching by George Cruikshank from "Sketches by Boz", 1836

and with threads of precious scarlet juices trickling out of his swelling midriff.

This old Dutch painter broods lovingly upon the sleekness of an ineffable young porker, all melting with tenderness, and weeping with his own succulence, a lemon popped in his mouth as the last seal of sensuous satisfaction. The brush pauses on Hare, in his dark rotten-ripeness, a decadence with tang; on jellied capons, transparent and luminous, decked in the frippery of ruffles, wearing green and red cockades on their bosoms and looking like the painted effigies of stout Elizabethan merchants and their wives in the memorials in old churches; on the juicy certainties of legs of mutton; on fatling lambs, corpulent ducks, aldermanic geese, mayoral turkeys, cherubic partridges; on tiny ortolans and wheatears dissolving in their own richness; on spiced pheasant, quail, snipe, woodcock, ptarmigan, guinea-hen, all the calendar of delectable birds and fishes presenting themselves dutifully to be eaten in their proper season.

Gaslight, this old Dutchman, paints on the walls prodigious shadows of the Cook—the Irish cook, that ogress of these lower regions—as she lifts the lids to peep in the bubbling pots, so that many clouds of sweet-smelling steam arise in this enchanted cave, or as she pokes and stirs up redder flames inside the stove. In this mingling of the fire's glare and the aromatic clouds, Cook towers up to the height of a giantess. Her eyes shoot sparks; her black hair tumbles around a burning face; she broods with a fanatical passion upon an orchestra of stewpots and boilers, oven trays, casserole dishes, stone urns of mystery, big saucepans, little saucepans. It is no wonder that Boy Buttons, plump and pink and rotund as a cupid on a Valentine, bursting out of his blue uniform, feels strange tremors as the ogress turns upon him a broken-toothed smile of cannibal ardour. "My," says she, "a'n't that a fine young porker!"

Those who still read the Victorian kitchen classics are perpetually astounded at the size of these dishes as well as at their diversity. On the dressers and tables of that ogress cook stand pies of solemn grandeur, some of a soaring, fanciful school of architecture, with minarets and crenellations, some of them with domes covered with edible conceits, Tudor roses, lover's knots, shamrocks, crossed swords and doves. These mighty pies, standing in a row, look as solid as an avenue of public buildings, a sort of Whitehall of pastry, but try them!—no monumental masonry *there*—they crunch, crumble and melt away like snow.

Still-life painter, what catches your eye on pewter platter and willow-pattern earthenware? The sheen of oysters, couched in their floriated shells; Whitstables and Colchesters, they are sixpence a dozen. Glorious age when that could be true! When Sam Weller could raise the philosophic inquiry why poverty and oysters should go together. Your light sparkles, old painter, on the lunatic armour of enormous lobsters, vermilion, spiky, double-clawed, with speared antennae and eyes of jet—lobsters mounted in pairs, too fantastic to own allegiance to this sober earth, but appearing like knights on the planet Mars, with an absurd, mad chivalry of look about them—primed to fight to the death on a field of gold—and with a creamy sweetness of marrow inside the armour. They could be bought for sixpence apiece when Victoria was young.

There is a vivid passage in G. M. Trevelyan's *British History in the Nineteenth Century* describing the tribute which was levied by the kitchens and larders. The great cities had to be fed and London demanded the fat of the land. Supplies came in by canal boat, and

> Night and day hundreds of horses in relays were coming up at trot and gallop from the South Coast and even from the Berwick and Solway salmon fisheries, bringing fresh to Billingsgate the best fish of every port. A hundred thousand

head of cattle and three-quarters of a million sheep yearly walked up to Smithfield for the slaughter, many of them from Scotland or from the borders of Wales. But strangest of all to the modern eye would be the droves of geese and turkeys, two or three thousand at a time, waddling slowly and loquaciously along all the roads to London for a hundred miles round, between August and October, feeding on the stubble of the fields through which they passed.

It is the law of the tribe that everything edible shall be eaten. Even the tiny larks, the most ethereal of God's creatures, beauty almost disembodied, must yield their fragile ounce of flesh to the cook, and Shelley's high-born maiden be miserably martyred to keep an alderman in good humour. "Larks!" cries the ogre Kitchiner, licking his chops. "These delicate little birds are in high season in *November*. When they are picked, gutted and cleansed, truss them; brush them with the yolk of an egg, and then roll them in breadcrumbs; spit them on a lark-spit and tie that on to a larger spit; ten or fifteen minutes at a quick fire will do them enough; baste them with fresh butter while they are roasting."

The horrid little books for the instruction and intimidation of the young, which multiply at this time, are full of warnings against the awful sin of gluttony. Helping himself to another leg of goose, with sage and onion reinforcements, the Reverend Doctor Antrobus proclaims, "A child should always rise from his meal with his appetite unsatisfied. The enervating and corrupting pleasures of the table are the worst snare that Satan spreads before a young person. There is a late Roman degeneracy in the spectacle of a gorging infant. Thus do Empires fall." To this the bluestocking Mrs. Amelia Evans, whose *Precepts and Homilies for Charity Children* have gone into three editions, puts in, looking up from her quails in aspic, "How true, sir. We may at times even learn wisdom from the French, do you not think, Dr. Antrobus?" "It may be, ma'am. The ways of God are inscrutable, ma'am," says the doctor, casting anxiously around him for the port, "and He chooses unlikely vessels. But of what were you thinking, ma'am?" "I was thinking of Pascal, the philosopher of that nation, who was grieved to find his thoughts turning towards a certain *dish* when they should have been fixed upon higher matters." "That is indeed a weakness of the flesh to which the French are prone," replies the divine, speaking through a mouthful of goose. "For that gross failing they were severely punished by their Revolution. Here in England, we wisely chasten, correct and chastise the frailties of the flesh early in life."

But even the compilers of the little books of morals for the nursery might well condone or overlook the pleasure which the child of the time finds in brooding upon the array of jellies, whipped creams and ethereal jam tarts glistening under the half turned-down gas in the pantry. To stern critics, whipped creams, it is true, may yield lingering satisfactions: in summer they can turn sultry and gross; and so it is conceivable they may appear on the menus of Old Nick in the restaurants of Tophet. And even the airiest jam tarts, strawberry, raspberry, greengage, must be crushed in the mouth and their fragments pursued by the tongue. But surely not even the tortured and noble Jansenist could think that the happy liquefaction by a child of these jellies that were concocted of isinglass, sugar, the juices of many fruits, and were stained a gorgeous crimson with the blood of the cochineal bug, has any likeness to the gross sin of eating. So rarefied as to be almost impalpable are these lustrous jellies of the Victorians; they *look* like a congealing of sunshine and air; they vanish on the palate immediately they are tasted, and are become a memory almost before there is time to isolate them as an experience. A pleasure that evades the senses can hardly be described as sensuous. Upon such honey-dew might the Blessed Spirits sup after their minuet to the music of Gluck in the asphodel fields.

In the dining-room the gas lamps dazzle. Their reflections bloom in the brimming lakes of mahogany; they strike showers of sparks from the silver ornamental monsters on sideboard and table, the stampeding elephants, the twisting serpents, Pocahontas and the Red Indians, the Greek slaves, the turtle that carries the world on its back, the rotund nymphs and the roly-poly cherubs that sustain the bowls wherein the fruits of the earth are heaped-up—peaches, apples, pears, bananas, black grapes and white, the pile being crowned always by the tufted pineapple.

"My heart sunk with our Claret-flask . . ." There Browning speaks. "Up jumped Tokay on our table, like a pygmy castle-warder." And then,

> Here's to Nelson's memory!
> 'Tis the second time that I, at sea,
> Right off Cape Trafalgar here
> Have drunk it deep in British beer.

Nationality in drinks is not constant. The consumption of whisky in those days was small compared with that of gin and rum. The aristocracy had a fine taste in wine, every kind of wine that the vineyards of Europe produced, but in the early part of the Victorian age the commercial classes drank chiefly sherry and port. The merchant coming home from his counting-house to an early dinner in Bloomsbury or Clerkenwell at five in the afternoon found palate, eye and spirit equally refreshed by the gold in the sherry and the deep rose in the port. These were manly liquors; port, warm as a fire inside a man, and with no poetic nonsense of beaded bubbles winking at the brim. Sherry, the aureate sherry, might be bullion etherealised in the vaults of the Bank of England. But after dinner, when the cloth was taken off and the women had retired, port was lord. A German visitor to London in the thirties complained that the middle-class Briton grew ever more haughty and less communicative, with each glass of port he took. The master of commerce mouldered on past midnight through sombre silences, like a fire that never flared up, but never went out. His Bacchus was a brooding god with locked lips. The flibbertigibbet Continental peoples might make fools of themselves on their champagnes, hocks and such-like: the mercantile Briton took to a wine that never babbled, and kept his secrets suspended in its rosy depths. These were not expensive weaknesses of the flesh. Crusted port stood at 25*s*. a dozen. Sherry was at 20*s*. to 24*s*., with brown sherry at 25*s*. a dozen.

Thorstein Veblen's theory of Conspicuous Consumption comes into one's head when reflecting upon these long, dull dinners. A society, or rather a dominant group in a society, becomes rich. Its standards are material ones. It does not use its surplus wealth in building cathedrals to the glory of God, nor in endowing poets, nor in becoming the patrons of painters and musicians. It makes a display, it puts on a show. It devotes itself to the most conspicuous and most obvious form of consumption, the dinner-party for twenty or thirty or forty stuffed owls. The silver and glass sparkle under the chandeliers. Mrs. Merdle's bosom is a show-case for jewels. The blinds are not drawn, and the lean and ragged wanderers of the night are able to stare in at the dazzling display.

CHAPTER FOUR

PHANTASMA

It was in 1807 that gas illumination was first tried in London streets. An ingenious German, Winsor by name, lighted the colonnade of Carlton House in honour of the birthday of its tenant, the Prince Regent. His Royal Highness, as he walked up and down the terrace inspecting the lamps, was invested in an infernal radiance, not at all unsuitable to him. The pantomimic glare made the Regent's palace look Babylonian, and bathed the trees and shrubs in the Park in a garish light of doom. Crowds came from all parts of London to see these illuminations. Brave London crowds! they pressed as near as they could get to the supernatural spectacle, despite the warnings of wise men that Carlton House would certainly blow up within an hour or so of the lighting of the gas—whish! bang!—like a volcano, and the Prince, his wicked cronies, the ambassadors with their stars and ribbons, and all the gay ladies at the height of Nebuchadnezzar's feast would shoot off like fireworks to the stars.

By 1837, the prejudice against gas had vanished, except among very old-fashioned people, and the clergy. Oil lamps still cast their mild, consecrated glow over congregations in church. We need not think too badly of the vicars, or call them hard-shelled old codgers, for the hiss, and the humming, and the gaudy flare, made gas at this stage unacceptable for any house of worship. But the publicans liked it. The gin palaces blazed. All that wild brilliance, sharpened and magnified by cut glass, and shot back from mirrors, made the eyes water. The chandeliers flung out waves of intolerable heat over the sweaty, smelly crew swarming the house, and the gas in the jets whined and buzzed. Horrible! But suppose you had been a workman pigging it in a dirty, cold room in St. Giles's, with a white-faced shrew of a wife and a brood of squalling, sick children, might not that glaring, garish place with all its heat and squalor indeed seem to be a palace? To you, then, its vulgar illuminations might well appear more beautiful than a whole heaven of stars, its tawdry decorations fairer than dawn or sunset. All the dreary over-and-over-againness of maudlin chatter might strike you as being spangled with gems of wit. Warmth, life, strong, stomach-warming liquor, at a penny a tot, companionship, a glory of lights blazing in a dismal world—why, if any of us were doomed to live in St. Giles's, in the eighteen-thirties, this might well look like the opening of a Mussulman's Paradise, so much kinder to the needs and desires of oor sensual man than the frosty Christian Heaven of gloomy saints and consumptive young angels plucking harps. Can anyone with the least acquaintance with the life and work of the poor in those days be astonished at the power and fascination of the gin palaces? The really surprising thing is that in 1837 there were no more than four thousand public houses in London, to serve its population of two million. In New York, in the last years of the Prohibition period, some twenty thousand speakeasies and blind pigs existed to satisfy the illicit thirsts of a population of some eight million.

But a century or so ago those who did tipple usually tippled inordinately. One has to be careful in taking George Cruikshank as a witness—he was such an exuberant and zealous Temperance propagandist—but there is a great deal of testimony from other hands to confirm the truth of that scaring series of drawings of his, "The Evils of Drunkenness". They are quite as gruesome as the pictures of the German artists of the Middle Ages with their dances of death, their masques of the plague, their grinning skeletons and bottle-nosed fiends stoking up the fires of Hell. Let us take a piece of evidence from a provincial source, the Vicar of St. Mary's, Nottingham, writing to ask the Home Secretary to establish a police force:

> The debauchery, the extreme licentiousness and the continual state of drunkenness of the lower orders are productive of the great evils. The streets are all day long thronged with intoxicated, lawless and obnoxious people, making it impossible for respectable females to pass without protection. On Sundays the public houses are vomiting forth drunken persons at all hours. . . The magistrates are most of them connected, if not actually engaged, in the trade of the town, and they are reluctant to act against those who are their customers, or those who support their political views.
>
> (From E. H. Glover's *The English Police.*)

Blue ruin! That is a name that brings a shiver; it belongs to the endless, unwritten poetry of the gutter. It is an expression, picturesque and chilling, coming from a time when a child really believed there were bogies and demons to be seen walking the streets, and when he shuddered at the hideous, wild, mad faces looking at him as he hurried on. From some magazine pieces Walter Besant wrote during the Queen's Jubilee year, describing London in the year when she came to the throne, I take this page, which has the unholy fascination of that bygone city in it, and is, by the way, a specimen of Besant's graphic manner of writing:

> As for the drinking of spirits, it was certainly much more common then than it is now. Among the lower classes gin was the favourite—the drink of the women as much as of the men. Do you know why they call it "blue ruin"? Some time ago I saw, going into a public-house, somewhere near the West India Docks, a tall lean man, apparently five and forty or thereabouts. He was in rags; his knees bent as he walked, his hands trembled, his eyes were eager. And wonderful to relate, the face was perfectly blue—not indigo blue, or azure blue, but of a ghostly corpse-like kind of blue, which made one shudder. Said my companion to me, "That is gin." We opened the door of the public-house and

looked in. He stood at the bar with a full glass in his hand. Then his eyes brightened, he gasped, straightened himself, and tossed it down his throat. Then he came out, and he sighed as one who has just had a glimpse of some earthly Paradise. Then he walked away with swift and resolute step, as if purposed to achieve something mighty. Only a few yards farther along the road, but across the way, there stood another public-house. The man walked straight to the door, entered, and took another glass, again with the quick grasp of anticipation, and again with that sigh, as of a hurried peep through the gates barred with the sword of fire. He went into twelve more public-houses, each time with greater determination on his lips and greater eagerness in his eyes. The last glass, I suppose, opened these gates for him and suffered him to enter, for his lips suddenly lost their resolution, his eyes lost their lustre, he became limp, his arms fell heavily—he was drunk, and his face was bluer than ever.

Now it is night in the strange city.

What a spell that old, primitive gaslight cast! Neither oil that was used before it, nor electric lighting which came after, had anything like its power to charm the imagination.

It is the Devil's own light, as it dances a jig with the shadows at the windy corner of Hanging Sword Alley. It shivers and hops up and down in a dance of wicked joy. Fixed in a square of iron, clamped to a blotched wall, it hums to itself as it dances, and all over London this night you will hear the humming of the gas jets. It is not a dulcet note. It can bring a touch of frost to your blood on the sultriest night when you come upon it in a lonely corner like this, in an alley that has a bad name. "What makes me shiver?" the wayfarer asks. "Somebody is walking over my grave."

That spark of Old Nick in the gas-lamp there, jumping up and down, and buzzing like an imp, looks as if it had seen a man's throat cut by thieves one night, and could never forget it, and waits to see it happen again. There is a heavy sweat on the walls, the alley reeks on this warm night, its breath is corrupt, the place is near enough to the river for a man walking here to be stifled by the river stenches. Upstream at Westminster, the great men of Her Majesty's faithful Commons gathered on this hot night in Committee Rooms to order the business of this blessed realm, seal the windows that look upon the Thames for fear they catch its infected breath. On the river, Rogue Riderhood plies his trade; his rat's eyes on the lookout for bodies to seize and strip of their money.

The shadows are ugly, they twist and writhe, sometimes they appear to be running away, then they come to a stand at the end of the passage, they collect and huddle together, in wait for the stranger. But don't they look now to be harder than shadows? Halt!—watch!—isn't that an ambush? Robbers? The light shakes in an ague of expectation. Wasn't that a ghost of a whistle, I heard, and a smothered "Hist!" at the turn of the alley?

In the black shades of old Waterloo Stairs, you may hear the creeping

THE THIRD PHANTOM APPEARS TO SCROOGE
Etching by John Leech from Dickens's "Christmas Books", 1869

and rustling of Fagin's pupils—then there is the dead stillness as the plod-plod-plod of the victim's steps grows louder—then the dart and scuffle—the scattering and scurrying—then the rat-a-tat-tat of thieves' feet scudding off at a great speed, becoming fainter down the endless streets, and the faintest echo of a crow of triumph a long way off.

The man out alone has reason for night fears and chills. Ruffians, cut-purses, cut-throats swarmed in the alleys and by-ways in those days, they whisked in and out of the rotting wharves with the rats; they hid themselves in tumble-down hovels on the water-front. The old watch, the

Charlies, who used to cry at nights, "Twelve of the clock and all's well", waving their lanterns to one another from the street corners—those Charlies who used to be plagued by the young bloods and bucks of the town playing tricks on them, beating them, pricking them with swords, had only lately been swallowed up in the night of time, along with Dogberry and Verges and with Master Double. Peel's New Police, business-like fellows, wearing blue jackets with pewter buttons and beaver top hats, had been brought in eight years before. Here is Mr. Secretary Peel, speaking in the House on the Metropolitan Police Improvement Bill, April 15, 1829:

> If, for example, they selected the last year, and calculated the proportion which the number of criminals in London and Middlesex bore to the population, they would find that not less than one person in every three hundred and eighty-three had been committed for some crime or other in 1828 . . . Surely, it was not surprising, when the great extent of the Kensington district, and its great wealth, were considered, that three drunken beadles should be no preventive of housebreaking and thievery in it. Indeed, as had been said of the Court of Chancery, three angels, under such circumstances would be a sorry protection (A laugh.) . . . He believed that a large proportion of the inhabitants resident in the neighbourhood of Twickenham and Brentford were under constant apprehensions that their lives and liberties would be attacked; and such fears were entirely inconsistent with the free enjoyment of liberty and peace.

It was not Bill Sikes alone who resented Peel's one thousand Peelers as an infringement on the liberty of the subject. Looking at George Cruikshank's ferocious little book, *Cruikshank v. The New Police*, one would suppose that Peel had raised up a horde of janissaries, Bashi-bazouks, and eunuchs with scimitars, to take the place of those tried friends of freedom, the "porochial" constables, the beadles, the watchmen and the Bow Street runners. Cruikshank concluded his fling with a sketch of one of these new oppressors of the people dangling from the gallows—so perish all tyrants!

What fantasies were spun around those constabulary top hats! They were symbols of Peel's plot to overthrow the liberties of his country. These fellows in the beaver hats were to be his Pretorian Guard. Surrounded by them, he would march to the Palace; under the shadows of their truncheons he would seize the mace in the House of Commons, he would make himself Lord Protector—perhaps even King—he would rob the Bank of its bullion, and Lord knows what other wicked things he would do, for there could be no satisfying the lust for power of this terrible man who had set up the Police Force. (Our ancestors dreamed such nightmares after their whitebait suppers, and that is very laughable to us, who, with our serene, smiling good sense, never get ridden by political hags and night fancies!) The New Police made a bad start in politics by using their night-sticks at the Coldbath Fields rally of the

MR. AND MRS. BARLOW IN THEIR HOUSE NEAR IPSWICH
Water-colour by an unknown artist

A MULLIONED VILLA NEAR CIRENCESTER, BUILT *c.* 1850
Lithograph from P. F. Robinson's "Designs for Ornamental Villas", 1853

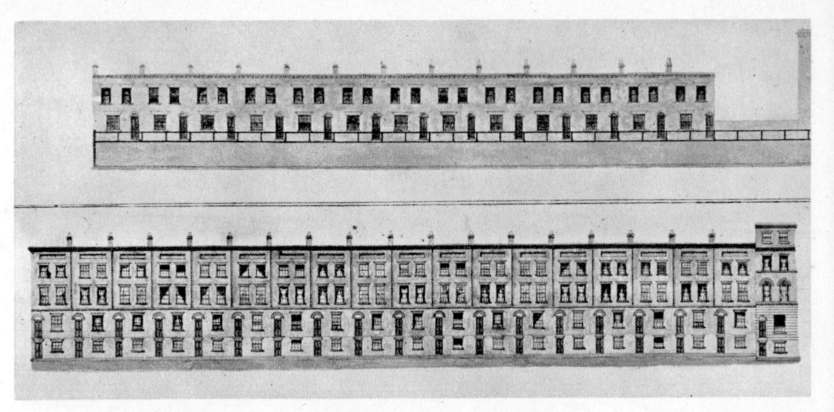

MONOTONOUS ROAD DEVELOPMENT IN LONDON:
SOUTH END OF BAZING PLACE
Water-colour by L. N. Cottingham, 1826
Crace Collection, British Museum

GREAT RUSSELL STREET AND MONTAGUE HOUSE BEFORE THE ERECTION OF THE PRESENT BRITISH MUSEUM
Water-colour by George Scharf, 1845–49. *British Museum*

National Political Union—that early expression of working men's discontent. This caused another fright—the Force had been assembled to trample down the Radical protest. It took the Peelers a little longer to learn the trick of keeping order at a political meeting than to catch burglars in "the great extent of the Kensington district". It could not be learned in a day, that tact in handling the excitable legions of protest and dissent.

Peel's Police were from the start successful in stilling those fears of the inhabitants of Twickenham and Brentford to which Sir Robert had feelingly referred. Indeed, a bit too successful, complained the provinces. For, pursued by those bloodhounds in beaver top hats, many of the companions of Sikes and the pupils of Fagin slunk off to Birmingham, Manchester, Liverpool, Leicester, Nottingham, Sheffield and Leeds. What had been Peel's count of the black sheep? One criminal in three hundred and eighty-three persons in London, he said, and something like one in eight hundred in the provincial cities. Now the balance shifted. Provincial aldermen who once had swelled with pride over their city's virtue now shivered at a knock on the door at nights. Silly jealousies between one city and another had denied Peel the national Police Force he longed for, and as time went on the provincial cities set up their own Forces, some good, some not. The name of Watch Committee still keeps the memory of that old bellman, Dogberry.

It was a period of brutish crimes and savage punishments. Sikes, when in a sportive mood, used to tighten an imaginary knot behind his left ear, then let his head fall limply on his right shoulder. That was a good joke to make old Fagin turn white. Jack Ketch was kept busy. In the early years of the century there were still a great number of crimes and misdemeanours that were hanging matters. In 1800 there were two hundred and twenty capital offences, in 1837, fifteen, in 1870, two only—murder and high treason.

I do not know where one can get a better notion of the smell and savour of crime, the taste of blood in the mouth, the utter *Godforsakenness* of the underworld of the eighteen-twenties and thirties than in the pages of *Oliver Twist*. It is not the most beguiling of Dickens's novels, though in Bumble it owns a comic character of Shakespearian amplitude. ("If the law supposes that, the law is an ass, an idiot. If that's the eye of the law, the law is a bachelor; and the worst I wish the law is, that his eye may be opened by experience—by experience.") But the book lacks the one-and-only magic, the dream-like quality in which Dickens's most Dickensian pages are bathed, the poetry of a child of genius for ever lost in an enchanted city. To read *Oliver Twist* is like looking down a dirty alley in the light of six o'clock of a March morning. The dustbin, the dead cat, the scattered filth, the broken bottles, the forsaken old grannie huddled up in her rags on a doorstep, the bully skulking home, casting a look over his shoulder at every step, are perceived as in a hard light before sunrise. *David Copperfield* and *Little Dorrit*, by contrast, are wanderings through the city of his inmost dream by moonlight, with a silvery haze spread over every ugly house, and every dull character transfigured into stone imps or comic hippogriffs. *Oliver Twist* has the powerful interest and the powerful boredom of police reports.

It ought to be the favourite novel of those stern sons and daughters of Gradgrind (or, maybe, Thomas Sapsea) who do not like Dickens because he writes sentimental fairy stories. In chapter after chapter, it is difficult to discern in that realistic crime-reporting a glimmer from the dreaming city of his imagination. When one samples the police-court columns in such papers as *The Morning Chronicle* one finds them very like the Fagin-Sikes chapters in theme and treatment, though Dickens is always infinitely the better writer. Is the murder of Nancy coarse melodrama? You will find it outdone in the criminal records of the time. The murders in low life of that time are mere sickening butcheries to read, unredeemed by the pathos, the tact of the heart and the reticences of the nerves of a literary artist. One thinks of the shining moments of that civilisation, the young Tennyson drawing "from the brown eggs of the nightingale the music of the moon", Newman preaching at St. Mary's, the figure of Darwin setting out on his journey of discovery, "the marble index of a mind forever voyaging through strange seas of thought alone"—and *there*, underlying the glory, is the raw, rank brutishness. For a hundred years and more, refined stomachs have turned against Dickens because of his sentimentality. "We can't stand all that suet in the pudding," they cry, "and all that treacle he pours over his pudding. Give us the dry sherry and biscuit which Miss Austen serves in her genteel parlour." But could there be anything less sentimental than his Rogues' Gallery in *Oliver Twist*, the drawings by a celestial policeman of the Artful Dodger and Charley Bates, with their "high cockolorum", their rapturous discovery of their own badness? The tiny homunculus glowing in the glass cries, "Man or boy, we are sure only of one thing, that we are remarkable and singular creatures, nothing like us was ever created before in the universe, nothing like us will ever happen again. We must make the dull world acknowledge our importance. If we cannot do so by our goodness and beauty, then we must achieve it through our grand, inordinate, spectacular wickedness". See the Artful Dodger entering the Police Office with his big coat sleeves tucked up, his left hand in his pocket, his hat in his right hand, coming in "with a rolling gait altogether indescribable".

> I'm an Englishman, ain't I? Where are my priwileges? . . . We'll see what the Secretary of State for the Home Affairs has got to say to the beaks, if I don't. Now then! Wot *is* this here business? I shall thank the madg'strates to dispose of this here little affair, and not to keep me while they read the paper, for I've got an appointment with a genelman in the City, and as I'm a man of my word and wery punctual in business matters, he'll go away if I ain't there to my time, and

then pre'aps there won't be an action for damage against them as kep me away. Oh no, certainly not.

Dickens doubtless had many illusions. He had few illusions about the reality of evil. For him, as for many sensitive creatures, cradled in poverty, Sin was hard, absolute, unalloyed, not foggy and variable. It is commonly those who have enjoyed curtained existences, who were born in soft beds and have grown up in cosy surroundings, who are sceptical of the powers of darkness, who smile away the doctrine of original sin as an old myth, and are sure the mystery of evil is to be resolved by politics, economics, medicine, by more soap and sermons or less beer, or by more hearty young chaps playing more football. Dickens *did* believe that damned souls put on human shape and find their awful fulfilment on earth in cruelty, in torture and the corruption of the innocent. The older he grew, the less inclined he seemed to be to accept the theory of the natural goodness of man. *Edwin Drood*, with its smell and rustlings of unnamed evils, is far more likely to keep one awake at night than *Oliver Twist*. Night often broods over his pages; there is often midnight brooding in his spirit. He describes Quilp in a wonderful phrase as a "dismounted nightmare". There are many dismounted nightmares in his streets.

Now it has grown very late, and most of the windows in the street have become blind eyes. The shadows of this night sweep up above our heads in the likeness of Gothic arches. The stone monsters are coming to life. The gargoyles are turning into creatures of flesh. The demons, hobgoblins and fiends—streaked with soot and rain, some with their faces half eaten away by the acids in the smoky air—are climbing down the towers and arches of the night, awkwardly, with strong, stiff motions, jabbering as they clamber down; they know their hour has come. Their hour!—it is here, it is here! The eyes of stone now have a gleam of coals in them. The scorings and annulations of the stone faces have now become the workings of scaly, dry skin over old bones. Some of these creatures are objects of pity and compassion, others of more than mortal loathing. Among the first kind are poor witless things that mean no harm, but prowl the streets with the starved cats till dawn. Under the dank arches of the Adelphi, amid the stench and the rotting straw, in the old burial grounds near the Fleet Prison, they creep and cluster, picking over the garbage heaps.

There are worse creatures abroad. These evil monsters weave their way through the city, turning their faces away from its lamps, but every now and again they are caught and forced to declare themselves in the play of crosslights. Then you must steel yourself to meet the white stare—the primal wickedness looking full at you, and then vanishing. In that moment, it fortifies a man if he has some medal against the dark to clutch, some spiritual amulet. Adam Smith, Jeremy Bentham, William Godwin, Macaulay—admirable characters and philosophers of the new enlightenment as they are, they are not enough at such a time, as they would not be enough, one suspects, when a man lay dying. The look of damnation pierces through the beautiful systems of the economists and speculators, through the pride of the State. In the House of Commons and in the newspapers confident voices proclaim the popular faiths. "In serving his self-interest, man advances the public interest." "The greatest happiness of the greatest number!" The ringing phrases sound queer in the dark street late at night.

The sin for which there is no forgiveness is the profanation of the child. The records of the society for dealing with child prostitution will not make pretty reading on the last day.

It has seemed to this writer that there are two elements in the great Victorian age which are not taken into sufficient account nowadays—the violent and the sinister. Its antimacassars covered up its creeping and crawling things. The daintiness of its sentimental art and writing masked its spiritual corruptions. The awful authority of Mrs. Grundy prevented its writers of genius, such writers as Dickens and Thackeray, from doing more than murmuring hints of the wickedness they knew. The villains in Dickens are commonly thought to be merely comical nowadays—stock figures from an old melodrama—and at their appearance the pennies begin to rattle down on the stage. From Monks in *Oliver Twist* to John Jasper in *Edwin Drood* they are pure villains, just as Iago was a pure villain. To the contemporary reader they were real enough in essence, if not in speech. They were emanations of that ferocious and concentrated malevolence, the joy in evil for its own sake, which lay beneath the enamelled surface painted with pretty scenes from the "Idylls of the King". It is hard to understand how a legend grew up that Dickens is primarily the celebrant of Christmas cheer, a kind of Santa Claus among novelists, with false whiskers and a horrible false joviality. He has, it is true, his hearty side—the side that gave us high jinks at Dingley Dell, and Mr. Fezziwig's ball, and the Cheeryble brothers. But how soon that was subdued to his deeper, darker preoccupations! There were many occasions when the genius of Dickens had a mediumistic quality. The cries of tortured and savage spirits burst through his lips. He was haunted by visions of murder. The thoughts and emotions of the murderer would take daemonic possession of him. We know from contemporary reports with what frightening power he acted the murder of Nancy by Bill Sikes, over and over again, on the public platforms. We know, too, that it was his favourite role, that it drained his vital force more than any other, and that when at the end of his days, he was a sick man, killing himself by those exhausting appearances, he flung himself into the part of Sikes with an increased, almost insane, frenzy. Dickens seems to have taken a morbid pleasure in the terror he communicated to his audiences—noting "so many faintings tonight", so many screams from the women.

Guilt and blood tormented his dreams. Sometimes he walked the streets in a trance, half-believing the brand of murderer was on him. That mind, so sensitive to all the deep impulses and quivering vibrations of his age, was obsessed by the barbarous savagery of its underworld. Carlyle said of De Quincey that he had the face of a child, but of a child that had seen Hell. That might have been applied to Dickens when he was wrestling with the lost spirits that called on him to make their torments articulate. Does anyone suppose that the account of Fagin's last hours in the condemned cell at Newgate, or the delirium of Jonas Chuzzlewit after he had murdered Tigg, was written without painful exhaustion of body and mind? Dickens, the medium, twists and writhes in the agony of Fagin as the boom of every iron bell in the city gives the "deep hollow sound of death".

> At one time he raved and blasphemed; and at another howled, and tore his hair. Venerable men of his own persuasion had come to pray beside him; but he had driven them away with curses. . . . It was not until the night of this last awful day that a withering sense of his helpless, desperate state came in its full intensity upon his blighted soul. . . . He had spoken little to either of the two men who relieved each other in their attendance upon him; and they, for their parts, made no effort to rouse his attention. He had sat there awake, but dreaming. Now he started up every minute, and, with gaping mouth and burning skin, hurried to and fro, in such a paroxysm of fear and wrath, that even they—used to such sights—recoiled from him with horror. He grew so terrible at last, in all the tortures of evil conscience, that one man could not bear to sit there eyeing him alone; and so the two kept watch together.

This is the other side to the security, the radiant assurance of the Victorian world. The cultured society of that time appears to us like a lighted ship sailing a dark, mysterious sea. On board there is every comfort, every refinement of pleasure. The food and wine are delicious, there is music, there are heaps of flowers, the company is most agreeable, and good talk never falters. In one saloon Michael Faraday, the magician, is amusing a distinguished group with some astonishing tricks; he has called the lightning down from the clouds and weaves it in dazzling patterns around his head. Charles Darwin is exhibiting his rare specimens brought back from far-away seas. Tennyson is reading to the ladies:

> For I dipt into the future, far as human eye could see,
> Saw the Vision of the world, and all the wonder that would be.

Gladstone and Mill are in earnest debate on the problems of Free Will, and in the royal cabin Sterndale Bennett is playing Mendelssohn to the Queen. The cat-like Arnold picks his fastidious way through the saloons, emitting at times a faint hiss, at other times revealing his elegant claws; he finds the society provincial, and lacking the Attic spirit, but that he is at such pains to disparage it is taken as an inverted compliment to the high order of civilisation represented by the company.

We see that glittering ship sailing on a sea of perils. A curmudgeonly old Scot, who is glaring into the night from the bows, mutters that they'll be running into evil weather soon, with pitch and flame pouring down from the skies he wouldn't wonder, and Lord have mercy on their souls then. This ship is so sure it is unsinkable that it has no boats. Underneath the bright ship, and weaving through the black waters around it, are shapes of evil inexpressible; images of sharks, with yawning mouths, and cuttle-fish and coiling snakes.

There is no writer of that age who conveys the sense of monsters in the deep, of the perils that wind about the ship, so well as Dickens does. Besides his absorption in the act of crime, in punishment, in prisons, in scaffolds, in the files in the police offices, there was a related theme which runs through Dickens's pages. It is the theme of the lost child who wanders through a world of unimaginable perils. The abandonment of the young David Copperfield—the old hag snatching at Florence Dombey—Pip caught by the convict in the churchyard—these were reflections of his own childhood dreads. He, too, had been cast away; he, too, had been exposed to the prowling monsters; and his mind retained the scars of that experience until the day he died. He identified himself with innocence lost in the jungle for an obvious psychological reason; he identified himself with the man of blood for some more subtle reason. On those long tramps through London streets in the middle of the night—looking in on some friendly police inspector at three in the morning—the lonely artist was both the destroyer and the destroyed, the tiger and the gazelle.

> Between the acting of a dreadful thing
> And the first motion, all the interim is
> Like a phantasma, or a hideous dream.

Dickens lived for long periods on end in that phantasma, and its strange light suffuses his greatest pages.

PART V

THE HAUNTED MAN

CHAPTER ONE

RELIGION AND POLITICS

The importance of religion in the lives of the Victorians is hard to exaggerate. It is a subject that deserves far more space than it usually receives in studies of the period. For, in touching it, we touch the inmost springs of action. And we touch, too, the inner doubts, despairs and terrors that lay beneath the marble self-assurance, and enable us to know the Victorians as men, not as mere pictures in an album of successful lives.

Few characters of the Age of Dickens were reticent about religion. Nowadays you may work side by side with a man for years and never have the faintest idea whether he is a Catholic, a Presbyterian, a Theosophist, a Seventh-Day Adventist or an Agnostic. It would be thought in bad taste for you to inquire, or for him to confess. Which of us could answer an examination paper on the religious links of the present members of His Majesty's Government? Yet in Victoria's day everybody knew, more or less, the Lord Chancellor's outlook on Hell—as Pusey said of Lord Chancellor Westbury, he had a *personal* interest in the question of eternal punishment—and everybody knew where the Home Secretary stood on the subjects of altar lights and the Reserved Sacraments. In this age of ours, religion is a confession as shy as first love. The Victorians debated the themes of Faith not only without self-consciousness but with positive zest. Sex was *their* embarrassment, as religion is ours. They entertained a realistic view of Heaven, and a practical notion of Damnation. An Evangelical lady-in-waiting gushed to the Queen one evening on the bliss that awaited her Majesty in Paradise. For example, what joy it would be for her Majesty to converse in the shadow of the sapphire-coloured throne with her Majesty's great ancestor, David, King of Israel. "King David is *not* a person I would wish to meet," said the Queen coldly.

Nowadays it is considered ill-bred to invoke Divine aid on a party platform, but the Victorians constantly called in the spiritual world to redress the balance of the political one, and they did so with the direct simplicity of children who truly believe that God is their Father in Heaven. After the Third Reading of the Factory Bill in 1847, Shaftesbury wrote in his diary, "I am humbled that my heart is not bursting with thankfulness to Almighty God—that I can find breath and sense to express my joy. What reward shall we give unto the Lord for all the benefits that He hath conferred upon us?" That is touching, beautiful and child-like; and, reading it, one says instinctively, "Blessed are the pure in heart for they shall see God."

Shaftesbury, who proved so often in Victorian affairs "the last restraint of the powerful and the last hope of the wretched", was an Evangelical. It was a faith of another order, a High Anglican faith, that inspired Gladstone's prodigious career. The young Gladstone, the rising hope of "those stern and unbending Tories"—he who wrote *The State in its Relations with the Church* (1838)—was as ardent a clerical in politics as M. de Maistre across the Channel. The contention of his book was that "the propagation of religious truth is one of the principal ends of Government, as Government".

In his *Chapter of Autobiography*, printed in 1869 when he had become a Liberal Prime Minister, Gladstone wrote in these terms of the clerical manifesto of his Conservative youth:

> The distinctive principle of the book was supposed to be that the State had a conscience. But the controversy really lies not in the existence of a conscience in the State, so much as the extent of its range. Few would deny the obligation of the State to follow the moral law. Every treaty, for example, depends upon it. The true issue was this: Whether the State in its best condition has such a conscience as can take cognisance of religious truth and error; and, in particular, whether the State of the United Kingdom, at a period somewhat exceeding thirty years ago, was or was not so far in that condition as to be under an obligation to give an active and an exclusive support to the established religion of the country.

(That last sentence, by the way, is highly Gladstonian, and is illustrative of his labyrinthine style.)

Gladstone came to change his mind about the moral obligation of the State to impose a Protestant Church upon Catholic Ireland, but he never faltered in his insistence that the State *has* a conscience and that politics must be ruled by the moral law. Many who saw and heard him when he was a very old man are still living to tell how Gladstone would become transfigured by some issue of right and wrong arising out of

A COUNTRY CHURCH ON CHRISTMAS MORNING
Etching by Robert Seymour from "A Book of Christmas" by Thomas Hervey, 1837

mundane affairs. The hooded eyes of the old eagle, dim with age, would then glow with a supernatural heat. His body would stiffen, he would throw back his head in an imperious anger. A power apparently beyond the reach of an old man's nerves and muscles would seize him. There was a light upon him from another planet. The voice would deepen, and call back all the notes of its magnificent prime—pity, scorn, valour, wrath, the indignation of a god at the baseness of men. He would cry out as for the sword of the Lord and of Gideon, and he all but forced men to anticipate the audit of Judgment Day.

Lord Melbourne, after listening to an Evangelical sermon on Sin, had said crossly: "Things have come to a pretty pass when religion is allowed to invade the sphere of private life." In that he spoke for the eighteenth-century aristocracy. It was impertinent to inquire if a gentleman was saved. God would always frank the privileges of the nobility. In Gladstone was manifest the high seriousness regarding life, and the concern over human destiny, that marked the prosperous merchant class from which he sprang—that upper middle class which, in the nineteenth century, took the place of the old aristocracy and became in turn the ruling caste. Religion to Gladstone was like the ether, which penetrates all substances, all temporalities. The cruelties of Bomba, the Bourbon King of Naples, were to him "the negation of God erected into a system of Government". He was in an everlasting anger against Disraeli for refusing to consider political matters as primarily moral ones, for behaving, instead, as the opportunist man of affairs, calculating the balance of advantage; for taking a monkey's joy in the exhibition of his agile cleverness; and for being as cynical as Walpole about human motives. In one of those phrases that distil the private disillusions of a genius, Disraeli wrote of "the dazzling farce of life". To Gladstone, life was a hard but glorious battlefield on which the struggle between Good and Evil was fought; a man must declare himself for God or Satan—there could be no neutrals in that war.

There is no figure more representative of the Victorian age than Gladstone, as there was none greater, yet of all Victorian figures his has appeared the most remote, cryptic and unsympathetic to the twentieth century. Surely, say the young, he must be a hypocrite using high-flown sentiments to mask the designs of self-interest. Labouchere's often-quoted gibe that he didn't mind the Grand Old Man concealing an ace in his sleeve, but objected to his pretending, when exposed, that God Almighty had put it there, is taken as a text by many modern writers for their studies of Gladstone. We may think what we please of religion and of its relation to politics, but we shall never comprehend the Victorians unless we recognise the force in such a passion as Gladstone's, with all its conceded ambiguities or violent swoopings to and fro, or the response it evoked among his countrymen. It moulded and coloured the age, it influenced the subsequent development of politics in Britain, and it insensibly affects even those who today write in a puzzled anger about the auto-intoxication of the illustrious hypocrite.

The religious impulses that animated the Age of Dickens had their origins in the eighteenth century. Or it would be more true to say they derived from the protests of the human spirit against the cold, brilliant, secular finality of that age. There were two streams of tendency that had an influence visible to this day in the religious and political life of the nation—the Evangelical revival in the Church of England; and the Methodist movement, which began within the State Church and, being driven out of it, carried a great accession of strength to the old, ineradicable forces of British Dissent. The shock of the French Revolution brought a rally to order and authority in Britain. This was predictable. What was less predictable was the religious awakening that the Revolution brought about on this side of the Channel. The breach in the Whig party could have been foreseen; so, too, might have been the conversion to Conservative principles of Wordsworth, Coleridge and Southey. What was more surprising was that the Duchess of Bolton should decide to go to chapel regularly and "have family prayers in the country".

The links between the British and French aristocracies had been close. No one, said Talleyrand, could know the true sweetness of life who had not shared the pleasures of the French aristocrats before the Revolution. Highly cultivated Englishmen cherished the graces and charms of this French civilisation. It was a blessed relief to them after enduring their own coarse, red-chapped society, where love was of the barnyard, where wit came from the stable, and bankers were esteemed above poets. When they left Dover they set sail for the Island of Cytherea. There, under the canopy of ancient trees, in the velvety shadows where a bust of old Silenus leered from his fluted pedestal, and the wine and loaves were spread out on a fair cloth on the grass, and Harlequin, beribboned and cross-legged, played a love ditty on his mandoline, a Queen, a young and lovely Queen, might suddenly appear in the guise of a shepherdess or a milkmaid. These passionate pilgrims of ours from the land of fogs and eternal dullness had their wits stolen away by the endless subtle refinings of physical pleasure, the airy and nimble play of wit, "the unbought grace of life", and that sensibility through which, in Burke's words, vice itself lost half its evil by losing all its grossness.

Now they had seen the dreadful end of that world of delicate enchantments. The heads of Athénée and Palamède had bent to the knife; the sawdust was blotched with the blood of friends. The faithful, foolish Princesse de Lamballe had been hacked in pieces by the mob and her head stuck on a pike. The Queen herself was butchered. With Burke, the English who had loved the old France, and had drawn their dearest happiness from her, cried out that the age of chivalry was gone, and the glory of Europe extinguished for ever.

But they were haunted by the fear that the wrath of Jehovah had been visited upon these entrancing and corrupt children in that they had mocked Him; and because reparation must always be exacted when responsibility has been dodged. To live without obligation—to take so much of the world's treasure without paying for it, no matter how exquisite a life one has lived on credit and on borrowed time—was that not the sin for which there was no forgiveness? The impulses of Puritan ancestors, long in a trance, began to stir again in the blood. Old fears, old doubts, old questionings that had slept since the Lord Protector's time awakened. The awful warnings of the Old Testament were remembered: the mysterious hand was seen to be moving across the wall. Fire had fallen from Heaven to consume these lovely parasites, as it had fallen long ago upon the inhabitants of Sodom and Gomorrah who had flouted the ultimate obligations of the human condition. Might not a like doom engulf Britain? For she, too, had tempted the wrath of God by the spectacle of an aristocracy indifferent to everything in life's call except the pursuit of its pleasures. The morals of that aristocracy were as shameless as French morals; its manners were far more gross. The Princes of the

Blood set the note of fashionable society; a note of lubricity unlightened by charm; a lout's horseplay passing for gaiety, and downright brutishness serving for wit. The Reign of Terror in France frightened many members of the British ruling classes into a repentance for the sins of their society; it aroused in not a few of them a sense of social and political duty. They, at least, must justify themselves by works. They made a hurried count among their friends—how many just men had been needed to save the city? Simple country folk gaped to see how many fine coaches, blazoned with coats of arms, drew up at the village churches on Sunday mornings.

It was a moment comparable to the end of *Don Giovanni* when the ensemble moralises on the fate of the wicked Don who has just gone down through the trap-door into the flames of Hell. Donna Elvira retires melodiously to a nunnery, Donna Anna begs a year of mournful meditation before she marries, Leporello seeks in the tavern "a better master", while Zerlina and Masetto, children of earth, go home to supper together. "*Questo è il fin di chi fa mal . . .*" The wicked shall be turned into Hell.

The Evangelical revival brought back family prayers and a strict observance of church-going. It restored Puritan rules of private conduct. It denied cards, dancing and the theatre to the faithful. Yet the Evangelicals were not ascetics. They relished the hundred and one sweet satisfactions of a well-ordered table, they took wine, they were generous hosts, and would brood lovingly upon the arrangement of a banquet. They augmented the comforts of the flesh while curbing its more primitive pleasures; they understood how cheering in this vale of woe are such consolations as a good meal and a warm bed. They cultivated the mind as well as the palate. If they thought meanly of the stage they, at least, showed a taste for what was good and fine between book covers. Like most of us, they had their contradictions. They were liberal critics of literature. Byron, for instance, was read with admiration by the cultivated Puritans, despite the scandalous associations of his name; though editions of his poems without *Don Juan* were preferred. I once owned a handsome copy of Byron that had belonged to an Evangelical family. Three-quarters of *Don Juan* had been cut out with scissors; *Childe Harold* was full of admiring underscorings.

Their culture may have been narrow, but it was deep. They extracted much happiness from the gentle pleasures of letter-writing and conversation. That distinguished Parliamentary figure, William Wilberforce, around whom the Clapham Sect revolved, confessed a Puritanical creed and was a very stern Sabbatarian, yet he could be the most cheerful of companions. Unlike most philanthropists, he abounded in the private virtues; unlike most friends of Man, he won and kept long the love of those men and women who knew him best. He, who could speak with such grave power against slavery and other large evils in the House of Commons or on public platforms, excelled in the winning art of small-talk, bubbled over with good nature, was sunny and eupeptic, was troubled by none of those knots in his nervous system or shadows across his brain which a harsh religion is generally supposed to bring about.

There is an agreeable sketch in *Pendennis* of an Evangelical lady's household:

> In Egypt itself there were not more savoury fleshpots than those of Clapham. Her mansion was long the resort of the most favoured among the religious world. The most eloquent expounders, the most gifted missionaries, the most interesting converts from foreign islands were to be found at her sumptuous table, spread with the produce of her magnificent gardens . . . a great, shining mahogany table, covered with grapes, pineapples, plum-cake, port wine and Madeira, and surrounded by stout men in black, with baggy white neckcloths, who took little Tommy on their knees and questioned him as to his right understanding of the place whither naughty boys were bound.

High thinking and cosy living formed the rule of these families. To their influence, more than to any other, the Victorians owed domestic arrangements of almost enervating ease: the parlours and the bedrooms with the big fires blazing in them, and the little maids eternally lugging coal-scuttles upstairs; the corpulence of cushions, the suffocating intimacy of all those velvet hangings, the feather mattresses, deep as the embrace, of sleep itself, the silky smother of enormous eiderdowns, the warming-pans, the hot-water bottles, the stifling warmth of wool and flannel. Such was the setting in which our strenuous ancestors sought their repose. Such were the balms of their mortified flesh.

You and I might not be at ease in this Evangelical company—finding their indulgences almost as insupportable as their prejudices, and their strenuous cheerfulness a little exhausting—but the soul of goodness and compassion was in them. Because they lived, the sum of the world's misery and pain was lessened a little. They were charmless; they were prim; and they were on the side of the angels. A contemplation of their lives and works leads one to place charm, wit, humour and imagination below the humdrum serviceable virtues in the salvation of society. There was many a poor wretch who had reason to be grateful that the innate zeal of the Evangelicals carried them from religious reforming into political activity; many a freed slave, many a madman rescued from the torments of public exhibition on Sundays at Bedlam; many a starved, half-naked mite spared from the mines.

Political sympathies softened the rancour of religious bigotry. The Evangelicals, and their Nonconformist auxiliaries, worked in loyal partnership with free-thinking Utilitarians, with Radicals and other unsanctified characters for the abolition of the slave trade and such admirable ends. The Saints acted as though they believed that politics provided the most direct and satisfying assurance of justification by works. A creditable record in the division lobbies would be recognised at the gates of Paradise. No writer caricatured the Evangelicals and the Dissenters with a more wicked pencil than Charles Dickens, but they forgave him, for the sake of certain life-and-death issues in which they and he were so manifestly on the same side. The nose of Stiggins glows for ever down the night of time, a star as fiery as the nose of Bardolph. In the figure of Chadband, the lambent flame of the comic genius is seen to play around certain quirks and weaknesses of the Evangelicals:

> "My friends, what is this which we now behold as being spread before us? Refreshments. Do we need refreshment then, my friends? We do. And why do we need refreshment, my friends? Because we are but mortal, because we are but sinful, because we are but of the earth, because we are not of the air. Can we fly, my friends? We cannot. Why can we not fly, my friends?"

Dickens's account of Mrs. Jellyby, sitting amid the litter and ruin of her neglected home, seeing nothing nearer to her than Africa, dictating letters to the Ramification Society, and extending to the natives of Borrioboola-Gha (on the left bank of the Niger) the affection she denied her husband and children, was a cruel satire upon those missionary enthusiasms which were dear to the Evangelicals. It deeply wounded Lord Denman as a Liberal, as an Abolitionist and as an admirer of Dickens, by its injustice to his friends. Yet Dickens, the anti-Puritan, was beloved by most men and women whose conscience had made them reformers. For they saw Dickens as their ally in the long struggle against cruelty and injustice, against the martyrdom of the poor and the massacre of the innocents. They saw his novels as sublime tracts. Shaftesbury, the noblest of all the Evangelicals, believed that the Lord had dowered Dickens with his great gifts in order that he might rouse attention "to many evils and many woes". "God gave him a general retainer against all suffering and oppression," said Shaftesbury. Could a great man hope for a finer epitaph?

The Evangelicals recoiled in genteel horror from the ecstasies of the flesh, and they seldom appear to have been touched by the true ecstasies of the spirit, which Catholics, High Churchmen, Methodists, Swedenborgians, Quakers and adherents of the Salvation Army, among others, have known. To outward view they had a habit of looking dull, complacent and fat, but at least they were never bored. They never knew the black *ennui* that descended upon the brilliant French civilisation of the eighteenth century, an *ennui* that failed to find a relief in the heightening of pleasure by the corruptions of pain, and by the profanation of the image of the beloved. Let us think of such characters as eccentric, frustrated, frantic—but they stayed the course, they were mysteriously compensated, and their ending was not pitiful.

To be an intelligent and cultivated Puritan is doubtless to be not quite civilised. But to be not quite civilised is a guarantee of survival in this harsh world. The inner strength of such characters as our Victorian Puritans is that they are always in a state of *becoming*, never of *being*. They will never know the disillusion of conquest; they will never hear the mocking voice that cries "Satis".

> Bold Lover, never, never canst thou kiss,
> Though winning near the goal—yet, do not grieve;
> She cannot fade, though thou hast not thy bliss,
> For ever wilt thou love, and she be fair!

A great deal of sympathy has since been expended upon the victims of Victorian Puritanism; usually seen in the likeness of thin, straggly shoots sprouting in the cellar, putting out pallid leaves and nervous tendrils, hungry for the warm sun, clambering up, so weak and so hungry, towards the little grating where the patch of daylight glimmers. But those tendrils, white and thin, are sensitive nerves. To be famished and to refrain—that heightens awareness. It increases the area of the sensibility, of the tragic, the comic and the poetic sensibility. Wild, refracted lights of frost and snow are cast upon that interior stage on which the shy, buttoned-up Englishman acts out his own life-long mimic *Hamlet* or spins those private lunacies of which the world becomes aware only through the disclosures of an Edward Lear or a Carroll, who must always take rank among our Puritan writers.

The Evangelicals were regarded by their own Church with that displeasure which any old institution, snug, comfortable, draped with ivy, understandably feels towards troublesome creatures inside it who are not content to leave well alone, but must always be fussing, fidgeting, asking questions, moving resolutions, disturbing the afternoon slumbers of their elders and betters. It is said that it is dreary drudgery being a Bishop nowadays, but a Bishop's life was most agreeable in the early part of the last century. There were Bishops then who kept up the state of Dukes, grew fat on a great rent-roll, gave splendid entertainments in their palaces, drove out in their carriages and four—one of them, at least, in his carriage and eight. Such prelates were not likely to take kindly to those among their flock whose zeal in spreading the Gospel was a standing reproach to their own sluggish ease. In the palace of Ely, where on festal occasions a string band pulsed, and the flowers were magnificent and the champagne perfect—in that palace where the county families danced at the Bishop's ball, the *Olney Hymns* were naturally accounted sad fudge.

> The dearest idol I have known,
> Whate'er that idol be,
> Help me to tear it from Thy throne,
> And worship only Thee.

Such a sentiment might be considered suitable on the lips of destitute widows; it was not a congenial meditation for well-fed Princes of the Establishment.

The Bishops, then—or nearly all of them—condemned the Evangelicals as meddlesome cranks, while the wordly-wise of the time poked fun at them as prigs. The half-grown schoolboys, lusty young barbarians Tory and Whig—"Eton boys grown heavy", as Praed said—who gave their tone to the House of Commons, called them "The Saints"; and any healthy schoolboy of today can reproduce for you the exact inflection in saying "Pi!" But the Evangelicals, infuriating fellows that they were, were unruffled by ridicule. The most implacable enemies they made were the enemies of most decent, kindly citizens; and so were more useful to them than fair-weather friends. The Evangelicals possessed tenacity of purpose together with that serene consciousness of being always right which, irritating though it is to the rest of the world, enables minorities to exert a power beyond their numbers.

Among the chief political allies of the Evangelicals were those Methodists with whom they had also found themselves in closer religious sympathy than with most of their fellow Churchmen. Some of the Bishops, indeed, said of the Evangelicals that they were Methodists in masks. The teachings of Wesley had made a deep impression on such figures as Clarkson and Wilberforce, the Abolitionists; on Howard, the prison reformer; and on Hannah More, that admirable bluestocking who had so real a care for the education of the children of the poor. At a time when Nonconformists were still kept out of the House of Commons by the bad old laws it was the Evangelical Churchmen who spoke for the Nonconformist conscience. The protest was none the less strong because it was vicarious. Wesley had made his converts among many classes, including the commercial well-to-do, but the majority of Methodists at this time were farm labourers and small farmers, working men and artisans in the towns, shopkeepers and tradesmen, and their wives. These classes were drawn by the democratic impulse of the new evangel, and they, in turn, lent to it the fervency of their own aspirations towards a fuller life.

The Methodists were called Enthusiasts. In our times, "enthusiasm" is a word in good standing. It is hard for us now to catch the meaning it carried for cultivated men of the eighteenth century and early nineteenth—to comprehend, for example, why it sounded such an odious word to a man so deeply religious as Samuel Johnson. Is "fanatic" today's synonym? Hardly—for it does not convey all the shades. In the abhorrence which the notion of Enthusiasts and Enthusiasm provoked, several elements were mingled—the dread of bad taste, the suspicion of humbug and moral fraud, the fear of levellers and of the undermining of authority, discomfort in the presence of the irrational, and a considerable dose of intellectual and social snobbery.

In one of his Peninsula despatches, Wellington pressed the "mysterious divinities of the Horse Guards", as Guedalla called them, to give their minds to increasing the numbers of "respectable and efficient clergymen"

TOWER BRIDGE, LONDON

Built by Sir Horace Jones and Sir John Wolfe Barry, 1885–94

Coloured lithograph

NINE ELMS STATION, VAUXHALL, SOUTH WESTERN RAILWAY

Water-colour by T. H. Shepherd, 1856

Crace Collection, British Museum

PLATE 20

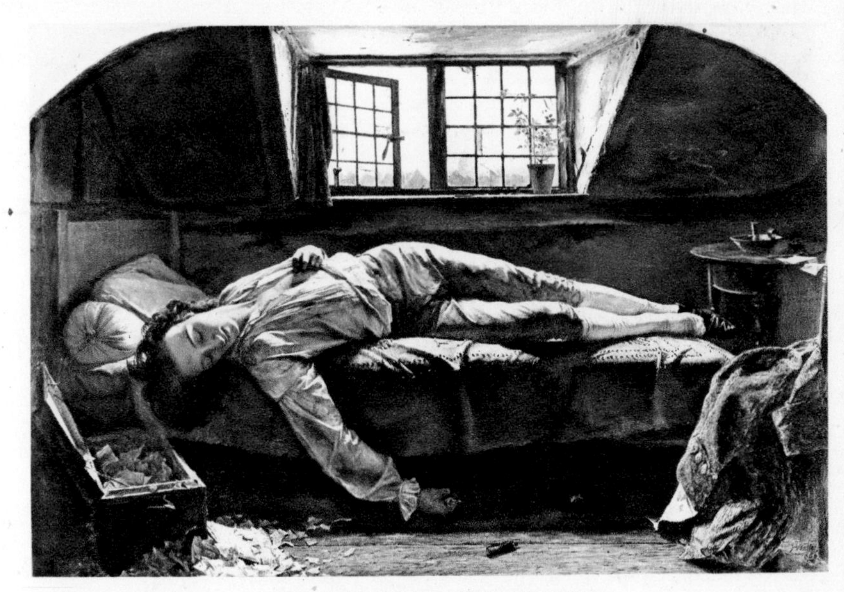

THE DEATH OF CHATTERTON
Oil painting by Henry Wallis, 1856
Tate Gallery, London

OPHELIA
Oil painting by Sir John Millais, 1852 (detail)
Tate Gallery, London

attached to the Army. Wellington was alarmed by the rapid spread of Methodism in the Army. "There are two, if not three, Methodist meetings in this town, of which one is in the Guards," he wrote.

> The men meet in the evening, and sing psalms; and I believe a sergeant (Stephens) now and then gives them a sermon. . . . These meetings likewise prevail in other parts of the Army. In the 9th Regiment there is one, at which two officers attend, Lieutenant —— and Dr. ——; and the Commanding Officer of the Regiment has not been able to prevail upon them to discontinue this practice. Here, and in similar circumstances, we want the assistance of a respectable clergyman. By his personal influence and advice, and by that of true religion, he would moderate the zeal and enthusiasm of these gentlemen, and would prevent their meetings from being mischievous, if he did not prevail upon them to discontinue them entirely. This is the only mode in which, in my opinion, we can touch these meetings. The meeting of soldiers in their cantonments to sing psalms or hear a sermon read by one of their comrades is, in the abstract, perfectly innocent, and it is a better way of spending their time than many others to which they are addicted; but it may become otherwise, and yet, till the abuse has made some progress, the commanding officer would have no knowledge of it, nor could he interfere.

Wellington was writing like a sensible Roman general, perplexed by the spread of the Christian cult among his legionaries, troubled by a feeling that it was even more dangerous than it looked, but unsure wherein precisely lay the peril.

Methodism was a return to ecstasy, the flame from the sky which darts in and out of our national life intermittently; governed by what mysterious laws, who can tell? In the seventeenth century, religion and poetry had both shone with that wild illumination; a kind of St. Elmo's fire flashing around the masts and in the rigging of our Ship of State. The eighteenth century had put out those lawless lights. Good Sense became lord in the two realms where Good Sense is most at fault, and where he finds the natives speaking a tongue he himself can never pick up. In the nineteenth century, ecstasy broke through the frigidities of religion and poetry; but the fetters were docilely assumed again by the end of the century. Wonder—the rapture of salvation—the intoxication of the Divine Love—the white madness of religion—these have largely passed from the lower middle classes, and there now largely prevails a formal cold ethic in the chapels such as would have commended itself to Wellington's "respectable clergymen". But in those early days the believers were transformed by a rhapsodic joy. In some of the hymns of Charles Wesley, sung not only in dingy conventicles but upon the wild heath, there was the child's freshness of ardour, even the breathless rhythms, of Blake's *Songs of Innocence*. As, for an example, in this hymn:

> In the heavenly Lamb
> Thrice happy I am,
> And my heart it doth dance
> At the sound of His name.

And, again:

O the rapturous height
Of the holy delight
Which I felt in the life-giving blood!

The Wesleyan revival was a rebirth of joy in a joyless time. The labouring man, often less prized than horse or ox, and the servant girl, held prisoner in a dark, beetle-haunted basement (like Snagsby's Guster) found themselves borne up and swept away on a flood of everlasting ecstasy whose source lay beyond the stars. The experience of conversion brought an excess and superflux of happiness transcending the power of words—how could it be expressed but by half-smothered cries, sighs, groans and by the pangs of a spirit struggling to break out of the clay? At the camp meetings of the Methodists, humble folk would spring to their feet, stand rigid as in a trance, their faces turned to the sky but with a brightness on their faces not shining from the sky, and then confess and cry out, as under torture, the particulars of their inner miracle. They had been born again. They bathed in the splendour of "a present free and full salvation". They were suffused by God's grace; it streamed through them; flesh, bone, heart, mind, were all irradiated; they were consumed by glory like the small clouds at sunrise. What mattered then the hardness of life's way, the bare feet bleeding from the sharp stones, the cold hearth and the empty belly at the day's end, the pain, the sickness, the broken hopes, the humiliations of the proud spirit, the cruelties of masters, the insolence of the educated and the amused contempt of the powerful? The New Man, as the convert called himself, was a free man, free, free, free, in a sense beyond all earthly freedoms. The load of his sins had rolled off his back; he had been cleansed in the blood of the Lamb from the stains of this life; he was no more the sharer of the world's large guilt. To the great noblemen of the town of Vanity, who caught sight of him from their coaches as he trudged the streets, he might appear a mean, ill-conditioned fellow, without comeliness or grace, his body deformed by toil and low breeding, his understanding narrow, his conversation tedious, his manners coarse. But the real man as he saw himself by his own inner vision was a tall, straight, handsome angel, the son of God, and the brother of Prince Jesus; and he was heir to the fields of Paradise.

These men and women brought to the contemplation of goodness and mercy something warmer than intellectual assent. They felt in their mortal substance the pressure of the Divine Love; it was manifest in the blood-stream and along the nerves; it made the body shake and quiver; the eyes rained tears of joy, and the senses were rapt away. And underneath them were the everlasting arms.

Nor was there lacking a daring luxuriance of imagery that contrasted with the Protestant plainness of worship of these simple hearts. The matter-of-fact, worldly country parsons, often more at home on a horse's back than in a pulpit, were scandalised by the prodigalities, the audacities, the bad taste, the stammering rhetoric of a genuine passion. There was, to their way of thinking, the rankness of Italian extravagance in these enraptured broodings upon the wounds of Christ, in that agonised vision of the precious blood pouring from His side which haunted the minds of these poor village fanatics.

No sacred incantations, no gorgeous rituals induced in them the state of removed contemplation in which the world, and the world's affairs, melted away in dark vapours. It was through words, and words alone, that the hours of exaltation were reached. The language of the hymn and prayers and the readings from Scripture, uttered in a plain daylight that shone through uncoloured windows—on a Sunday morning in an ugly little chapel where a congregation of rustics had met—boughs brushing against the panes and satirical cawings of the rooks audible from outside—it was this language that did service for swinging censers, the seven candlesticks, the paintings of the Holy Family and the Descent from the Cross, the music of a Mass by Vittoria, the ringing of the bell, and the awful moment of the Elevation of the Host. As the conventions of respectability and education took hold upon these sectaries, the incandescence of their early ecstasies died away. In the later years of the century sleek, comfortable men who had done well in trade and had absorbed the standards of the upper classes discouraged the use in prayers of the lovesick images of *The Song of Songs* and tried to keep out of the hymnal the hymns of fire and blood. Modern taste, replacing religion by religiosity, turned against an ardour as innocent and candid as this:

> There is a fountain filled with blood
> Drawn from Immanuel's veins;
> And sinners plunged beneath that flood,
> Lose all their guilty stains.

When frankness of passion dies out in religion what remains but a cold propriety? The embarrassing nakedness of the soul is covered up in the wool and flannel of ethical platitude. For what is religion if, like poetry, it is not a wild, lawless thing?

The appearance of ecstasy in low life nearly always creates uneasiness among the educated classes. Nobody can tell what havoc may be wrought in polite society by a God-intoxicated man from the lower orders. The Duchess of Buckingham wrote to Selina, Countess of Huntingdon:

> I thank your ladyship for the information concerning the Methodist preachers; their doctrines are most repulsive, and strongly tinctured with impertinence and disrespect towards their superiors, in perpetually endeavouring to level all ranks and do away with all distinctions. It is monstrous to be told you have a heart as sinful as the common wretches that crawl on the earth; and I cannot but wonder that your ladyship should relish any sentiments so much at variance with high rank and good breeding.
>
> (From G. W. E. Russell, *Collections and Recollections.*)

The Nonconformist sects grew in political vigour through the middle years of the century, after the striking-off of their civil disabilities. The sober, grey weather of that age suited them. Miall's powerful journal *The Nonconformist* took as its motto "The Dissidence of Dissent and the Protestantism of the Protestant Churches", an aggressive motto that unduly irritated Matthew Arnold.

Such communities as the Congregationalists and the Baptists who, steadfast under persecution, had kept in their souls the stubborn iron of Cromwell's England, now felt a new access of power. The declaration of faith, adopted when the Congregational Union was set up in 1833, has a note characteristic of those times:

> It is not intended that the following statement should be put forth with any authority, or as a standard to which assent should be required. Disallowing the utility of creeds and articles of religion as a bond of union, and protesting against subscription to any human formularies as a term of communion, Congregationalists are yet willing to declare, for general information, what is commonly believed among them, reserving to every one the most perfect liberty of conscience.

The ends sought by this union were not only the strengthening of a link among highly independent brothers but a help "in procuring perfect religious equality for all British subjects and *in promoting reforms bearing on their moral and social condition*". The Baptists, insisting on the spiritual equality of all their members, the humblest and the richest, the stupidest and the cleverest, and on the right of each of their communities to order its own affairs, gave something of their own to nineteenth-century notions of democracy.

In the eighteenth century, the great breach in Methodism had been between those who thought men were either damned or saved before they were born, and those who believed they had a very good chance to save themselves in this life. But in the nineteenth century the splits were nearly all brought about through the clamour of the laymen for more power and authority in their chapels. Those who were crusty individualists in religion, who set such store on the sacredness of the conscience, were not likely to be toadies to authority in politics. They were hardly of a mind to bob and scrape to privilege because it was of old standing. The cry of "One Man, One Vote", heard on the moors and in the workshops, was echoed in the chapels. The self-reliant lay preacher who felt within him grace abounding, and was sure that he was closer to God than any priest or parson, also made a highly self-reliant mechanic; sometimes he rose in the world and became a tradesman or small manufacturer; then he would often provide satisfying religious reasons to bolster up the teachings of the Manchester School. The great Wesley, himself as good a Tory as Dr. Johnson, proved in turn an inspiration to *laissez-faire* Liberalism, to the Radical revolt and to Trade Unionism.

The Quakers, then as now, were a community small in numbers, but

"THE EMPTY PURSE": STALL AT THE ST. BRIDE'S ANNUAL FAIR
Oil painting by James Collinson, *c.* 1857
Tate Gallery, London

EVENING AFTER THE HUNT
Water-colour by Louis Eugène Lami, 1850
Victoria and Albert Museum, London

A BRIGHT LITTLE DINING-ROOM
Water-colour drawing by George Cruikshank for "The Bottle", 1847
Victoria and Albert Museum, London

powerful by the quality of their virtues; they were withdrawn from the world, waiting in quietness upon the inner light. Yet it was the Quakers who made the first stir against the wickedness of the slave trade. They pursued their kindly offices by stealth. By their example they sought to teach philanthropists the virtue of modesty and reformers the wisdom of restraint. Philanthropists and reformers were equally poor pupils.

We cannot escape our ancestors. The influences of these bygone generations of devotees and sectaries are apparent in a hundred ways in English life today. Names have changed, loyalties have withered away, the churches and chapels have lost much of their power, but the old habit of applying moral touchstones to political issues remains. Most Britons have in their veins the blood of some evangelical great-grandfather, haunted by the sins of the world, or some contumacious Baptist who shook his fist at my Lord Bishop's coat of arms, or some ecstatic Methodist who had walked apart with God on the cliffs of Cornwall. The Christian Socialist of Charles Kingsley's day, the High Anglican of Gladstone's persuasion, the Welsh Calvinist and the Shorter Catechist, they are visible —shadowy but constant figures—behind the veils of the present. In following the movements of our times it is of recurring interest to see how men and women who have broken with the beliefs of their fathers, and regard all religions as childish superstitions, yet speak and act in the old terms and display the old passions and prejudices, sometimes the old crochets. Nor has the foreign accusation of hypocrisy been silenced; this is a humiliation to some, a comfort to others; and at least an assurance of continuity.

Morality and religion are not the same thing, although the Victorians came in the end to believe that they are. The hungers of man's soul are not to be stayed by an ethical code. Yet in the highly practical business of survival an ethical code is of considerable value to a nation. On the whole it has proved so to the British.

The influence of the Evangelical and Puritan revival upon Victorian culture was strongly marked. In his preface to *A Collection of Hymns for Use of the People called Methodists*, John Wesley had written, "That which is of infinitely more moment than the Spirit of Poetry is the Spirit of Piety. . . . When Poetry thus keeps its place, as the handmaid of Piety, it shall attain not a poor perishable wreath but a crown that fadeth not away." That was a definition very different from Wordsworth's, "Poetry is the breath and finer spirit of all knowledge; it is the impassioned expression which is in the countenance of all science." Shelley regarded the poets as the unacknowledged legislators of the world; Wesley commanded that the Muse should wear the mob cap of Selina, Countess of Huntingdon. That poetry, that indeed all the arts should serve as the handmaids to religion and ethics, was commonly accepted in the nineteenth century. I cannot recall any Victorian artist of substance—at least of the middle period of the century—who would have argued against that assumption. We in our day, who have seen the artist humbly accept the role of a propagandist of political theory, should not find it hard to comprehend the pressure of the all-surrounding atmosphere of Victorian ethics upon writers, painters and musicians. Moral values were placed above artistic ones; the virtuous was preferred to the beautiful; the didactic supplanted the romantic. Across the Channel, Jules Lemaître pointed out that the differences between English and French literature in the nineteenth century were rooted in the deepest differences of race, in the essential Protestantism of the one, and the essential Catholicism of the other. In France, said Lemaître, there was a religious, or rather ecclesiastical, literature with which only the devout were acquainted; and there was a profane, *laic* literature, which everybody read, a literature that was quite free from "reflections on the inner nature of souls, moral curiosity, and religious sentiment". The Protestant mind, even when it had freed itself from every variant of orthodoxy as expressed by a score of sects, remained the Protestant mind. For, so argued Lemaître, to abandon, after unrestricted examination, a religion of which unrestricted examination is an inherent attribute, is not properly speaking to abandon it at all. "Among Protestant peoples, where the faithful soul depends only upon his conscience, and allows no intermediary between himself and God, the universal habits of thought and discussion which result, cause a mingling of religious sentiment and anxiety in all their literature—even profane—and unbelievers retain at least the manner and tone of believers."

Carlyle was a prophet, an Elijah. Ruskin was his Elisha. "The Religious Teaching of Tennyson" became the subject of many a sermon by popular preachers. So did "The Moral Influence of Robert Browning". We have already seen how the Evangelicals and Nonconformists clasped Dickens to their bosoms. As for Thackeray, he was an incorrigible preacher, and his favourite text was *Vanity of vanities, all is vanity*. Of all the writers of that age none had a greater moral displacement, none was more deeply reverenced as an ethical teacher than George Eliot. This was all the more remarkable in that she had rejected faith in God and had defied conventional morality. But who dared apply the name of Sin to her austere adultery with George Henry Lewes, and who could charge with impiety the lady who was the incarnation of Duty, stern daughter of the voice of God? The vision rises of F. W. H. Myers walking with her in the garden of Trinity on that evening "of rainy May": she, "taking as her text the three words which had been used so often as the inspiring trumpet-call of men—the words God, Immortality, Duty—pronounced with terrible earnestness how inconceivable was the first, how unbelievable the second, and yet how peremptory and absolute the third. . . . I listened and night fell: her grave, majestic countenance turned towards me like a sibyl's in the gloom."

George Eliot is as concerned as any theologian with the consequences of human action. The characters in her didactic novels are weighed down by a sense of duty and responsibility. "We cannot remain passive and inert," they seem to say, "for that in itself is a state of sin. We exist, therefore we must act. Yet action can never take place in emptiness. Whatever we do, however light the word, however trivial the deed, it may touch off an appalling train of consequences. The act—that is at once the necessity, the snare and the crushing burden."

The introspection, the constant examination of the conscience and the absorption in scruples that are displayed by George Eliot's characters represent that Protestant tradition of writing which Lemaitre found puzzling and distasteful. The weight of sin, the burden of obligation and the oppression of guilt overshadow all kindly and happy human relationships. They give a desperate poignancy to the brief loves of men and women and to the smile on a child's face.

CHAPTER TWO

SUNDAY AT HOME

Long were the Sunday afternoons of summer in the country—in the hours after tea, long ago—the minutes passing slow as hours to the child sprawling in discomfort on the horsehair sofa; *The Lamplighter* unopened on his knees; the prickles on the horsehair rasping his legs, the lace antimacassar's knots and nodules chafing his neck, his small stomach tight and round from Sunday's high feeding, and his small soul loaded with the doom looking down on him from the walls—the steel engravings, stern and grim, of the Massacre of the Innocents, of the Sack of Jerusalem and of Resurrection Morning, with graves yawning, and the sun turned to blood, and a myriad wretched spectres rising in their cerements and crying, "Oh that the hills would cover us!"

Not a sound in the house except the intermittent buzz and ping of a flying beetle that has lost his way. The chimes of the parlour clock have been muffled on this holy day. The striped hood has been drawn over the cage of Joey the parrot, his whistling being unseemly on such a day, and the bird sits huddled in a melancholy decline in a sickly twilight of yellow and red. A button dangles by a thread from the child's coat, it has irked grandmamma a great deal, she cannot keep her eyes from it, her fingers itch for her sewing basket, but the day must not be profaned by needle and thimble. All playthings are locked away, all games forbidden, all light thoughts censored. If the contemplation of the infinite mercy and goodness of God is beyond the range of that little brain, then that little brain must content itself with a blank respectful nothingness, a child's Nirvana. The one concession to the frailties of an infant mind is the production by grandmamma after tea of two or three such improving books as *The Fairchild Family*, Dean Farrar's *Eric, or Little by Little* and *The Wide Wide World*. The book-case which contains the Waverley Novels, Captain Marryat's *Masterman Ready* and Lever's *Charles O'Malley* is locked—and the key is in grandmamma's reticule that hangs from her waist.

No sound in the house—but it is alive with smells and scents and *tastes*. The heat of the summer afternoon in the house, the pressure of those long, sultry, silent hours, squeezes and wrings the inmost savour, the stuffy secrets from the thick curtains, the horsehair sofa and the plump cushions, from all fabrics and dyes. The musty brown smell of velvet and velveteen, an *underground* smell, is the same smell that the earth yielded when one had dug up, out of theological curiosity, the tiny corpse of a blackbird, buried on the day before, under the wet autumn leaves, with the aid of the Book of Common Prayer. Lace gives up a bright smell from its starch and soap—smelling fragrantly like grandmamma's brew of elderberry tea—a very good smell, says she, for the chest, that part of a boy which was of constant concern to Victorian grandmammas. When the kitchen door furtively creaks, there steals through the house the most heavenly perfumes, heightened in the voluptuous heat of the silent summer afternoon almost to the point of torture, redolences of roast beef and an intoxicating gust of cherry pie. Not *all* the happiness of sensual man is denied him on this penitential day. There is never fasting. Through the windows giving on the garden, through those Venetian blinds that, half-opened, show dazzling bands of azure and green, comes the breath of heliotrope, of stocks and cloves. In that soundless atmosphere the perfumes and aromas seem to take on a triple pungency, or it may be that in the suspension of the other senses all the pleasures of consciousness are pressed together in the sense of smell. Speech is sealed, song is sealed, there is nothing that may be touched, but the redolences and scents of the earth float and unfold themselves upon the motionless air, immoderate and uncontrollable. It is they alone that on this day of stern restraints carry across the silent land and into all quiet houses with drawn blinds, the rebel word of beauty—beauty, that old disturber of the peace—beauty with her train of impossible longings and foolish regrets and wicked discontents. The house of the senses, the fortress of the Victorian Puritans, was never safe, so long as there was one cranny through which a whiff of heliotrope or clove might creep. So potent are these various scents and smells, moving like spirits through the silence, that in the after-years the boy, having become a man, will suddenly catch the exhalation of horse-hair or velvet in an old house, then find the world dissolving around him, and he will be back again, lost, friendless, half-happy, half-unhappy, half-dreaming, half-revolting, in that unending Sabbath with grandmamma.

The boy turns his eyes from the awful lightnings and earthquakes of the Apocalypse to the blue, the green and the golden wash of the late summer afternoon that streams in through the interstices of the blinds. Over the meadows is spread the cloth of gold of king-cups and buttercups. Out of doors nothing stirs in the languorous heat. The cattle are sheltering from the sun under the pavilions of the oaks or are cooling their flanks in the little stream, under the shadow of the willows. Over all the land lies the spell of a sleepy peace and quietness. "I turn to thee as some green afternoon turns towards sunset and is loth to die." There is no wheel to stir up white dust in the lanes, and the wild rose and the honeysuckle breathe their unvexed enchantments, out of time, out of space, out of people. Not a cart rattles. The monstrous motor-car has still to be thought of. The far-off hills take on peacock colours as the sun slants west. Those are the Delectable Mountains where the happy shepherds, whom God loves, look after their sheep. And there, over there, says grandmamma, is the land of Beulah, the shining land, where pain is stilled, and losses mended, and griefs assuaged, the land of everlasting summer afternoon, no more than two steps this side of Paradise. But when one is as young as that one has no broken things to mend, no rest to woo; one longs for freedom and fights, for pride and money, for Famagusta, and the cascading seas off Valparaiso.

The child waits and waits for the spell of silence to be broken at last by the tinkling of the cracked bell of the little church whose spire, snub and black like an old witch's hat, peeps above a row of poplars whose volatile, silvery leaves for once hang in dead stillness in this breathless late afternoon. Then on the paths across the drowsy fields appear the village families going to church, and the landscape takes on again the warmth, the curiosity and the animated absurdity of humanity. They walk with hushed decorum. They live in a world in which on one day of the week a dead man is always lying upstairs, a great-grandfather's corpse lying in a silver-plated coffin somewhere up there in the ineffable azure. They are dressed in their Sunday best; such decent black habit as becomes a funeral. How sleek the men's hair, and the cowlick under the awkward hard hat; how snowy the pinafores of the children. How stiff they look, like family portraits in a daguerreotype.

Over them all, and over all the smiling, sleepy land, lies the spell of the great prohibition. It is the Sabbath day and Victoria is Queen.

The British Sunday that appalled such visitors from across the Channel as Heine and Taine, and such native sons as Dickens and Thackeray, was one notable consequence of the religious revival of the late eighteenth and early nineteenth century. The Evangelicals and their Dissenting allies were harsh Sabbatarians. They set up the Society for the Better Observance of the Lord's Day; under its pressure governments framed, and magistrates enforced, the severest ordinances. They sought to match in rigour the repression which marked the rule of those implacable Presbyterians who had so long served the Lord across the Border. The easygoing Sabbath ways of the Georgians were put down with a hard hand: dancings, debauches, cock-fighting, prize-fighting, all public worship of Bacchus and Venus. Families were imprisoned in their homes, as soldiers are confined to barracks, with a dispensation for church-going. In the country it was a tolerable tyranny, for no Society for Better Observance of Sunday can stop thrushes from fluting, or censor the fragrance of the honeysuckle; and it is very pleasant to be forced to do nothing in the country. But in the cities, in the industrial centres, the Victorian Sabbath was purgatorial.

"It was a Sunday evening in London, gloomy, close and stale." So opens that chapter in *Little Dorrit* which brings back the desolation of all urban Sabbaths.

> Maddening church bells of all degrees of dissonance, sharp and flat, cracked and clear, fast and slow, made the brick-and-mortar echoes hideous. Melancholy streets in a penitential garb of soot, steeped the souls of the people who were condemned to look at them out of windows, in dire despondency. In every thoroughfare, up almost every alley, and down every turning, some doleful bell was throbbing, jerking, tolling, as if the Plague were in the city and the dead-carts were going round. Everything was bolted and barred that could by possibility furnish relief to an over-worked people. No pictures, no unfamiliar animals, no natural or artificial wonders of the ancient world—all *taboo* with that enlightened strictness, that the ugly South Sea gods in the British Museum might have supposed themselves at home again. Nothing to see but streets, streets, streets. Nothing to breathe but streets, streets, streets.

To Arthur Clennam, come home from abroad, the dismal tolling of the bells revived an endless chain of such Sundays.

> There was the dreary Sunday of his childhood, when he sat with his hands before him, scared out of his senses by a horrible tract which commenced business with the poor child by asking him in its title, why he was going to Perdition?—a piece of curiosity that he really in a frock and drawers was not in a condition to satisfy—and which, for the further attraction of his infant mind, had a parenthesis in every other line with some such hiccupping reference as 2 Ep. Thess. c. iii, v. 6 & 7. There was the sleepy Sunday of his boyhood, when, like a military deserter, he was marched to chapel by a picquet of teachers three times a day, morally handcuffed to another boy, and when he would willingly have bartered two meals of indigestible sermon for another ounce or two of inferior mutton at his scanty dinner in the flesh. There was the interminable Sunday of his nonage; when his mother, stern of face and unrelenting of heart, would sit all day behind the Bible—bound, like her own construction of it, in the hardest, barest and straitest of boards, with one dinted ornament on the cover like the drag of a chain, and a wrathful sprinkling of red upon the edges of the leaves—as if it, of all books! were a fortification against sweetness of temper, natural affection, and gentle intercourse. There was the resentful Sunday of a little later, when he sat glowering and glooming through the tardy length of the day, with a sullen sense of injury in his heart, and no more real knowledge of the beneficent history of the New Testament than if he had been bred among idolaters. There was a legion of Sundays, all days of unserviceable bitterness and mortification, slowly passing before him.

We all remember the famous phrase about the Puritans putting down bear-baiting not because of the pain it gave the bear but because of the pleasure it gave the spectators. Did the Sabbatarians of the nineteenth century enjoy the thought of the unhappiness they caused or were they moved by some more benevolent purpose? Reading the chronicles of that age, one sometimes suspects that they were unwitting instruments of the instinct of race preservation. Was the *taboo* set up in order to save the tribe from being worked to death? In the early years of the century there were no more active opponents of the Sabbatarians than a number of the manufacturers in the North of England and Midlands. They complained that "through religious prejudice" a day's work was being lost every week. How many tons of coal, how many yards of cotton, how many ingots of steel, how many tin trays and Staffordshire mugs, and how many zeroes on the balance sheets, were lost through pandering to the superstition of these psalm-singing humbugs? Protestantism was coming into conflict with the profit motive to which it had given a theological sanction. In answering these arguments the Evangelicals made a mean defence of a decent position. Instead of replying that the working man had earned the seventh day's rest by his exhausting work on the other six, they made a sneaking, sanctimonious plea that it would be better in the long run for the masters to be sure that they had God-fearing workmen, because such creatures would be docile, and could be trusted not to burn down the mills and cut their masters' throats. It was by such methods that the Victorians justly acquired their reputation for hypocrisy. The Evangelicals might so easily have pointed to the slaves of the factories stretching out their worn bodies in a coma of grateful exhaustion on a Sunday and have said: "That, gentlemen, is our case."

Crankiness, that endearing British quality, marked the Sabbatarians. What absurdity could be more comical than the behaviour of William Wilberforce when he learned that Louis XVIII, the poor gouty old man who had been kept from his kingdom so long, had taken coach out of London one Sunday to reclaim the throne of St. Louis. Had he but waited for peep of day on Monday Wilberforce would have cried "Vive le Roi!" with the best of them. But to travel on Sunday, even to win back France to Christian order, to legitimacy, to rightful authority—ideals that Wilberforce cherished—that was unforgivable. "What ingratitude," cried Wilberforce, "and without temptation. What folly! Is this the Roman Catholic religion? Is it philosophical enlargement of mind? . . . How sad that none should have the courage to tell them. O shame, shame! Forgive, O Lord, and punish not our land for this ingratitude and cowardice." It struck none of Wilberforce's friends that it would be a little unreasonable of God to wreak vengeance on *Britain* because the French king had broken the Sabbath on its soil. The Evangelical Deity was kind and generous in big things, but capricious in small ones.

The Sabbatarians suffered their rebuffs. On one Sunday in 1849 Disraeli, after attending divine service, left Hughenden by train to attend political affairs of moment in town. He received a solemn admonition from the Vicar to set a better example to his "poorer and less intellectual neighbours". Disraeli replied that public circumstances of urgency had compelled him to travel, then went on to crush the Vicar in these terms: "Had you made any temperate inquiry, you might perhaps have ascertained that it is not my habit to travel on Sunday, and I would venture also to observe that my object in attending Divine Service is not merely or principally to set an example to others. The duties of a spiritual pastor should be fulfilled without regard of persons, but those duties are often of a delicate nature, and it is therefore desirable that they should fall to the lot of those who act with reflection and not in a hasty and

PLATE 23

DERBY DAY

A detail from the oil painting by William Powell Frith, 1858

National Gallery, London

"APRIL LOVE"
Oil painting by Arthur Hughes

"LOVE'S MISSIVE"
Water-colour by William Henry Hunt

"RIPE STRAWBERRIES!"
Water-colour by William M. Craig
for his "London Cries", 1804

"THE SONG OF THE SHIRT"
Steel engraving by G. Finden
after Doré

precipitate spirit." That Vicar shortly afterwards left the neighbourhood.

The Sabbatarians were beaten in their efforts to stop the running of trains on Sundays. In this they met the resistance of a sentiment as powerful as their own—that faith in the moral mission of railways which I have already touched upon. To the middle Victorians God was plainly on the side of the big locomotives. Mechanical Progress was a clear fulfilment of the purpose of the ages. So the Bishop of London, who was an old-fashioned fellow with the rust of the coaching times upon him, was driven back on that last desperate recourse of cornered men—statistics. In his great, gloomy palace at Fulham his Lordship would sit analysing the accident returns in a fever of happy expectation. It must, it *must* turn out that more trains went off the rails on Sundays—that more travellers were killed and maimed on that day through their impious flouting of God's law.

The Bishop and his friends had more success in stopping the opening of museums, picture galleries and zoological gardens on Sundays. It was sad to find the gentle, kind-hearted Shaftesbury on the side of those zealots who thought it a sin that the naked beauty of the gods of Greece should be beheld by mortals on the Sabbath, or that the eyes of the people should be raised from the grime and the mud in which they lived to the pure celestial gold of Fra Angelico. It might even have been that some blind, hobbled souls in our big cities would have been lifted out of their darkness for a little space by the playing of *The Pastoral Symphony*, by a scratch band in the Mechanics' Institute, or by hearing even an indifferent actor speak Romeo's farewell:

> Thou art not conquered; beauty's ensign yet
> Is crimson in thy lips and in thy cheeks,
> And death's pale flag is not advanced there.

No, there was no chance for that. The virtuous forbade. If the common people would not spend the Sabbath in rest, meditation and going to church, then it was better that they should be driven to the gin palace and worse places than that Shakespeare and Beethoven should corrupt them.

Thackeray made one excursion into politics. In the General Election of 1857 he was candidate for Oxford City, standing against Edward Cardwell, he who afterwards became the great War Minister. Thackeray drew upon himself all the anger of the Sabbatarians. A broadsheet of theirs accused him of saying at the Mitre Hotel on July 9th, 1857, "I would not only open the Crystal Palace, the British Museum and the National Gallery, but I would go further, and open the CONCERT ROOMS and THEATRES on Sundays." Thackeray's answer to this, in a speech to the Oxford electors, suggests how hard pressed he was:

I never spoke or thought of opening Theatres on Sunday—I would try to multiply the means of procuring peace and harmless pleasure for the people on that day, and know that in many Theatrical Pieces there are jests, and allusions, and situations ill-fitted indeed to any, but especially to the Sacred Day. I would consent to and encourage good Band-Music, which has been played before our Sovereigns for a hundred years past; but would object to Songs, for the same reason that renders me averse to Plays—because Songs may be made vehicles for jokes and buffoonery, which, on such a day, might justly shock the sense of religious persons. And I believe the relaxation of the present system would make many people friendly to the Clergy whom they now suppose to be hostile to their honest pleasures; would be a means of happiness and union amongst the families of the Poor; and ought not to offend the feelings of any Christian man.

Thackeray lost the election.

CHAPTER THREE

THE ROAD TO ROME

There was the Oxford Movement. That is all a part of bygone fears, hopes, disillusions—dead embers now. Yet there are many middle-aged men and women reared in Evangelical households for whom the name of Oxford must still glow with an angry light. They will hear again an anxious whisper, "Children, be careful not to cross Father today; he is in a great taking about the Puseyites." The sinister words "Popery" and "Ritualism" vibrate once more on the air, and with them there comes again a childhood shudder at the thought of heretics burning at Smithfield, among them Father. Cartoons in the Evangelical papers of wolves in sheep's clothing rise up before the inner eye—monkish wolves flinging off their false wool in the middle of the fold and grabbing plump little Protestant lambs. For many men and women the crossing-over of John Henry Newman to Rome was the spiritual crisis of their own lives. J. A. Spender said that so late as the middle of the First World War—amid all those miseries and horrors—his father was still "deploring the secession of Newman and anxiously considering the point at which he took the wrong road". Many Victorians went on doing that until the end of their days. Keble's Assize Sermon on National Apostasy which set off the whole train of the Oxford Movement was preached at St. Mary's in 1833. A reader coming to Keble's sermon for the first time might well wonder why so reasonable a statement of an understandable position made so great a noise in the world, nor would he be much wiser after burying himself in the *Tracts for the Times*, which ran from 1833 to 1841, took up Keble's themes, and played skilful variations on them. But the young reader's father might, on seeing the bound numbers of the *Tracts*, remember a home of strict piety in which they shared the fascination of the dangerous with—of all unlikely companions, but it *could* be so in those days—Swinburne's *Poems and Ballads*. Across this gulf of time, it might appear to a moderate mind that if devout young Churchmen believed that their Church was of divine origin they could not but be moved to their depths by seeing it treated as though it were a docile department of State. Even to many who did not like the Romish ways of these young men it was odious that an old rake of a Prime Minister should make a Bishop as he made a Governor of Mauritius—that is, as awarding a prize to a sound party man—or from an English gentleman's family feelings that Uncle Harry should never be left to starve.

"The Apostolic Succession and the Holy Catholic Church were principles of action in the minds of our predecessors of the 17th century"; and it was to the revival of these principles that the Tractarians dedicated themselves. "If the trumpet gives an uncertain sound, who shall prepare himself to the battle?" was inscribed on the title page of Tract Number One—*Thoughts on the Ministerial Commission, respectfully addressed to the Clergy*—written by the master hand of Newman. These trumpets of the youthful trumpeters were shrill; they rang through drowsy cloisters, and among cobwebby studies; they roused dead souls to life; the echoes lasted long.

Nothing, one supposes, would be thought more insulting to Tractarians and Methodists alike than to suggest a resemblance between them. Each entertained a contempt for the other, strong even for those times, their religious differences being sharpened by social ones. Even in our more easygoing age, a comparison is likely to be taken amiss, but to an uncommitted mind, is it so far-fetched? Both of them were in their separate ways *enthusiasts*. Both took up arms against a mocking, pagan system under which the civil power called upon the Augurs to support it, and worked the Oracles to soothe the public mind. Both were hungry for ecstasy, the flame that shone not in the Erastian Church. Those altars were cold. Who might ever discern a flash of angels' wings in Barchester Cathedral? Who was ever brought closer to celestial matters by the attentions of such a cleric as Jane Austen's Mr. Collins? Of these two communities of spiritual starvelings, one found their happiness and their peace by discovering God's abounding grace within them. The other rested all upon the supernatural authority of the Church and in the restoring of the majesty of its sacraments; through its ancient symbols they comprehended those mysteries that are beyond the grasp of logic, ethics and the senses.

At the time the Oxford Movement began, the High Church itself could not be called ritualistic. Its force was most apparent in the realm of political ideas. It provided a philosophy for High Toryism, it invested the person of the King in a sacred aura. The Oxford Movement must always attract the sympathy of those undogmatic characters who think of religion, as of music and poetry, as carrying us above this world of political and economic struggle.

There is more than one road to ecstasy. Ecstasy may descend upon the solitary man walking across a moor in a December twilight—a sky of lead above him—no birds calling—no companionable signs of life to cheer him—the single sound he hears the creaking of the wind in the scrub—a vast, chill, sombre loneliness spreading around him. Then this friendless man is suddenly possessed by an overwhelming sense of the love of God. Through the cope of lead rain down burning arrows. The landscape is all transfigured, the air full of light, and the rank grasses shine like wires of

JOHN HENRY NEWMAN
Sketch by Richard Doyle
British Museum

silver. The solitary goes on his way shouting and singing, for, if he could not cry out, the joy inside him would split his heart. Such a rapture may come without any intervening agency. But it betokens a very limited acquaintance with the religious experiences of our fellows not to acknowledge that other state of ecstasy achieved by the one who kneels before the illuminated altar, his eyes half-blinded, his whole being crushed down with awe. Then he is seized with a consciousness of a world of light beyond the ring of these poor shadows. He is aware of a communion of presences gathering in cloud on cloud, wings of azure and vermeil and wings of golden grain, presences like Milton's squadrons of angels, soaring up in endless flights from the chimneys of the city to the threshold of Heaven, and, in their numberless hosts and assemblies, undiminished in the vistas of Time. The Bride of Christ has dressed herself in fairest raiment, the mystic marriage is celebrated. For this rapt believer, though the church he kneels in be poor and dingy and set in a slum, it is now filled with a glory almost insupportable. The roof has melted away and shafts and beams of radiance more dazzling than the sun descend upon him. He is raised out of himself, he is drawn upwards into that brightness streaming from the throne. The angels, saints, martyrs and apostles have become to him presences far more substantial than the men and women who kneel beside him, and through this communion he attains the glory of the height.

The vivid differences between the classes which gave such subtle colourings, such interplay of light and shade, such a mixture of comic and ironic flavours to the Victorian period, affected its religious life. People chose their faith according to their places in the caste system.

The Methodist labourer of 1840 who, in a tiny chapel in a Dorset village, sang "Jesu, lover of my soul" and, in doing so, felt all earthly griefs assuaged, all losses recompensed—what might he have in common with the young gentlemen of good families who at Oxford sat at the feet of Pusey and idolised Newman? He had gone to school with Bunyan and Foxe; and could he have talked with those young men at Oxford he would have been in some doubt as to whether they were the children of Giant Pope or Giant Pagan. There could have been no proposal less inviting to the peasantry and the lower middle classes than that they should have taken part in any kind of *Oxford* Movement, Oxford being at that time a by-word of class privilege and religious discrimination. To the Dissenters, the Tractarian movement was not only a Papist revival, it was in large part a gentleman's revival; its leaders combined the haughtiness of caste with the arrogance of dogma. It is a hard truth to learn that not only out of the mouths of peasants and workmen, but out of the mouths of the upper classes may come wisdom and enlightenment.

This was a revival that moved even its enemies, in their own despite. There was a quickening of life throughout the whole body of the Church of England in the forties and fifties. The hunting parsons, the three-bottle parsons of the eighteenth century, the chaplains who ranked a little lower than the butlers in the great mansions, some of them being treated as poor zanies and clowns, could no longer be drawn as truly representative characters, even by such Radical satirists of the Establishment as Douglas Jerrold. The Church, to do it justice, showed that power to keep alive by moving with the times, and by learning from its critics, that marked other old English institutions. It profited from those two very different revolutions of faith, the Evangelical and the Ritualist. Gladstone said truly that the Ritualists had carried forward the enlightenment begun by the Evangelicals. The Ritualists, he thought, had not paid sufficient respect to the value of man's personal intuition of God, and the Evangelicals had been blind to tradition. The Church in the fifties shook off its sloth, and, being awake, its soul was ever after full of conflict; but the stress and divisions were themselves proofs of life. None who troubles to look into the history of our fathers' time can doubt the vigour of the Church of England in the second half of the last century, nor fail to be struck by the quality of the talents it attracted to its service.

Graham Wallas complained once that accounts of the religious movements of the nineteenth century were either written out of glum sectarian prejudice or were "chatter about Newman". The first is unreadable, but Newman is unavoidable because he wrote so well, and is so touching and lonely a figure amid the drums and banners of the Victorian pageant. The truth is that controversy survives its generation only through some insinuating grace of style, through the accents of a voice so winning that men will heed it for its own sake when the brawling of faction is stilled. Today it is still possible to hear talk for or against Dr. Pusey in some churches—but who, outside High Church scholars, ever turns the pages of the *Literary Remains of Richard Hurrell Froude*, that amiable young zealot who said that the best thing he knew about Archbishop Cranmer was that he burned well (an emanation of Christian charity much admired by the fine gallants of the Movement)? Keble's hymns, that are like gentle snowdrops of the faith, are still cherished. But what of Bowden, Perceval, Isaac Williams and W. G. Ward—"Ideal" Ward, "most generous of all Ultramontanes"? The best in this kind are but shadows. No longer do Parliamentary bulldogs growl and show their teeth over altar lights, the vestments of priests, the Reserved Sacrament or the Eastward position. It is many years since *The Times* has edified us by a leading article against restoring the images of saints in a village church. No Cabinet of our age has met to consider prosecuting Anglican clergymen for reviving the service of the Mass or for hearing confessions. The tides of the world have rolled on. In the period we live in now the religious quarrels of the nineteenth century appear as far away as that dismal long-ago dispute of the Eastern Church as to how many fingers should be outstretched in the benediction.

Of all dead books that cumber the shelves none gather thicker dust than volumes of religious contention—but Newman's *Apologia* lives, and will, I think, live a great while. It is a considerable advantage to a saint to possess charm, and a style that winds itself into our thoughts like music is one of the most uncommon gifts that God bestows upon his theologians. Most readers who have a taste for the fine things of the English tradition will surrender to the spell of Newman's patrician irony. In the clear amber of his writings he has preserved midges and flies that once had fretted him. He was subtle, and he was often merciless. Poor Charles Kingsley, for example, would have taken a much higher place in modern repute if he had not been so unlucky as to engage himself in a controversy with Newman that involved Newman's honour and truthfulness. We avert our eyes from the spectacle of Kingsley, the honest fellow blundering to his doom. This fine Catholic gentleman raises his eyebrows, utters half a dozen cool, ironical words, and our hearty Protestant hero is shown to be a bounder. "Away with you, Mr. Kingsley, and fly into space", writes Newman on an early page of the *Apologia* and one has the image of a coarse, red-faced, blustering Anglican clergyman, in his dog-collar and stuffy black clothes, being shot off the earth altogether, sent somersaulting for eternity through a night of scornful stars. It is an unjust fate for the father of Christian Socialism, for so good and kind a man as Kingsley; but what can be done against the pitiless magic of a master?

The attaching power of Newman's personality gave a painful and thrilling interest to his going over to Rome. The Oxford Movement had begun with the declaration that nothing but the faithful preaching of the neglected doctrines of the Anglican divines of the seventeenth century would "repress the extension of Popery". And then the Movement ended in the "acceptance of Popery" by its most renowned and attractive figure. The abandonment of a cause by a leader who has won his followers as much by the graces of his personality as by the persuasiveness of his arguments is bewildering to those who have loved him. They can never believe it to be quite true. What could have broken that destined union of souls? They puzzled, they grieved, and they re-enacted all the scenes in the tragedy in their minds, over and again, wondering if it could have been averted had somebody at this point behaved differently; had Pusey spoken at one moment, or had Ward held his peace at another. And, as with a well-beloved prodigal, those who could never think ill of him were always of a mind to lay the blame upon the wiles of the dark Italian enchantress. How strong must have been the spell that ensnared so gentle a knight! The fear of Rome was greatly spread by Newman's fate.

Newman lived until 1890. To the end the bulk of his contemporaries remained puzzled by him. In the Victorian newspapers and Reviews you may find endless conjecturings as to why so fine an intellect could accept the notion of paying for Indulgences or could believe that miracles were wrought by the bones of a saint. These matters were thought to be far more important than the subtleties of *The Grammar of Assent* which Newman published in 1870 and in which he treats of the "illative sense", that intuition, delicate but profound, which leads to certainty where logic fails us. In this book he wrote as a poet, and usually those who sit attentive for the hard crusts of theology are disappointed when they are given the ambrosia of poetry. His delicate illuminations and perceptions about the soul, the tremblings of the veil that hangs before the dweller in the innermost, were of a very different order from the harsh logic and cut-and-thrust of theological disputation. Newman's mind was like a quiet pool that one comes upon when walking in the country at night. In it are reflected the quiverings of the willow-leaves, and the silvery mist of the fields, as well as the great wheel of the stars. In that mirror the terrible majesty of the heavens is made gentle, and Orion and the Pleiades are tangled in a web of shadows of the leaves. He of all men could lighten "the burden of the mystery". His confessions and his shrinkings, his doubts and divinings, belong to the intimacies of the lonely heart rather than to the melodrama and thunderings of pulpits and platforms.

It is little wonder that Newman aroused suspicions of his orthodoxy in the sinewy, soldierly mind of Manning, the second most illustrious convert of that age. For Cardinal Manning was a leader of practical wisdom, who knew well the frailties of flesh and blood and the obligation those frailties laid upon their pastors to sustain dogma, to vindicate authority and to repress the eccentricities of private judgment. The dislike between Manning and Newman was strong; their rivalry apparent. Manning was such a man as old institutions love. He was the seneschal, the warden, the engineer, the soul of the garrison, the defender of the outworks; and when one is in his company, reading his life and acts, one thinks of the Faith as being like that impregnable Palace of the Popes at Avignon, that grand specimen of the military architecture of the thirteenth century, towering up like a mountain, indestructible as a mountain, blazing, and beetling, and looking twice as big as it is, across the vineyards of Provence. In the contest with Newman the verdict lay with Manning.

Manning exhibited in the highest degree the proverbial zeal of the convert. There never lived a stronger Papalist, said G. W. E. Russell, who knew and respected him.

> He was more Ultramontane than the Ultramontanes. Everything Roman was to him divine. . . . He believed that he had been divinely appointed to Papalise England. The cause of the Pope was the cause of God; Manning was the person who could best serve the Pope's cause, and therefore all forces which opposed him were in effect opposing the Divine Will. . . . A power independent of, or hostile to, his authority was inimical to religion, and must, as a religious duty, be . . . destroyed. Exactly the same principle animated his dealings with Cardinal Newman. Rightly or wrongly, Manning thought Newman a half-hearted Papalist. He dreaded alike his way of putting things and his practical policy. . . . When Newman died there appeared in a monthly magazine a series of very unflattering sketches by one who had known him well. I ventured to ask Cardinal Manning if he had seen these sketches. He replied that he had, and thought them very shocking; the writer must have a very unenviable mind, etc., and then, having thus sacrificed to propriety, after a moment's pause he added, "But if you ask me if they are like poor Newman, I am bound to say—*a photograph.*"

I do not ask to see
The distant scene; one step enough for me.

But the Mannings must win else there would be no more institutions, and then where would we all be?

Newman, too, died a Prince of that Church whose pillars are Certainty, Authority, Submission, Logic and Affirmation. Yet he is enduringly attractive to us because we see him always as a pilgrim soul, groping, stumbling, stretching out his hands in the mist.

> Lead, kindly Light, amid the encircling gloom,
> Lead thou me on;
> The night is dark, and I am far from home,
> Lead thou me on.

There comes back to us the cry of Gerontius in the hour of death:

> I can no more; for now it comes again,
> That sense of ruin, which is worse than pain,
> That masterful negation and collapse
> Of all that makes me man; as though I bent
> Over the dizzy brink
> Of some sheer infinite descent;
> Or worse, as though
> Down, down for ever I was falling through
> The solid framework of created things,
> And needs must sink and sink
> Into the vast abyss.

There is nothing of the ringing brass of spiritual success in Newman. There are strewn about him "the bright ambiguities" of Heaven.

The dread of Rome's mysterious power, heightened by the Oxford Movement, and the circumstances of Newman's conversion, created a hysteria over Popery in 1859. In that year the Pope created half a dozen Cardinals; among them there was the Englishman, Wiseman. A Papal Bull, issued shortly afterwards, set up a Roman Catholic hierarchy in Britain, and in his pastoral letter, "given out at the Flaminian Gate", Wiseman, the new Cardinal, announced with some precipitancy that Catholic England had been restored "to its orbit in the ecclesiastical firmament". Protestant sentiment in the country recoiled sharply. The Prime Minister, Lord John Russell, was a son of that Whig house which had given its blood in the defence of the Protestant faith in bygone years. Old loyalties, historic passions, lent fire and spirit to his protest. Lord John's manifesto, addressed to the Bishop of Durham, indignantly repelled the claims of the Papacy, and expressed alarm at the spread of Ritualism in the Church of England—calling it the "danger within the gates" or, as we should say today, a fifth column. Disraeli, observing the stir with his bright alien eye, was disposed to be cynical at first, writing that "even the peasants think they are going to be burned alive and taken up to Smithfield instead of their pigs". He was inclined to suppose that Lord John had simulated his rage, pouncing on a good issue at a time when things were going badly for his party. But in the end the mood of the country assured Disraeli "of the essential Protestantism of the British character", and, at a later day, he himself was to bring forward a Bill to put down Ritualistic practices in the Church of England. If you would know how intemperate was the opposition excited by the "Papal aggression", look at the bound copies of *Punch* for 1850–1. The cartoons of Wiseman and the Catholic Bishops revive the brutality of Gillray. The Russell Ministry brought in a Bill to make illegal the assumption of the new titles by the Catholic Hierarchy; the Bill was passed by great majorities; but it was never enforced, and in the seventies it was repealed.

Religious intolerance is not a pleasant subject. It is infectious to handle. But even the slenderest sketch of the Victorian age must touch in passing on the squalls over ritualism in the Church or the unceasing flurries about Catholic intentions. The ghosts of Elizabethan times, of Stuart times were never laid, there were moments in the century when it seemed that the spectre of crazy Lord George Gordon in his cocked hat, with white face, lank hair tumbling over his blazing eyes, was abroad in the streets again. A good many people, it seems, can manage very well without loves or loyalties, but they must have something to hate to keep themselves alive. Before the Jews became the chief object of this irrational hating, the Catholics served the purpose. Fanatical men at street corners exposed the conspiracies and plots hatched by the Jesuits to overthrow the realm. The Catholics in mid-Victorian days became the object once again of primitive fears; they drew upon themselves the dread of the unknown, the loathing of the alien; and patriotism reinforced spite. The Anglo-Catholics did not escape their share of the odium. Father Ignatius, the Anglican Benedictine, was stoned in the streets and more than once came near being lynched.

CHAPTER FOUR

AND THIRDLY . . .

Over the loaded Sunday dinner-table the morning's sermon was a main topic of conversation. Orthodoxy being taken for granted, the manner was usually more eagerly discussed than the matter. For the sermon was a Victorian art form, as it had been a seventeenth-century and eighteenth-century art form. Among strict Evangelical and Nonconformist families who regarded the playhouse as being under Satan's management and the novel as a corrupter of the young, the pulpit was in some part a moral substitute for both. It supplied dramatic interest, narrative power, analysis of character, passion and humour in addition to the vindication of sound doctrine. The connoisseurs of this ancient art expected, too, that a sermon should exhibit the same regard for form as a sonata. The text from the Bible on which it was built up was like a theme in music; and the firstly, secondly and thirdly of the preacher were the variations and fantasies upon the theme; and there was very often a thundering finish to the sermon in which the text was heard, so to speak, in the triumphant key of C major and in four-four time. The quality of the performance was accounted quite as important as the composition. "How did Dr. Parr do this morning?"—"He was in excellent voice."—"What was his greatest moment?"—"Oh, without doubt, his account of the Crossing of the Red Sea. Everyone sat spellbound. It was so vivid one could see and hear the waves, and feel the terror of the moment before their parting. When the miracle happened, Dr. Parr's voice rang out like a trumpet. It was hard to keep one's seat and not to jump up crying 'Hallelujah'."

What consummate professionals and specialists those old preachers were! The biographer of that commanding figure, Canon Henry Liddon, speaks of "his charm of feature, his exquisite intonation, his kindling eye, his quivering pose and gestures", and his power to vary fiery sarcasm with gentle humour, authority with tenderness. Liddon, when a tiny child, had robed himself in sheets of *The Times* newspaper and, mounting a nursery chair, lisped his first sermons; as a boy he rehearsed endlessly for the pulpit; as a young man he studied attentively the methods of the most successful preachers in Paris, the inheritors of the grand manner of Bossuet, those who wore so magnificently the ceremonial robes of a great tradition, stiff with gold tissue and gems, majestical, solemn—but, none the less, underneath the heavy brocade there was palpable the beating of the human heart.

Liddon perfected his natural gifts by intense application. To him a sermon was not an easy chat or causerie based on a few scribbled notes, it was a work of art, designed to persuade, to woo, to conquer the imagination. In this conquest, the skills of the rhetorician and the actor of sacred drama were blended. When he preached in St. Paul's men and women —middle-class people, working-class people—came from all parts of London to hear Liddon. His themes were conventional, he was orthodox and unoriginal in thought, he did nothing to startle, he never perplexed by intellectual subtleties—with him it was the *style* that mattered. In this regard, Liddon, like other celebrated Victorian preachers, resembled those Italian painters of the old days whose subjects were provided for them by the Church—the Nativity, the Flight into Egypt or the Crucifixion. They had no need to dissipate their energies in the search for fresh objects, they could concentrate all their natural force on treatment and manner.

The Dissenters had a number of preachers who excelled in the sacred dramatic style, such men as the Rev. W. J. Fox who had eyes like burning coals and long white hair like a comet's tail. Fox was a mesmerist. He would transfix his congregation. Their hearts would be in their mouths as he enacted in the pulpit some such scene from Holy Writ as Jacob wrestling with the angel. By his hypnotic arts Fox would make his auditors feel in their own muscles the agonies of that struggle of mortal flesh with supernatural powers. They would groan, they would writhe in their seats, sweat would spring out on their brows. Some of us can recall being taken as small children to hear the preachings of some venerable man who had been brought up in that school and kept its style; some fierce, eloquent old man who was like Keats's pale-mouthed prophet dreaming. I am thinking now of one such. By some trick of the imagination, in recalling him, my head is filled with images of walking through a great, gloomy mansion with painted ceilings, smoky and dimly seen, filled with swirling draperies of red and blue, foaming horses, the writhing limbs of martyrs, babies spitted on swords, shooting stars, and, over all, God, a terrifying old man, with lightnings darting out of his eyes and a beard like a thundercloud. This was childhood's response to the dramatic, to the spectacular, to the concrete in the discourses of one of those old-time preachers. Their method was to impress the mind by a literal reporting of the supernatural and fantastic. They would give the cubit measurements of the Heavenly City as though they had just returned from it, and they raised their hands in wonder at the memory of its shining jasper walls. The bears that ate the wicked children who mocked the prophet's bald head—I could hear their stealthy padding in the street outside, where the trams were silent, and could almost feel their stinking breath behind my ears. In my imagination Jezebel, painted red as a doll, is still falling shrieking from the palace window to be devoured by the dogs; blind Samson pulls down the pillars with tremendous convulsions of his mighty thews, and the roar and the white dust is all around me. The legends of the Old Testament when they are recounted in this dramatic style seem to draw a response from the depths of our common consciousness or memory; a child appears to know that they have happened and that he has had a part in them; his listening is a recognition. These old preachers had access to those deep springs.

In one of his books Sir William Robertson Nicoll, himself a Nonconformist divine, writes in disparagement of the old-fashioned rhetoricians of the pulpit. As a specimen of the "big bow-wow" manner that became unfashionable by the turn of the century, he quotes a sermon by the Rev. J. W. Boulding in which the ascent of Elijah to Heaven is described in this picturesque language:

> At last, when the darkness began to fall, and the form of the prophet faded from their view, suddenly the snorting of horses was heard in the distance, and the rumbling of wheels, like the murmur of a storm, and lo! when they looked, the mountains seemed to burn as in a furnace, and all the sky was red as blood; for, rising out of the sea, a chariot came, and the breath of its steeds was smokeless flame, and its living wheels were a rolling blaze, and, swift as thought, the whirlwind on which they swept in their pauseless course caught up the prophet into the mantling fire; while, standing in the midst of the burning car, his own wild heart became the centre of the blaze, fanned by the whirlwind and kindling in the flames, till the lightning's rapture was but the reflection of his own, and, streaming with the trail of a comet through the night, he faded among the stars into the depths of heaven; while the mantle wearily floating to the earth was the proof that the prophet's recompense was rest, and the whirlwind's history the peace of God.
>
> (Robertson Nicoll, *A Bookman's Letters*, 1913.)

Robertson Nicoll asks indignantly—does anyone wonder that a generation subjected to this sort of stuff become sick of gravy? I can, on the other hand, imagine that a generation starved of gravy might find "this sort of stuff" an agreeable change. A sermon, like a play, can only be truly judged in performance—it is not intended to be read by the firelight. Mr. Boulding was, one presumes, like all his successful contemporaries of the cloth, a well-trained elocutionist; he had taken pains with his diction, exercising his voice in his bedroom with *Marmion* and *The Lays of Ancient Rome;* he swelled his diapason; he gargled; he took lozenges. Above all, it is quite clear that when composing a sermon, this admirable fellow did precisely what those other wooers and seducers of the public, Shakespeare and Mozart, did—he wrote with an eye on the dramatic effect and an ear cocked for the musical effect. This account of the ascent of Elijah might have sounded very well indeed when declaimed by Boulding. Was it not there, at the mysterious moment when the darkness began to fall, that Boulding pulled out the bourdon stop in his voice—and there at the rhapsodic phrase, "till the lightning's rapture was but the reflection of his own", that his fine organ was extended to the utmost, that he blew out all the breath in his bellows so that the trumpet notes went rolling about the chapel petrifying poor old women and making the gas-globes ring? I seem to hear, too, the caressing, carrying whisper of the words on which Boulding ended—"the whirlwind's history the peace of God", followed, surely, by a thrilling silence in the chapel. It is unlikely that any who heard that discourse went to sleep in the middle of it. Let us compare Boulding's gravy, its ruddy juices and its rich body, with the thin-lemonade, modern style used by crushed young parsons today, scared of being thought pious or priggish, addressing a congregation of old ladies and gentlemen, as though they were Boy Scouts: "God, you know, asks no more of us than that we should all play up and play the game. Let us think of Him as the Great Sportsman. In His wisdom we may sometimes find ourselves playing on a very sticky wicket, but He expects us, you know, always to keep a straight bat. Let us so behave in the Test Match of life that when we are bowled out for the last time we may hear His cheery voice calling from the Heavenly pavilion, 'Oh well played, sir, well played!' " No—meat gravy, with its succulent juices, still sits better on the stomach than lemonade.

Our grandfathers and great-grandfathers took an artistic pleasure in sermons. Some of them would move from church to chapel, from High to Low, untroubled by differences in doctrine but vastly curious as to the performance. In this they were like those lovers of singing who would not care whether the opera was by Verdi, Meyerbeer or Wagner so long as the voices were mellifluous. At one time they would contrast the styles of Pusey, Keble and Channing; at another Liddon, Stanley, Dale, Martineau; as in another sphere they compared Lind and Patti. The last eminent Briton who was of these enthralled tasters of sermons was Admiral Fisher.

Among the lower middle classes there was no preacher more highly venerated than Charles Haddon Spurgeon, who was born in 1834. Spurgeon broke with the Baptist Union because his fellow religionists were moving away from Fundamentalism, from a literal interpretation of the Scriptures. As he saw it, by departing from the full rigour of the old tenets, they were "going down hill at breakneck speed". At the Metropolitan Tabernacle at Newington Causeway, built for a congregation of six thousand, Spurgeon, the independent divine, preached Sunday after Sunday with unflagging zeal; men and women flocked from all parts of London, and from the provinces, to hear him. His sermons, published weekly, sold in their hundreds of thousands. Spurgeon looked like a hairy lion with shaggy mane and large soulful eyes—Androcles' lion—and in the pulpit he grew larger than life through the swelling of his own afflatus. He had a voice like a 'cello, orotund and deeply vibrating; a good voice for wooing sinners to the penitent form. The stern Calvinism he professed involved the future misery of all the human race, save a tiny handful of the elect, and yet the power of his appeal resided in his obvious liking for his fellow men. He had out-givingness. He exhaled warmth. He established a personal relationship between himself and the humblest, least-regarded beings in his congregation. He gave to many thousands of lowly characters moving dimly through those depths of the lower middle class where life is drearier than among working folk, the sense of important identity that all of us crave. Spurgeon's portrait still hangs on the walls of many cottages in Britain, and his sermons are still read aloud in the small chapels of the stricter sects in East Anglia and the Home Counties. Spurgeon was a man of the people. He could compass the sacred dramatic and the denunciatory styles, but his most effective vein was the homely. Here is a characteristic passage that I have picked out from an old volume of his sermons:

> A mouse was caught in a trap, the other day, by its tail, and the poor creature went on eating the cheese. Many men are doing the same; they know they are guilty, and they dread their punishment, but they go on nibbling at their beloved sins. They remind me of the soldier in the old classic story. The army marched through a certain country, and the commander-in-chief ordered that there should be no plundering; not a man must touch a bunch of grapes in going through the vineyards, or he should die for his disobedience. One soldier, tempted by a bunch of grapes, must needs pluck it and begin to eat it. He was brought before the captain, who declared that the law must be carried out and the thief must die. He was taken out to die; and tho' he knew his head would be cut off, he went on eating the grapes as he walked along. A comrade wondered that he should do this; but the condemned man answered that no one ought to grudge him his grapes, for they cost him dear enough. Such are the bravadoes of sinners. The breasts of wicked men are steeled rather than softened by a sense of condemnation; but once let the Holy Spirit remove the burden of their guilt, and they will be dissolved by love.

Spurgeon also set a fashion in the conventicles for a certain heartless, mirthless facetiousness of which this is a specimen:

> I have heard of a minister who preached for several years before he was converted, and when converted he became a very earnest preacher of the gospel; but one day as he rode along the street he was observed to stop and cane a dog which was lying in front of a door. When they said to him, "Mr. McPhayle, why did you beat the dog?" he said, "He was so exactly like myself, lying in the sun sleeping—a dumb dog that didn't bark—that I could not but give him a touch of the rod; though I meant it all the while for myself."

CHAPTER FIVE

THE SIDE OF THE ANGELS

I see him now, as I saw him when I was a boy, a survival from a period long before my own. A venerable figure in seedy, shiny black, with a triangle of yellowing piqué at his throat, his face shaded by a black straw hat, he advances stolidly along the beach. The afternoon is hot—as hot as afternoons of long ago by the sea alone could be—but the fierce white sun cannot melt him inside that beetle-like carapace of rusty black. His nose keeps in July its January look of incurable frost-bite. By comparison with his gloomy solidity, the thin bodies of the young bathers racing down the beach to leap into the dazzle of spray appear pallid, almost transparent. They are the young Oceanides, phantoms of the azure sea. Their laughter is part of the multitudinous laughter of the waves, their arms and shoulders, as they swim out from shore, become lost in the whiteness of the foam as the waves curve and dissolve, in lines of endless beauty, reaching to the faraway skyline. These young Oceanides, and the afternoon which is so completely theirs; the sapphire of the sky, so clear, so hard, making the universe appear as one jewel; the sea, the lovely pagan, the unconverted heathen, casting her smiles around her, sparkling, glittering, baring her breasts to the sun, flinging her garlands of spray in the blue air—these young Oceanides and the afternoon belong together to the old mythology, to the white sunshine of Hellas. But he, *he* is Gothic, Victorian Gothic, a solid shadow irresistibly advancing. Fragile and pale in the hot sun appear the bodies of the Oceanides, but *he* is a chunky figure carved out of wood, and painted in harsh primary colours, by a Nuremberg craftsman. There is a dreadful invincibility about him. He is a Fundamentalist pastor of the old school, a vessel of the Lord, honest, pig-headed, vindictive, brave, with a physical *density* much greater than that of flesh. He carries a stick, an oak stick. It is not so much an aid to walking as an extension of his own wooden forefinger. He uses it to explore and to warn the wicked sensual world as he walks through it—he pokes—he wags—he stirs up. He jabs at a stranded starfish. He waves this wand in remonstrance at the nakedness of a little child. Poor little wretch! he was conceived in sin, his frail body is evil and corrupt, and there is no health in him. With little grunts of pleasure, the pastor explodes the tiny bubbles and blisters on the seaweed. Now he draws near, and I can see with how rough a hand the Nuremberg toymaker has dabbed the red and blue on that face to create the illusion of wintriness. The enormous lean forefinger, three feet long, is now prodding the little colony in a rock pool, tiny exiles from the sea, left behind when the tide ebbed, an infant crab hiding under the vivid streamers of the sea-grasses, a razor-shell or two, lustrous and opalescent, some dead cockles and a nameless agitation of microscopic life. The ferrule stirs up a vortex of sand in the clear water between the rocks.

"Boy!" croaks the old man, "Boy, take notice and praise the Creator. His wonders are infinite."

The wooden forefinger prods the boy's thin ribs, and the boy painfully takes notice.

Then the boy, embarrassed and uncomfortable, indicates that the neighbouring cliff, rearing its tawny heights from the sands, provides some interesting new exhibits. A recent landslide has made that old familiar cliff look like a new cliff; it is naked and fresh, its secrets are out. There, in exquisite drawing, are the lines of some prehistoric small children of Ocean, delicate whorls and spirals of rainbow shells that once had "paddled in a halcyon sea" at a period measurelessly remote when the sun was just as white as it is today, but there were no human cries on the beach, no fragile creatures of our own flesh and blood—only the sun and silence—all the beauty of the world unfolding there without any lover to observe it.

The old pastor blinks his red-rimmed eyes at the delicate engravings on the face of the cliff, then looks at the bustle of tiny life in the rock-pool, then looks back again at the cliff. "The wonders of the Lord are infinite," he repeats, and sets his jaw.

He looks at me with a sparkle of suspicion. "Boy," says he, "there are men in the world who talk in their blind ignorance about fossils." He thrusts the stick with such anger at the cliff that flakes fall away, but no hurt is done to the exquisite traceries of the shell, now glittering in the sun again for the first time in a million years.

"What fools those men were to think that *this* proved their blasphemies," says the pastor, stabbing away at the rock. "God Himself may have put those relics there in just that way to make a mock of their wicked pride." He cackles in contemplation of this divine practical joke. "Or Satan may have put them there—I can't say which. A thousand ages in God's sight is but an evening gone. In His own Good Book, God has told us how He created the world in six days. That is the gospel truth, and all else must be a snare and delusion of the Father of Lies. Proclaim that, boy, to clever fools who go about with little hammers chipping shells out of rocks. They cannot alter the blessed truth that Creation took place six thousand years ago, not a million years ago, nor a million million as some of them pretend. The Father of Lies talks through many mouths nowadays. Boy, the godless will try to poison your soul by the vanities of so-called science. I have seen the scientist flourish like the green bay tree. When I was

CHARLES DARWIN
Pencil sketch by Marian Collier, 78
National Portrait Gallery

young there was a limb of Satan, a man called Darwin, who in his wicked pride said that man had descended from a monkey. That, boy, is such mad blasphemy as turns men's brains when they abandon the Book of Life, which is the only rock we have to cling to. Where is that man Darwin now? He is surely back in Hell with his master, and with all other evil spirits. Keep to the Book, sonny, keep to the Book. If a schoolmaster showing you fossils or monkeys makes you doubt one line of it, then you will be led to doubt the whole of it, for it all hangs together, and *then* you will certainly burn."

He passes on, muttering "fossils and monkeys", thrusting at a viewless Satan with his stick, the brilliant flash of gulls' wings over his head, until he is lost in the blue distance. He is to me the archetype of the stubborn resisters to the march of science. On this granite orthodoxy the waves of new thought had beaten and broken in vain. He was the incarnation of lower-middle-class England in Darwinian times.

The old pastor was right in supposing that to yield one text, even in Deuteronomy, was to imperil the whole fabric of the literal inspiration of the Bible, and to be lost in a sea of uncertainties. Edmund Gosse's father was a naturalist of repute, but he was also a member of the Plymouth Brethren, and the naturalist was subdued by the sectary. Such a character would never surrender the certainty of his emotions to the reservations of his intellect. He died secure and happy.

"Fossils and monkeys" exercised the mid-Victorians considerably. Charles Darwin's *Origin of Species* was published in 1859. The idea of an evolutionary process working through the method of natural selection brought a deathly chill to many hearts. Lyell's *Geological Evidence of the Antiquity of Man*, which came out in 1863, proved as severe a shock to them as Darwin's theory. To thousands of men and women who, though reared in the old faith, lacked the unshakable dogmatism of my Fundamentalist pastor, the theory of Evolution brought agonies of doubt. They had been born into a tidy, cosy, shipshape world which, like a big Noah's Ark, floated on the sea of Time. In this Ark God had arrayed the insects, reptiles, beasts and birds in their proper order; and He had placed Man in governance over them—Man that He had made in his own image. Now the Ark began to break up. The lamps suddenly went out, the collapsing walls revealed outside the wastes of a dark ocean under the arch of a sky hung with sombre stars—and, looking on this prospect, men's souls were filled with the cold and terror of the night. Where might they find a refuge? Where now was God?

Darwin had shown them that the comforting notion of the special creation of immutable species was quite false. The life force which fulfilled its purposes through natural selection, through the survival of the fittest, had taken the place of the God of our fathers, the paternal Deity, the personal God, enthroned on high, to whom a believer might, as a trusting child to a father, take his troubles. And Man himself, the lord of the universe—how ambiguous now appeared his ancestry, and how dubious his future! He, too, was subject to the ordinances, and to the caprices, of blind necessity. The diligent excavators at Les Eyzies showed that Man was an old inhabitant of a very old planet; and a dizzying vista opened up of endlessly receding centuries in which the ancestors of Queen Victoria, Mr. Gladstone, the Archbishop of Canterbury, Tennyson, Father Newman and George Stephenson were indistinguishable from wild beasts, skulking in dark wet caves, hunting their prey and being in turn hunted as prey. The agitating thought persisted—*how* near to the creatures of the jungle, to the ape and the tiger, were the forefathers, the first men? How near were *we*? Could the first chapter of Genesis be accepted even as poetic truth? To the anguishing uncertainties caused by the naturalists, the biologists and the geologists were soon added those doubts which the anthropologists supplied. In the Britain of the sixties, the young science of anthropology appeared garbed in the Quaker habit of E. B. Tylor. After the publication of Tylor's *Researches into the Early History of Mankind*, it was more difficult than ever for men and women to accept the Biblical account of how Man came to be upon the earth. The inner confusion and dismay brought about by the scientists were in striking contrast to the outer confidence, optimism and material progress of the sixties.

> For the world, which seems
> To lie before us like a land of dreams,
> So various, so beautiful, so new,
> Hath really neither joy, nor love, nor light,
> Nor certitude, nor peace, nor help for pain;
> And we are here as on a darkling plain
> Swept with confused alarms of struggle and flight,
> Where ignorant armies clash by night.

Matthew Arnold's father, the formidable Arnold of Rugby, had, as a young man, suffered a prolonged spiritual crisis over the doctrine of the Trinity, and great was the concern among the Arnold clan. But the poet of *Dover Beach* sang his exquisite elegy for loss of faith in all dogmas.

But we must not forget the others—those thoughtful and sensitive if somewhat impetuous beings who felt the intoxicating joy of seeing a Bastille overthrown. The brutal systems of theology that had enslaved men's minds, the doctrine of eternal punishment that had tortured them—how could they exercise their jungle sorcery any longer in the bright air and sunshine of these new truths? The glorious promise of Shelley's *Prometheus Unbound* was fulfilled: Demogorgon, the ultimate Fate to which even the gods must surrender, had arisen in the Car of the Hour and was about to tear cruel Jupiter from his throne. For these free spirits, the theory of Evolution gave a dignity and enlargement to all existence; it supplied a series of exciting new clues to the riddles of nature; it broke the iron matrix of the old, dogmatic religion and offered boundless possibilities of progress; it made the visible world not less marvellous but more so; and, by destroying superstition, it exalted Man. That air was so bracing that it was not at first perceived how arid and killing it might be.

We can see today, better perhaps than they could see in the nineteenth century, that the ground had been well tilled for Darwinism. A generation in which the idea of the irresistible march of Mechanical Progress had already been instilled did not find it hard to comprehend evolutionary theory. A generation whose hero was the self-reliant man of the Manchester School confirmed from its own experience the truth that the fittest survived. And a generation that had learned to expect daily miracles from applied science was of a mind to accord respect to any scientific theory. There were old Calvinists, men who had done well in steel and cotton, who grimly noted a correspondence between natural selection and the doctrine of the elect.

Darwin, a great, original mind, was not well served by his intemperate followers and by those who sought to bend his theories to their own ends.

He was sometimes as much maligned by admirers as by the vulgarians who made their silly jokes about the ape ancestor. There was a suspicious eagerness among big business men of the sixties to agree that the world of men and women presented a striking illustration of that struggle for existence by which the evolutionary process was advanced. Our North Country friends, Mr. Gradgrind and Mr. Bounderby, were eager to pick out any theory from theology, philosophy, economics or science which suggested that the battle was to the strong and that the weakest must go to the wall—in the interests, of course, of the general good. The justification of worldly success which at one time successful men had derived from the teachings of Protestantism, and at another from Adam Smith's *Wealth of Nations*, they now seized upon in Darwin. The cotton-spinners, the ironmasters, the shipbuilders, the heads of the great exporting houses, the bankers, the engineers—they were manifestly the fittest of the fit in the struggle for survival.

One imagines that to a lonely student in a Tibetan monastery in a thousand years' time, poring over such records of the Victorian age as may still survive, the voices of that age may at last all come to sound very like one another—the politicians, the theologians, the scientists, the believers, the agnostics. The best men among the Evolutionists were lifted up by a sense of righteousness as strong as that which had sustained the Evangelicals in their assault on slavery. It was characteristic of the age that rationalism was itself often a form of religious experience, and the enemies of orthodoxy were inspired in the attack by the belief that they possessed a superior ethic and a nobler moral purpose. Thomas Henry Huxley rebuking Bishop Wilberforce seems to echo Gladstone denouncing Disraeli over the moral wickedness of his foreign policy. In the voice, there is the same note of scorn for the trifler with truth, the same wrath over the substitution of cleverness for principle. The agnostic is the high moralist, the Bishop becomes the frivolous worldling. Huxley's debate with Gladstone over the Virgin Birth furnished a fine example of two men of exalted faith, each of whom was seeking to save the other's soul from mortal error. Huxley was peerless in exposition, and there is no scientific writer more stimulating to read, but the more one reads him, the more one feels in the presence of one of the eminent preachers of that age. It was very right that he should call a collection of his best papers *Lay Sermons*. There is always the roll of theological thunder in Huxley's style. How well he could use the anathematising manner perfected by generations of English divines in their holy war with one another. Take, for example, so typical a page from Huxley as the following:

> In this nineteenth century, as at the dawn of modern physical science, the cosmogony of the semi-barbarous Hebrew is the incubus of the philosopher and the opprobrium of the orthodox. Who shall number the patient and earnest seekers after truth, from the days of Galileo, until now, whose lives have been

> embittered and their good name blasted by the mistaken zeal of Bibliolaters? Who shall count the host of weaker men whose sense of truth has been destroyed in the effort to harmonise impossibilities—whose life has been wasted in the attempt to force the generous new wine of Science into the old bottles of Judaism, compelled by the outcry of the same strong party? It is true, that if philosophers have suffered, their cause has been amply revenged. Extinguished theologians lie about the cradle of every science as the strangled snakes beside that of Hercules; and history records that whenever science and orthodoxy have been fairly opposed, the latter has been forced to retire from the lists, bleeding and crushed, if not annihilated; scotched if not slain. But orthodoxy is the Bourbon of the world of thought. It learns not, neither can it forget; and though, at present, bewildered and afraid to move, it is as willing as ever to insist that the first chapter of Genesis contains the beginning and end of sound science; and to visit, with such petty thunderbolts as its half-paralysed hands can hurl, those who refuse to degrade Nature to the level of primitive Judaism.

What a fine, ringing, *pulpit* style this is. The image of the strangled snakes must have excited the envy of half the Presbyterian divines in Scotland.

The argument over Darwinism went rattling on far beyond the period of this sketch; but long before the century was out a Broad Church marriage was, so to speak, solemnised between religion and science. The honest fundamentalists on both sides continued to bite their thumbs at one another, but there grew up a middle group which brought about a beautifully British accommodation between the claims of the apes and the angels. In that mild, moist atmosphere of compromise which envelops our island it was suddenly perceived that there was no difficulty at all in reconciling science and faith. God, as defined by the Liberal churchmen, had ceased to be the arbitrary despot of the Universe, and was now become a strictly constitutional monarch, who could be trusted to accept the advice of the British Association for the Advancement of Science. By 1889 Alfred Russel Wallace was writing that there were in man's individual and moral nature distinct parts which could not have been developed by variation and natural selection alone. The mathematical, artistic and metaphysical faculties were, said he, altogether removed from utility in the struggle for life, and were therefore unexplained by the doctrine of natural selection. In the Romanes lecture of 1893 Huxley said, "Social progress means a checking of the cosmic progress at every step and the substitution for it of another, which may be called the ethical process; the end of which is not the survival of those who may happen to be the fittest in respect of the whole of the conditions which obtain but of those who are ethically the best." Benjamin Kidd, the evolutionary diehard, felt that this was a shameless backsliding. The theory explained everything. If Wallace and Huxley doubted its universal application, then so much the worse for them. An Evolutionist like Kidd, and my Fundamentalist pastor who on the beach that summer's day had warned me that to concede one text in Holy Writ was to jeopardise the soul's salvation, were brothers under the skin.

CHAPTER SIX

OUT OF THE DEPTHS

I have written of the search for ecstasy. It was sometimes found by another way, a dark and tortuous way that led to the edge of madness.

Cultivated and delicate intellects among the adherents of the dogmatic Faiths wrestled painfully with the doctrine of Hell and eternal punishment. To any sensitive spirit, outside the Church, the notion of everlasting damnation might well be the most terrible suspicion that ever darkened the human mind, as Morley said it was. But for the believer, there it was—the enormous dogma, no more easy to overlook than a mountain—and it sustained all the other dogmas. To gentle, devout souls, who recoiled from killing a mouse, it was agonising to reflect that they could not even save those they loved from an eternity of misery if they had not been sealed to redemption by the blood of the Lamb. The slightest fall from grace might entail an immortality of torment.

> There's a great text in Galatians,
> Once you trip on it, entails,
> Twenty-nine distinct damnations,
> One sure, if another fails,
> If I trip him just a-dying,
> Sure of Heaven as sure can be,
> Spin him round, and send him flying
> Off to Hell, a Manichee?

What to do? inquired the sensitive believer. How could one move happily in civilised society, meet Dizzy and Lord Palmerston at dinner, attend a Royal Drawing-room, read *The Times*, go to the Academy banquet, cut a figure at Ascot, debate Browning's hieroglyphic verse, discriminate between Macready and Phelps, follow zestfully the twists of the Evolutionary argument, with the ghastly fear gnawing at one's heart that nine out of ten of the men and women one so agreeably met were doomed after the death of the body to suffer unutterable tortures for ever?

The tender-hearted usually comforted themselves by the reflection that Hell was probably a state of mind rather than a place, and that the wicked heart, which steeled itself against the infinite pity and goodness of God, made its own damnation. Kindly men and women fixed their hopes on the uncovenanted mercies of God; and Newman, when, with a sweet smile, he assured the old Quaker that God would somehow find a way of saving him, stood for all such Victorians whose natures were gentler than their creeds. One benevolent Anglican theologian suffered the rebuke of his Bishop for toying with the heretical notion of a universal salvation. Some there were who even thought that one day, long after the world had passed away, Satan himself might find grace at last and be restored to Paradise, and in hoping this might be so reflected the humane emotion of my Uncle Toby. When the parson told him that the Devil was damned already, to all eternity, "I am sorry for it, quoth my uncle Toby".

But in the dim underworld of religion, in the corrugated iron chapels of the stricter sects at the end of gas-lit alleys, there were no metaphysical compromises with the doctrine of damnation. Hell was as real a place as London, and of all the millions, and trillions, and quadrillions of human souls that had been born into the world since the Creation, no more than a tiny handful of the elect could hope to escape burning endlessly in its flames. When my mind is forced back to this frightening, yet horribly attaching theme, I am haunted by childhood recollections of hearing of men and women who would pace up and down their narrow rooms at nights, like animals in a cage, moaning that they had sinned the unforgivable sin, and were for ever out of the reach of God's mercy. It was of no avail their crying out "What must I do to be saved?" for they now knew they could never be saved, and they anticipated in their quaking flesh the everlasting tortures of perdition. Fanatical men and women, with sleepless red eyes, would press into the hands of a young boy whom they caught on the streets hideous tracts concerning the sin against the Holy Ghost, the sin for which even God himself would not grant a pardon, and the poor little wretch would lie in a sweat till morning broke, feeling the cold of that incomprehensible terror in his bowels. Sometimes in the street at morning there would be seen the apparition of a man, a decent working man, rushing out of his house, dishevelled and with a mad look, crying that his soul was damned and that the pit was yawning for him. Whenever I see on the streets of London or New York those Solomon Eagles of our age, the characters who run up and down carrying placards that read "The wages of sin is death" or "The wicked shall be turned into Hell", I re-enact in my imagination those older scenes of misery. There is the dark room in Flooden Road, Camberwell, a name charged with blood; and the unforgiven sinner, half-insane with dread, is staring out of the window at the unfading glare hanging over London—the clouds above the city reddened with his prefigured doom.

All over the world, wherever that gospel of eternal damnation was carried, men, women and children suffered these torments of mind. The family memories of the United States and Canada, as I was to learn in after years, were full of testimonies to this supreme fear that had darkened my own mind when a child. The light of the African moon poured down upon this mortal wretchedness. In Olive Schreiner's *The Story of an African Farm*, a fine book now almost forgotten, there is a heart-freezing description of the young boy who lies awake listening to the ticking of his father's great silver hunting watch. Every time it ticked a man died.

> He thought of the words his father had read that evening: "*For wide is the gate, and broad is the way that leadeth to destruction, and many there be which go in thereat.*"
> "Many, many, many," said the watch.
> "*Because straight is the gate, and narrow is the way that leadeth unto life, and few there be that find it.*"
> "Few, few, few," said the watch.
> The boy lay with his eyes wide open. He saw before him a long stream of people, a great dark multitude, that moved in one direction; then they came to the dark edge of the world, and went over. He saw them passing on before him; and nothing could stop them. He thought of how that stream had rolled on through all the long ages of the past—how the old Greeks and Romans had gone over; the countless millions of China and India, they were going over now. Since he had come to bed, how many had gone!
> And the watch said, "Eternity, eternity, eternity."
> "Stop them! Stop them!" cried the child.
> And all the while the watch kept ticking on; just like God's will that never changes or alters, you may do what you please.
> Great beads of perspiration stood on the boy's forehead. He climbed out of bed, and lay with his face turned to the mud floor.
> "O God, God! save them!" he cried in agony. "Only some; only a few! Only, for each moment I am praying here, one!" He folded his little hands upon his head. "God! God! save them."
> He grovelled on the floor.
> Oh, the long, long ages of the past, in which they had gone over! Oh, the long, long future, in which they would pass away! Oh God, the long, long, long eternity which has no end!
> The child wept, and crept closer to the ground.

Among the sects that flourished in the shadowy vast realms of the lower middle classes of Victorian England, there was to be found an animal terror of Hell, but there was, too, a fierce pleasure at the thought of the unsaved sinner's doom. The preachers gloated upon the tortures of the unquenchable fires, and their congregation groaned, but, being sure their own names were inscribed in the Book of Life, rejoiced to see cruelty done. The fierce satisfaction that Lazarus felt when from Abraham's bosom he gazed upon the torments of Dives was shared by the shopkeepers' apprentices, and the poor, pinched old women, who attended the Little Bethels. The congregation at Zion Chapel observed by Robert Browning on that cold, drenching Christmas Eve of 'forty-nine, was composed of such. How brilliant is his hitting-off of the characters!—the shoemaker's lad, his wizened face in want of soap, a wet apron round his waist, stopping outside to get his fit of coughing over, "poor gentle creature"; the fat weary woman, her umbrella "a wreck of whalebones"; then "the many-tattered, little old-faced, peaking sister-turned-mother" who was carrying the sickly babe with spotted face and wringing the poor suds dry of a draggled shawl; and "close on her heels the dingy satin of a female something"; and then:

> A tall yellow man, like the Penitent Thief,
> With his jaw bound up in a handkerchief,
> And eyelids screwed together tight,
> Led himself in by some inner light.

While the old fat woman "maternally devoured the pastor",

> The man with the handkerchief untied it,
> Showed us a horrible wen inside it,
> Gave his eyelids yet another screwing,
> And rocked himself as the woman was doing.

This was a *milieu* far removed from the Universities of Oxford and Cambridge, from Lambeth Palace and Whitehall—dark, mysterious region at the bottom of the sea where blind fishes moved about with cold flames in their head. It is only those who have ever lived in that *milieu* as children who can understand what a *consolation* the belief in Hell brought to the downtrodden. The scarecrow standing in rags in Belgrave Square could watch the pageants of Vanity Fair roll by and reflect that the jaws of Hell would gulp down all its actors: the profligate lords and the lovely rakes in petticoats, the judges, the merchants and their rosy coachmen, the stock-jobbers, the lawyers, and, most gratifying of all victims, the rich, proud Bishops. No earthly revolution, substituting one set of masters for another, could ever afford so complete a satisfaction to under-dogs as the assurance that the orders and persons they hated most would be condemned to everlasting torments. How few would be the brands snatched from the burning! How rapturous for a Bethnal Green Lazarus "to quench the gin-shop's light in Hell's grim drench" and to contemplate my Lord Dives, one of Her Majesty's principal Secretaries of State, crying piteously for water out of the fiery pit! What could Marx offer to those who had the glare of the everlasting bonfire in their eyes?

The higher critics of the Bible, the Evolutionists and the Rationalists between them, succeeded in destroying this satisfying faith in damnation. In the year after the publication of *The Origin of Species* there appeared *Essays and Reviews*, a collection of Broad Church papers to which Benjamin Jowett, Frederick Temple and Mark Pattison, among others, contributed. This book, which caused two of its contributors, Henry Bristow Wilson and Roger Williams, to be tried for heresy by the Court of Arches, was critical of dogma and of the literal interpretation of the Bible. The writings of such Continental critics as Strauss and Renan were becoming widely read in Britain—the sibylline George Eliot herself had translated Strauss's *Life of Jesus*. The enlightened Victorian intellect devoted itself to extinguishing the flames of Tophet. A cool dawn of reason glimmered over the dead volcanoes and the calcined bones of Hell and in that pallid light the soul of man might walk in peace. The liberators never questioned that man was a reasonable animal, and, optimists that they were, never doubted that he was born to create his own happiness. It was only a chilly sceptic who was also a critic of Liberal optimism, such as Fitzjames Stephen, who could deplore the abolition of Hell on grounds of social necessity. In putting out the flames of Hell, Victorian Liberalism robbed the depressed lower middle classes of a dreadful inner certainty and hope. Hell fire and damnation gave meaning, appalling meaning, to many a wretched existence. The flames of perdition, illuminating the waking thoughts and the dreams of men and women, transfigured many starved lives. A supernatural glow filled the back rooms of tenements and shone on the greasy coats, the dirty sinks. An everlastingness of bliss or an everlastingness of pain—to contemplate either made the heart shake and the flesh quail, and dimmed the poor hopes of the world. What were earthly humiliations, squalor, pain, neglect, filth, compared with that tremendous destiny? Those who had this sense of doom upon them might be desperately frightened men, or insanely exultant men, but they could never be silly, empty creatures, fixed in meanness, and drugging themselves with dull pleasures.

The abolition of Hell also robbed the revolt against orthodoxy of its most powerful emotion, the Promethean impulse to defy a brutal Deity. I have a wry, silly picture in my head of a boy discovering the mediaeval romance of *Aucassin and Nicolette* and crying out at the top of his voice the glorious blasphemies of Aucassin's speech:

> In Paradise what have I to do? . . . For into Paradise go none but such people as I will tell you of. There go those aged priests, and those old cripples, and the maimed, who all day long and all night cough before the altars, and in the crypts beneath the churches; those who go in worn old mantles and old tattered habits; who are naked, and barefoot, and full of sores; who are dying of hunger and of thirst, of cold and wretchedness. Such as these enter in Paradise, and with them have I nought to do. But in Hell will I go. For to Hell go the fair clerks and the fair knights who are slain in the tourney and the great wars, and the stout archer and the loyal man. With them will I go. And there go the fair and courteous ladies, who have friends, two or three, together with wedded lords. And there pass the gold and the silver, the ermine and all rich furs, harpers and minstrels, and the happy of the world. With these will I go, so only that I have Nicolette, my very sweet friend, by my side.

"I wonder God Almighty does not strike you dead," said the old woman who overheard the proclamation of this blasphemy. "Since it has pleased Him not to, get on with your supper. All French trash should be burned."

The restoration of Hell might be an aid to poetry as well as religion.

PART VI

DIVERSIONS

CHAPTER ONE

THE STROLLER'S TALE

Our entry into the Early Victorian theatre is inevitably made on the heels of Vincent Crummles. We have travelled with him along the road from Guildford to Portsmouth, behind that pony whose mother was on the stage—"she ate apple-pie at a circus for upwards of fourteen years; fired pistols, and went to bed in a night-cap; and, in short, took the low comedy entirely". We plunge into the dark passages, smelling of orange-peel and lamp-oil, "with an under-current of saw-dust"; we thread the maze of canvas screens and paint-pots, and emerge into the twilight of "bare walls, dusty scenes, mildewed clouds, heavily daubed draperies and dirty floors", where everything looks coarse, gloomy, cold and wretched.

Vincent Crummles's inclination of the head, it will be recalled, was something "between the courtesy of a Roman emperor and the nod of a pot companion". In a like manner, the Crummles theatre blended magnificent make-believe with a dismal poverty. The scenical banquets were made up of jewelled goblets of pasteboard, a little vinegar, a biscuit or two and a black bottle—a splendid feast, but not very filling. The Infant Phenomenon in her dirty white frock, her frills and her bonnet of pink gauze, must sometimes have been short of the gin and water which was the inspiration of her artistry. Portsmouth, like other provincial towns, did not always respond to "refined theatrical entertainments properly conducted".

"To the Infant's benefit last year," complained Crummles, "on which occasion she repeated three of her most popular characters, and also appeared in the Fairy Porcupine, as originally performed by her, there was a house of no more than four pound twelve."

"And two pound of that was trust, pa," said the Infant. "Two pound was trust," repeated Crummles.

The note of Vincent Crummles, as of the Early Victorian stage, was one of happy and romantic humbug, the grand swagger that carries off the squalor of vagabondage and turns a ragged coat into ermine robes. There was superb gammon in Crummles's use of the pump and the two washing tubs bought cheap at a sale. The London theatre, as he said, bought dresses and properties and then wrote a play around them. Crummles would show them something fresh and daring in this line. "We'll have a new show piece out directly . . . Let me see—peculiar resources of this establishment—new and splendid machinery—you must manage to introduce a real pump and two washing tubs . . . Real pump! Splendid tubs! Great attraction!" As Thackeray said of Fielding, Crummles may have had low tastes but his mind was not mean.

There was another aspect of the Crummles drama which was endearing. That was its child-like innocence, the simple faith in the moral purpose of the Universe which underlay its wildest sensations.

Mr. Lenville asked what part there was for him in young Nickleby's adaptation from the French.

> "Anything in the gruff and grumble way?"
> "You turn your wife and child out of doors," said Nicholas, "and in a fit of rage and jealousy, stab your eldest son in the library."
> "Do I though!" exclaimed Mr. Lenville, "That's a very good business."
> "After which," said Nicholas, "you are troubled with remorse to the last act, and then you make up your mind to destroy yourself. But, just as you are raising the pistol to your head, a clock strikes—ten."
> "I see," cried Mr. Lenville. "Very good."
> "You pause," said Nicholas, "you recollect to have heard a clock strike ten in your infancy. The pistol falls from your hand—you are overcome—you burst into tears, and become a virtuous and exemplary character for ever afterwards."
> "Capital," said Mr. Lenville, "that's a sure card, a sure card. Get the curtain down with a touch of nature like that, and it'll be a triumphant success."

The London stage in Dickens's youth was a strange institution. Covent Garden and Drury Lane enjoyed a State monopoly of theatrical performances. It was, however, no breach of privilege to "give musical performances of a dramatic nature". By 1843, when Parliament brought the monopoly to an end, more than twenty other theatres had opened in London. They gave operettas and burlettas—musical performances of a dramatic nature, indeed—but what judge could decide how much spoken dialogue was necessary to sustain the comic interest of a burletta, or to carry forward the plot of a ballad opera?

Very little ingenuity was required to get around the law. In these early nineteenth-century musical performances, the speeches grew longer and the interludes of music shorter. The Act of 1843 did little more than recognise an accomplished fact. Parliament gave majestic permission to

"GRIMALDI'S LAST SONG"
Etching by George Cruikshank from "Grimaldi's Memoirs", 1839

the theatres to do what they were already doing. If any reader has a morbid interest in that bygone form of entertainment, the burletta, he may like to look at the three examples of it that Dickens wrote in 1836–7. *The Village Coquettes* is the liveliest of the three, but the reader will find nothing of the radiance of *Pickwick* in it. There is a great deal of dialogue and very few ballads. The exquisite bathos of Dickens as a lyric-writer may be judged from the first two verses of Squire Norton's song:

The child and the old man sat alone
  In the quiet peaceful shade
Of the old green boughs, that had richly grown
  In the deep thick forest glade.
It was a soft and pleasant sound,
  That rustling of the oak;
And the gentle breeze play'd lightly round,
  As thus the fair boy spoke:—
Dear father, what can honour be,
  Of which I hear men rave?
Field, cell and cloister, land and sea,
  The tempest and the grave:—
It lives in all, 'tis sought in each,
  'Tis never heard or seen:
Now tell me, father, I beseech,
  What can this honour mean?

The two old monopoly theatres, Covent Garden and Drury Lane, suffered from the disadvantage of bigness. In each there was a cavernous stage confronting a vast auditorium. Covent Garden seated more than 3,000. What availed fine strokes of dramatic portraiture, subtle looks, by-play, whispers, delicate shadings of expression, in the wastes of those barns? Love was compelled to bawl its shyest secrets; a witticism had to be fired off like a cannon to reach the galleries; and the whisper of an aside was magnified to a bellow. The players were driven to grimacing, gesticulating, mouthing and ranting, and, in the end, even the sublime Mrs. Siddons was said to have "grieved like a cheesemonger's wife". It is not surprising that comedy and tragedy both took refuge in the smaller houses, nor that the huge arenas of Covent Garden and Drury Lane were given over in the end to spectacle. The pageants, waterfalls and transformation scenes of the Victorian stage are commonly looked upon as marking a decay of the dramatic art. Is that so certain? Any pilgrim who has ever tried to struggle across the sandy desert of the poetic drama of the early decades of the nineteenth century must surely view the transformation scene in a Victorian *Cinderella* as an oasis of waving palms and bubbling springs. There was one stage-struck boy I knew for whom the very list of *dramatis personae* in those old plays—Khaled, a Moorish chief, Leonora, a beautiful captive, Don Guzman, her betrothed, and the rest—and the stage directions—Act v, scene 1: *A ruined Gothic Abbey by moonlight*—held an excitement indescribable. But even his infatuation could not survive the speeches of the heroes of Joanna Baillie and the heroines of Hannah More. The passion to write five-act tragedies in blank verse possessed blue-stocking ladies, lawyers, young bloods, politicians, and country clergymen. Macready, the chief actor of his time, was pursued by a horde of playwrights, and you may read in his diary how he groaned at the sight of his table piled high with unreadable manuscripts.

The footlights are glowing. "*Enter the Guards*", reads the author's stage direction. The Guards enter. The enormous stage shakes from their trampling feet. What do the Guards say? They speak in chorus:

> GUARDS. Fly with him! Fly, Sir Loys, 'tis too true!
> And only by his side thou may'st escape!
> The whole tribe is in full revolt—they flock
> About the palace—will be here—on thee—
> And there are twenty of us, we, the Guards
> Of the Nuncio to withstand them. Even we
> Had stayed to meet our death in ignorance,
> But that one Druse, a single faithful Druse,
> Made known the horror to the Nuncio! Fly!
> The Nuncio stands aghast.

And so on, and so on. It is not only the Nuncio who stands aghast. But it is not the hooves of those plodding cart-horses of the Muse, Sheridan Knowles and Dean Milman, clattering downhill that we hear in that speech. The lines are those of a genuine, indeed a great, poet in the flush of his young manhood's power. He is Robert Browning. The play is *The Return of the Druses*. There are few things sadder in the chronicles of squandered genius than the plays Browning wrote for Macready—unless it be those even more tedious plays which, later in the century Tennyson, in fever and travail, wrote for Irving. It is to be feared that the poetic dramas of that benevolent judge and kindliest of men, Thomas Noon Talfourd—his much-admired *Ion*, for example—must now rank with the bound volumes of Dr. Channing's sermons and the church music of Spohr among the tastes of our great-grandfathers whose attractions for ever escape us. But spectacle, now!—that is something we can understand. The Victorian stage mounted pictorial splendours as diverse as Charles Kean's Shakespearian revivals, the burlesques on classical themes at the Olympic Theatre, and the Christmas pantomimes. Charles Kean, Edmund's second son, had a fine eye for stage palaces and gorgeous pageantry. He was reproached for relying too much upon the scene-painter, the wardrobe mistress and the archaeologist, and too little upon Shakespeare, but the designs for his stage sets, preserved in the Victoria and Albert Museum, have a lasting charm for the imagination: for one thing they carry us back into that vanished Princess's Theatre on whose boards in 1856 the child Ellen Terry made her appearance as Mamillius in *A Winter's Tale*.

When gas illumination was brought in, the stage manager acquired a necromancer's wand. It was an illumination that achieved a hundred different broad or subtle effects in witchcraft. One who as a tiny boy, clinging to his father's shoulder, saw the last gas-illuminated pantomimes at the Surrey Theatre, remembers, as he might remember glimpses of

Paradise in a dream, the almost unbearable brilliance of that lighting when it was in full blaze; and its unearthly mystery when it was subdued to a glimmer. When the light was imprisoned in the caverns of Neptune's Kingdom on the floor of ocean, it was little more than a luminous cloud, a floating phosphorescence hinting secret chambers of wonder in endless recession, but, faint though it might be, it had the power to strike a sudden flash of lightning from the emeralds in a mermaid's crown, and to send pulsations of an electric fluid through all the shadowy grottoes, so that one made out, in the depths of the stage, the dim pallor of the swimmers' arms, moving in time with the ballet music, and to feel, even more than to see, the prodigious anemones, with quivering streamers, and the huge trees of coral, between whose branches the mermaids swam.

That light, so mysteriously diffused beneath the waves, became as dazzling as the glare of tropical sunshine when it shone upon Ali Baba and the Forty Thieves in the Street of the Bazaars. The golden cups turned into molten gold—there were rubies of blood dropping from the eunuchs' scimitars—and the sapphires and diamonds in the Sultan's turban burst and crackled like fireworks whenever the monarch rubbed his nose, and cried, "Chop off his head".

It was the true light of lost fairyland in the last transformation scene, when the stage became the court of Oberon and Titania, and a caressing voice fading into a limitless distance sang, "I know a bank where the wild thyme grows—where the wild thyme grows". I live again those moments when one veil after another of gossamer mist fell away, dissolving in the midnight brightness. Now an enormous marigold moon climbs up the back-cloth; a thing out of Nature; but it is the only moon one could dream of on such a night. Robin Goodfellow, perched on the branch of an oak, swinging himself to and fro in ecstasy, is cut out in black against that yellow moon. Elves and fairies are descending endlessly from the flies; they glide above the sacred bank, and make the transit of the moon, uttering cries of a pure happiness beyond the reach of words. They are creatures in flower-bell skirts, with iridiscent wisps of wings, merest dragon-fly wings; there are stars tangled in their locks, sparkling under the garlands of rosebuds; and we are too young and drowned too many fathoms deep in the illusion to know or care if the elves are sustained by wires.

When the whole Court has come together, they raise their wands, and in a shrill chorus cry hail to Oberon and Titania, now blissfully united again after their mimic war. The light blazes upon the King and Queen of fairyland, standing with locked hands upon a bank of the greenest green moss and most brilliant flowers ever seen, and as they, the great ones, are spangled from crown to heel in jewels, they are almost too bright for mortal eyes to look on. Then with the orchestra rising to a frenzy of fiddles, flutes and drums, and the white flower-bell skirts swirling around their monarchs, one mist of gauze after another slowly comes down again to dim the scene; the preposterous moon fades; Puck vanishes; the light on the bank dwindles to a faint glow; and presently the morning star begins to sparkle diamond-bright in the cloud of gauze. We are not sad, for there is the harlequinade still to come, and it seems there is to be no end to the unfolding of happiness, to the linked pleasures, and the discoveries of enchantment in this world that you and I have been so luckily born into.

That was a magic of the old-fashioned stage having nothing to do with wit, intelligence, poetry or the high arts of tragedy and comedy. Who shall say what is reality? Heaven knows how cheap and trashy by one set of standards were those spectacles, and how cruel it would be to peep behind those scenes. We may suspect that most of those fairies were drabs, or pert baggages like Fanny Dorrit. The tinsel and the flares must have hidden a great deal of dirt. And it was that snuffy, decrepit old man, in the orchestra well, Frederick Dorrit, whose flute's ecstatic squeakings expressed the ardours of Oberon after the long parting. But what more can we ask of the stage, as of life itself, than that the illusion should be strong, no matter how contrived?

We might indeed steal from Balzac one of his best titles and call the whole history of the Victorian stage *Lost Illusions*. It is usually said that the first night of Tom Robertson's *Society* in 1865 set the Victorian theatre free from fustian and bombast, broke the bonds of absurd conventions and unreal situations. *Society* brought in naturalism. The audience would now be able to see themselves mirrored on the stage. Mr. and Mrs. Belgravia could rise from their coffee-cups, break off a conversation about the unwisdom of allowing Margaret to marry the baronet, drive to the theatre, and there listen entranced while Mr. and Mrs. Belgravia on the other side of the footlights discussed the unwisdom of allowing their Margaret to marry the baronet. "Why, look," whispered Mrs. Belgravia in ecstasy, "those coffee-cups! They are the image of our own blue and gold!" What a home-like place the theatre had become. What a relief to have no more boring poetry to listen to, and to be spared the embarrassment of seeing passions skinned alive.

Tom Robertson, the revolutionary of the Victorian stage, made the discovery that the well-to-do middle classes had the fondness of Narcissus for looking at their reflected images. His plays were realistic, which meant they concerned themselves largely with the uninteresting misadventures of unremarkable people. His lines were true to life, which meant they were often as tame as life. An actor himself, he knew the tricks of the stage and how to tell his gentle stories with skill, while in Squire Bancroft or Marie Wilton he commanded the services of well-graced players. But it was not so much the naturalism of Robertson's situations and dialogue as the appurtenances of the new school of tea-cup drama that made the mid-Victorians catch their breath and clap their hands. Why, there are silver spoons to stir the tea from Twining's, the furniture is the Tottenham Court Road's heaviest, the bell-pulls are of real velvet brocade, and see! the door-handles in Mrs. Belgravia's drawing-room are actually of shining brass. ("Real pump! Splendid tubs!") Could Thespis or Crummles soar higher into the heaven of invention? Poor Shakespeare!—all he could employ in his day at the Globe was a loutish boy to hold up a sign marking a change of scene, *The Forest of Arden*, as it might be, or *Elsinore: a platform before the castle*.

So the fashionable drama of polite society, and worldly wisdom, of drawing-rooms and country houses, of "nice normal people with five thousand a year", established itself. It was to dominate the West End for a long time. It enfeebled the public imagination and made large fortunes for a number of eminent actors, managers and playwrights.

The theatre of Kean, of Phelps, of Barry Sullivan was no doubt a fallen angel, the feathers bedraggled, the halo drunkenly askew, but at least it was an angel, and it had wings. Tom Robertson and the new young actor-managers of his school, shook their heads at that dilapidated seraph, "Tut! We shall never get *you* into the enclosure at Ascot looking like that. Permit us to remove that old-fashioned halo. Haloes are no longer worn. A silk hat would suit you much better. Allow us to unhook those soiled pinions. They *do* collect dust, don't they? Why, here is Mr. Bancroft with his own tailor from Savile Row who will fit you out in a beautifully cut frock-coat in place of those absurd robes which trip you up. Here, also, are two very charming people, Mr. and Mrs. Kendal, who will be delighted to show you how to ingratiate yourself with archdeacons."

There was, of course, Irving. This greatest of Victorian actors, who made his first appearance on the stage in Bulwer-Lytton's *Richelieu* in 1856 and lived until 1905, revived the poetic drama, and adorned it with the splendours of artistic spectacle, so serving two traditions, and so opposing the cup-and-saucer school of society drama on two sides. In the end, he bankrupted himself by his Lyceum productions. Some accused Irving of treating Shakespeare shabbily, through spoiling the most glorious poetry in the world by a showman's artifices. Some barely allowed him to be an actor at all—he lacked the physical graces, they said, he was stilted and awkward, and his voice was full of odious affectations. But while Irving lived who could forget Shakespeare?—who could believe that pumps, washing tubs and Tottenham Court Road furniture were the final illusion of the stage?—who could be unaware of the sacred powers of the imagination?—who could forget the grandeur of passion or the redemption of man's soul through poetry?

There was a figure haunting this period who was far less splendid than Irving. He was a ludicrous creature, too ridiculous even to be accounted pitiful. His soiled linen, the high stock he affected, his shiny frock-coat, his cadaverous looks, his discoloured nose, his tragic eyes and his long dirty fingers grasping his lank hair, were drawn a thousand times by the comic artists of the period, and may still be seen surviving in those repositories of Victorian tradition, the minor humorous journals that one gets in barbers' shops. He was the actor of the old school. Sometimes he was drawn standing in a manager's office in a greatcoat with collar and cuffs of astrakhan, a battered silk hat in one hand, the manuscript of a poetic drama in the other, and, by an exquisite stroke of the artist's fun, a moth was shown fluttering out of the greatcoat. We knew his doom, poor fellow, before we glanced at the text beneath the drawing. He had played *Hamlet* more than once at Leamington Spa. He had in his—ahem —leisure hours (and one feared he now had many) indited a drama which very good critics had assured him equalled in poetic fire Talfourd's *Ion*, and whose principal part, they said, Macready himself would be delighted to play were that great man still living. You saw in the drawing the manager, a well-fed man, flashing diamond rings, and sitting under a playbill of *Hearts and Diamonds*, waving the wretch away with cutting comments on his appearance, and we were expected to laugh heartily at his humiliation. What place was there for this absurd scarecrow among the sleek young men and pretty young women of society drama who modelled themselves upon the smart set? Who wanted to look at another *Ion* or even another *Strafford?*

Yet if we had stopped laughing at the actor of the old school long enough to observe him, we might have detected in him the traces of fallen majesty. Did we not think it very comical to see him collecting his pride on the pavement outside the manager's office and stalking off with his head absurdly high and his left arm trailing behind him? Yet in that walk was preserved, though now lamed by the infirmities of age, the grandeur and dignity of John Philip Kemble when he was acting in his "high Roman fashion"—it brought back the way Kemble entered the Forum as Caesar, or, as Coriolanus, bade his last farewell. Was it not amusing to see the old actor at the Market Cross of a provincial town, where he had essayed his Readings from Shakespeare, surrounded by a hooting crowd, with the dogs snapping at his elastic-sided boots? What a figure he cut on that occasion when he broke down in Hamlet's last speech, and, striking the stones with his tall stick (his only property), cried out in an access of pathetic rage, "I will do such things—what they are I know not?"—while his torturers uttered a chorus of jeers. Yet that must have been very like the gesture Garrick employed at the peak of King Lear's fury when, as Bannister said, "his very stick acted". This wild motion of an old, mad king—its despair heightened by the private torments of the player, a tattered exile from his own kingdom—was itself of royal lineage, although now mocked and dishonoured. It was a gesture that had come down to us through Heaven knows what flittings and migrations from the wings of provincial Theatres Royal, through draughty passages smelling of oranges and dirty-clothes-baskets, descending by how many devout repetitions—the youth in his ardent apprenticeship learning from some decrepit old trouper, whose loyalties had outlived his ambitions, the very clench of the fist and force of the stroke as he, in turn, had been instructed in these actions by his granddad who had copied direct from some living model.

Edmund Kean died in 1833, the "small man, with Italian face and fatal eye" whose volcanic soul enthralled the poets of his time and raised the pit of Drury Lane to a frenzy. "Kean is gone," wrote Fanny Kemble, "and with him are gone *Othello*, *Shylock* and *Richard*." Not altogether. Something of Kean lived on, something of Othello. For our barnstorming old actor retained in his seediness, in his moonlight flits from one frowsy lodging-house to a frowsier, in his stilted mannerisms, some lingering glow of the lava glare of Kean. When he had borrowed a shilling from you, and the warmth of rum was animating his worn old carcase again, he would recite, needing no persuasion, Shylock's speech,—"Hath not a Jew eyes? hath not a Jew hands, organs, dimensions, senses, affections, passions?"—and you could then behold again, although through many mists and fumes, the wonder of that night, the 26th of January, 1814, when Kean came upon the stage of Drury Lane for the first time, when the house "was empty of nearly all but critics and those who came in with oranges or orders; and the listlessness of the small spiritless audience at the first night of a new *Shylock* was 'the languor which is not repose' ". Was the old actor's voice rasping, his action abrupt and singular? So were Kean's on that first night. In the grip of a power, in whose tyrannical service he had found only hunger, humiliation, debts and the sores of a pariah dog, the actor of the old school was transfigured; for a fleeting minute or two he seemed to draw upon some stellar stream of energy which enabled one to understand what a fury of life must have raged in Edmund Kean, what tumults and upheavals of the soul, shaking the body to pieces. So through the Victorian twilight, in dreary lodgings in by-streets, there were preserved, by creatures who excited only contempt and pity, glittering fragments of an immortal treasure, covered over with grime and dust; the phrasing of a Shakespearian line that might be as old as Quin or Cibber, and a laugh, spectral and mannered, that was the echo of some seventeenth-century Falstaff; and what made the comfortable Victorian, detained by this scarecrow, most uncomfortable in these eerie manifestations was precisely that which startled the very first audiences who heard them, namely their force of novelty.

In the eye of the old actor who quivered with the supernatural energy of Kean there was visible not only the ancestral sorrows of the Jew, and the study of revenge, but also the light that had ceased to burn on the fashionable stage. The players who belonged to the society drama of Robertson, on which Pinero and Henry Arthur Jones were later to build their fashionable problem plays, might lead lives as easy as those of the characters they represented, they might lunch with duchesses and become friends of the Prince of Wales. But the old actor, a beggar prince of the royal house that marked its proud descent from Richard Burbage, wandered the roads, baring his head to the wind and the planets. Yet if the destiny that ruled him was cruel, it had entrusted to him an imperishable heritage. While the popinjays and young minxes who had driven him from his estate were prisoners in their eternal drawing-room, repeating their endless empty chatter, he, the old actor, tramping under the stars, could put on the broken crown of Lear, or cry with Antony,

> Let's have one other gaudy night: call to me
> All my sad captains, fill our bowls; once more
> Let's mock the midnight bell.

It was this disreputable tramp, this indisputable ham, who was the drama's rightful heir, and, under his dirty linen and frayed coat, he hugged the jewel of the ages to his breast.

CHAPTER TWO

WITCHES AND WARLOCKS

"Now that the schools are gone, and the regular sight-seers exhausted," said Mrs. Jarley, of Jarley's Moral Waxworks, "we come to the General Public and they want stimulating."

Mrs. Jarley sat rattling silver coins at the entrance to the stupendous collection of upwards of One Hundred Wax Figures, "all others being impostors and deceptions". The discerning and enlightened General Public was cool to her wooing. The population of the town, "though they manifested a lively interest in Mrs. Jarley personally, and such of her waxen satellites as were to be seen for nothing, were not affected by any impulse moving them to the payment of sixpence a head. In this depressed state of the classical market, Mrs. Jarley made extraordinary efforts to stimulate the popular taste, and whet the popular curiosity."

There is little occasion for us to pity our great-grandparents their narrow opportunities for entertainment. They needed no lectures on the use of leisure—they had somewhat less of it than their descendants enjoy—and they had a fair notion of how to amuse themselves in their homes with dancing, music and games; when they went out, they could choose between opera and burletta, theatre and concert hall, the panorama or Daguerre's diorama (on which by an ingenious system of lighting a smiling landscape would be changed in a twinkling to a stormy sea), the circus, masquerades, the zoos, the exhibitions of dwarfs and freaks, the waxworks, the fairs on the heaths, and the mixed pleasures provided by such gardens as Vauxhall, Cremorne, Marylebone, Kensington, Ranelagh —and Bagnigge Wells—on top of countless small tea gardens where brews stronger than tea were served. According to the London guides of that time, the prices of admission to Drury Lane were five shillings for boxes, three shillings for the pit and the gallery two shillings and a shilling. At the smaller theatres the prices were four shillings for boxes, two shillings for the pit and the gallery one shilling. The Strand Theatre at the end of Waterloo Road on the Surrey side of the river halved these charges. The Surrey Theatre had the bad habit of charging the playgoer an extra shilling for a seat once he had got inside.

It is unlikely that all the amusements of a century ago would possess tang for a modern palate. The panoramas, for example? Great-grandmamma was inexpressibly thrilled by the sight of Vesuvius in eruption—a cardboard crown stuffed with fireworks and washed by crimson light.

PLATE 25

THE BAR OF THE "HALF MOON" TAP
Coloured etching by Isaac Robert Cruikshank
From Pierce Egan's "Life In and Out of London", 1869

THE GIN SHOP — A GIN PALACE AT NIGHT
Wood engravings by George Cruikshank from "The House That Jack Built", 1853

BRIXTON PRISON: FEMALE CONVICTS AT WORK
DURING THE SILENT HOUR
Wood engraving from Henry Mayhew's "Great World of London", 1856

Does that seem childish to those of us who are familiar with the marvels of the cinema? I remember being taken, as an infant of very tender years, to see in some church hall a survivor of these Victorian panoramas, stranded, like so many other Victorian survivors, on that far, suburban beach, there to break to pieces amid the babble of urchins. It was *The Earthquake at Lisbon;* formed on that event which made so profound an impression on Voltaire and came to rank as a rationalist miracle, disproving the existence of a beneficent Creator. Though I live to be a hundred, I shall never wipe from my mind the violent shock of that night. I doubt if it is through the rawness of babyish impressions alone that I see such an infernal glare spread over the scene. There must surely have been a wicked skill in stage carpentry, a diabolical lighting, to raise the effects which appal me still—even with more recent shocks in my head. I can comprehend the morbid fascination which the panorama held for the Victorians when I close my eyes and see again the fearful moments of the earthquake. What brought the sharpest freezing to the heart then, and brings it now, is the particular circumstance of the mad jangling and clamour of all the bells of all the city's host of churches, as the earth in its convulsions shook them, flinging their towers and campanile to and fro. That was the device of a grand and sinister imagination—to heighten the terror of the visual illusion by that demented clanging.

The palaces of the Lisbon dukes, smothered in flowers, crumbling down with a roar—the tenements tumbling upon the poor, fleeing people in the streets—the frantic mother rushing this way and that with a naked child in her arms—the wild streamers of fire shaking above the ruins—the earth opening, and the mouths of Hell yawning in the avenue of Kings—all this was conveyed with a horrid exactitude. They knew their business, these makers of panoramas.

The Victorians believed in the purification of infant souls through pity and terror. Their Gothic imaginations rejoiced in physical and spiritual horrors, although their own world was so fat, secure and comfortable. They promised the child an entertainment, and his eyes sparkled, and then they thrust him into a coal-cellar saying, "It's dark, horribly dark, isn't it? And there are wild beasts, and cannibals and bogy men there. Can't you see the red flame of their eyes flashing down there in the dark?" It is too much to suppose that they were possessed of a prophetic sense that the world which would come after them would not be secure and comfortable; that the young should be brought up to know that they would sup on horrors; and that the twentieth century would turn out to be very like the fifteenth century.

Spring has come, it has come to an England still in large part undefiled, the woods stand in a mist of green, and there are the breakers of hawthorn blossom on the hedges. Nature's small children shake themselves, stretch and yawn out of their winter sleep, and take a peep at the strengthening sun. And now, many odder creatures, who have been sleeping all winter long in the city begin to move along England's many-winding roads. The caravans set out for the small towns and villages. A mangy old lion, dim of sight and smelling strong, blinks at the sunlight on the country cottages. Amiable veteran with broken teeth, he is due to petrify the yokels and servant-girls of the West Country. He will enter into a friendly fraud with an old actor, as mangy as himself, to tear a pound of raw steak out of the actor's jacket to create the illusion of the fearful act of eating a man alive. In carts and wagons move the circus people, the mathematical horse, the learned pig, the human skeleton, the bearded woman, the frog boy and the rest. The members of Sleary's company are striking out for new fields—"all the fathers could dance upon rolling casks, stand upon bottles, catch knives and balls, twirl hand-basins, ride upon anything, jump over everything, and stick at nothing—all the mothers could (and did) dance upon the slack wire and the tight rope, and perform rapid acts on bare-backed steeds". In this Canterbury pilgrimage go Mrs. Jarley and her waxworks, Codlin and Short and their Punch and Judy show, and a swarm of tumblers, gymnasts, singers and fortune-tellers. Doublethrust, in Cruikshank's *Comic Almanack* for 1844, though drawn in burlesque, may be taken as a fair specimen of these strollers. He, having "long occupied the honourable position of second cut-throat on the national boards, finding that the managers had taken to cutting each other's throats, and consequently left nothing for him to do, got together a select company for the purpose of performing Shakespeare in the provinces". This is how Doublethrust advertised his season:—

MACBETH,

From the Text of Shakspeare:

Followed by

A NAVAL HORNPIPE,

From the Text of T. P. Cooke:

Preceded by

AN ADDRESS,

Written expressly for the occasion, by the

PRESIDENT OF THE LOCAL INSTITUTION FOR THE ADVANCEMENT OF SCIENCE.

From the text of Shakespeare be it noted—that was common form. "*Macbeth* wore a plaid shawl, commonly called a horse-cloth, and a pair of stocking-drawers, with a breast-plate formed of the brass ornaments used to cover the screws of tent bedsteads. . . . By the way of an over-flow at half-price, the rain came on in such torrents at about half-past eight that in the fourth act Macbeth came on under an umbrella." That is so near to the truth, as one may see it peeping out of the corners of old country newspapers, that it can hardly be called a caricature.

The country fairs and race-courses drew the wanderers. There was a great deal of noise, dust, hearty vulgarity, horseplay, honest happiness and animal vitality in these assemblies, and little in the way of tired, mechanical fun. Through spring, and the golden weeks of summer, the vagabonds wandered the country, often going hungry, often living more by their wits than by their art, and chivvied by the constables and magistrates. Few slept so snugly as Mrs. Jarley in that cosy, shiny caravan of hers. The little inns that look so pretty in the picture-books with their diamond-paned windows and creeper-covered walls, were not all sweetness inside, and we may be glad that it never fell to us to try the beds of tenth-rate lodging-houses in country towns in the forties. On any fine night it was wholesomer to sleep under a hedge wrapped in an old coat.

Summer! The throb of the drum across the fields of shimmering wheat, across the lazy dominion of the cornflower and the poppy, calls us to a stretch of common land on which these entertainers have settled. From the folds of their tent, the actors poke their heads and sniff the country air. Their faces are daubed with ochre, crimson lake and lamp-black, and under the green reflections of the sun in the chestnut-trees they look the most comical of goblins and demons; the village girls gape and giggle. A sheeted ghost gibbers at the rear of the tent to be let out to swallow a mouthful of fresh air. A spurt of powder and blue flame makes a stench. It is the Demon King rehearsing his effects. The First Hired Assassin lies on his back gazing with sad eyes at the drift of snowy clouds. A Highlander in yellow drawers exchanges memories of Kean with a broken-down Indian brave who has had half his feathers pecked out. When the drum outside the tent has brought a crowd together, the theatrical entertainment begins. It is as likely as not a fine confused medley of a melodrama from Renaissance Italy, filled with hissing vipers, and an allegorical dance by the Princess Pocahontas and Captain Smith; while Bussy D'Ambois, with a saucepan-lid on his chest, will fight a duel to the death with the Master of Ravenswood. In the productions of these strolling players, given in the tents on the village greens, there were visible fragments of the drama of the seventeenth and eighteenth centuries, baleful gleams from the Jacobean playwrights, situations from Otway's *Venice Preserved* and from Congreve's *Mourning Bride*, as well as broad grins inherited from the farces of Sam Foote and George Colman.

There is a captivating account in Dickens's *Greenwich Fair* of the performance of one of these companies of actors of the early Victorian times. The immense booth, with the large stage in front,

> so brightly illuminated with variegated lamps, and pots of burning fat, is "Richardson's" where you have a melodrama (with three murders and a ghost), a pantomime, a comic song, an overture, and some incidental music, all done in five-and-twenty minutes. . . . A change of performance takes place every day during the fair, but the story of the tragedy is always pretty much the same. There is a rightful heir, who loves a young lady, and is beloved by her; and a wrongful heir, who loves her too, and isn't beloved by her; and the wrongful heir gets hold of the rightful heir, and throws him into a dungeon, just to kill him off when convenient, for which purpose he hires a couple of assassins—a good one and a bad one—who, the moment they are left alone, get up a little murder on their own account, the good one killing the bad one, and the bad one wounding the good one. Then the rightful heir is discovered in prison, carefully holding a long chain in his hands, and seated despondingly in a large arm-chair; and the young lady comes in to two bars of soft music, and embraces the rightful heir; and the wrongful heir comes in to two bars of quick music (technically called a "hurry") and goes on in the most shocking manner, throwing the young lady about as if she was nobody, and calling the rightful heir "Ar-recreant ar-wretch!" in a very loud voice, which answers the double purpose of displaying his passion, and preventing the sound being deadened by the sawdust. The interest becomes intense; the wrongful heir draws his sword, and rushes on the rightful heir; a blue smoke is seen, a gong is heard, and a tall white figure (who has been, all this time, behind the arm-chair, covered over with a tablecloth) slowly rises to the tune of "Oft in the stilly night". This is no other than the ghost of the rightful heir's father, who was killed by the wrongful heir's father, at sight of which the wrongful heir becomes apoplectic, and is literally "struck all of a heap", the stage not being large enough to admit of his falling down at full length. Then the good assassin staggers in, and says he was hired in conjunction with the bad assassin by the wrongful heir, to kill the rightful heir, and he's killed a good many people in his time, but he's very sorry for it, and won't do so any more—a promise which he immediately redeems, by dying off-hand without any nonsense about it. Then the rightful heir throws down his chain; and then two men, a sailor, and a young woman (the tenantry of the rightful heir) come in, and the ghost makes dumb motions to them, which they, by supernatural interference, understand—for no one else can; and the ghost (who can't do anything without blue fire) blesses the rightful heir and the young lady, by half suffocating them with smoke: and then a muffin-bell rings, and the curtain drops.

Meanwhile in the meadow behind the players' tent, two brawny young men have peeled off their shirts and are pounding one another with bare knuckles. Sweat and blood glisten on the play of a blacksmith's and a ploughboy's muscles. They are plucky, game chaps, they will take and give blows doggedly, and they will be good for at least fifteen rounds. The crowd that rings them round cheers, spits and jeers at the to and fro of the fight, priding themselves on being erudite patrons of the Corinthian Fancy.

In those days boxing was outlawed. A society which for so long tolerated the barbarities of child labour professed to be shocked by the pagan brutality of the prize fight. So boxing took refuge in open country where the constables seldom troubled to follow it.

"Dear, dear, what a place it looked, that Astley's!" The name brings up the image of Andrew Ducrow, the most accomplished and picturesque horseman in the history of the ring, and of that ethereal Miss Woolford.

Astley's was the place for the family man. It amused Dickens to observe there Papa and Mamma shepherding nine or ten children; three little boys in blue jackets and long trousers, "with lay-down shirt collars"; and a little girl, then two more little girls, then three more little boys; and a round-eyed infant in a braided frock lifted over the seats, "a process which occasioned a considerable display of little pink legs".

Astley's was generous in its entertainment, it had a stage on which melodramas and spectacles were presented, and a wide arena for the feats of horsemanship. Such pageants as *The Burning of Moscow* and *The Crusaders of Jerusalem* were startling enough to make any small boy's eyes bolt out of his head. The great thrill of Astley's was, of course, *Mazeppa And the Wild Horse*. What glorious nonsense that was! See the handsome Tartar prince tied by cords to the horse. See the torches lighted and brandished, flaring up the mountain side, row on row. Ladies and gentlemen, grapple yourselves to your seats, stuff handkerchiefs in your mouths, while the blood-chilling spectacle unfolds. Look!—the wild horse is madly rearing and plunging and foaming. The waving torches have driven him frantic. His eyes are ablaze with fire, blood and lunacy. He is off, off with the wind in his tail. The little children shriek and shut their eyes and kindly matrons press their hands over their hearts. Papa gives an ironical cheer. Up the rocky defiles flies the demented horse, with the Prince of Tartary lashed to his back. Lightning blazes, thunder rolls, prodigious cataracts fall from heaven to accompany that infernal ride. Wolves raven, carrion birds wheel. At the back of the stage an endless panorama unfolds. After a million miles of riding ruin, dawn breaks in Tartary, the exhausted horse yields up the invincible youth, insensate, but still breathing. And we know now that youth, beauty, virtue, high birth, can never be destroyed. Hurrah! We proclaim Mazeppa KING OF THE TARTARS. The small girls wave their handkerchiefs loyally, and Papa's outburst of ironical cheers is worthy of the House of Commons.

I wish I could have been at Astley's to see the experiments in equestrian Shakespeare, particularly Richard the Third mounted on "White Surrey", the heroic beast dying nightly in a most beautiful and affecting manner, melting the small girls in the boxes to tears. I would like, too, to have seen Henry V and Macbeth prancing and curvetting around the stage. One day, I suspect, the notion will be revived; everything in turn comes round again. Some clever young producer will stage a cycle of equestrian Shakespeare at the National Theatre.

In *The Newcomes* you may find preserved a pleasant memory of the drama at Astley's.

> Who was it that took the children to Astley's but Uncle Newcome? I saw him there in the midst of a cluster of these little people, all children together. He laughed delighted at Mr. Merryman's jokes, in the ring. He beheld *The Battle of Waterloo* with breathless interest, and was amazed—yes, amazed by Jove, sir!—at the prodigious likeness of the principal actor to the Emperor Napoleon. . . . It did one good to hear the colonel's honest laugh at the clown's jokes, and to see the tenderness and simplicity with which he watched over this happy brood of young ones.

Joey the Clown is a traditionalist. They say he is always called Joey after Grimaldi, but his japes and his patter come down to us from remoter origins. "Here we are again!" is a very old cry echoing down the corridors of history. That comic figure with the floured cheeks and big red mouth that the children laughed at last Christmas as he scampered into the ring, and turned his somersaults, is an aristocrat of a long line, and all his conventions, the faces he pulls, the tricks he plays, bring us into touch with generations of Joeys. The dialogue between the clown and the ring-master at Astley's that Dickens records—is that not a ritual recitation lovingly handed down from father to son?

> "I say, sir!" the clown begins the exchange.—"Well, sir?" (It's always conducted in the politest manner.)—"Did you ever happen to hear I was in the army, sir?"—"No, sir."—"Oh yes, sir, I can go through my exercise, sir."—"Indeed, sir."—"Shall I do it now, sir?"—"If you please, sir; come, sir—make haste." (A cut with the long whip, and "Ha! done now, I don't like it" from the clown.) Here the clown throws himself on the ground, and goes through a variety of convulsive gymnastics, doubling himself up, and untying himself again, and making himself look very like a man in the most hopeless extreme of human agony, to the vociferous delight of the gallery, until he is interrupted by a second cut from the long whip and a request to see "what Miss Woolford's stopping for?" On which, to the inexpressible mirth of the gallery, he exclaims, "Now, Miss Woolford, what can I come for to go, for to fetch, for to bring, for to carry, for to do, for you, ma'am?"

Through revolutions and world wars, the line of clowns endures, unbending conservatives all of them, but where in this modern age shall we find such a creature of dazzling phantasmagoria as Ducrow? He was a horseman without rival, but he was not content simply to be the best horseman of his time. Like Tom o'Bedlam, he was attended by a host of furious fancies. He dreamed of himself as the god of love, as the god of war, as Osiris, as Sardanapalus, as the great Cham—he lived a hundred lives, all of them prodigious. He ransacked the centuries for barbaric splendours, covered himself with the jewels of the Moguls, wore the armour of Hector, looted the silks and brocades of the Manchu emperors.

There were a number of Victorians of note who expressed in their varying ways that powerful vein of phantasmagoria which ran through this age of mahogany and ormolu, of triumphant science and mechanical

A MUSIC-HALL TRAPEZE ARTIST
Cartoon by Richard Doyle from his "Bird's Eye View of Society", 1864

prowess, of fat living, bovine materialism and the blessed certitude of the five per cents. There were, for example, the architects of Victorian Gothic; there was the great poet who wrote that masterpiece of delirium, *Maud*; there was Edward Lear, the Queen's drawing master, who knew that a pobble is better without his toes; there was the mathematical lecturer at Oxford who hunted the Snark and wrote "Jabberwocky"; there was Rossetti painting *How They Met Themselves;* there was Dickens in a thousand pages, from Jonas Chuzzlewit's flight and Carker's end to the opium dream that opens *Edwin Drood*.

Among these angels and demons of the Victorian phantasmagoria, we must put the circus performer Ducrow. For he expressed in the most direct form the longing to break through the dull ordinariness of life into the bizarre and the fantastic—into that wonderland where the writ of the King's Bench did not run, where everything was violent or absurd, and the improbable had become the conventional. Lord knows what havoc Ducrow's devouring lust for grandeur might have caused in respectable society if he had not been able to glut his towering passions in his circus roles. What felicity to ride through life on a fiery steed—sometimes on three horses together, sometimes controlling six of them!—through an ever-changing landscape of gorgeous hashish visions. What roles!—and what backgrounds! The hanging gardens through which he rides—their million roses dim under the Babylonian stars—dissolve in a few seconds into subterranean halls, reared on soaring pillars of basalt, and illuminated by naphthaline torches that will never be put out; halls in which lie buried the treasure of the kings who reigned before Adam, guarded by enormous serpents as old as the rocks around which they are curled. Now the back-cloth behind the magnificent Ducrow is changing again. The panorama brightens, the sun rises and we are in a festival at Baghdad, and all the gems of the Arabian Nights are scattered around us, the minarets and crescent domes shed dazzling light; the fountains fling up their showers of diamonds; the nightingale pours out its heart even by daylight within the walled gardens, and its passion is not drowned by those musicians in coloured silks who pluck their melancholy strings behind the lattices. There is sherbet, sweetmeat and sweet preserves, and a wilderness of flowers, and there is she, the fairest among women, the full moon of all delight. Then the light congeals, and the air grows harsh. Again the painted scene changes to yield Ducrow another triumph. He now becomes the genius of the gloomy North. We are among the pines that fledge the dark, cold mountain slopes. Castles on giddying peaks—thunder-clouds streaming from their thin towers—precipices coiled like dragons' tails around them. Crevasses, and Alpine witches muttering spells of death among the frozen rainbows, trolls, gnomes, the howlings of werewolves, the echoings of treacherous horns among the defiles and a black north-east wind blowing. Presto!—the backcloth is transformed. Ducrow lifts his head, and sniffs a more rarefied air. We are on the unending plains of the New World. Their primeval silence is torn by the cries of the Red Indians, there is the intoxication of the war dance, the fire and the plumes, the ecstasy of cruelty, and the madness of dripping blood.

Against these backgrounds of phantasmagoria moves always one lonely, prodigious figure—now king of Babylon, now Tyre, now Nineveh, now a king before Adam, now Commander of the Faithful, now the Champion of Christendom, now Great Chief Rain in the Face—always Ducrow, but always more than Ducrow. To be able to dress himself up in his day-dreams and to spread his private visions like the tail of a peacock in the sight of cheering thousands, this was the happy fate of Ducrow. When he came riding out on a horse fantastically caparisoned, he had the posture of a conqueror of the world, balancing on one foot on his fire-snorting Bess; the lord of creation showing off his muscular calves and thighs, his torso encased in Greek armour, exquisitely ornamented, armour such as Juno might have presented to her favourite hero in the Trojan war, a plume in his helmet, and on his face the glow from the burning of the topless towers.

The impersonations were always melting one into another, as in the opium-eater's dreams. Now, cries he, I am Tamburlane the Great, my chariot is dragged by captive kings. "Holla, ye pampered Jades of Asia: what, can ye draw but twenty miles a day?" Now I am Genghis Khan, and I come with the scorching wind that drives across the desolation of the wilderness and on that wind is carried a continuous wailing note of grief and lamentation that is older than Time itself, and it will sustain its awful monotone until this planet is no more. I am Pizarro in the Temple

THE ANTI-SLAVERY SOCIETY CONVENTION, 1840
Detail from the oil painting by B. R. Haydon
National Portrait Gallery, London

WILLIAM EWART GLADSTONE IN HIS OLD AGE
Grisaille on millboard by Sydney Prior Hall
National Portrait Gallery, London

A VILLAGE CHOIR
Oil painting by Thomas Webster, 1847
Victoria and Albert Museum, London

of the Sun. I am Antony in Egypt. I am Henry pacing the Cloth of Gold. Is not all existence illusion? And could there be a grander hallucination than this—to be Mr. Ducrow?

Such a being appears as an emanation of the dream-life of his age, an embodiment of the insane fancies that were buttoned up inside the formal frock-coats. An album of Victorian worthies shows square earthy shapes and heavy faces, whiskered or bearded, under stove-pipe hats. The images melt upon the page, and there in the gilt-edged pasteboard frames appear Tamburlane, Antony, Childe Harold and Mr. Ducrow.

Ducrow was without education, yet in some way he had managed to pick up a good deal of knowledge about gods and heroes, kings and victorious generals, about the shows and pageants of the past. He was a foul-mouthed showman and charlatan, with shocking manners, yet he had a sensitive feeling for scenical colour and design, and something of the disinterested frenzy of the poet. Ducrow had been ill-used in boyhood, but if you brand such a desperate boy with hot irons every time he is caught hiding a book in his jacket, if you whip him every time he looks at a picture, if you keep him starved and tied to the galleys, he will yet, by an unerring instinct, find his spirit's sustenance, somehow divining the books he cannot read. Ducrow died at fifty, burned out by glory, having lived in a fever through many centuries of existence. But how happy a man he had been!

Miss Woolford, I suppose, was the archetype of all the princesses of the circus ring the world has seen since, the beautiful bare-backed equestriennes of our boyhood. But none of them has ever attracted that particular idolatry, none has provoked such vain regrets. These others, these later ones, were, I fear, merely gracious and lady-like, while she was always *La Belle Dame Sans Merci*, "full beautiful, a faery's child", though, in fact, she was the child of mercenary parents who treated her badly. She was born in the year before Waterloo. She died in the time of the Boer War—a gruff, grim and snobbish old woman. To say that she was an eminent Victorian is rather like claiming Titania and Puck as eminent Elizabethans. She was there, she was part of it, but she did not belong to it.

The great singers of the bygone opera are ghosts; we can catch no echo now of the notes of Malibran—then how on earth are we to bring back out of the blackness the phantom grace of a young girl who did little more than ride horses in a ring? Yet the matchless Miss Woolford—it must always be, one notes, in this context, respectfully *Miss* Woolford—she, who was the bright star of Astley's, so charmed the imagination of the age that lovers of the past, of that Victorian past, have toyed ever since with the nonsensical fancy that her shade would somehow yield to their incantations. "Miss Woolford knows me; she smiled at me," squeaked the clown, rolling in the sawdust. I have read lines in praise of her, written long after Astley's was gone, which display the same sense of recognition, as though the dreamers had just caught a glimpse of that elfin rider and the most delicate milk-white hands in Christendom. What can one ever keep of her, whose glory brightened, and went, and then came again always in the most fugitive moments? Those moments of beauty that stilled the groundlings at Astley's to a religious hush—the lyric movements of her arms as she twined the flags above her head—the graceful way she leaped through the hoop or the circle of flames—all these were bubbles of the air. Yet still the illusion persists, among those who dream and brood about the past, that there is some compensating principle in nature which gives to the most fleeting things a second chance, a second revelation. They are not content to see their Miss Woolford through the eyes of Dickens, Thackeray and Dicky Doyle.

The Victorian daemon was merciless to the young who showed any talent. It was, in particular, harsh to its artists in their making. Nothing was spared them. The effortless grace of movement, the ease that cast its spell over audiences—these were nearly always rooted in a squalid, wretched childhood, a childhood spent on the treadmill. "My father whipped me as a child to make me stand on my toes," said Taglioni. How revealing is that pun of Grimaldi's—an awful pun in two senses. He was once watching Ducrow using his whip on a boy he was training in horsemanship. "I must make an *impression* on him, you see," said the master. "Does it need such a lot of *whacks*?" asked the sad clown, who had himself been a whipped puppy. Those children were acquainted early with one of the grim truths of the world that the triumphs of the artist are usually wrought in pain and a sweating out of the very heart's blood. "All things excellent are both difficult and rare," said Spinoza, and the great Victorian artists knew how cruelly high was the purchase price of their excellence. As a child, Miss Woolford had been trained, not at all gently, by her father to walk the wire and to dance on a nag's back. It was he who taught her to sail like thistledown over the twenty-nine ribbons. As a child, too, she had danced as Columbine in the pantomime. It is as the eternal Columbine that one sees her, in her floating gauze, light as a flower and of unearthly loveliness, standing on her rushing horse, leaning far to one side in the speed and wind of the race, with the orchestra dashing into its crescendo; an airy spirit who might at any moment rise and soar through the roof. On her face is a tranced smile, she is happy in her own happiness, as though the wall of all the other faces, and the noisy band, and the blazing lights had no existence. Her grace is unconscious, she is like a bird in unawareness of the motions of her flight. And yet, it seems, she was loathing and despising it all the time, longing for prim respectability in Bayswater.

Did she—I sometimes wonder—really exist? Was she not, perhaps, a beautiful myth, a projection of a dream? All those drawings of her, unworthy things that they were said to be, "not *getting* her, at all", and all those enraptured foolish scribblings are they not the forgeries of desire? In inventing the figure of Miss Woolford, were not those Victorians embodying an idea of romantic beauty—the beauty that is beyond possessing? Pater's defining of romance as the quality of strangeness added to beauty—now, that would have suited Miss Woolford. It is true that historically there *was* a Miss Woolford, a rider at Astley's who married Ducrow at twenty-three, married again after his death a rich, dull husband, gave up the ring at twenty-five, and lived to be eighty-six. But there was also a historic Richard Whittington and a historic Bluebeard, and what are they to us? The forbidding old lady who hated the thought of the circus, of which, long, long ago, she had been the queen, and would not talk of it, had nothing to do with the folk-lore of the Victorians.

There are no statues to Mr. Ducrow and Miss Woolford in London, no three-volume biographies were composed; they are very frail ghosts. He was fantasy. She was beauty. And those round, sound men of the time who worked so hard, made so much money, were so right-thinking, read *The Times*, voted for Lord Palmerston and ate such very heavy meals were troubled by these apparitions, and found them hard to forget.

CHAPTER THREE

JACOB'S LADDER

At choir practice on Friday nights, the choirmaster would often show a restless spirit. Not Mendelssohn *again*, he would cry querulously, throwing up his hands. And *not* Spohr. Let me see, how many times have we done "As pants the hart" in the past eighteen months?

Not Stainer, not Barnby, not Goss! Suddenly those solid characters—the three old reliables of choir nights, Stainer, Barnby and Goss—had become unendurable bores. For my own part, I had always thought of these composers as an old-fashioned firm of solicitors, Stainer, Barnby and Goss, commissioners of oaths, with brass plates and roll-top desks—paragons of respectability, wearing mutton-chop whiskers which they stroked all day long, and handsome gold Alberts setting off the impressive rotundity of their paunches. Their music was written on stiff law foolscap, it had fine red seals attached, it was tied up at night in pink tape, and tucked away in deed boxes. To escape these old friends whose faces had grown too familiar, our choirmaster began ransacking some old cabinets, tall and rickety, where, concealed behind the barricades of surplices and cassocks, there were kept great, grimy, cobwebbed piles of Victorian church music—anthems and cantatas. That all his earlier huntings through these wastes had brought him no gleam of treasure never discouraged him. On each new march into this desert he was confident he would turn up some forgotten early anthem of Sullivan, an Ouseley that had been overlooked, or an unknown piece by Sterndale Bennett which would be a model of gentlemanly behaviour in music. He never found any of these gems. At last, in desperation—the floor being littered with discarded sheets—he would plunge his hand into the black recesses, and pull out a sooty bundle, then deal out to us the parts of *Jonah's Deliverance*. The boys would stumble and squeak through a page or two, our master at the piano, peering through his spectacles at the anthem, first in hope, then in loathing. Then he would stop, give a sick grin and cry, "Enough! —more than enough", and gather up the sheets. I recall one anthem, snatched from the back of a cabinet, in which the genial promise, "Their children shall be dashed to pieces before their eyes" (*Isaiah*, xiii), was chanted to a lively tune that brought to mind children dancing in the streets around a hurdy-gurdy, and we went on with the rollicking theme until the choirmaster broke down, resting his head on the top of the piano, and shaking with an inner storm of laughter.

The usual end of such evenings was his saying sharply that it was getting late, we must attend to business, and that we would now turn to Mendelssohn's *Hymn of Praise*. "And let us try to get a sharper attack this time—more bite, more decision." We knew well enough the page to turn to, "I waited for the Lord", inscribed—do I remember aright?—"for two soprani and chorus". Our first soprano was a big, plump, rosy boy who would have made a good Cupid on an old-fashioned valentine. Out of his round body he brought forth a small, shrill treble that was like a little lark piping up from a big pie. First soprano lacked the easy temper of the fat; he was full of twitches and doubts, and he had a trick of wrenching his topmost notes out of the twisted corner of his mouth, with a grimace of pain, as though he were touching the nerve in a tooth. Second soprano was a slim, cool, feline boy, who had a way of smoothing the back of his head with his hand, his dark eyes half-closed like a cat's, as though he were very pleased with himself. He warbled his chest notes with a bird's ease, casting meanwhile from under his lashes glances of malice at his rival. They were not aware of it, but these two boys were living examples of a debate which in its day aroused much passion: should choir-boys be trained to use the head voice or the chest voice? Our master was a natural Liberal, he saw virtue in both schools, and he compromised. So first soprano brought forth his tiny tinkling, musical-box notes from the head, and second soprano, preening his back-hairs, fluted like a thrush from his chest.

"Back to Mendelssohn," cried the master. Now began the familiar thrum—thrum—thrum—*thrum* of the piano accompaniment which, when I had heard it in infancy, seemed to me to be like the trailings of liquid light that a lifted paddle shakes out of the water. And now, second soprano (with an impish look at first soprano who was beginning to squirm like an impaled beetle, as he usually did before he sang) raised his melodious wail, "I waaai-ted for the Lord, He incliii-ned unto me". Then, above the honeyed sweetness of second soprano's notes, first soprano took flight.

"Oh Lord!—the attack, the attack," groaned the master, bringing his right hand down on the keyboard in a rending crash. The plump boy turned crimson, the thin boy gave a pitying smile, cast down his eyes and folded his hands in his lap. So in later years I was to see that same compassionate smile, dispersed in empty air, on the face of a celebrated Donna Anna at a rehearsal of *Don Giovanni* in a far-away land, when the equally renowned Donna Elvira had been brought to a halt by the conductor. Across all seas and across the gulfs dividing age, race and sex, the soprano temperament remains constant in a world of change.

"Let us try again!"—thrum—thrum—thrum—*thrum*. We were in flight once again, the room vibrating from the enthusiasm of the accompaniment. Now the piccolo voice soared up over the flute voice, the lark over the thrush, the bee above the butterfly—and then we, miserable grubs of choristers, with our snuffles, false starts and cracked notes joined in, and the choirmaster, who, though the idea of hearing Mendelssohn again might bore him, could never resist the old spell once it began to unfold, moved his head from one side to another in tender ecstasy. The choirmaster appeared conscious of a presence at once mild and insistent, amiable yet dominating. It was as though the ghost of his *own* master was in the room. He had rebelled against that influence, but was now subdued to it. It asserted a tradition, and it carried him back to the pleasures and certainties of his boyhood. Those gentle melodies had charm, and they had authority.

Then one could understand how it was that long ago Victoria and Albert and so many solid burghers and their wives, so many pensive maidens, and so many amiable young men, had found in Mendelssohn treasures of sensibility. Was he not made for them, this engaging young German Jew, all compact of good breeding and melody? He was a genius who never forgot that he was a gentleman. He had ardours, but they were controlled. He was not like Beethoven, who was sublime but ill-mannered, and who in his boorish passions would knock over the tea-tables in the drawing-room. Chopin was feverish, Schumann introspective, Schubert smelt of the beer-cellar, but Mendelssohn combined the fascination of the artist with the eligibility of a young banker. The first performance of *Elijah* at Birmingham in 1846, with the composer conducting, was a genuinely moving affair. At the invocation of this music the marble heavens opened and were kind. At the end of the oratorio, Mendelssohn was half-killed by the embraces of his audience. The business men of Birmingham were lifted out of themselves by a religious sentiment that matched their own—that was Protestant and was without mysticism—and by a beauty that was new but had no strangeness to disturb them. Mendelssohn caught up in himself some part of the spirit of that age. He expressed the longings of the comfortable middle classes for the seemly, the dignified, the pure, the comely, the high-minded in their art; and if to us today those feelings, as reflected in his music, appear shallow, we should remember that fashions in emotion are always changing. The symphonies, the oratorios, the violin concerto, may now appear to us insipid—*Elijah* may be treasured only by suburban choral societies, and *St. Paul* neglected even by them—pianists may hide the *Songs Without Words* inside their piano-stool—but there is the principle of life in Mendelssohn. The composer of *The Midsummer Night's Dream* music and *Fingal's Cave* is not likely to pass with Raff and Reinecke into the darkness. Even that large part of his music which now seems tepid has an enduring historical interest. When we hear it, we are brought close to one side of the Victorian soul.

Those Friday evenings were like a search for a familiar headstone in a graveyard of the middle Victorians. Blowsy angels of discoloured marble stood there, blowing broken trumpets, or nursing enormous harps whose wires had rusted away. There were waxen lilies of the valley under glass bells, and over the glass the damp of that place had spread a green mould and a ghastly sweat. A foreigner or two has been buried in this Kensal Green of music. At the feet of a gilded seraph carrying a wreath of laurel, sacred to the memory of Charles Gounod, were piled crackling bunches of immortelles whose withered reds and purples looked frowsy and arch. None who was not condemned as a boy to sing the anthems of the forgotten middle Victorians can imagine how dismal was the mass of this religious music. It lacked the vital spark which animated bad Italian music, the *Stabat Mater* of Rossini, for example. That music of Rossini was stagy, full of explosions of blue fire and flighty tunes swooping down from the wings, but it had gusto and it caught the ear. When that theatrical manner of writing sacred music, remote from any recognisable religious experience of Evangelicals and Puritans, reached its perfection, far later in the century, in Verdi's *Requiem*, it gave us a secular masterpiece to admire. This *Requiem* was not like a church, it was a grand baroque palace, all crimson curtains, marble pillars and encrustations of gold. One came to regard it as being among Verdi's best operas, as good as *Traviata* or *Aida*, though not so fine as *Otello* and *Falstaff*. It was the flesh that quaked, rather than the spirit, at the piercing shouts of the trumpets in the *Dies Irae*. Yet how splendid appeared the dramatic power and rich melodies of Verdi by comparison with some dreary *Nunc Dimittis in B Flat* or *Magnificat in C Major* droned by our choristers to the accompaniment of a foggy November's coughs and sneezings. Our thin and consumptive Muse would have done well from an infusion of the happy, full-blooded vulgarity of even the lesser Italians. They, at least, believed in making a cheerful din, and in stirring and exciting an audience.

I find myself chanting again an anthem that began, "I was glad when they said UNto me, let us go into the house OF the Lord". It was like sitting in a cart behind an old mare that went along at a jog-trot, but that every now and then reared and whinnied for no visible reason. The stress in the melodic line in these compositions often had nothing at all to do with the meaning of the phrases, and the trivial tunes could often quite well have been married to a villagers' chorus in a light opera, "Three cheers! The squire is home again".

It is strange that the Victorians, to whom religion was so real and whose inner spiritual struggles were so painful, should have left us so little music of spiritual quality and understanding. They did not give us a composer who is the match of Emily Brontë or Christina Rossetti, or Newman, or the architect Pugin. Yet music is held to be the most spiritual of the arts, the art which is beautifully free from the hungers, frettings and slumbers of our wretched flesh, and, being so pure and disembodied, can best express the maladies and transfigurations of the soul.

There was very little church music to be heard at the beginning of the nineteenth century when the Church itself was asleep. When the awakening came in the early fifties, the flood of oratorios, anthems and sacred cantatas, of which my choirmaster had such a collection, began. It was a response to a demand, but it was a mechanical response. The chief spur to the revival of church music came from the Oxford Movement, which sought to give colour and warmth to religious life, to enrich it with the symbolism of ritual and the splendour of the arts. But the Pentecostal flames seldom descended upon the composers. English music had to wait a considerable time for a Hubert Parry and an Elgar.

During the Victorian time there was a more potent spirit than Mendelssohn's abroad, a grand, masculine, heroic spirit that one comes to admire more and more as time passes—Handel. Mendelssohn had the interest of a contemporary; Handel was the congenial classic. Of all the demi-gods of the eighteenth century, none retained a stronger authority over the nineteenth. "To perform in one's head one of Handel's choruses is better than most of the Exeter Hall performances," wrote Edward FitzGerald, but the Victorians insisted on singing him in every hall in the land. The Crystal Palace was, of course, the great temple of Handel-worship. The Palace is gone, it was burned up in 1936, but who can guess how many copies of programmes of the Handel Festivals are still to be found, tucked away at the back of writing-desks, or among the lumber of an attic, with magazine drawings or photographs of Sims Reeves, Charles Santley and Madame Albani pasted in the front? Taine wrote of "that vague desire for sublimity" which has animated the British people from their origins, and is likely to endure in them to the end. Nothing represented a more conscious striving after sublimity than the Handel Festivals. Was it reached? At least ENORMITY was achieved. The central transept of the Crystal Palace, where the festivals took place, was chosen for its monstrous size. At the first festival in 1857, when Michael Costa conducted, the choir numbered 2,000 and the orchestra 386, and a four-manual organ was used, a huge cave of the winds, blowing harmonious gales. The *Messiah*, *Judas Maccabaeus* and *Israel in Egypt* were performed at this first festival; a generous feast. As the years went on, the choir swelled to 3,500, and the players to 500. The choral singing and the playing at the festivals were rough and ragged, though, by contrast, there has never been a group of solo singers more accomplished in their art than those who sang Handelian airs in the old Crystal Palace. But what did jumbled choruses, spoiled orchestral rhythms, false notes and missed cues matter? In 1857 any such flaws were overlooked in the innocent delight of discovering how very big a big noise could be. The Victorians loved the colossal for its own sake, and were often inclined to confound size with grandeur, a fault with which they reproached both the Germans and the Americans. The largest attendance at a Handel Festival was

87,784 in 1883; at the bicentenary commemoration in 1885 85,000 persons attended. The Victorians took pride in rolling such figures on their tongues. Solemn characters often liked to reckon them as so many *souls*, as though that made the tally all the more impressive. "When your Papa was here many years ago," I once heard an old woman say, "there were no fewer than eighty thousand *souls* gathered under the Palace roof. And dear knows, how many of them have since gone to Glory—fewer, perhaps, than thought were going."

"*All we like sheep have gone astray*." The words were penitential but not the tune. Were there ever fatter sheep with more silvery fleeces than those that trotted back to the fold at the Crystal Palace? And when the enormous congregation rose to sing the Hallelujah Chorus, their very rising made a prolonged roar like the waves breaking on a mile length of rocks. The jubilant shout, "Hal-le-LU-jah, Hal-le-LU-jah" (*terra-BOM-bom*), was repeated and repeated in a thundering crescendo, as one imagines the cries of the army that marched round and round the walls of Jericho were reiterated, till the air was dizzy, and the towers rocked. *Terra-BOM-bom!* What lung-power those well-fed sheep possessed; what relish they took in their own strong voices! It was a wonder that all those ten thousand panes of glass of the Crystal Palace were not blown out. *Terra-BOM-bom!* Passers in the streets used to marvel at that saintly din and solemn jubilee. Scientific tests were made of its carrying power. Could it be heard at a further distance than the roar of Niagara? Half a mile? Three-quarters? *What!* a whole mile away? Or was that a fairy-tale of science? Penge heard it. Anerley gave back the jocund cry. It penetrated into the laurelled recesses of Norwood. This was a shout of liberation. How many fears, doubts, gnawing worries about this world and the next were shaken off in the rising ecstasy of Hallelujahs! It was like that moment in *The Pilgrim's Progress* when Christian's burden falls from his shoulders, and he watches it roll down the hill, and he knows that at last he can stand up straight and look at the sun. *Hallelujah!* If ever a cry could shake the throne of Grace it was this. But the victorious moment passed. Exhausted by aspiration, the eighty thousand sank back into their seats. A cold sense of mortality was to take the place of the brief exaltation. The cheerfulness of the strayed sheep and the jubilation of the Hallelujahs were but illusions, and soon done for. "*Though worms destroy this body, yet in my flesh shall I see God*." . . . "*Since by man came death, by man came also the resurrection of the dead*." Those frightful paradoxes of the faith, uttered with ravishing sweetness by the purest of solo voices, diffused a religious melancholia, struck a chill to the heart, and made one conscious what a place this central transept was for icy draughts.

A child has but one way of subduing the startling experiences which each day brings him and of making them tolerable to his consciousness, that is by spinning an imaginative web around them, and placing them at a remove; setting them, it may be, in the clouds. For my part, my mind was full of the colossal winged bulls of Assyria that I had seen in the British Museum, especially when I heard the pounding of the side-drum with its stretch of skin eight foot across reinforcing the terrors of death. Without those images, at once frightening and assuring in their concrete reality, I could not have translated those fears into any form of experience. Vast was the roof of this mysterious temple, the effect of its height and size not diminished by the shell, or boarding, pitched under it to catch the sounds. The wreaths of fog, floating languidly in the height, caught the shafts of sunshine, broke them, and diffused them in an ominous glow, so that those coiling vapours seemed to be reflecting the flames of a pillaged city. That light of sombreness and doom was spread over the numberless tiny white faces, specks of humanity, that filled the temple. "*But who may abide the day of His coming? And who shall stand when He appeareth? For He is like a refiner's fire.*" The grip of a dead hand was on my heart. The crowd was so vast that no matter where one looked it melted into a grey mist of people. All the attractive marks of human individuality, the blue eyes and the brown, the ruddy cheeks, the young hair or the white crest, all expressions of liking or disliking, were reduced to a swarming of ants. Beyond the immediate ring of vision, men and women ceased to be persons, they became tribes, they became atoms in a historical process. When the bass voice cried out, "*Why do the nations so furiously rage together, and why do the people imagine a vain thing?*" one was aware that the massed abstraction of a nation lay all about one, blind, brooding and menacing, and that one was on an island in an angry sea of people, people, people, raging furiously together and all imagining a vain thing.

The immensity of a stage thronged with seventy or eighty thousand actors, and lighted by that sinister glow from above, filled one with the desolation of some remote epoch in which the unique grace of the individual, the charm of a smile, the partings and meetings of lovers, were lost, trampled down, in the movements of nameless hordes, driven by an animal instinct towards fresh feeding-grounds. "*Their sound is gone out into all lands, and their words unto the ends of the world.*" And that sound had the mournfulness of a great wind, hot and dry, that has come wailing and creaking out of the heart of a desert.

In that setting, the noble choruses of *Judas Maccabaeus* or of *Israel in Egypt* increased the sense of the burden of the past, and of the generations of men that had spent an hour or two in the sun and were now dust. Under that vast arch of smoky crystal the words of Hebrew prophets and poets, wedded to music whose copious ease and familiarity can never stale for us its hypnotic power, and sung before these solemn tribes, carried us back to the waters of Babylon and the deserts of Egypt. Even *The Messiah* left one thinking little of the promise of Christ, but much of

Jehovah, the fierce avenging God of battles. We are the bondsmen of the Old Testament, said the music, and there is no deliverance for us. The sublimity that was achieved by the Victorians was the sublimity of the Hebrews.

The iron admonitions struck down into our hearts. The skies reverberated with the angry voice of the all-mighty, all-seeing Father. "*Yet once a little while and I will shake the heavens and the earth, the sea and the dry land.*" The fatalism and the blood-guilt of the Old Testament lay upon us. Not even the tenderness of the alto air, "*He shall feed His flock like a shepherd*", nor the morning light suffusing "*How beautiful are the feet of them that preach the gospel of peace*" could reconcile us to the gloomy weight of mortality.

Christian's load was bound to his weary shoulders again. Like the monuments of the antique world that were built to defy Time and magnify man's works, the temple of iron and glass oppressed us with a sense of the fleetingness of man and the foolishness of all his wretched little dreams and loves.

In the night I could hear the metallic clanging of the wings of the Assyrian bulls as they rose one after another in flight, and a voice crying, "*But Thou didst not leave His soul in hell, nor didst Thou suffer Thy Holy one to see corruption.*"

Dr. Percy Scholes in his two-volume *The Mirror of Music*, recounting the history of a century as reflected in the pages of the *Musical Times* (1844–1944), has a very pleasant chapter on the mania for sight-singing which swept over Britain in the forties. It carried away the populace, writes Dr. Scholes, "almost as did some of the dancing manias or religious manias of the Middle Ages". This remarkable craze was started by the arrival of a German ex-priest and singing master, Joseph Mainzer, whose text-book *Singing for the Million* had a big sale. Mainzer conducted crowded classes of all ages, including tiny children, in London and the provincial cities. No revivalist camp could have presented scenes of more infectious enthusiasm. Wherever this mesmerist went, he left behind him trains of jubilant choirs. He was talked down as a charlatan, his method of teaching singing called humbug, but what a very great amount of harmless pleasure he seems to have given! The descriptions that Dr. Scholes quotes out of his researches into the early numbers of the *Musical Times* make cheerful reading. Parties of working men and women would march out into the countryside chanting their happy choruses, boats were chartered to carry the sons and daughters of harmony down the river to Gravesend, and the shores echoed their ringing part-songs. This Pied Piper, Mainzer, led the people out of their dingy towns to the hills and meadows, singing, ever singing. At Brighton, Mainzer's followers hailed him in an anthem that included these delicious words:

Mainzer! foremost of this throng,
Teaching us sweet Music's strains,
Take our thanks and take our song,
Small return for all thy pains;

Hail! Professor Mainzer thou!
God upbear thee by His love,
Go teach Heav'n's sons Music *now*
Then go sing with them above!

Only a leader assured of the devotion of his flock could accept that last line without a twinge of suspicion.

Dr. Scholes points out that the enthusiasm for "teaching Tom, Dick and Harry to sing music at sight" was part of the larger movement of the period for improving the condition, intellectual, moral and religious, of the working classes. It allied itself to the Mechanics' Institutes, it was linked to such organisations as the Rechabites; while the Temperance societies welcomed Mainzer's innocent intoxications.

Dr. Scholes shows us from his files that 1841 was the start of a choral century. Mainzer came to England in that year; and in that year, too, John Curwen "took the first step along a road leading him to the development of a system that was at last to drive these other systems into complete oblivion". Tonic Sol-fa, despised though it was, opened the gates of musical understanding to very many, particularly to the children in the elementary schools. Curwen's system greatly increased the numbers of working people who were drawn into the activities of the choral societies. In describing the condition of the working people in the middle years of the century one must set down among all the other things, this one—that many of them had a deep love of music, and they sang as their great-grandchildren do not sing. They sang a good deal of rubbish in those days, it is true—how banal many a mid-Victorian glee could be!—but they also sang much fine, heart-stirring music by Handel, Haydn and Mendelssohn. The list of choral societies in the provinces during the middle Victorian years, especially in the North, is very striking. One seems to hear the singing of these honest voices, with their Yorkshire or Midlands burr, against the ever-growing thunder of the machines. Let the din of the machinery increase, the human voice will soar above it. When the wages and hours struggle was at its grimmest, working men and women, gathering in some shabby hall in the cotton towns, would find their inspiration in singing with full-throated energy, "Lift up your heads, O ye gates, and be ye lift up ye everlasting doors, and the King of Glory shall come in". That is a cry of children of the captivity who are not without hope.

Such enthusiasts produced the big audiences for the oratorios whose popularity through the century puzzles us today. I am not thinking, of course, of the *Messiah* or *The Creation* or *Elijah*, but of the compositions in this form by the Benedicts and Costas, and such works as Barnby's *Rebekah*. FitzGerald was premature when, in 1848, he wrote, "I think the day of oratorios is gone, like the day for painting Holy Families". The flood, indeed, came after 1848. We have now lost the taste for these Namaans and Women of Samaria, Daughters of Jephtha and Priests of Baal.

Apparently we are not the men our fathers were; they were hearty feeders who gobbled up good, bad and fairish music with an equal enjoyment. They had an appetite for every dish on the table, Spohr as well as Beethoven, Dvořák in his day as well as Schumann in his. There is no charge made against the Victorians more false than that they were cold to new genius. When in the fullness of time Wagner appeared, he called to him his own following as Verdi before him had done. The response of ordinary members of the public was usually far warmer and more understanding than that of the newspaper critics. At a period when such pundits of music criticism as Chorley and Davison were horrified by the vulgarities of Wagner, upper-middle-class and lower-middle-class audiences were already welcoming his "music of the future"—although it is true that many of them also responded with almost as much pleasure to the dronings of the worthy Doctor Crotch. It was not the refusal to recognise originality—they would welcome almost anything new—but the omnivorousness of these Victorians that now surprises us. As Dr. Scholes reminds us, a fine talent such as Henry Hugo Pierson's was not denied admiration, but Dr. Bexfield, who appears to have had no talent at all, enjoyed an equal respect. One gets the bewildered feeling of listening to the conversation of a reader of Victorian literature who shows a liking for the "dappled things—for skies as couple-coloured as a brindled cow" —of Gerard Manley Hopkins, but also recites Martin Tupper's verses with enthusiasm.

The really unaccountable thing about these nineteenth-century music lovers was their slow awakening to the grandeur of Bach. No other great composer has had to wait so long for his just honour in England. Going over a list of choral performances, in the Victorian age, Dr. Scholes finds that "in 1846 Mendelssohn stands next to Handel, while Bach's name never once appears and must, indeed, have been quite unknown to ninety-nine out of a hundred British choralists, whilst to the remaining odd one in a hundred that remote composer was merely vaguely known historically and not loved or reverenced. Even as late as 1886, Mendelssohn still easily maintains his place as runner-up to Handel." To the old people from whom I received my first impressions of the composers, Bach was a tedious, dry old fellow, he was that most arid of all kinds of professors, a German one, an arithmetic master of music, working out his sums on a blackboard. Having labelled him as a great musical bore, they put him aside with Piccinni and Salieri, as men who had once made a stir but had no meaning for a later age. They stopped their ears to Bach's other-worldly passion, and his lyrical power. One must except, of course, the devoted minority, among them Mendelssohn himself, and Barnby who, when he was organist at St. Anne's, Soho, began the yearly performances at that church of the St. John Passion Music. The missionaries of Bach were in the end to convert the world, but in the fifties and sixties their cause appeared almost hopeless. I recall an old lady who had been persuaded against her will to hear some parts of the *St. Matthew Passion* saying, "But this music has no *soul*. Music is the language of the soul, or it is nothing. Beethoven and Schumann, Mendelssohn and Chopin—they are all very different, but, at least, they all have *soul*. Even Wagner, noisy brute that he is, has soul. This Bach is a fossil." She had kept the prejudices of her contemporaries.

I think it may be because they had committed themselves to their own notion of the romantic that the free spirits, the strong spirits, in the Victorian times refused for so long to listen to Bach. There never was a more absurd argument than the one over romanticism and classicism. It sometimes became mysteriously entangled with politics—and a man's attitude to Church and State, to Home Rule, the New Woman, the single tax became involved with his musical tastes. There was a disposition to regard Beethoven, Mendelssohn, Schumann and Schubert as staunch Liberals, whose support in the division lobby Mr. Gladstone could always count upon; Wagner was a revolutionary Socialist like William Morris; Mozart and Haydn were tolerable Tories, rather like Derby and Salisbury; while Bach was a crabbed old reactionary as embarrassing to his own party as a Wellington Tory would have been in the Parliament of 1874. When the music of Brahms first reached this country, it suffered from the assumption that the composer was abstract, classicist, conservative, and therefore would, if given a chance, be certain to vote against Welsh Disestablishment and Municipal Banks. Mr. Bernard Shaw's early musical criticism amusingly reflects the prejudice of these progressives, though his recantation was handsome. If the word "romantic" has any meaning in music at all, it would appear to us today that there could be no more romantic composer than the Brahms of the symphonies, the songs and the B flat major piano concerto. Do we look down our noses at the Victorians for arranging the composers under such ridiculous categories? What of our own?

In a raw, wet English winter, in a dark city, in surroundings that are unspeakably dingy, with a dull job and a cheerless home, with wrangles about politics and family life going on around one, music is Jacob's adder. We can but dimly guess from signs and tokens, from faded letters and diaries, and conversations with old people, how much the traffic of angels meant in the inner life of those Victorians who were restless and unhappy. The streets of back-to-back houses in a Lancashire town on a rainy November morning, with the knocker-up scuttling from door to door, rap-rap-rap, bang-bang-bang, and yellow lights moving behind the dripping panes—was that not a good place to remember the end of the C major symphony of Schubert which says better than words can say that men are the sons of God, that the whole universe of planets and stars is theirs to conquer, and that the power which moves "the sun and all the other stars" is divine love and divine joy? There were many, oppressed by a gloomy religion, who found in this art their pardon and their peace.

In our northern climate, the exiles from the sun, huddling under scowling skies, chilled to the bone by the rain; pursuing the ghosts of uncertain pleasures; haunted by the undying Calvinist in their blood—these exiles longed for the South, for the sun, the olive and the vine. "November weather breeds blue devils," wrote Edward FitzGerald, who had a great love for music. "In October de Englishman shoot de pheasant; in November he shoot himself." To one living in a provincial town filled with fog, shadows and harsh memories, the discovery of such a name as Teresa Carreño or Sarasate, pasted on a hoarding—coming soon, coming in a month's time, next week, then the day after tomorrow—filled the mind with pictures of orange groves, deathly still at noon; the streets of old cities shimmering in the heat haze; the candle-lit darkness of cathedrals; the royal children of Velasquez, dressed in silver, rose and black; haughtiness and chivalry and a white, strong sun; and the long sierras gleaming far, far away on the skyline, crowned with cooling snows. Few pianists, it is to be supposed, have played better than Teresa Carreño, the Venezuelan, few violinists have been so ingratiating in their charm as Sarasate, the Spaniard, but these fine artists were sometimes almost lost in the dazzle of their names—names which glowed with the radiance and colours longed for throughout a northern winter. In January, by the North Sea, its yellow waters heaving under a low ceiling of frozen clouds, and an east wind blowing pain and sickness, the exiles from the sun often became obsessed with such mere names and images, and fell into reveries that were incomprehensible to the hard, practical, humorous Latins, who drove hard bargains and loved money as much as any Manchester man. The lucky ones who were born in the lands of vine and olive never knew, never could comprehend, such longings: music, for all their love of it, was part of the practical business of life and could never mean so much to them as to the disinherited children, the skinny ones, the hungry ones, the ardent ones.

What is one to say about the opera? Was it all a fraud and deception? Was it a holus-bolus of various arts in a stage of degeneration? Or was it summed up by Adelina Patti, that sharp business woman rapping the table and announcing, "The fee will be a thousand pounds payable by two o'clock on the day of performance". A thousand pounds! "All this was to be had for five shillings," said another voice. Thinking of the old opera, and its monkey tricks and its flummery, there comes back into the mind a page in De Quincey.

> I seldom drank laudanum, at that time, more than once in three weeks; this was usually on a Tuesday or a Saturday night; my reason for which was this: In those days Grassini sang at the Opera, and her voice was delightful to me beyond all that I had ever heard. I know not what may be the state of the Opera-house now, having never been within its walls for seven or eight years, but at that time it was by much the most pleasant place of public resort in London for passing an evening. Five shillings admitted one to the gallery, which was subject to far less annoyance than the pit of the theatres; the orchestra was distinguished by its sweet and melodious grandeur from all English orchestras, the composition of which, I confess, is not acceptable to my ear, from the predominance of the clamorous instruments, and the absolute tyranny of the violin. The choruses were divine to hear; and when Grassini appeared in some interlude, as she often did, and poured forth her passionate soul as Andromache, at the tomb of Hector, etc., I question whether any Turk, of all that ever entered the Paradise of opium-eaters, can have had half the pleasure I had. . . . All this was to be had for five shillings. And over and above the music of the stage and the orchestra, I had around me, in the intervals of the performance, the music of the Italian language talked by Italian women; for the gallery was usually crowded with Italians; and I listened with a pleasure such as that with which Weld, the traveller, lay and listened, in Canada, to the sweet laughter of Indian women; for the less you understand of a language, the more sensible you are to the melody or harshness of the sounds; for such a purpose, therefore, it was an advantage to me that I was a poor Italian scholar, reading it but little, and not speaking it at all, nor understanding a tenth part of what I heard spoken.

In that passage sounds the unappeasable longing of the northern soul, drifting amid the fogs or the icy sleet, wandering through the defiles of the stone office buildings when the lamps are all lighted at noon—the longing for the foreign faces and the entreating voices of the south. This was the mood of the lovers of opera.

The secret of the old opera certainly did not lie in its truth to nature nor in its artistry. Its fatuous conventions and silly stories, its choruses of villagers and soldiers, its leading ladies, bursting with corpulence, while affecting to be flower-like girls, its wooden acting, its shoddy stagecraft, its vulgarising of love and its cheapening of tragedy—all this made the sensitive squirm and the ribald laugh. When one thinks of the old opera, then across the little stage of memory that a man carries about under his hat trip some of the most foolish young women ever created, all of them great favourites with the Victorians. There is that sweet innocent, Linda of Chamonix—and all her troubles with the wicked marquis, the foreclosed mortgage on the old farm, maidenly virtue in peril, guilty splendour in Paris, the booming chorus of highly moral Savoyards and Linda going off her head and recovering her sanity with suspicious ease and readiness. Here comes Dinorah, tumbling into the raging flood after her pet goat, and being fished out by faithful Hoel the goatherd, who will surely live to rue that rescue. Next appears Amina, *La Sonnambula*, throwing off glittering cascades of notes as she walks in her sleep over a bridge which (as one English translator innocently remarked) "sinks under her weight". Now we salute stout Norma, casting horoscopes and telling fortunes for the Druids—and Marie, the daughter of the regiment, frisking like a war-horse whenever she hears the drum and fife from afar—and Elvira of *I Puritani* driven crazy, as well she might be, by those ineffable British aristocrats, "Lord G. Walton of the Puritans", Lord Arthur Talbot "of the Cavaliers", and Sir Benno Robertson, whom one suspects of civil war profiteering. Then there is Lucia di Lammermoor, surrounded by her ridiculous black-whiskered chorus in kilts—and Little Arline, the Bohemian girl, roaming with the gipsies, but dreaming she dwelt in marble halls in a song that struck FitzGerald as "a dreadful vulgar ballad". What a crew they were, those beauties of the old opera! What poor weak intellects the dear girls had! Linda, Dinorah, Elvira and Lucia all went mad, usually in white silks and satins, to the accompaniment of the happiest organ-grinder's tunes imaginable.

Malibran, Grisi, Mario, Tamburini, Lablache, Garcia, Jenny Lind, Sontag, Patti and the rest—it is easy enough to mock them as the pedlars of profitable follies. Few of these singers appear to have had great depth of intelligence, or sensitiveness of understanding. They were for the most part marionettes, each endowed with a voice of uncommon beauty, and a most uncanny skill in using it. Some master doll-maker had artfully contrived a flute inside the throats of the little creatures, and when they were set in action liquid notes of heart-easing melodies would flow from their painted wooden lips. How could these marionettes of music be judged by the standards of truth or the imagination?

The runs and shakes of the old operas, the floweriness of the arias, the vocal filigree work, having nothing at all to do with human emotions, almost belonged, in a phrase of a later day, to an abstract art. The operagoer was not invited to decide whether a woman whose lover had left her, or a man about to be shot, would be likely to express emotion in a prodigious trill that was a wonder of breath control and production. He was expected to admire certain notes in the human voice that were of ravishing beauty, and an art in using them learned in a very hard school whose secrets seem now almost lost. We know from the memoirs of those times how real an emotion was evoked by the warblings of these toy nightingales. If Jenny Lind adorned a sacred air with the same vocal decorations and sparkling fountains of notes that she gave to Lucia's mad song, she did so from a desire to give pleasure by displaying to the full the resources of her marvellous instrument. In a like manner, years afterwards, Edward Lloyd was to enrapture the Handel Festival audience by his singing of "Love in her eyes sits playing", and those critics who protested that this, though finely done, was out of keeping with an occasion consecrated to the adoration of God, were thought to be strait-laced. The voices of these singers touched emotions that were far removed from the empty words of their songs and from the business of the stage. Owen Meredith's *Aux Italiens* is, I suppose, to be accounted no more than Victorian elocution-class doggerel, but it is agreeable doggerel, and keeps a pleasant flavour of the period:

> Of all the operas that Verdi wrote,
> The best, to my taste, is the Trovatore;
> And Mario can soothe with a tenor note
> The souls in Purgatory.
>
> The moon on the tower slept soft as snow;
> And who was not thrilled in the strangest way,
> As we heard him sing, while the gas burned low,
> "*Non ti scorda di me*"?

Non ti scorda di me. "Do not forget me!" Mario was by all reckonings far and away the finest tenor of his times. (He was born in 1810 and lived until 1883.) He had all the gifts—at least, all the physical gifts—that the gods can give to a singer: he cut a fine figure, he had romantic looks, and on the boards dressed himself as splendidly as a nobleman in a Paul Veronese painting; he had a grace that won the eye; and, above all, he possessed a voice of most attaching quality. In *La Favorita*, singing the role of the lover who renounced the joys of the world for the cold cell of the monastery, he melted the house to tears at the thought of so elegant a sacrifice. But if Mario had done no more than sing the twice-one table, or the names of the railway stations between York and Darlington, he would have brought a pang of sentimental tenderness even to Becky Sharp. It was no wonder that Mario singing in *Trovatore* should move Owen Meredith to think of his first love—it was an effect Mario appears to have had on many Victorians:

> I thought of our little quarrels and strife;
> And the letter that brought me back my ring.
> And it all seemed then, in the waste of life,
> Such a very little thing.

The tunes—are they, or, rather, *were* they, after all, so shoddy? I doubt if I would have thought so had I been living then to hear them sung by those mellifluous voices; for example, by that quartet, Grisi, Rubini, Tamburini and Lablache. Then there were the duets that Donizetti wrote for Mario and Grisi; they provoked Heine's extravagance about the duets of the rose and the nightingale—"the rose is the nightingale among flowers and the nightingale the rose among birds." Happy, lucky, innocent world in which a poet could write like that and not be laughed at.

Delicacies of shading and subtleties of understanding—one should not look for *them* in the melodies of Donizetti. He was not Fauré nor Hugo Wolf. But what music this is of the sunshine and the vine—music made to be sung by plump beauties, with lustrous corkscrew curls and flashing eyes. In hearing the sextet from *Lucia* nowadays, if the voices are good Italian ones, it is not hard to live again some of the emotions of our great-grandfathers. We don't care a fig, and neither did *they*, about the sorrows of Lucy and the Master of Ravenswood, but when that tune begins to swing to and fro like a pendulum I wish it might go on for hours. I have heard it at Covent Garden in the old days sung by fairish singers, and I have played it over in gramophone recordings numberless times, but I can never remember what, in fact, the sextet is *about*—what crisis in the dark traffic of Lammermoor it marks. That, indeed, is the proper eighteen-fortyish state of mind. All that matters is the pure pleasure of the sounds. There is a part of one, stirring underneath the surface, that takes a kind of purring, animal joy in the rise and fall of the music and in its pressing forward to its peak. Who troubles about sense, or meaning, or dramatic aptness, in the primitive enjoyment of hearing the fat little Italian soprano, with olive oil and honey in her throat, riding those waves? Now the seventh wave mounts. It curves and then crashes—now, surely, she's swamped. Her five noisy fellow singers, stretching their lungs, and aided by the orchestral gale, have drowned her this time. But no! She rises from the boiling trough, like a gull in a storm, and at the uproarious end is heard above the tumult shrieking her last triumphant *eck-eck-eck*.

There is no other art in which one can laugh at one's enthusiasms, and yet become so taken out of oneself; and, as for the aesthetic impurities of opera, its mongrelisms, let the professors argue them out. The spell cast by voices of uncommon beauty and power in the Victorian time may explain in part some mysteries that baffle us today. For example, whatever did our great-grandfathers see in Meyerbeer and his patchwork quilt of other men's styles? Who could now endure the thought of sitting through the long hours of *Le Prophète* or *L'Africaine*? Yet Meyerbeer was a mighty man to the Victorians, and it may be there are still old men alive who, remembering their childhood, and their own fathers taking them to the opera for the first time, think of him as a finer composer than Wagner, more tuneful, more apt and expressive. Meyerbeer could write in any style that would be likely to give pleasure, the Italian, the Freuch, the German, or he could obligingly concoct a mixture of all three, but he took care to write lush melodies that would give scope to the voices of that age. How much did his fame owe to such a singer as Pauline Lucca? It may be that those who for the first time heard the Lucca sing Valentine in *Les Huguenots* at Covent Garden, filling the house with the opulence of her voice, not unreasonably felt that Meyerbeer was better than Wagner and Verdi rolled into one.

"No lady is a lady without having a box at the opera: so my Jemmy, who knew as much about music—bless her!—as I do about Sanskrit, algebra, or any other foreign language, took a prime box on the second tier. It was what they called a double box; it really *could* hold two, that is, very comfortably; and we got it a great bargain—for five hundred a year." Thackeray's Cox was writing his snob's diary at a time when the aristocracy paid for their boxes according to their rank, a royal duke paying the most. "What a place the opera is, to be sure! and what enjoyments us aristocracy used to have!" recorded Cox.

> Just as you have swallowed down your three courses (three curses I used to call them;—for so, indeed, they are, causing a deal of heartburns, headaches, doctor's bills, pills, want of sleep, and such like)—just, I say, as you get down your three courses, which I defy any man to enjoy properly, unless he has two hours of drink and quiet afterwards, up comes the carriage, in bursts my Jemmy, as fine as a duchess, and scented like a shop. "Come, my dear," says she, "It's *Normy*[1] to-night (or *Annybalony* or the *Nosey di Figaro* or the *Gazzylarder*, as the case may be); Mr. Coster[2] strikes off punctually at eight, and you know it's the fashion to be present at the very first bar of the aperture"; and so off we are obliged to budge, to be miserable for five hours, and to have a headache for the next twelve, and all because it's the fashion.

Even Cox, though, confessed that he found pleasure in the voices of Lablache and Rubini.

There was another form of entertainment linked in those days to the opera. Cox, the martyr to fashion, complained, "The opera is bad enough; but what is that to the bally?" Memories of Taglioni, of Carlotta Grisi and Cerito were cherished by their worshippers for a whole long life-time. In commending Fanny Elssler and her sister to Mrs. Cox, when she was shocked by their antics, Tag said, "Those are the most famous dancers in the world, and we throw myrtle, geraniums and lilies, and roses at them in token of our immense admiration." We may judge of the quality of the great dancers of the time from Miss Kemble's account of Fanny Elssler: "She was the most intellectual dancer I have ever seen. Inferior to Taglioni in lightness, grace and sentiment, to Carlotta Grisi in the two latter qualities, she excelled them all in dramatic expression." She danced, said Miss Kemble, as much with her head as her feet. Mrs. Cox (Jemmy), the newly-rich matron, was taken off her guard on the first night that she stopped on after the opera to see the dancers.

> When Madamasalls Fanny and Theresa Hustler[3] came forward, along with a gentleman, to dance, you should have seen how Jemmy stared, and our girl blushed, when Madamasall Fanny, coming forward, stood on the tips of only five of her toes, and raising up the other five, and the foot belonging to them, almost to her shoulder, twirled round and round and round, like a tee-totum

[1]These being translated read *Norma, Anna Bolena, Nozze di Figaro* and *Gazza Ladra* (The Thieving Magpie of Rossini).

[2]Michael Costa.

[3]Fanny Elssler and her sister Therese, who, being so far the taller, usually took the male role.

for a couple of minutes or more; and, as she settled down at last on both feet, in a natural decent posture, you should have heard how the house roared with applause, the boxes clapping with all their might, and waving their handkerchiefs; the pit shouting "Bravo!"

Mrs. Cox was shocked that a woman should act so immodestly, but what at last drove her out of the house was the appearance of a figure that came "skipping and bounding in like an Indian-rubber ball", flinging itself up, at least six feet from the stage, and there shaking about its legs like mad.

"That's Anatole," says one of the gentlemen. "Anna who?" says my wife, and she might well be mistaken, for this person had a hat and feathers, a bare neck and arms, great black ringlets, and a little calico frock which came down to the knees. "*Anatole;* you would not think he was sixty-three years old, he's as active as a man of twenty." "*He,*" shrieked out my wife; "What, is that there a man? For shame! Munseer. Jemimarann, dear, get your cloak, and come along; and I'll thank you, my dear, to call our people, and let us go home."

Yet Mrs. Cox was so quick in picking up the notions of the world of fashion that within three weeks of this night of disgust, why, "law bless you! she could look at the bally as she would at a dancing-dog in the streets, and would bring her double-barrelled opera glass up to her eyes as coolly as if she had been a born duchess".

There is to be found in Cox's diary, by the way, a good bit of description of what it looked like behind the scenes at the ballet. It is a picture by Hogarth rather than by Degas. "Fancy lots of young and old gents of the fashion, crowding round and staring at the actresses practising their steps. Fancy yellow, snuffy foreigners, chattering always and smelling fearfully of tobacco. . . . Fancy old men, dressed in old nightgowns, with knock-knees, and dirty, flesh-coloured cotton stockings, and dabs of brick-dust on their wrinkled old chops, and tow-wigs (such wigs!) for the bald ones, and great tin spears in their hands, mayhap, or else shepherds' crooks, and fusty garlands of flowers, made of red and green baize. Fancy troops of girls, giggling, chattering, pushing to and fro, amidst the black canvas, Gothic halls, thrones, pasteboard Cupids, dragons and such like; such dirt, darkness, crowd, confusion and gabble, of all conceivable languages, was never known. If you *could* but have seen Munseer Anatole! Instead of looking twenty, he looked a thousand. The old man's wig was off, and a barber was giving it a touch with the tongs; Munseer was taking snuff himself, and a boy was standing by, with a pint of beer, from the public-house at the corner of Charles Street."

CHAPTER FOUR

REMEMBERING CREMORNE

There was Cremorne—the gardens by the river. It became, if you like, a Victorian burlesque of a day-dream of the eighteenth century, but at the end, there was drawn out of it another kind of beauty, preserved in perfect keeping for years to come in the floating lights and shadows of Whistler's Cremorne paintings. Cremorne will always be a fine and lovely name.

This day-dream of the eighteenth century had been spun around grottoes, waterfalls, a deep-cleft valley of rocks; stone urns heavy with moss; a broken Gothic arch wreathed in ivy; and the scene was pavilioned by clouds of leaves, bronze leaves, through which the beams of noon found it hard to pierce. There would be a labyrinth of little paths through the wilderness. The paths wound and twisted up the slopes of a hill to a sunlit temple of Flora, or they skipped down the rocks to the cavern of a hermit who had fled from the hurly-burly of Richmond or Twickenham to meditate there in quiet the relations of the Sublime and the Beautiful. They were paths that dodged, tacked, wheeled back on themselves, and would sometimes take half a mile to go from the bottom of a little hill to the top. The scene had an elegant pensiveness, the not unpleasant ache of indefinable longings. Zephyrs sported among the clouds of leaves, those bronze thunderclouds that rose, cloud on cloud, into the far skies, as in Gainsborough's landscapes. The whisperings and murmurs of leaves, which even so far inland remembered the sea, mingled with the sound of the little streams splashing among the rocks to make an agreeably sad music that was never still. There was a dim richness of violets and mosses apparent in the shadows by the stones. Their dark colours, the deep violet and the green, were refreshed continually by the mist of waterfalls. Above the rocks were spread lawns as smooth and bright as green enamel; and these lawns were starred by tiny white and blue flowers. There was a sense of closed enchantment in the place, as though a sorcerer had drawn a circle around a great lord's park, and the trees, the stones and the statues were waiting in a trance for the naiad to rise from the lake. A wizardry older even than that of the Augustan Age hung in the air of Cremorne and there were echoes along its walks of that voice which on the lawn of Ludlow Castle on a summer day in the seventeenth century had sung:

Sabrina fair
  Listen where thou art sitting
Under the glassy, cool, translucent wave,
  In twisted braids of lilies knitting
The loose train of thy amber-dropping hair,
  Listen for dear honour's sake
  Goddess of the silver lake,
    Listen and save.

This was the day-dream, so we must imagine, of that Lord Cremorne who in the gardens of the mansion by the river which he bought from the Huntingdons—this was the family of Selina, the Methodist Enthusiast, who set up the Countess of Huntingdon's denomination, and built the round churches to foil the Devil from lurking in corners—had made a retreat that would wed a sylvan peace with the excitement of scenes of fashion; one of his gates opening on a wilderness, the other giving upon the glare of routs, assemblies, balls, the chatter of well-bred monkeys and the intrigues of elegant rakes.

There was something else besides the longing for the picturesque. In each age the romanticism of the lover expresses itself through chosen conventions in life and art. These vary greatly from one generation to another. We know that the letters Lord Orville wrote to Evelina brought tears of sensibility from Fanny Burney's readers. The phrases in them that to us seem frigid and stilted were for contemporaries charged with sincere emotion. So in the early Victorian times the trills and runs of the old operas, which we think absurd, served as expressions of a genuine sentiment. The eighteenth-century day-dream, the dream of an artistically arranged wilderness, met the need of the lover of that age to provide the right setting, *the shut world*, for the beloved. It was there, in that tamed wilderness, where the runnels spilled over the rocks, under the spread of the beeches—there, in that endless July weather of the imagination, in that little island world outside the world (but yet not far from Richmond Park)—in those glades, where it was not astonishing to see Greek gods wearing perruques and flowered waistcoats, and where the Æolian harp murmured the tunes of Dr. Arne, it was there that the lover and the beloved could find their contentment at last, their happiness.

There are arias in Handel's operas that bring back something of that world in which a nymph walks in hoops and lilac-sprigged gown. Listen!—Jupiter, Semele's Jupiter, in full-bottomed wig, lace ruffles and diamond buckles is singing:

Where'er you walk, cool gales shall fan the glade;
Trees, where you sit, shall crowd into a shade,
Trees, where you sit, shall crowd into a shade.

Above our heads soar again the pavilions of July leaves, sultry, swaying, full of the murmurs of bees; bronze clouds hanging in a milky sky. There is the music of pigeons, an alto melody, wooing and lovesick, a sensuous incantation lulling that shaggy hermit to a summer afternoon sleep and to troubled summer dreams. And where the falling waters brim into a pool, filled with the streamers of brilliant green weeds and patterned with the creamy water lilies, she waits her lover—she who wears panniers, red heels, patches, ribbons and laces, but in this dream is a classical shepherdess, too; Daphne or Chloë or Doris. She has escaped the stenches, the dirt, the smallpox, the leeches, the bodystealers and the raddled old lechers of the town. She is safe for ever in the green recesses of the imagination. Where'er she walks, cool gales shall fan the glade.

It was long in dying, this dream. It was still possible in the eighteen-forties, long after Wordsworth had given poetry a new tongue, stern and pure, in *Poems and Lyrical Ballads*, to inscribe in the album of Miss Charlotte Louisa Evans, the Inconstant Fair of Upper Norwood, the fond aspiration that Hope's glowing car and Fancy's painted wings might bear her to Tunbridge Wells to "quaff in Fashion's temple from Hygeia's chalybeate springs". It was long, long before the middle Victorian time that Burns had written

> The pale moon is setting beyond the white wave
> And Time is setting with me O,

but the poetesses of the school of Mrs. Leo Hunter, and the literary Dick Swivellers, still used words as deeply dyed by the sentimental fashion of the earlier time as "bosky" and "vermeil", and did not even hesitate to invoke the finny and the feathered tribes. Nor did the clear, bright landscape painting of the young Tennyson, in which every flower and leaf was cherished by a Pre-Raphaelite of verse, nor the glorious gusty vigour of the young Browning change a taste formed on Collins and Gray. So in the grottoes, twining paths, fountains and arcades of the pleasure gardens of our Victorians there was kept some part of the private dream, some colours of the interior scenery of the eighteenth century, although much coarsened and tarnished. One may still see from Rosherville Gardens at Gravesend, the last survivor of a forsaken fashion, how inviting that setting might be: the water sparkling through the screen of trees, the paths skipping and leaping in circles up and around the hills, the tangled ivy on the stone, the artful blending of rustic and urban, the affectation of innocence.

All that is now left of Cremorne is the gates, freshly painted by an owner who has a decent care for the past. They stand in that "misty mid-region" where one can never be certain where Chelsea ends and Fulham begins; they stand there lost in a featureless desert of bricks, where once the strawberry fields spread for miles on miles. These gates, with their lightness of design and their fine filigree—they might serve as the

SONGS,
DIVINE AND MORAL,
FOR
THE USE OF CHILDREN.
BY THE
REV. ISAAC WATTS, D.D.
See p. 37.
LONDON:
CHARLES TILT, 86, FLEET STREET.

AN EVENING SONG.

AND now another day is gone,
I'll sing my Maker's praise;
My comforts every hour make known
His providence and grace.

EMILY CONSTABLE'S HYMN BOOK
With the woodcuts coloured for her by her father, John Constable, 1834

XX.

AGAINST IDLENESS AND MISCHIEF.

How doth the little busy bee
Improve each shining hour,
And gather honey all the day
From every opening flower!

I.

THE SLUGGARD.

'TIS the voice of the Sluggard: I heard him complain,
"You have waked me too soon! I must slumber again!"
As the door on its hinges, so he on his bed
Turns his sides, and his shoulders, and his heavy head.

WATTS'S "DIVINE AND MORAL SONGS FOR CHILDREN"
Edition of 1848 with woodcut illustrations by C. W. Cope

PLATE 30

"THE BELLE OF THE SEASON" PUT TO SHAME BY THE IMMODESTIES OF THE BALLET

Mezzotint by A. E. Chalon, 1840 (illustration for Lady Blessington's poem)

entrance to the palace of Cinderella or the Sleeping Beauty—open no more upon enchantments. The gates closed upon the gardens for the last time in 1877. The morals of Chelsea had been shocked by the spectacle of the harlots who flocked there. The people of church and chapel held meetings, wrote letters of complaint incessantly to the Home Secretary and the Police Commissioner, and the end came shabbily and meanly. It was this last disreputable phase, though, that produced those images of magical grace that come first into our heads when we hear the name Cremorne.

On a fine summer evening, the stars over Cremorne showed faintly in the hazy, smoky sky of dirty London, the lights of a swarm of small craft danced their reflections in the river, and the lanterns under the bridge looked mysteriously Venetian. The trees in the gardens were threaded with coloured lamps, and, at the end of the evening, to crown all, there was the firework display. One had to wait until it was quite dark, and the shadows on the river were velvet black; then the rockets were touched off, and soared up with a whistle, and a swu-u-ush like tearing silk; then, to the chorus of long-drawn Ahhhhhh-hs they burst in the heat mist and sluggish smoke over Chelsea Reach in a shower of rubies without lustre, and blurred sapphires, or spun round in wheels of tarnished gold. Dreamy, dim festivals of lights! Who now remembers them? But there was a man born to save those most fugitive of moments, to preserve the joy of some child who, in the seventies, watched the falling lights, and to communicate that emotion to those whose fathers were not even thought of then. He was an American, born at Lowell, Massachusetts and he had been a West Point Cadet.

Whistler deepened the London sensibility. There had been a time when the intimate vision was in the keeping of Congreve and Handel, and the foliage was steeped in that august sombreness of Sir Joshua which is spread around *Mrs. Siddons as the Tragic Muse*. Then an arch Victorian "picturesqueness" overlaid the imagination of the Georgians. The heart-strings were now plucked by the melodies of Tom Moore; and "Rich and rare were the gems she wore" supplanted "O ruddier than the cherry". The brooding majesty of the trees of Reynolds and Gainsborough vanished; in its place was the moonshiny prettiness of Sir Noel Paton, and the lawns at Cremorne, hung with fairy lamps, looked very like Sir Noel's paintings of Oberon's court, a realm of tinsel and paper flowers. And then, at the end of it all, came this genius from across the Atlantic to turn tinsel into thread of gold, to turn pretty Victorian doggerel into real poetry. It was not only the Cremorne lights that Whistler saw. He saw also Battersea across the river, the smoking factories and the huddle of waterside streets. To some, at least, among those who heard the message of the *Ten O'Clocks*, there came a transforming experience—the understanding that beauty is boundless, that it is not locked up in a few books, or hung on a few walls, but is an unending revelation. In that period, of all periods, when the pursuit of ugliness had religious as well as economic approval, there was need of this Lochinvar of art who had come out of the West.

> When the evening mist clothes the riverside with poetry, as with a veil, and the poor buildings lose themselves in the dim sky and the tall chimneys become campanile, and the warehouses are palaces in the night, and the whole city hangs in the heavens, and fairyland is before us—then the wayfarer hastens home; the working man, and the cultured one, have ceased to see, and Nature who, for once, has sung in tune, sings her exquisite song to the artist alone, her son and her master, her son in that he loves her, her master in that he knows her.

The Muse of History smiles her ironic smile. I was thinking of Whistler's *A Nocturne in Black and Gold—The Falling Rocket*. Then the Muse whispered, "You remember what happened to that picture of the fireworks at Cremorne, don't you?" It was a sorry tale of pride, of a noble character who behaved like an ass; and it is a humbling tale for all great men. In 1877 Whistler showed eight pictures at the Grosvenor Gallery. One of them was marked for sale. It was *A Nocturne in Black and Gold—The Falling Rocket*. The price he asked for it was two hundred guineas. John Ruskin was in those days the supreme pundit of art criticism. Of Whistler's *Nocturne in Black and Gold* Ruskin wrote this criticism: "I have seen and heard much of Cockney impudence before now, but never expected to hear a coxcomb ask two hundred guineas for flinging a pot of paint in the public's face." Whistler sued for libel. He might have reflected that it would be as easy to find a pair of scales to weigh a sunset as to find a court to decide what is art. It was a very bemused jury that decided this issue. It was so much at sea in the debate over art that it behaved at times like the jury in the trial of the Knave of Hearts in *Alice*. One cannot but think that the jurymen who held a picture upside down to look at, and who considered a Titian to be a bad daub of Whistler's, must have been related to Bill the Lizard. The Attorney-General conducted Mr. Ruskin's case, and awed the jury by showing how great a man his client was. Whistler was awarded a farthing damages, and was bankrupted by bearing his costs. There was an exchange in his cross-examination which came to be widely quoted. The Attorney-General asked, "The labour of two days, then—is it that for which you ask two hundred guineas?" Whistler answered, "No, I ask it for the knowledge of a lifetime." He might also have said that he asked it for an eye that had seen new and subtle wonders in Cockneydom.

The man who ruined Whistler was the dedicated prophet of beauty, the teacher who had taught that ugliness was a moral evil. It was Ruskin, too, who, in an earlier day, had with matchless eloquence defended the Pre-Raphaelite painters against the barbarians. The critics of the fifties had written of Rossetti, Millais and Hunt in phrases very like those that he had used about Whistler. Did no echoes of them ring in Ruskin's head as he sat down to write those words about the Cockney impudence of the American coxcomb?

The pleasure gardens of London provided a mixture of entertainments; concerts, farces presented on open-air stages, puppet shows, dancing and fireworks. And there were the balloon ascents. The argosies of magic sails, "the pilots of the purple twilight", gave an air of pleasant fantasy to the London sky on summer afternoons. Looking out of Victorian windows in the fifties one might see a dozen or more balloons in a race, drifting in the currents of blue air, flashing in the sun. Their jackets were of bright colours, striped red and white like peppermint sticks, or covered in gilt. The Barnum streak, the "liking for circuses and stunts", was marked in the Victorians, and the aeronaut Charles Green, who made hundreds of ascents from the Gardens, carried up with him some strange companions. In September 1845 he rose with "a lady and her pet leopard". In 1852 an acrobat on a trapeze was attached to his car; this performer swung to and fro, twirled and gyrated as the balloon sailed over London roofs, and ended the act by hanging down by his heels. The same year a French actress, in the character of Europa, riding a young bull, was carried up to the clouds amid cheers and laughter, the animal being slung by ropes under the belly of the car. Ponies had been hoisted up to the clouds without protest from the humane, but public opinion, always uncertain in its boiling point, was outraged by the sight of a bull soaring through the air. At Ilford, where the balloon came down, Europa and her manager were fined by the magistrates for cruelty to the animal.

At Cremorne, as at Vauxhall, there were experimenters in flight who lost their lives. The newspapers of July 1837 contain accounts of the melancholy end of Robert Cocking, a landscape painter, sixty years old, who had long cherished a desire to test a parachute of his own contriving. For months Cocking had plagued Green to take him up; at last, on a clear, windless morning, the aeronaut did so. Cocking's parachute was an inverted umbrella made of fine Irish linen; its circumference was 107 feet 4 inches; and the artist sat in a basket underneath the cone. At a height of a mile and a half, his parachute was set free, but the umbrella folded up; Cocking fell—in the words of a man who watched him—"like an oyster shell cutting through water". When he was picked up, Cocking uttered one groan, and died. The Coroner, at the inquest, was curious to know if the speed of the fall might in itself have killed Cocking. Could the human frame sustain so great a speed without bursting? The physician assured the Coroner that on the new railways "it has been no uncommon thing for persons to travel at an enormous speed *up to sixty miles an hour without loss of life*".

In the seventies Vincent de Groof, a Belgian, drew great crowds by his promise to show men how to fly like birds. He modelled his wings on the bat and his tail on the peacock. The wings of silk were stretched over canes that gave "the folding continuity of the bat"; they were thirty-seven feet from tip to tip. His peacock tail was eighteen feet long. De Groof shut himself in a wooden cage twelve feet high. Three levers controlled the movements of his wings and tail, and the man who had become half-bat, half-peacock was attached to the balloon by a thirty-foot rope. This story belongs to that intricate Gothic phantasmagoria that lies beneath the starched conventions of the Victorian age; it belongs to the frightening shadows on the wall, and the red glare through the cracks.

> The balloon soared to a great height, but for fully half an hour continued to hover over the gardens. Then the wind bore it rapidly away in the direction of St. Luke's Church, Chelsea, till the machine was perilously near the church tower. No one quite knew what happened at this moment. Simmons (the balloonist) seems to have called out, "I must cut you loose", and De Groof to have responded, "Yes, and I can fall in the churchyard". Suddenly the rope was severed, the machine, without resistance to the air, was seen to collapse, and wind round and round in its descent, till it fell with a heavy thud near the kerbstone in Robert Street (now Sydney Street, Chelsea). A great crowd had collected, De Groof was picked up in a terrible state, and taken to Chelsea Infirmary to die. The fate of the balloon was an anti-climax; it was carried away to Springfield in Essex, where it came down on the Great Eastern railway line, after a narrow escape from a passing train. The whole affair caused great excitement in London, and the details were copied into papers like the *Indian Mirror*. A street-ballad sold in the Chelsea streets drew the obvious morals, and appealed to the tender-hearted passer-by:
>
> You feeling hearts, list to my story,
> It is a most heartrending tale;
> And when the facts are laid before you
> To drop a tear you cannot fail.
>
> (From *Cremorne and the Later London Gardens*, by Warwick Wroth, assistant keeper of Coins in the British Museum.)

That scene haunts one like a bad dream, dreamed by a child long ago who looked out of the window over the mysterious higgledy-piggledy landscape of London roofs, at the undulations of slates and tiles, the peering eyes of garrets, the clumps of puffing chimney-pots, and then beheld with crawling terror, far off, at first—then coming nearer, the swoopings of the prodigious bird. So—dreams the child—might the winged monster, the enormous bat, hover above me, and pursue me, through that city, infinitely older and more perilous than London, its streets more crooked, the unsleeping eyes of witches staring out of its windows, the city which claims us when we fall asleep. In that city which is an endless continuation rather than the counterpart of the London of living men, a child might scramble in terror, in moonlight, across the wilderness of roofs, half-choked by the belchings of the chimneys, burning his hands on the cowls, slipping, struggling to keep a foothold on the crazy gables, trembling on the edge of parapets, hearing always the rush of these wings behind him; then at last tumbling over the brink of the corniced cliff, which by now had become a hundred miles high, and falling, falling, falling for ever in the darkness of the crevasse with the terrible wings beating above him, and following him, and falling too.

It was a Victorian nightmare imposed upon the grottoes, waterfalls and enamelled lawns of the eighteenth century, where the bewigged Jupiter sang to Semele, "Where'er you walk".

POSTSCRIPT

We cannot escape the Victorians. We may think of them as museum pieces, despise their standards, and detest their cruelties, but they haunt us. They are in our blood. Ever since the gloomy sunset of the nineteenth century, when the old Queen lay dying and Britain's credit in the world was sadly impaired by the disasters of the South African war, there have been I know not how many rebellions against Victorianism. "I have seen four and twenty leaders of revolt." What has come of it all? Who, in the end, can escape his father and grandfather?

The repute of the Victorians stood at its lowest in a time that most Britons now look upon with some shame, the nineteen-twenties and thirties—the Shoddy Age. The bright wits of that period, hard, neurotic, disloyal, sterile as mules, could conceive of nothing more ridiculous than those pompous old buffers with their preoccupation with man's duty to his neighbour and man's duty to God. Darwin was as comical an ass as Gladstone, Huxley as big a prig as Newman, Browning as great a bore as General Gordon, Tennyson as sweetly silly as Millais, Carlyle a ranter, Dickens as trumpery a writer as Mrs. Henry Wood. In the early thirties Dr. H. D. A. Major was making this protest: "It is the fashion of our complacent Georgian idealists to regard the Victorian Age as a sort of Cimmerian chaos of competitive industrialism, scientific materialism and smug hypocrisy, and to ignore the extraordinary amount of work the Victorians accomplished in the spheres of intellectual enlightenment and of social and political reforms. The Victorians had their ignorances and their limitations, their sickly sentiment and their bad taste, and the age that follows them is highly sensitive to their defects. But the Victorians had great courage, great energy and great kindness of heart." Courage, energy and kindness were not national virtues greatly esteemed in the nineteen-thirties.

The Age of Shoddy is dead, and who now would lay a wreath on its grave? Nowadays we speak more civilly of our grandfathers. There is a visible respect for the achievement of the Middle Victorians, and a serious curiosity about their motives. We no longer see them as freaks and frumps. In our chastened mood we are even prepared to concede that they may have some wisdom to pass on to us from beyond the tomb. We are like a family for whom nothing has fallen out well—fortune gone, hopes disappointed, faith lost—a family suddenly remembering the peaceful and secure lives that its grandparents lived, and wistfully returning to its springs and origins for health and strength. We turn over the leaves of their gilt-edged album, and by a scrutiny of those placid faces hope to spell out the secret of their happiness. A generation that has known two world wars, and is always shadowed by the fear of a third, envies the long peace of the Victorians. Amid our current economic and political discontents, we remember that in the nineteenth century the world followed the leadership of Britain in political ideas, in trade and industry, in applied science and invention. We contrast the riches of that proud estate with our present beggary. It was Britain's century. The image of John Bull, muscular and portly, very rich, very energetic and able, insensitive, insolent, purse-proud, his cheeks ruddy with roast beef and brown ale—a benevolent uncle when not worsted, but a tough fellow when his dander was up—the friend of the slave and the foe of the tyrant—is printed all over the nineteenth century. Thousands of poor devils in Continental countries owed their necks to the feeling of their czars and kings that this hard bright eye of John Bull was upon them.

We cannot talk of the Victorians as though they were a race that all thought alike, always acted together. They were split by parties and sects. They engaged in frantic political controversies, they were divided by religious faiths and philosophies. There were many angels among them, many devils, and a great number of them were moral neuters. All changes of any order, whether for good or evil, were brought about by impassioned minorities. But it *is* possible to discern a "stream of tendency" in that age. It is fair, too, to say that certain general attitudes towards life were shared by a majority of the intelligent men and women of the time. These men and women were well aware of belonging to the most powerful nation in the world, they were proud of their settled, comfortable society, they were proud, too, of their country's achievements in mechanical progress. Possessing every material excuse for that self-satisfaction which is the death of the soul, they did *not* sink into complacency, and their souls did not die. Few societies have housed sterner critics than Carlyle, Dickens, Ruskin, Arnold and Morris; yet these prophets were not stoned, they were crowned. The capacity for self-criticism and for laughing at themselves was very strong among the Victorians. The Victorian age saw the triumph of the British middle classes. Never before was a ruling class buttressed by greater physical power or endowed with greater wealth. Yet it was from the heart of this prosperous, triumphant middle class that there sprang the movements for social justice for the working people. Lady Dorothy Nevill, herself an aristocrat, used to say that Charles Dickens was the perfect reflector of the opinions and ardours of the middle classes.

Do the faces in the family album look like those of opinionated characters, sure of themselves in this world, certain of their place in the next? The truth is that for many of them the private crisis of the soul was long and painful. Economic interest was not the sole spring of action for rich and poor; religious certainty and doubt played a part in daily life which is almost unknown in our age. Amid the treasures of their material civilisation, among all the ornaments of their culture, the subtler minds among the Victorians were weighed down by a tragic sense of man's destiny. Those trite old questions—"What shall a man do to be saved?" and "For what shall it profit a man if he shall gain the whole world and lose his soul?" pierced through the tumult of the Industrial Revolution. Existence had meaning. As we have seen, even the damned were invested in the awful grandeur of their doom. The Victorian free-thinker, in breaking away from the old faith, still retained his sense of the unique value of the individual. He opposed to the old faith not a negation but a new religion, the religion of humanity. Those who believed in God and those who did not believe in God believed equally in the dignity of man. Science brought astonishing news of the magnitude of the universe and the age of the earth, but this did not dwarf man to the insignificance of an insect, it increased his majesty, for it was through him that this vast cosmos was made conscious of itself. The serious-minded Victorians saw the Moral Order displayed in the splendours of the night sky. The stars were "the armies of unalterable law". Above all, the Victorians had a sharp sense of the struggle between Good and Evil, and they saw not only history but their daily lives as its battleground.

It is the Puritan qualities that one detects as uppermost in many of the representative men and women of the Middle Victorian time—an inner unrest, an obscure feeling of guiltiness and a fear of Hell, which are always sharp spurs to make men work hard to forget their ultimate fate; a joy in the world of action and heroic venture as a relief from the despair of contemplation; fear going together with a stubbornness of spiritual pride; a sense of responsibility to one's neighbour; a belief in the ethical value of mechanical Progress, a wistful hope that Paradise might one day be stormed by machines.

After living in their company for any length of time, one's final emotions spring from respect and admiration, not from affection. Their legacy of material achievement and of imaginative literature is overwhelming to contemplate. They lack the Greek qualities, they lack the Gallic qualities. Above all, they lack charm. One comes to appreciate the justice of their most searching critic, Matthew Arnold. They were, on the whole, Philistines, they were, in the mass, barbarians. They could be brutally insensitive to women, children, servants and artists. The way a Victorian Liberal could treat the Irish shocks a modern Conservative by its stupidity. But they were men cast in a large mould. And what manly Roman virtues they exhibited!

On the physical side they believed in the strength of their sinews, in the power of their brains, in their capacity to outwork and outwit any people on earth. They believed, too, in the divine purpose of Britain and in its noble destiny to lead the world into the ways of peace. Now whatever we

ADELINA PATTI AS ESMERALDA
in Giulio Campana's opera
Coloured lithograph, *c.* 1860

MACREADY AS MACBETH
Coloured engraving from Tallis's
"Dramatic Magazine", 1850

TAMBURINI AS RICCARDO
in Bellini's "Puritani"
Lithograph by A. E. Chalon, 1836

GIUDITTA PASTA AS SEMIRAMIS
Coloured lithograph by A. E. Chalon,
1837

"SCENE IN A ROMAN CIRCUS"
Ducrow in one of his favourite tableaux. Lithograph, *c.* 1830–40

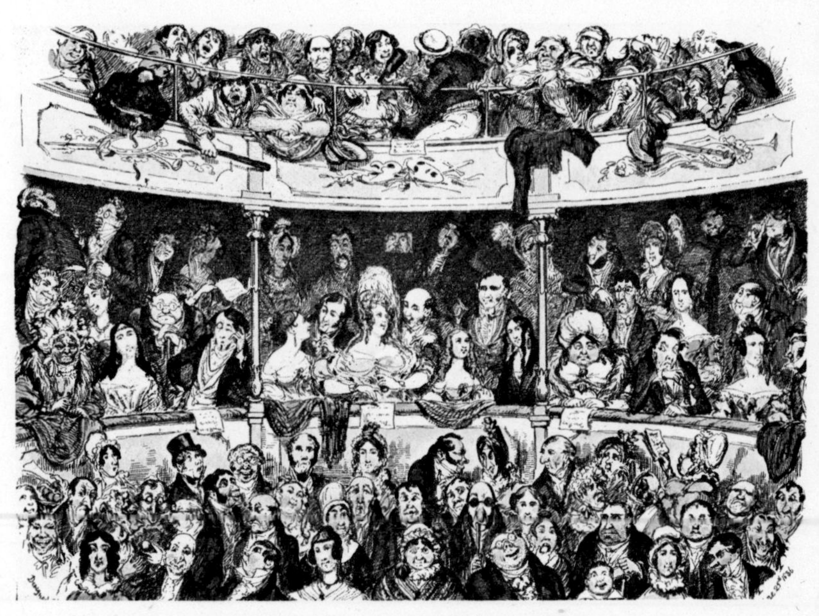

THE AUDITORIUM OF ASTLEY'S AMPHITHEATRE
Coloured etching by George Cruikshank, 1836
From "Volume One of My Sketchbook"

may think of the validity of such notions, the truth is that when strongly held by considerable masses of men and women they have an invigorating effect upon the national fortunes and tend to raise the standards of national behaviour. These ideas were as good as battleships; they were worth armies in the field.

None could pretend that the Middle Victorians were a wholly virtuous people, that all they did was done finely. They left their descendants some damnable inheritances: the hideous sprawl of our big cities, for example, and the neglect of the land which enfeebled the nation and brought it near to its utter undoing in two world wars. Modern Britain has suffered, too, because social reform moved at far too slow a pace in Victorian times. In this regard, the more far-seeing of the statesmen were either not true to their own best instincts when they held power, or were frustrated by their parties, or deflected by events. Then again, we must chiefly credit the Victorians with inflicting upon us that meanest of British vices, social, intellectual and spiritual snobbery, a bad quality that stands quite apart from class distinctions and that seems unaffected by political revolutions.

At a time when things are not going well for Britain, it is tempting to let the mind dwell upon a period when she was prosperous and strong, and was the master power in the world. The frescoes of our past always have a consoling interest in the lean years. The walls glow with mural paintings that record the victories of the Age of Elizabeth and the Age of Anne, and they stir a patriot's blood, but in their problems and their aspirations, in the intimate texture of their passions, the Elizabethans and the Augustans are remote from us. The Victorians are very close—as close as the spirit of a man's father. They have something still to say to us. With all their virtues and with all their sins upon their heads, they send us a signal of courage. Never lose heart, they seem to say; all will be well.

On the very eve of the splendour of the Victorian age, Britain seemed physically, morally and intellectually bankrupt. When all is said and done, when the account is struck, all that matters is the staunch heart of a people, its flow of creative ideas, its capacity to set free its own energies and its faith in itself. That is the grand testimony of the Age of Dickens.

CHRONOLC

	GREAT BRITAIN AND COLONIES: POLITICAL AND ECONOMIC	SOCIAL AND CULTURAL
1830	Death of George IV. William IV succeeds to thrones of England and Hanover. Earl Grey becomes Premier on resignation of Duke of Wellington.	King's College, London, founded for members of the Established Church. Tennyson's *Poems, chiefly Lyrical* published. Auguste Comte's *Philosophie Positive*. Deaths of Hazlitt, Huskisson.
1831	Reform Bill introduced (March). New elections, big Whig majority. Reform Bill rejected by Lords (September). Riots in Bristol. Reform Bill reintroduced (December).	British Association for the Advancement of Science founded. Death of Hegel.
1832	Reform Bill passes Commons (March). Amendment by Lords leads to Grey's resignation but Wellington fails to form ministry. Grey returns and Bill is passed (June). England occupies Falkland Islands. England blockades coast of Holland.	Capital punishment abolished for a number of crimes. Deaths of Bentham, Goethe, Sir Walter Scott.
1833	Slavery abolished throughout British Empire and £20 million compensation granted. Children under nine excluded from cotton mills. Inspectors of Factories appointed. National Trades Union organised by Robert Owen and Fielden, but lasted less than a year. British rule in New Zealand begins.	Keble's Assize Sermon on National Apostasy marks beginning of the Oxford Movement. First Government grant (£20,000) made to English schools.
1834	New Poor Law forbids outdoor relief and sets up Poor Law Commission. Melbourne succeeds Grey as Premier (July). South Australia Association formed. Houses of Parliament destroyed by fire. Peel succeeds Melbourne (December).	Deaths of Coleridge, Lamb, Malthus, Lafayette.
1835	Peel resigns. Melbourne Premier once more (April). Municipal Corporations Act makes mayors and corporations elective.	De Tocqueville's *Democracy in America* Death of William Cobbett.
1836	Newspaper Stamp Duty reducedf rom 4*d*. to 1*d*. a copy. House of Commons divisions lists published for the first time.	
1837	Accession of Queen Victoria. Parliamentary publications placed on sale by the House of Commons following the case of Stockdale *v*. Hansard of 1836. Formation of the Working Men's Association. New Zealand Association formed.	Dickens's *Pickwick Papers*. Carlyle's *French Revolution*. Jenny Lind's first performance. Death of Constable.
1838	Anti-Corn Law League formed in Manchester by Cobden and Bright. People's Charter (published May) inaugurates Chartism. Unrest in Canada. Lord Durham appointed Governor (January); resigns (October).	

AL TABLE

SCIENCE, INVENTION AND DISCOVERY	FOREIGN AFFAIRS	
iverpool and Manchester Railway; "Rocket" ngine.	July Revolution in France; Charles X flees and Louis Philippe becomes King. Revolution secures the independence of Belgium from Holland. Risings in Germany, Switzerland, Warsaw. Cholera appears in Europe. French capture Algiers.	1830
'araday's electro-magnetic discovery.	Belgian independence under King Leopold recognised and its neutrality guaranteed. Russian Army overruns Poland.	1831
	Dutch oppose independence of Belgium; French take Antwerp. Poland declared a Russian province. Carlsbad Decrees mark reaction in Germany and Austria.	1832
	Zollverein is adopted by all German States. France adopts elementary education. Turkish treaty closing the Dardanelles to all except Russian warships arouses British hostility to Russia.	1833
'irst photography by Fox Talbot.	Carlist Civil War begins in Spain. Riots in Paris and Lyons.	1834
	September laws curtail liberty of Press in France.	1835
'irst patentf or an electric telegraph. 'itman's shorthand invented.	Spanish Civil War ends with defeat of Don Carlos. Dutch found Natal.	1837
ondon and Birmingham Railway opened. 'Great Western" crosses Atlantic and first regular teamship service begins.	Louis Napoleon settles in England. Afghan War (1838–42). France attacks Mexico. Death of Talleyrand.	1838

	POLITICAL AND ECONOMIC	SOCIAL AND CULTURAL
1839	Melbourne resigns (May). Peel called to office, but Queen refuses his stipulation that Ladies of the Bedchamber appointed by his predecessor should be removed. Peel refuses to take office and Melbourne returns. First Factory Inspector's Report.	Committee of the Council of Education formed.
1840	Queen Victoria marries Prince Albert of Saxe-Coburg-Gotha. Rowland Hill introduces penny post. Trafalgar Square designed. Committee on Health of Towns. Maoris acknowledge the sovereignty of Queen Victoria by the Treaty of Waitangi.	
1841	Peel becomes Premier; Disraeli leads Opposition. New Zealand becomes a Colony.	Newman censured for Tract No. 90, ceases publishing *Tracts for the Times.*
1842	Chartist riots. Peel reintroduces income tax for three years. Modified corn tax on a sliding scale. Chadwick's report on Sanitary Condition of the Labouring Population. Report on employment of women and children in mines. Young Ireland movement begins.	Macaulay's *Lays of Ancient Rome.*
1843	Queen Victoria visits Louis Philippe, ratifying Entente Cordiale with France. Railway boom begins.	Free Church secession from the Established Church of Scotland. Carlyle's *Past and Present.* Ruskin's *Modern Painters,* Vol. I. Death of Robert Southey.
1844	Bank Charter Act. Rochdale Pioneers found Co-operative Store. Natal becomes a Crown Colony.	
1845	Peel removes all duties on exports, abolishes or reduces many import duties. Failure of Irish potato crop. Railway speculation.	J. H. Newman and Ward join the Roman Catholic Church. Disraeli's *Sybil.*
1846	Second failure of Irish potato crop results in famine. Repeal of Corn Laws; Peel provides for gradual abolition of duty on corn. Lord John Russell succeeds Peel as Premier. Palmerston becomes Foreign Secretary.	*Daily News,* first cheap newspaper, started with Dickens as editor. Evangelical Alliance opposes Romanism. Robert Browning and Elizabeth Barrett marry. Mendelssohn's *Elijah* produced at Birmingham.
1847	Population of Ireland, in spite of relief measures, reduced by three million through famine and emigration. First Jewish M.P. (Rothschild) elected, but cannot take his seat. Financial panic caused by railway mania.	Charlotte Brontë's *Jane Eyre.* Bohn's Libraries begin. British Museum built.
1848	Chartist movement collapses after mass meeting tries to present huge petition to Parliament. Unrest in Ireland. Crown and Government Security Bill. Act passed limiting work in factories for women and for children of 13–18 to ten hours.	Thackeray's *Vanity Fair.* Pre-Raphaelite Brotherhood formed. Macaulay's *History,* Vol. I. Mill's *Political Economy.* Bacon-Shakespeare controversy begins. Deaths of George Stephenson and Emily Brontë.

SCIENCE AND DISCOVERY	FOREIGN AFFAIRS	
	Aden annexed. First Chinese War (Opium War), 1839–42. Hong Kong taken.	1839
	Louis Napoleon's unsuccessfu linsurrection results in his capture and imprisonment. Remains of Napoleon brought from St. Helena and buried in Les Invalides, Paris.	1840
	Convention signed by Great Powers closing Dardanelles to all warships. List in Germany attacks free trade as an obstacle to nationalism.	1841
	Opium War in China ends; Hong Kong ceded; Canton and Shanghai opened to English traders. Second Afghan War (1842–49).	1842
	Scinde War.	1843
	French war in Morocco ends.	1844
	First Sikh War (1845–46); Sikhs invade British India and are defeated. Anglo-French expedition against Madagascar.	1845
	Spanish marriage of French heir destroys British Entente Cordiale with France. United States at war with Mexico. Polish insurrection. Pius IX becomes Pope (1846–78). Civil war in Portugal and Switzerland. Kaffir War.	1846
Chloroform used by Simpson as an anaesthetic. Joule discovers mechanical equivalent of heat. Gold discovered in California. Mountains of Kenya discovered. Franklin perishes searching for N.W. Passage.	Salt Lake City founded by Mormons. Charles Albert of Savoy introduces liberal reforms in Piedmont.	1847
	Second Sikh War (1848–49). Revolution in France; creation of National Workshops; Socialists, excluded from executive of New National Assembly, revolt but are suppressed; Republic is proclaimed (February); after riots Louis Philippe flees to England (March); Louis Napoleon selected President of the Second Republic (Dec.) Riots in Italy; Mazzini and Garibaldi in the Constituent Assembly attempt to abolish temporal power of the Pope.	1848

	POLITICAL AND ECONOMIC	SOCIAL AND CULTURAL
1848 (*cont.*)		
1849	Navigation Laws of 1651 and 1661–62 repealed. Punjab annexed.	Kingsley's *Alton Locke*. Sainte-Beuve begins *Causeries de Lundi*. Ruskin's *Seven Lamps of Architecture*. Bedford College for Women founded.
1850	Palmerston's action in support of Don Pacifico. Pope appoints Catholic Bishops to England. Representative government established in South Australia, Tasmania and Victoria.	Dickens's *David Copperfield*. Tennyson's *In Memoriam*. Free Libraries begun under Ewart's Act. Deaths of Peel, Wordsworth.
1851	Great Exhibition in Hyde Park. Palmerston dismissed. Gold discovered in New South Wales.	Herbert Spencer's *Social Statics*.
1852	Lord John Russell succeeded by Lord Derby, with Disraeli as Chancellor. Disraeli's Budget defeated. Whigs return to office under Lord Aberdeen.	Mrs. Stowe's *Uncle Tom's Cabin*. Meryon's "Etchings of Paris." Deaths of Turner, Wellington and Daniel Webster
1853	Gladstone's Budget abolishes duty on soap, reduces 133 taxes, imposes death duty. Indian Civil Service opened to competition.	Professor F. D. Maurice dismissed from King' College, London. Gautier's *Emaux et Camées*. Mommsen's *History of Rome*.
1854	Indian railways begun.	
1855	Lord Aberdeen resigns; Palmerston becomes Premier. Newspaper Stamp Duty abolished. Queen Victoria and Prince Albert visit Napoleon in Paris All Australian Colonies, except Western Australia, given responsible government.	Deaths of Charlotte Brontë, Kierkegaard. *Daily Telegraph* begun.
1856	Oudh annexed. Tasmania achieves self-government.	Holman Hunt's *Scapegoat*. Deaths of Heine, Schumann.

SCIENCE AND DISCOVERY	FOREIGN AFFAIRS	
	Venice proclaims a Republic under Manin. Charles Albert, King of Sardinia, attacks Austrians and is defeated (July). Unrest and revolts in Prussia, Baden, Bavaria, Saxony and Hanover. Federal Parliament of two Chambers meets at Frankfort and publishes *Fundamental Rights of the German People.* Insurrection in Vienna; Metternich escapes to England; Emperor abdicates and is succeeded by his nephew Francis Joseph. Attempted revolts of Czechs in Prague and of Poles in Warsaw and Cracow are suppressed; Kossuth appointed Minister for Hungary. Swiss civil war ends with establishment of Federal Government. Holland and Denmark obtain liberal Constitutions. Mexico gives up Texas, New Mexico, California, Nevada, Utah, Arizona and parts of Wyoming and Colorado to U.S.A.	1848 (*cont.*)
	Charles Albert of Sardinia abdicates in favour of his son Victor Emmanuel. Mazzini controls Republic in Rome until French troops restore the city to the Pope; French remain in garrison until 1870. Hungarians proclaim their independence under Kossuth, but are defeated. Gold rush in California. Second China War. Second Afghan War.	1849
	First Burmese War. Universal suffrage abolished in France and freedom of the Press curtailed. Death of Louis Philippe.	1850
irst submarine telegraph laid from Dover to Calais. I. Perkin discovers aniline dyes. old discovered in New South Wales.	Napoleon carries through *coup d'état* and is elected President for 10 years. Second Kaffir War (1851–53).	1851
	Napoleon chosen hereditary Emperor of France. Cavour becomes Premier in Piedmont. Francis Joseph abolishes Austrian Constitution. Second Burmese War (1852–53).	1852
teinway begins to make pianos.	Turkey declares war on Russia. Americans gain right to trade in Japan.	1853
	Crimean War (1854–56). England and France declare war on Russia (March); battles of Alma, Balaclava and Inkerman; siege of Sebastopol.	1854
	Fall of Sebastopol (September).	1855
essemer and Siemens improve steel production. eanderthal skull discovered. urton discovers Tanganyika and Speke the ictoria Nyanza lakes.	Peace of Paris ends Crimean War; England, France and Austria guarantee independence and integrity of Turkey; Black Sea declared neutral and navigation of Danube made free. Persian War (1856–57). Third China War (1856–60); Canton bombarded	1856

	POLITICAL AND ECONOMIC	SOCIAL AND CULTURAL
1857	Commercial panic; Bank Charter Act suspended. Indian Mutiny breaks out (March).	Hughes's *Tom Brown's School Days.* Miss Mulock's *John Halifax, Gentleman.* Flaubert's *Madame Bovary.* Baudelaire's *Fleurs du Mal.* Buckle's *History of Civilisation.* Trollope's *Barchester Towers.* Calendar of English State Papers and Ro Series begin. Deaths of Auguste Comte, de Musset. Universities founded in Calcutta, Bombay, Madra
1858	Palmerston defeated; Lord Derby becomes Premier. Indian Mutiny suppressed. Queen Victoria proclaimed Sovereign of India; Lord Canning appointed Viceroy. Volunteer system begun. Property qualification for Members of Parliament abolished. Jews admitted to Parliament.	Tennyson's *Idylls of the King.* Carlyle's *Frederick the Great.* Frith's "Derby Day". Death of Robert Owen.
1859	Lord Derby resigns on defeat of Disraeli's Reform Bill; Palmerston returns as Premier. Rise of Fenianism in Ireland. Queensland becomes a self-governing Colony. Ottawa chosen as capital of Canada.	Darwin's *Origin of Species.* George Eliot's *Adam Bede.* Gounod's *Faust.* J. S. Mill's *On Liberty.* Deaths of David Cox, de Tocqueville, Henry Halla and Macaulay.
1860	Commercial treaty with France reduces many customs duties. First Maori War.	*Essays and Reviews* published. Tolstoy's *War and Peace.*
1861	Excise Duty on paper abolished. End of First Maori War. Cotton famine (lasting until 1864). Gladstone reduces income tax from 10*d.* to 9*d.* in the £. Death of the Prince Consort (14th December). Lagos ceded to England.	George Eliot's *Silas Marner.* Spencer's *Education.* William Morris begins work as a decorator.
1862	House of Commons debates Education. Tea duty reduced.	George Meredith's *Poems.* Spencer's *First Principles.* Mill's *Utilitarianism.* Albert Memorial designed by Gilbert Scott an national subscription fund opened.
1863	Government makes unsuccessful efforts to oppose Germany on Schleswig-Holstein question and Russia over Poland. Ionian Isles ceded to Greece. Second Maori War.	Renan's *Vie de Jésus.* George Eliot's *Romola.* T. H. Huxley's *Man's Place in Nature.* Death of Thackeray.
1864	Government refuses aid to Denmark in war against Prussia. First Ashanti War.	Newman's *Apologia pro Vita Sua.*

SCIENCE AND DISCOVERY	FOREIGN AFFAIRS	
	Chinese fleet destroyed. Financial crash in U.S.A. Dred Scott decision upholds slavery in U.S.A. Algeria conquered by France.	**1857**
William Thompson invents the mirror galvanometer. S.S. "Great Eastern" launched.	China and Japan opened to trade. Turks massacre Christians at Jeddah and are bombarded by H.M.S. "Cyclops".	1858
	John Brown executed at Harper's Ferry. Louis Napoleon supports Victor Emmanuel in war against Austria, but after victories at Magenta and Solferino makes armistice at Villa Franca; Austria retains Venetia and the Quadrilateral; Sardinia gains Lombardy. Death of Metternich.	**1859**
Speke and Grant discover source of the Nile.	Tuscany, Parma, Modena and Romagna joined to Sardinia after plebiscite. France gains Savoy and Nice, antagonising England. Garibaldi takes Sicily. Umbria and Sicily annexed to Sardinia with Papal States. China wars (1860–62). Massacre of Christians in Syria provokes intervention of Great Powers.	1860
	Victor Emmanuel becomes King of Italy. Death of Cavour. Serfs in Russia emancipated. Civil war between south and north U.S.A. (1861–65). English and French embassies established in Peking. France, England and Spain send an expedition to Mexico, which had suspended payments.	1861
	Bismarck becomes chief minister in Prussia. Unsuccessful insurrection by Garibaldi. Representative institutions established in Greece under George, second son of King of Denmark. French declare war on Mexico, but English and Spaniards withdraw. French annex Cochin-China.	1862
	Bismarck controls Prussian Press, dismisses Parliament. Polish revolt suppressed. Lincoln declares abolition of slavery in U.S.A.; Battle of Gettysburg. French conquer Mexico.	1863
	Austria and Prussia attack Denmark and seize Schleswig and Holstein. Maximilian accepts Mexican crown. War in Bhutan.	1864

	POLITICAL AND ECONOMIC	SOCIAL AND CULTURAL
1865	Palmerston dies (October); Lord John Russell succeeds him as Premier. General Booth begins work in East London. Fenian movement in Ireland collapses. Convicts no longer sent to W. Australia. End of Second Maori War.	Matthew Arnold's *Essays in Criticism.* Lewis Carroll's *Alice in Wonderland.* Wagner's *Tristan and Isolde.* Seeley's *Ecce Homo.*
1866	Gladstone's Reform Bill fails. Lord Derby succeeds Russell as Premier; Disraeli Chancellor of the Exchequer. Failure of Overend and Gurney; commercial panic. All restrictions on admission of Jews to Parliament removed.	Froude's *History of England.* Swinburne's *Poems and Ballads* (withdrawn by th publisher). Bancroft, Hare, Irving and Wyndham on Englis stage.
1867	Disraeli's Reform Bill. Co-operative Wholesale Society founded at Manchester. Fenian movement in Ireland revives. Federal Government of the Dominion of Canada established at Ottawa.	Strauss's "Blue Danube" waltz. Marx's *Capital.* Bagehot's *English Constitution.* Death of Faraday.
1868	Disraeli succeeds Derby as Premier. After General Election, Gladstone becomes Premier. Privy Council condemns altar lights in the Church of England. Fenian movement grows. Third Maori War.	Browning's *Ring and the Book.* Wagner's *Mastersingers.* Death of Lord Brougham.
1869	Irish Church disestablished. Hudson Bay Territories incorporated with Canada. End of Third Maori War.	Matthew Arnold's *Culture and Anarchy.* J. S. Mill advocates emancipation of women. Deaths of Lamartine and Sainte-Beuve.
1870	Civil Service entry made competitive. Forster's Education Act provides free public elementary education in Board Schools. Diamond mines started at Kimberley. West Australia given representative government.	Newman's *Grammar of Assent.* Infallibility of Pope in matters of faith and morals proclaimed by Vatican Council. Newnham College founded. Jowett becomes Master of Balliol. Death of Dickens.

SCIENCE AND DISCOVERY	FOREIGN AFFAIRS	
Lister begins antiseptic surgery. Benzine analysed by Kekule.	Prussia administers Schleswig and acquires Kiel. Austria rules Holstein. U.S. Congress abolishes slavery. Lincoln assassinated (April). Revolt in Jamaica suppressed by Governor Eyre.	1865
Atlantic cable laid.	Prussia defeats Austria at Sadowa (Königgrätz) and secures Schleswig, Holstein, Hanover and Hesse-Cassel; Victor Emmanuel, as Bismarck's ally, gains Venetia; Louis Napoleon asks for part of Bavaria and Hesse, but Bismarck refuses.	1866
	Napoleon makes liberal reforms. Bismarck prevents Louis Napoleon buying the Grand Duchy of Luxembourg, whose neutrality is then guaranteed. North German Federation established. Hungary given responsible government under Dual Monarchy with Austria. Maximilian of Mexico assassinated. U.S.A. buys Alaska from Russia. Abyssinian War (1867–68).	1867
	Poland incorporated with Russia. Rise of Young Turk Party.	1868
Mendeleeff classifies chemical elements by atomic weight.	Opening of Suez Canal. Feudal system in Japan abolished. Republican movement grows in France.	1869
	Franco-Prussian War begins. Louis Napoleon defeated at Sedan, and abdicates. Italian troops occupy Rome on withdrawal of French garrison.	1870

TABLE I

Total Number of Persons Living in the British Isles on

	27–28 May 1821	29–30 May 1831	6–7 June 1841	30–31 March 1851	7–8 April 1861	2–3 April 1871
ENGLAND AND WALES						
Males	5,850,000	6,771,000	7,778,000	8,781,000	9,776,000	11,059,000
Females	6,150,000	7,126,000	8,137,000	9,146,000	10,290,000	11,653,000
Total	12,000,000	13,897,000	15,914,000	17,928,000	20,066,000	22,712,000
SCOTLAND						
Males	983,000	1,114,000	1,242,000	1,375,000	1,450,000	1,603,000
Females	1,109,000	1,250,000	1,378,000	1,513,000	1,612,000	1,757,000
Total	2,092,000	2,364,000	2,620,000	2,889,000	3,062,000	3,360,000
IRELAND						
Males	3,342,000	3,795,000	4,020,000	3,191,000	2,837,000	2,640,000
Females	3,460,000	3,973,000	4,156,000	3,362,000	2,962,000	2,773,000
Total	6,802,000	7,767,000	8,175,000	6,552,000	5,799,000	5,412,000
UNITED KINGDOM						
Males	10,175,000	11,681,000	13,039,000	13,347,000	14,063,000	15,302,000
Females	10,719,000	12,348,000	13,670,000	14,021,000	14,864,000	16,183,000
Total	20,894,000	24,029,000	26,709,000	[illegible]7,369,000	28,927,000	31,485,000

NOTE: These figures show that the population of England and Wales
almost doubled in fifty years;
that of Scotland was more than half as large again in 1871
as it was in 1821; while that of Ireland,
which was nearly half that of England and Wales,
declined sharply after the disastrous potato famine of 1845–46,
so that by 1871 there were four people in England and Wales
for every one Irishman.

These summary totals do not show such factors
as the numbers of people of working age,
neither do they reveal the appalling mortality
of children of under five years of age during the earlier period.

The great increase of population
was largely the result of improvements in public health,
which enabled more young children to survive.

TABLE II

Housing in England and Wales

Date	No. of inhabited houses *No. of families o separate occupiers*	No. of business premises including uninhabited houses	No. of houses building	Percentage increase of inhabited houses over previous ten years *Percentage increase in population in same period*
1821	2,088,156 *2,493,423*	69,707	19,274	!6.16% *!8·06%*
1831	2,481,544 *2,911,874*	119,915	24,759	18·83% *15·80%*
1841	2,943,945 *not known*	173,247	27,444	18·59% *14·27%*
1851	3,278,039 *3,712,290*	153,494	26,571	11·57% *12·65%*
1861	3,739,505 *4,491,524*	184,694	27,305	!4·04% *11·90%*
1871	4,259,117 *5,049,016*	261,345	37,803	13·92% *13·21%*

NOTE: These figures, taken from the decennial Census Returns,
show that the number of dwellings
in England and Wales doubled in fifty years,
while the number of business premises and factories
trebled in the same period.

They illustrate one aspect of the growth of capital investment
during the early Victorian era.

The percentage increase in the number of houses exceeded,
on the whole, the percentage increase in population,
but clearly many families shared houses.

Apartment houses and large blocks of flats
were then very few.

Comparable figures for Scotland and the United Kingdom
are not available until the Census of 1881.

TABLE III

Public Finance—Revenue Amount of the GROSS PUBLIC REVENUE of the United Kingdom distinguishing the Principal Branches thereof. Charges for collection not deducted.

Years Ended 5 Jan.	CUSTOMS	EXCISE	STAMPS	TAXES	PROPERTY and INCOME TAX	POST OFFICE
	£	£	£	£	£	£
1841	*23,387,269*	14,871,597	*7,353,819*	4,164,877	—	1,324,342
1842	*23,492,884*	14,762,371	*7,319,252*	4,712,783	—	1,393,169
1843	*22,594,475*	13,592,392	*7,158,777*	4,508,515	*580,886*	1,585,504
1844	*22,609,957*	13,955,430	*7,121,581*	4,398,714	*5,340,992*	1,575,651
1845	*24,085,442*	14,379,791	*7,334,857*	4,431,563	*5,345,582*	1,676,111
1846	*21,801,918*	14,648,719	*7,886,830*	4,434,657	*5,190,997*	1,878,594
1847	*22,185,852*	15,023,003	*7,680,047*	4,487,715	*5,543,057*	1,983,745
1848	*21,674,721*	13,903,761	*7,704,947*	4,549,771	*5,604,407*	2,119,520
1849	*22,645,493*	15,170,833	*6,811,985*	4,526,522	*5,496,195*	2,218,251
1850	*22,264,259*	14,965,525	*7,025,010*	4,512,607	*5,558,919*	2,156,563
1851	*22,041,651*	15,278,208	*6,724,729*	4,567,237	*5,524,228*	2,277,363
1852	*22,219,214*	15,376,236	*6,545,542*	3,790,534	*5,439,644*	2,373,164
1853	*22,137,045*	15,746,055	*6,919,429*	3,568,420	*5,654,678*	2,373,907
1854	*22,506,443*	16,303,237	*7,148,787*	3,339,971	*5,731,777*	2,522,680
Quarter to 5 Apl., 1854	*5,122,042*	2,573,913	*1,838,431*	241,024	*2,731,299*	733,625
Years ended 31 March						
1855	*21,630,081*	16,883,507	*7,109,196*	3,179,008	*10,642,621*	2,369,709
1856	*23,241,063*	17,491,108	*7,090,753*	3,119,985	*15,070,958*	2,811,247
1857	*23,531,747*	18,338,295	*7,389,616*	3,136,103	*16,089,933*	2,921,992
1858	*23,109,105*	17,825,000	*7,415,719*	3,154,053	*11,586,115*	2,920,000
1859	*24,117,943*	17,902,000	*8,003,769*	3,162,000	*6,683,587*	3,200,000
1860	*24,460,902*	20,361,000	*8,043,598*	3,232,000	*9,596,106*	3,310,000
1861	*23,305,777*	19,435,000	*8,348,412*	3,127,000	*10,923,817*	3,400,000
1862	*23,674,000*	18,332,000	*8,590,945*	3,160,000	*10,365,000*	3,510,000
1863	*24,034,000*	17,155,000	*8,994,000*	3,150,000	*10,567,000*	3,650,000
1864	*23,232,000*	18,207,000	*9,317,000*	3,218,000	*9,084,000*	3,810,000
1865	*22,572,000*	19,558,000	*9,530,000*	3,292,000	*7,958,000*	4,100,000
1866	*21,276,000*	19,788,000	*9,560,000*	3,350,000	*6,390,000*	4,250,000
1867	*22,303,000*	20,670,000	*9,420,000*	3 468,000	*5,700,000*	4,470,000
1868	*22,650,000*	20,162,000	*9,541,000*	3,509,000	*6,170,000*	4,630,000
1869	*22,424,000*	20,462,000	*9,218,000*	3,494,000	*8,618,000*	4,660,000
1870	*21,529,000*	21,763,000	*9,248,000*	4,500,000	*10,044,000*	4,770,000[1]

[1]Includes £100,000 from Telegraph Service.

CROWN LANDS (net)	MISCELLANEOUS includes Army contributions from India, surplus fees, unclaimed dividends, etc.	TOTAL GROSS REVENUE	RATE OF INCOME TAX IN THE £		
£	£	£			
167,500	415,362	51,684,766	1842–43	7*d.* in the £ on incomes of	
162,000	385,861	52,228,320	to	and above £150	
133,000	968,864	51,122,413	1852–53		
117,500	1,686,256	56,806,081			
155,000	894,466	58,302,812		£100—£150	£150 and
120,000	1,594,771	57,556,486			upwards
120,000	1,270,769	58,294,188	April 1853		
77,000	500,530	56,134,657	to		
81,000	1,209,129	58,159,408	April 1854	5*d.*	7*d.*
160,000	933,390	57,576,273	1854–55	10*d.*	1*s.* 2*d.*
160,000	946,554	57,519,970	1855–57	11½*d.*	1*s.* 4*d.*
150,000	878,196	56,772,530	1857–58	5*d.*	7*d.*
260,000	1,067,456	57,726,990	1858–59	5*d.*	5*d.*
402,888	1,140,884	59,096,667	1859–60	6½*d.*	9*d.*
65,000	289,306	13,594,640	1860–61	7*d.*	10*d.*
			1861–63	6*d.*	9*d.*
272,572	882,975	62,969,669	on incomes of and above £100 with abate-		
281,516	1,237,511	70,344,141	ment of £60 on incomes under £200		
284,857	1,200,770	72,893,313	1864–65	6*d.*	
276,654	1,715,009	68,001,655	1865–67	4*d.*	
280,041	2,271,841	65,623,181	1867–68	5*d.*	
284,479	1,916,993	71,205,078	1868–69	6*d.*	
290,568	1,557,511	70,388,085	1869–70	5*d.*	
295,000	1,938,112	69,865,057			
300,000	2,754,562	70,604,562			
305,000	3,036,065	70,209,065			
310,000	2,993,787	70,313,787			
320,000	2,878,292	67,812,292			
330,000	3,073,568	69,434,568			
345,000	2,586,218	69,600,218			
360,000	3,355,992	72,591,992			
375,000	3,205,252	75,434,252			

Note: *Receipts from Stamps consisted of revenue from Deeds, Probates, Legacies and Successions, Fire and Marine Insurance, Bills of Exchange, Receipts and Drafts and were fairly uniform with slight rise throughout the period.*

TABLE IV

Public Finance—Expenditure Amount of the GROSS PUBLIC EXPENDITURE of the United Kingdom distinguishing the Principal Branches thereof inclusive of payments for Collection of Revenue (£)

Years ended 5 January	*Interest and management of National Debt, funded and unfunded*	*Civil List and civil charges of all kinds*	*Army and Ordnance*	*Navy, including Transport and Packet Services*
1841	29,467,475	5,256,236	8,521,907	5,597,511
1842	29,714,873	5,630,000	8,233,554	6,489,074
1843	29,577,132	5,631,061	8,162,594	6,640,163
1844	29,390,013	5,954,570	7,907,860	6,606,057
1845	30,613,833	5,941,911	8,103,026	5,858,219
1846	28,588,567	5,427,733	8,854,297	6,809,872
1847	28,257,987	6,308,281	9,061,233	7,803,465
1848	28,417,646	8,095,755	10,488,274	8,013,873
1849	28,742,877	7,164,001	9,723,408	7,922,287
1850	28,503,779	6,989,207	8,881,140	6,942,397
1851	28,297,584	6,758,209	8,955,061	6,437,883
1852	28,220,242	6,878,662	8,723,940	5,849,917
1853	28,114,533	6,615,848	9,509,962	6,625,944
1854	28,054,659	7,225,884	9,425,079	6,640,596
1854 (qtr. to 5 Apl.)	6,566,260	2,052,859	2,190,000	2,007,769
Year ended 31 March				
1855	27,976,582	7,735,515	13,831,601	14,490,105
1856	28,191,977	8,679,372	27,806,603	19,654,585
1857	28,785,808	8,420,102	20,811,242	13,459,013
1858	28,738,298	10,146,918	12,915,157	10,590,000
1859	28,666,474	9,110,129	12,512,291	9,215,487
1860	28,747,228	9,685,913	14,057,186	11,823,859
1861	26,328,207	10,728,029	14,970,000	12,331,668
1862	26,323,777	10,821,956	15,570,869	12,598,042
1863	26,224,750	10,881,512	16,264,790	11,370,588
1864	26,204,884	10,771,490	14,638,051	10,821,596
1865	26,362,491	10,205,412	14,382,672	10,898,253
1866	26,226,381	10,250,065	13,804,450	10,259,788
1867	26,074,871	10,523,019	14,675,540	10,676,101
1868	26,564,843	11,193,758	15,418,582	11,168,949
1869	26,611,419	11,966,643	15,000,000	11,366,545
1870	27,046,653	12,254,700	13,565,400	9,757,690

[1] Includes Canadian insurrection (£553,249) and Chinese expedition (£150,000). [2] Includes Canadian insurrection (£117,153) and Chinese expedition (£400,000). [3] Includes Canadian insurrection (£253,344), China and India (£1,102,929). [4] Includes Canadian insurrection (£25,300), China War and Opium Compensation (£1,661,879). [5] Includes expenses in China (£416,757). [6] Includes Kaffir War (£1,100,000). [7] Includes Kaffir War (£300,000). [8] Includes Kaffir War (£370,000). [9] Includes Kaffir War (£260,000). [10] Includes Kaffir War (£30,000).

Total Forces	Charges of collection of revenue	Total gross expenditure	Total expenditure after deducting charges of collection	Expenditure out of loans for fortifications
14,822,667	3,698,116	53,244,494	49,546,378	
15,239,781 [2]	3,730,130	54,314,844	50,584,714	
16,159,030 [3]	3,733,945	55,101,168	51,367,223	
16,201,096 [4]	3,814,833	55,360,512	51,545,679	
14,378,002 [5]	3,906,772	54,840,518	50,933,746	
15,664,169	4,056,098	53,736,567	49,680,469	
16,864,698	4,016,647	55,447,613	51,430,966	
18,502,147	4,112,218	59,127,766	55,015,548	
18,745,695 [6]	4,302,615	59,955,188	54,652,573	
15,823,537	4,161,397	55,477,920	51,316,523	
15,392,944	4,243,440	54,692,177	50,448,737	
14,873,857 [7]	4,073,372	54,046,133	49,972,761	
16,505,906 [8]	4,073,041	55,309,328	51,236,287	
16,325,675 [9]	4,191,928	55,798,146	51,606,218	
4,227,769 [10]	1,169,358	14,016,246	12,846,888	
30,121,706	3,291,005	69,124,808	65,833,803	
51,661,188	4,533,351	93,065,888	88,532,537	
34,270,255	4,671,037	76,147,202	71,476,165	
24,995,850	4,358,988	68,240,054	63,881,066	
22,510,301	4,515,969	64,802,873	60,286,904	
26,739,102	4,438,548	69,610,791	65,172,243	
31,345,564	4,487,448	72,889,248	68,401,800	50,000
29,452,342	4,699,581	71,297,656	66,598,075	970,000
27,635,378	4,553,461	69,295,101	64,741,640	1,050,000
25,545,572	4,527,433	67,049,379	62,521,946	800,000
25,280,925	4,606,472	66,455,300	61,848,828	620,000
24,829,067	4,601,937	65,907,450	61,305,513	560,000
25,351,641	4,823,958	66,773,489	61,949,531	450,000
28,587,531	4,883,203	71,229,335	66,346,132	530,000
31,366,545	5,021,302	74,965,909	69,944,607	525,000
24,622,690	4,933,802	68,857,845	63,924,043	200,000

This, and the preceding table showing the main sources of public revenue, illustrate the relatively simple structure of Public Finance in the early Victorian era. Revenue was raised mainly by indirect taxation (customs, excise and stamp duties). The most serious item of public expenditure was interest on the National Debt, which explains why Gladstone was constantly preoccupied with efforts to reduce the size of the National Debt.

TABLE V

Shipbuilding Number and tonnage of sailing and steam vessels built and first registered in the United Kingdom

YEAR	SAILING VESSELS		STEAM VESSELS		TOTAL	
	NO.	TONS	NO.	TONS	VESSELS	TONS
1830	732	75,666	18	1,745	750	77,411
1831	729	82,958	31	2,749	760	85,707
1832	726	90,064	33	2,851	759	92,915
1833	695	89,243	33	2,928	728	92,171
1834	770	97,582	36	5,128	806	102,710
1835	830	110,798	86	10,924	916	121,722
1836	646	80,878	63	8,758	709	89,636
1837	927	124,253	78	11,669	1,005	135,922
1838	1,063	151,910	84	9,549	1,147	161,459
1839	1,216	180,764	62	6,139	1,278	186,903
1840	1,296	201,111	74	10,178	1,370	211,289
1841	1,063	148,215	48	11,363	1,111	159,578
1842	856	116,213	58	13,716	914	129,929
1843	652	76,968	46	6,129	698	83,097
1844	624	88,882	65	6,113	689	94,995
1845	788	112,336	65	10,894	853	123,230
1846	732	109,394	77	15,956	809	125,350
1847	830	129,664	103	16,170	933	145,834
1848	733	107,218	114	15,334	847	122,552
1849	662	105,455	68	12,498	730	117,953
1850	621	[illegible]	[illegible]	[illegible]	[illegible]	[illegible]

1852	608	136,749	104	30,742	712	167,491
1853	645	154,956	153	48,215	798	203,171
1854	628	132,687	174	64,255	802	196,942
1855	865	242,182	233	81,018	1,098	323,200
1856	921	187,005	229	57,573	1,150	244,578
1857	1,050	197,554	228	52,918	128	250,472
1858	847	154,930	153	53,150	1,000	208,080
1859	789	147,967	150	38,003	939	185,970
1860	818	158,172	198	53,796	1,016	211,968
1861	774	129,970	201	70,869	975	200,839
1862	827	164,061	221	77,338	1,048	241,399
1863	881	253,036	279	107,951	1,160	360,987
1864	867	272,499	374	159,374	1,241	431,873
1865	922	235,555	382	179,649	1,304	415,204
1866	969	207,678	354	133,511	1,323	341,189
1867	879	174,507	279	94,573	1,158	269,080
1868	787	237,687	232	78,510	1,019	316,197
1869	688	230,762	283	123,525	971	354,287
1870	541	117,032	433	225,674	974	342,706

TABLE VI

Shipping Number and Tonnage of Registered Sailing and Steam Vessels of the U.K. (exclusive of river steamers) employed in Home and Foreign Trade and number of men, exclusive of Masters, employed in them

	SAIL			STEAM			TOTAL		
Year	*Vessels*	*Tons*	*Men employed*	*Vessels*	*Tons*	*Men employed*	*Vessels*	*Tons*	*Men employed*
1849	*17,807*	2,988,021	*144,165*	414	*108,321*	8,446	*18,221*	3,096,342	*152,611*
1850	*17,466*	3,032,532	*142,730*	426	*104,680*	8,700	*17,892*	3,137,212	*151,430*
1851	*17,664*	3,216,194	*131,277*	520	*144,741*	10,660	*18,184*	3,360,935	*141,937*
1852	*17,270*	3,215,665	*146,286*	549	*165,219*	13,277	*17,819*	3,380,884	*159,563*
1853	*17,567*	3,511,827	*155,006*	639	*218,260*	17,519	*18,206*	3,730,087	*172,525*
1854	*16,869*	3,516,456	*146,522*	538	*212,637*	15,894	*17,407*	3,729,093	*162,416*
1855	*17,074*	3,701,214	*147,288*	754	*288,956*	21,249	*17,828*	3,990,170	*168,537*
1856	*18,149*	3,825,022	*151,080*	851	*331,055*	22,838	*19,270*	4,156,077	*173,918*
1857	*18,429*	3,830,119	*151,434*	899	*381,363*	24,953	*19,328*	4,211,482	*176,387*
1858	*19,209*	3,956,038	*152,655*	862	*369,204*	25,177	*20,071*	4,325,242	*177,832*
1859	*18,675*	3,879,592	*146,208*	895	*389,517*	26,298	*19,570*	4,269,109	*172,506*
1860	*19,090*	3,852,245	*145,487*	929	*399,494*	26,105	*20,019*	4,251,739	*171,592*
1861	*19,288*	3,918,511	*144,949*	997	*441,184*	27,008	*20,285*	4,359,695	*171,957*
1862	*19,059*	4,011,501	*146,047*	1,003	*461,793*	27,816	*20,092*	4,473,294	*173,863*
1863	*19,757*	4,283,528	*153,651*	1,120	*511,751*	31,076	*20,877*	4,795,279	*184,727*
1864	*20,184*	4,589,475	*158,276*	1,329	*618,993*	37,480	*21,513*	5,208,468	*195,756*
1865	*20,207*	4,706,752	*158,589*	1,419	*701,699*	39,054	*21,626*	5,408,451	*197,643*
1866	*20,212*	4,705,049	*156,568*	1,506	*747,813*	39,802	*21,718*	5,452,862	*196,371*
1867	*20,161*	4,681,031	*153,229*	1,616	*812,677*	43,111	*21,777*	5,493,708	*196,340*
1868	*20,525*	4,691,820	*153,840*	1,725	*824,614*	43,662	*22,250*	5,516,434	*197,502*
1869	*20,156*	4,677,275	*152,186*	1,725	*880,028*	43,304	*21,881*	5,557,303	*195,490*
1870	*19,940*	4,519,141	*147,207*	2,240	*1,039,969*	48,755	*22,180*	5,559,110	*195,962*

Note: This table and the last show that steam had not overtaken sail by 1870, despite the increasing number of steamships being built.

U

TABLE VII

Railways England and Wales

Year	Length of lines open at end of each year	Total capital paid up (shares, loans, etc.) at end of each year	Total number of passengers conveyed, including season-ticket holders	Total traffic receipts	Total working expenditure	Net receipts
	Miles	£			£	£
1854	6,140	240,235,025	93,346,149	17,342,925	7,870,487	9,472,438
1855	6,210	249,805,306	99,175,923	18,363,369	8,845,924	9,517,445
1856	6,447	257,489,431	108,368,901	19,728,309	9,359,414	10,368,895
1857	6,773	263,198,206	115,858,806	20,527,748	9,707,498	10,820,250
1858	7,001	270,871,643	115,956,957	20,244,095	10,105,384	10,138,711
1859	7,309	277,665,518	124,881,202	21,723,926	Not available	
1860	7,583	288,691,611	136,989,404	23,472,946	11,258,104	12,214,842
1861	7,820	299,446,182	145,831,425	24,021,928	11,802,349	12,219,579
1862	8,176	318,237,038	152,437,927	24,529,062	12,050,581	12,478,481
1863	8,568	333,514,818	173,648,476	26,212,822	12,659,618	13,553,204
1864	8,890	352,855,395	197,216,575	28,563,632	13,535,813	15,027,819
1865	9,251	379,604,827	216,693,538	30,054,408	14,560,826	15,493,582
1866	9,701	402,224,274	238,137,282	32,274,869	15,894,526	16,380,343
1867	10,037	418,277,679	250,598,982	33,398,222	16,764,520	16,633,702
1868			No figures available			
1869	10,773	430,772,858	274,707,152	34,698,985	17,504,308	18,600,814
1870	11,043	440,169,455	295,173,920	36,691,138	18,227,739	19,894,422

Note : Official figures are not available before 1854 except for the U.K. as a whole from 1842 onwards. Like the statistics on housing, these figures illustrate another aspect of the steady process of capital investment during the period up to 1870.

TABLE VIII

Railways United Kingdom, including Scotland and Ireland. (Comparison with Table VII shows that the greatest railway development was in England and Wales)

YEAR *to 30 une*	MILES	CAPITAL £	PASSENGERS *Total*	PASSENGERS *Per mile*	RECEIPTS (£) *Total*	RECEIPTS (£) *Per mile*	EXPENDITURE £	NET RECEIPTS £
1842	1,875	(unknown)	18,453,504		3,820,522			
1843	1,952	65,530,792	23,466,896		4,535,189			
1844	2,148	72,351,567	27,763,602		5,074,674			
1845	2,441	88,481,376	33,791,253		6,209,714			
1845	3,036	126,296,369	43,790,983		7,565,569			
1847	3,945	167,321,856	51,352,163		8,510,886			
1843	5,127	200,173,059	57,965,070		9,933,552			
Year ended 31 Dec. 1849	6,031	229,747,778	63,841,539	10,585	11,806,498	1,957		
1850	6,621	240,270,745	72,854,422	11,003	13,204,668	1,994		
1851	6,890	248,240,896	85,391,095	12,309	14,997,459	2,176		
1852	7,336	264,165,672	89,135,729	12,150	15,710,554	2,141		

1853	[illegible]	[illegible]	[illegible]	[illegible]	[illegible]	[illegible]		
1854	8,054	286,068,794	111,206,707	13,807	20,215,724	2,510	9,206,205	11,009,519
1855	8,280	297,584,709	118,595,135	14,323	21,507,599	2,597	10,299,709	11,207,890
1856	8,707	307,595,086	129,347,592	14,855	23,165,491	2,660	10,837,456	12,328,035
1857	9,094	315,157,258	139,008,888	15,395	24,174,610	2,659	11,240,239	12,934,371
1858	9,542	325,375,507	139,193,699	14,587	23,956,749	2,516	11,668,225	12,288,524
1859	10,002	334,362,928	149,807,148	14,980	25,743,502	2,573	—	—
1860	10,433	348,130,127	163,483,572	15,669	27,766,622	2,661	13,187,368	14,579,254
1861	10,869	362,327,338	173,773,218	15,988	28,565,355	2,628	13,843,337	14,722,018
1862	11,551	385,218,438	180,485,727	15,625	29,128,558	2,522	14,268,409	14,860,149
1863	12,322	404,215,802	204,635,075	16,607	31,156,397	2,528	15,027,234	16,129,163
1864	12,789	425,719,613	229,272,165	17,928	33,911,547	2,651	16,000,308	17,911,239
1865	13,289	455,478,143	251,862,715	18,953	35,751,655	2,691	17,149,073	18,602,582
1866	13,854	481,872,184	274,293,668	19,799	38,164,354	2,754	18,811,673	19,352,681
1867	14,247	502,262,887	287,688,113	20,193	39,479,999	2,771	19,848,952	19,631,047
1868	—	—	—	—	—	—	—	—
1869	15,145	518,779,761	312,631,812	20,643	41,075,321	2,712	20,780,078	21,915,849
1870	15,537	529,908,673	336,545,397	21,661	43,417,070	2,794	21,715,525	23,362,618

TABLE IX

Imports Quantities and value of the principal articles imported into the United Kingdom

Years	*Oxen, Bulls, Cows, Calves*	Sheep and Lambs	*Butter (cwts.)*	Coffee (cwts.)	*Eggs (No.)*	Guano (tons)	*Caoutchouc (cwts.)*	Gutta Percha (cwts.)
1861	*107,096*	312,923	*992,772*	83,532,525	*203,313,360*	178,423	*57,834*	19,749
£	*1,558,065*	616,020	*4,902,394*	2,628,776	*550,557*	2,022,283	*435,923*	130,602
1862	97,887	299,472	*1,037,371*	94,041,883	*232,321,200*	141,636	*59,703*	18,284
£	*1,301,602*	569,315	*4,923,100*	3,303,387	*593,813*	1,635,322	*483,934*	195,399
1863	*150,898*	430,788	*986,708*	1,047,806	*266,929,680*	233,574	*65,649*	21,655
£	*1,931,814*	669,573	*4,537,157*	4,155,330	*673,638*	2,658,856	*512,399*	224,961
1864	*231,733*	496,243	*1,054,617*	975,691	*335,298,240*	131,358	*71,027*	35,636
£	*3,208,851*	873,905	*5,652,704*	3,606,236	*835,028*	1,457,088	*502,645*	275,000
1865	*283,271*	914,170	*1,083,717*	1,232,120	*364,013,040*	237,393	*71,392*	29,077
£	*4,401,482*	1,787,866	*5,945,884*	4,600,887	*928,247*	2,675,995	*530,538*	160,565
1866	*237,739*	790,880	*1,165,081*	1,134,329	*438,878,880*	135,697	*72,176*	15,134
£	*4,092,941*	1,504,312	*5,962,455*	4,089,329	*1,105,653*	1,439,679	*728,416*	78,109
1867	*177,948*	539,716	*1,142,262*	1,229,730	*397,934,520*	192,308	*79,756*	15,289
£	*3,054,310*	945,661	*5,854,271*	4,362,760	*989,837*	2,109,506	*696,377*	92,945
1868	*136,688*	341,155	*1,097,539*	1,552,701	*383,969,040*	182,343	*145,584*	16,279
£	*2,067,822*	527,164	*6,340,718*	4,858,107	*1,009,285*	2,039,478	*1,195,226*	91,850
1869	*220,190*	709,843	*1,259,089*	1,584,360	*442,172,640*	210,010	*136,421*	15,398
£	*3,833,850*	1,219,014	*6,923,210*	4,927,805	*1,126,853*	2,640,983	*1,134,585*	95,616
1870	*202,172*	669,905	*1,159,210*	1,606,267	*430,842,240*	280,311	*152,118*	34,514
£	*3,147,061*	1,151,373	*6,793,877*	4,942,769	*1,102,080*	3,476,680	*1,597,628*	496,951

Petroleum (gallons) *Unrefined*	Refined	*Raw Silk (lb.)*	Spirits (gallons)	*Raw Sugar (cwts.)*	Tea (lb.)	*Unmfd. Tobacco (lb.)*	Wine (gallons)
361,746		*8,710,681*	10,879,002	*10,399,405*	96,577,383	*50,761,116*	11,052,436
23,558		*7,705,277*	1,814,023	*12,163,308*	6,850,562	*1,919,815*	4,200,929
5,584,208		*10,372,123*	10,558,415	*9,884,191*	114,787,361	*39,982,123*	11,960,676
349,987		9,824,*148*	1,768,179	*10,929,406*	9,175,940	*1,999,401*	3,862,233
4,706,100	4,201,265	*9,221,145*	11,186,030	*10,724,522*	136,806,316	*51,318,284*	14,185,195
297,919	392,779	*9,380,758*	1,828,607	*11,530,242*	10,666,017	*2,482,978*	4,497,343
2,381,652	2,929,687	*5,655,401*	11,736,445	*10,754,453*	124,359,243	*61,042,667*	15,451,593
160,675	295,238	*6,336,903*	2,275,049	*14,404,150*	9,438,760	*2,650,009*	5,002,884
1,426,824	2,112,831	*7,732,450*	11,729,582	*10,250,524*	121,271,219	*66,084,857*	14,269,752
113,828	316,171	*10,185,855*	1,699,693	*11,302,624*	10,044,462	*2,781,968*	3,914,196
1,456,812	6,321,417	*5,453,804*	14,660,478	*10,639,085*	139,610,044	*54,374,797*	15,321,028
98,577	598,062	*7,243,199*	2,254,810	*10,795,015*	11,208,815	*2,101,351*	4,733,475
293,832	5,374,532	*5,849,648*	13,067,342	*10,545,315*	128,028,726	*57,586,287*	15,442,581
13,451	354,271	*7,556,462*	2,259,081	*11,501,961*	10,068,324	*1,841,942*	4,835,251
603,792	3,720,476	*7,036,177*	12,393,435	*11,796,161*	154,845,863	*49,016,586*	16,953,429
26,778	272,078	*8,741,045*	2,301,673	*13,339,758*	12,431,454	*1,743,287*	5,440,991
168,084	5,234,621	*5,573,366*	11,457,758	*11,033,653*	139,223,298	*52,588,590*	17,184,330
8,741	434,117	*6,812,831*	2,106,781	*13,540,917*	10,311,465	*1,854,220*	5,265,600
507,276	6,352,109	*6,307,575*	17,261,612	*12,798,631*	141,020,767	*45,557,887*	17,774,782
27,511	507,761	*8,204,993*	3,218,387	*14,440,502*	10,097,619	*1,680,140*	4,817,294

TABLE X

Wages

Occupation	Wages in shillings per week						
	1823–30	*1830–36*	*1836–45*	*1845–55*	*1855–65*	*1865–70*	*1870–75*
Woollen Cloth Weaver:							
Hand Loom—Men	15–18	14–17	14–17	14–16	14–16		
Power Loom—Women						12–14	13–15
Worsted Stuff Weaver:							
Hand Loom	17–20	11–14	11–12, etc.				
Power Loom				11–12	one loom 11–12½	two looms 14–16	two looms 15–18
Woollen Spinners:							
Jenny—Women	11–12	8–10	7–9				
Mule—Men	24–26	24–26	24–26	26–29	27–30	28–31	28–31
Wool Sorters	28–30	28–30	28–30	28–30	28–30	28–30	28–30
Dyers	16–18	16–18	16–18	16–18	17–20	17–20	19–22
Cotton Weavers:							
Hand Loom	14–18						
Power Loom				four looms 13–15	four looms 14½–16	four looms 15–17	four looms 16½–18½
Carpenters	23–24	23–24	24–26	24–26	26–28	28–30	32–34
Masons	23–26	23–26	26–28	26–28	28–30	32–34	34–36
Boot and Shoe Makers	21–23	21–23	24–26	24–26	24–26	25–28	26–29
Journeymen Tailors	21–26	20–25	20–25	21–26	22–27	22–27	23–30
Coal Miners	16–18	16–18	16–18	17–20	18–21	21–23	24–28
Agricultural Labourers	9–10	9½–11	10–12	10–12	12–14	12–14	12–16
General Labourers not in Agriculture	13–15	13–15	15–18	16–19	16–19	17–20	18–20

TABLE XI

Prices

COMMODITY OR SERVICE	*1823–1830*	*1830–1836*	*1836–1845*	*1845–1855*	*1855–1865*	*1865–1870*	*1870–1885*
Wheat (*mean average price a quarter*)	67*s.*	51*s.* 6*d.*	57*s.* 11*d.*	51*s.* 7*d.*	52*s.* 7*d.*	54*s.* 7*d.*	47*s.* 4*d.*
Beef (*per lb.*)	8*d.*–8½*d.*	8*d.*–8½*d.*	6½*d.*–7½*d.*	7½*d.*–9*d.*	8½*d.*–9½*d.*	9*d.*–10*d.*	10*d.*–11*d.*
Fresh Farm Butter (*per lb.*)	12*d.*–13*d.*	11*d.*–12*d.*	10*d.*–11*d.*	12*d.*–14*d.*	13*d.*–15*d.*	13*d.*–15*d.*	15*d.*–17*d.*
Eggs (*number for 1s.*):							
Summer			20-24			16–18	14–16
Winter			10–12			6–8	6–
Rent of workman's cottage with garden plot (*per year*)	£4–5	£5–6	£5–6	£6–8	£6–9	£7–10	£8–12
Agricultural rents (*per acre of average farm land*)		30*s.*–35*s.*		30*s.*–35*s.*		30*s.*–35*s.*	35*s.*–45*s.*
Cheese (*per lb.*)	7*d.*–7½*d.*	7*d.*–7½*d.*	6*d.*–6½*d.*	7*d.*–7½*d.*	7½*d.*–8½*d.*	7½*d.*–8½*d.*	8*d.*–9*d.*
Board of working man, with lodging, food, washing (*per week*)	8*s.*–9*s.* 6*d.*			8*s.*–9*s.*			11*s.*–13*s.*

NOTE: These figures, based on those in Palgrave's DICTIONARY OF POLITICAL ECONOMY (Macmillan, 1913), Vol. III, pp. 634–37, give a good general indication of the main trends in prices of some important factors in the cost of living and in the movements of wages in some principal occupations. But it must be remembered that they are averages, and that conditions probably varied considerably over the country as a whole. This is particularly true of agricultural wages (for which see in greater detail ENGLISH FARMING PAST AND PRESENT by Lord Ernle, Appendix IX.

BOOKS

To be really adequate, the bibliography should be larger than the rest of this book. The literature of the Victorian age is so vast that a fairly young reader might give his whole life to it, saving up for his eightieth year such joys as the poetry of J. Stanyan Bigg ("Night and the Soul"), whom George Gilfillan thought such a fine fellow "with a rich Arabian-Night kind of fancy", and the *Memorials* of the Rev. John McLeod Campbell.

In this huge ocean, the most one can hope to do is to mark certain islands where one has found instructive or entertaining experiences, or where one has met with out-of-the-way adventures. There is, of course, the majestic archipelago formed by the novelists and poets of the time—Dickens himself, Thackeray, the Brontës, George Eliot, Trollope, Disraeli, Mrs. Gaskell, Charles Kingsley, Bulwer Lytton, Tennyson, Browning, Arnold, Clough, Dante Gabriel and Christina Rossetti. These islands are humming with the tourist trade all the year round, and the fastidious sometimes complain that they have become commercialised. In their cheerful bustle they contrast with a lonely little atoll, a Robinson Crusoe kind of place, marked on my map as Richard Henry Horne, "Orion" Horne, who published his epic poem at a farthing, and then, giving up verse, took charge of the convoys of gold nuggets from Ballarat to Melbourne in the grand, exciting days, and wrote one of the liveliest of books on Australia. The writings of Carlyle, Ruskin, Arnold, Macaulay, Mill, Darwin, Huxley, Newman are, I suppose, what the Americans call required reading. There are also the formidable collections of the speeches of Russell, Peel, Palmerston, Gladstone, Disraeli and Bright which give one an immense respect for the staying powers of both orators and auditors. For a serious background to this light, superficial book, I would suggest the Cambridge Modern History.

As for the rest, any short list can only be the hugger-mugger of one man's arbitrary choice, limited by his caprices and prejudices on the one side and by his ignorance and indolence on the other. At the top of this individual list I would put the 1884 edition of the *Encyclopaedia Britannica*, which to my mind is one of the great, grand monuments of Victorian culture and intelligence. I would recommend, too, excursions into the dusty old files of some daily newspaper, *The Times* or the *Daily News* (begun by Dickens in 1846), as well as a renewal of acquaintance with those old friends of our childhood, the bound volumes of *All the Year Round*, *Household Words* and the *Illustrated London News*. There is a flavour in an old newspaper or magazine which evaporates when one tries to transfer it to a book of history; some precious topicality, some immediacy, is preserved in the old files.

Here, then, follows a list of a few of the books which have influenced this writer's view of the Early Victorian period or the times immediately before it, all of them being fairly easy books to borrow from our larger libraries:—

I. General Histories and Works of Reference

Cambridge Modern History, vols. 10, 11, 13 and Atlas. Cambridge University Press, 1907–10.

Cambridge History of English Literature, vols. 12–14. Cambridge University Press, 1915–16.

Encyclopaedia Britannica, 9th ed. 1875–89.
Clapham, Sir John: *An Economic History of Modern Britain*, vols. 1 & 2. Cambridge University Press, 1930–32.
Martineau, Harriet: *The History of England During the Thirty Years' Peace, 1816–46.* 1849.
Traill, H. D. (ed.): *Social England.* 6 vols. 1893–97.
Porter, G. R.: *The Progress of the Nation.* 1851.
Woodward, E. L.: *The Age of Reform* (vol. 13 in *The Oxford History of England*). Oxford University Press, 1938.
Young, G. M. (ed.): *Early Victorian England, 1830–1865.* 2 vols. Oxford University Press, 1934.

II. Memoirs, Diaries, Biographies and Contemporary Descriptive Work

Bagehot, Walter: *Literary Studies.* 1879.
Balfour, Lady Betty (ed.): *Personal and Literary Letters of Robert, First Earl of Lytton.* 1906.
Bamford, Samuel: *Passages in the Life of a Radical.* 2 vols. 1841–43.
Chesterton, G. K.: *Robert Browning.* 1903.
Cobbett, William: *Rural Rides.* 1830 (J. M. Dent, Everyman's Library, 1934).
Duff, Sir Mountstuart Grant: *Notes from a Diary, 1851–72.* 1911.
Egan, Pierce: *Life in London; or, the Day and Night Scenes of Jerry Hawthorn and his Elegant Friend Corinthian Tom.* 1820.
Emerson, Ralph Waldo: *English Traits.* 1856.
Forster, John: *The Life of Charles Dickens.* 3 vols. 1872–74 (J. M. Dent, Everyman's Library, 1927).
Gammage, R. G.: *History of the Chartist Movement, 1837–1854.* 1854.
Hammond, J. L. and Barbara: *Lord Shaftesbury.* Longmans, 1923.
Hawthorne, Nathaniel: *Our Old Home.* 1865.
Hunt, James Henry Leigh: *Autobiography.* 1850.
Leon, Derrick: *Ruskin: The Great Victorian.* Routledge & Kegan Paul, 1949.
Martin, Sir Theodore: *Queen Victoria as I Knew Her.* 1908.
Maxwell, Sir Herbert (ed.): *The Creevey Papers.* 1903.
Mayhew, Henry: *London Labour and the London Poor.* 1851.
Mill, John Stuart: *Autobiography.* 1873.
Monypenny, W. F., and G. E. Buckle: *The Life of Benjamin Disraeli, Earl of Beaconsfield.* 6 vols. John Murray, 1910–20 (new ed. 1929).
Morley, John: *The Life of William Ewart Gladstone.* 3 vols. 1903.
Nevill, Lady Dorothy: *Under Five Reigns.* 1910.
Owen, Robert: *The Life of Robert Owen, Written by Himself.* 2 vols. 1857–58.
Parker, C. S.: *Sir Robert Peel from his Private Papers.* 3 vols. 1891–99.
Parker, J. (ed.): *Essays and Reviews.* 1860.
Payn, James: *Some Literary Recollections.* 1884.
Peel, Ethel (ed.): *Recollections of Lady Georgiana Peel.* John Lane, 1920.
Pückler-Muskau, Prince von: *Tour in England, Ireland and France in the Years 1828–9.* 1832. (A sharp-eyed German observer who merits reprinting.)
Ray, Gordon N. (ed.): *The Letters and Private Papers of William Makepeace Thackeray.* Oxford University Press, 1945. (A triumph of American scholarship.)

Reeve, H. (ed.): *The Greville Memoirs.* 8 vols. 1874–87.
Russell, G. W. E.: *Collections and Recollections.* 1899.
Russell, Lord John: *Memoirs of the Affairs of Europe from the Peace of Utrecht.* 1824–29.
Sadler, T. (ed.): *Diaries, Reminiscences and Correspondence of Henry Crabb Robinson.* 1869.
Taine, H. A.: *Notes on England.* 1872.
Tennyson, Hallam: *Alfred, Lord Tennyson, a Memoir.* 1897.
Trevelyan, Sir George Otto: *The Life and Letters of Lord Macaulay.* 1876.
Ward, Mrs. E. M.: *Memories of Ninety Years* (ed. Isabel McAllister). Hutchinson, 1924.
Wright, Aldis (ed.): *Letters of Edward FitzGerald.* 1894.

III. Books on Special Subjects

Ashton, T. S.: *Iron and Steel in the Industrial Revolution.* Manchester University Press, 1924.
Bagehot, Walter: *Lombard Street.* 1873. *Physics and Politics.* 1872. *The English Constitution.* 1867.
Baines, E.: *History of the Cotton Manufacture.* 1832.
Bennett, James: *The History of Dissenters During the Last Thirty Years.* 1839.
Bentham, Jeremy: *Works* (ed. John Bowring). 1843. (Especially *An Introduction to the Principles of Morals and Legislation*; *Panopticon, or, the Inspection-House*; and *Leading Principles of a Constitutional Code for Any State.*)
Brougham, Henry Peter, Baron Brougham and Vaux: *Observations on the Education of the People.* 1825. *The Life and Times of Henry, Lord Brougham.* 3 vols. 1871.
Catalogue of the Great Exhibition of 1851. 3 vols. 1851.
Chadwick, Sir Edwin: *The Health of Towns.* 1889.
Chesterton, G. K.: *The Victorian Age in Literature.* 1913.
Chorley, H. F.: *Thirty Years' Musical Recollections.* 2 vols. 1862.
Cook, E. Dutton: *Nights at the Play.* 2 vols. 1883.
Cruikshank, George: *The Comic Almanack.* 1835–53.
Darwin, Charles: *On the Origin of Species by Means of Natural Selection.* 1859.
Davison, James William: *Music During the Victorian Era: From Mendelssohn to Wagner.* 1912. (Memoirs of the music critic of *The Times.*)
Eastlake, Sir Charles L.: *A History of the Gothic Revival.* 1872.
Elliott, Ebenezer: *Corn Law Rhymes.* 1831.
Engels, Friedrich: *The Condition of the Working Class in England in 1844.* 1892.
Fay, C. R.: *The Corn Laws and Social England.* Cambridge University Press, 1932.
Francatelli, C. E.: *The Modern Cook.* 1846.
Gladstone, W. E.: *The State in Its Relations with the Church.* 1839.
Grove, Sir George: *Dictionary of Music and Musicians.* 4 vols. 1879–89.
Hammond, J. L. and Barbara: *The Village Labourer, 1760–1832.* Longmans, 1911. *The Town Labourer, 1760–1832.* Longmans, 1917. *The Skilled Labourer, 1760–1832.* Longmans, 1919. *The Rise of Modern Industry.* Methuen, 1925. *The Age of the Chartists, 1832–54.* Longmans, 1930.
Haydon, Benjamin Robert: *Autobiography.* 1853.
Hole, Dean Samuel R.: *A Book about Roses.* 1869.
Hood, Thomas: *Comic Annual.* 1830.

Huxley, Thomas Henry: *Lay Sermons, Addresses and Reviews*. 1870.
Jones, H. Bence (ed.): *The Life and Letters of Michael Faraday*. 1870.
Kay-Shuttleworth, Sir James: *Four Periods of Public Education as Reviewed in 1832—1839—1846—1862*. 1862.
Kingsley, Charles: *Two Years Ago*. 1857. (As far as I know, the only novel written about sanitation; it should be read with Chadwick's Reports.)
Lennox, Lord William Pitt: *Plays, Players and Playhouses at Home and Abroad*. 2 vols. 1881.
Lewes, George Henry: *Actors and the Art of Acting*. 1875.
Lyell, Charles: *Biological Evidence of the Antiquity of Man*. 1863.
Martineau, Harriet: *Poor Laws and Paupers*. 1833.
Methodist Hymn Book, The.
Mill, James: *Analysis of the Phenomena of the Human Mind*. 2 vols. 1829.
More, Hannah: *Village Politics*. 1792. (Published under the pseudonym "Will Chip".)
Morley, H.: *The Journal of a London Playgoer, 1851–86*. 1886.
Newman, John Henry, and others: *Tracts for the Times*. 1833–41. *Lyra Apostolica*. 1836.
Parker, J. (ed.): *Essays and Reviews*. 1860.
Penrose, Elizabeth: *Mrs. Markham's History of England*. 1823. (Shows us what the young were taught to think about their country.)
Reade, Charles: *It Is Never Too Late To Mend*. 1856. (The cruelties of the old prison system described by a master of documentation.) *Hard Cash*. 1863. (A lurid exposure of the horrors of private lunatic asylums.)
Scholes, Percy A.: *The Mirror of Music, 1844–1944*. 2 vols. Oxford University Press, 1947. (Centenary volumes of the *Musical Times*.)
Smiles, Samuel: *Lives of the Engineers*. 3 vols. 1861–62. *Self Help*. 1859. *Character*. 1871.
Smith, Frank: *The Life and Work of Sir James Kay-Shuttleworth*. John Murray, 1923.
Smith, George: *History of Wesleyan Methodism*. 3 vols. 2nd ed. 1859–62.
Spurgeon, Rev. Charles Haddon: *Gleanings Among the Sheaves*. 1864.
Stanley, Dean Arthur P.: *The Life and Correspondence of Thomas Arnold*. 2 vols. 1844. (Arnold of Rugby.)
Stephen, Leslie: *The English Utilitarians*. 3 vols. 1900.
Taine, H. A.: *History of English Literature*. 1871.
Tyndall, John: *Fragments of Science*. 1871.
Williams, Sir S. C. Stuart, and Ernest Short: *Railways, Roads and the Public*. Eyre & Spottiswoode, 1939.

ACKNOWLEDGMENTS

Particular acknowledgment must be made to the Controller, H.M. Stationery Office, for permission to include figures from the *Statistical Abstracts for the United Kingdom 1840–54, 1851–65* and *1863–77* in the statistical tables on pp. 284–299.

INDEX

Literacy

1841

1871

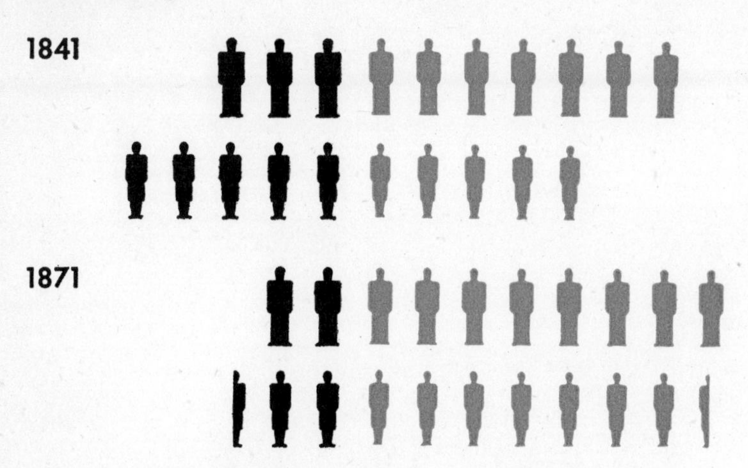

Each blue symbol represents 1 literate among 10 men and women

Treasury Grants for Elementary Education

1840

1870

Each circle represents £100,000

Books Published

1841

1871

Each symbol represents 100 books

CHART II

London's Theatres 1836

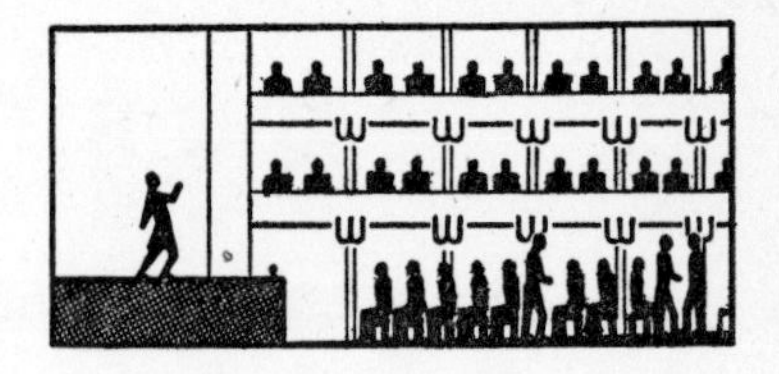

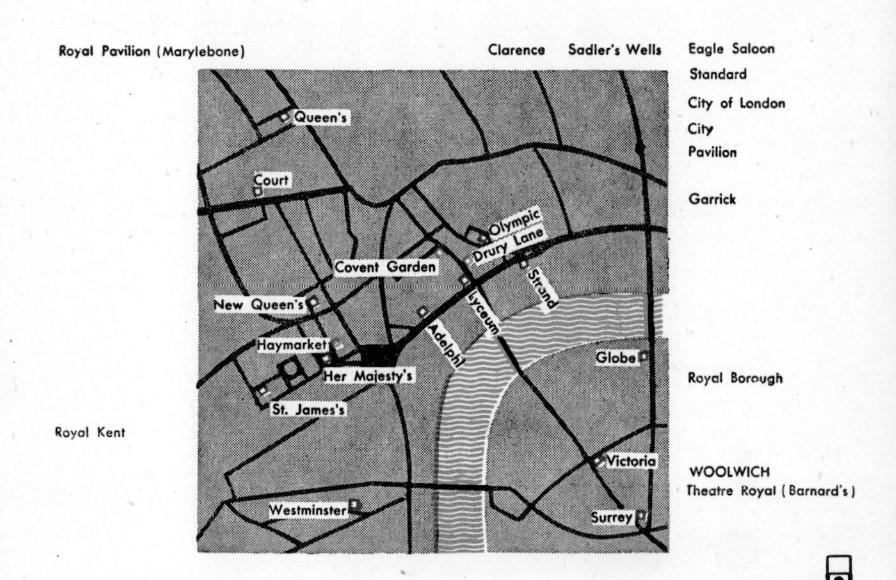

ISOTYPE INSTITUTE

London's Theatres 1870

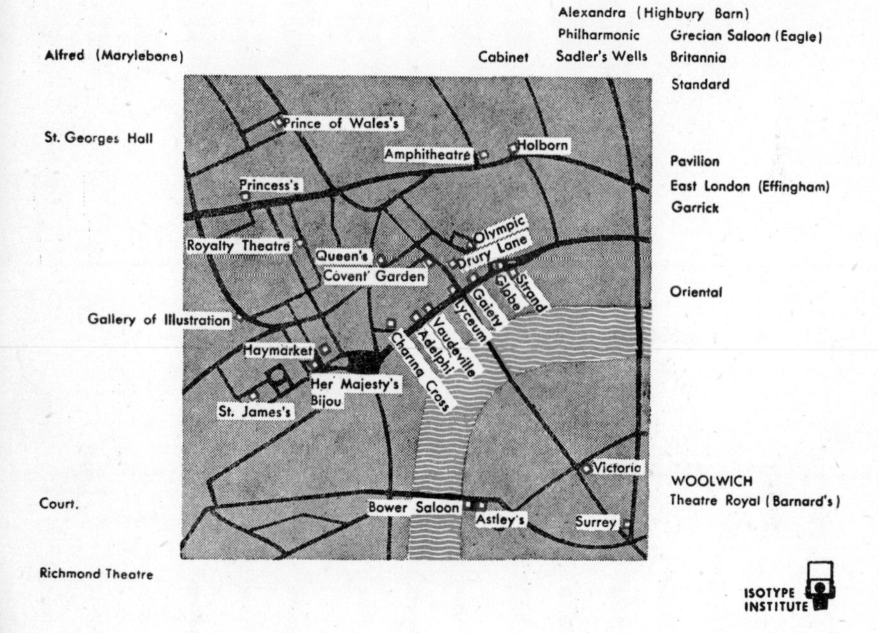

ISOTYPE INSTITUTE

Population

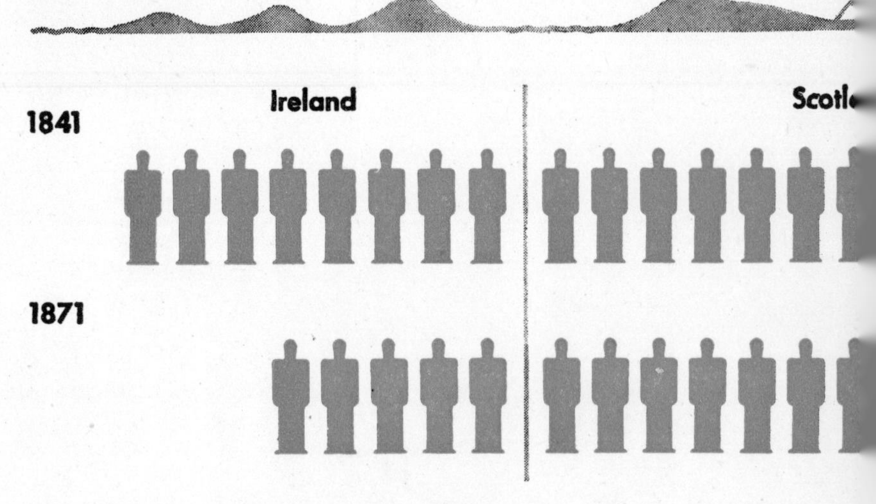

Each man symbol represents 1 million population

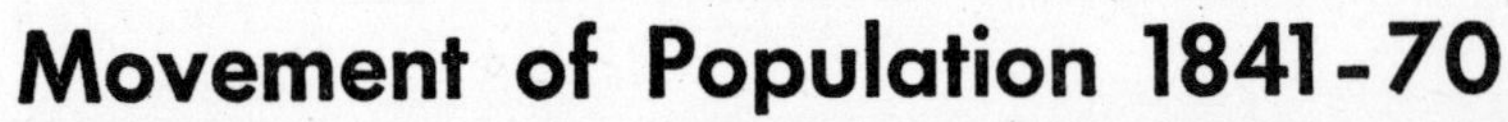

Movement of Population 1841-70

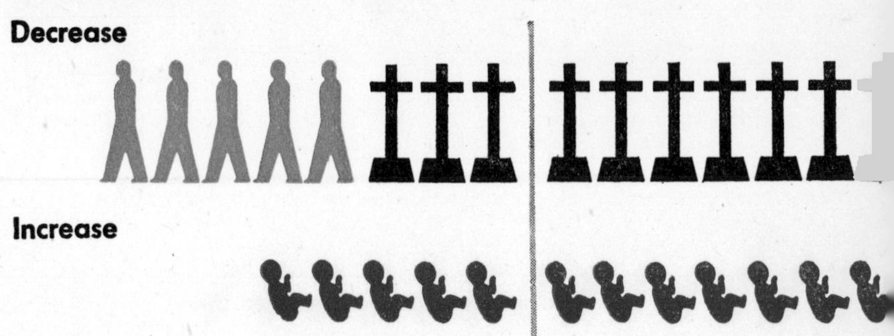

Each blue symbol represents 1 million net emigration
Each black symbol represents 1 million deaths
Each red symbol represents 1 million births

ngland and Wales

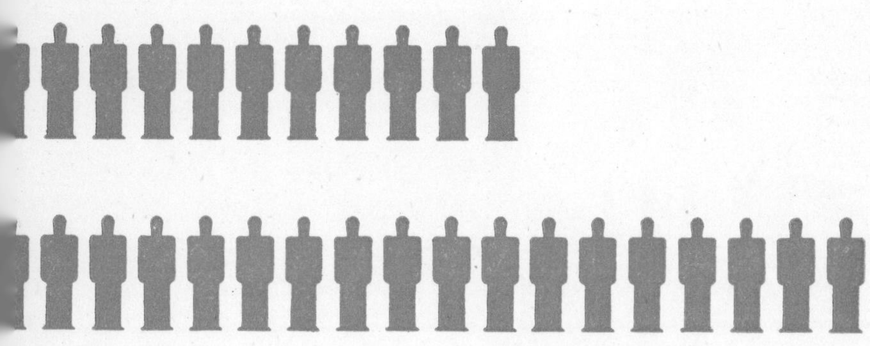

CHART V

Emigration from the British Isles 1835-69

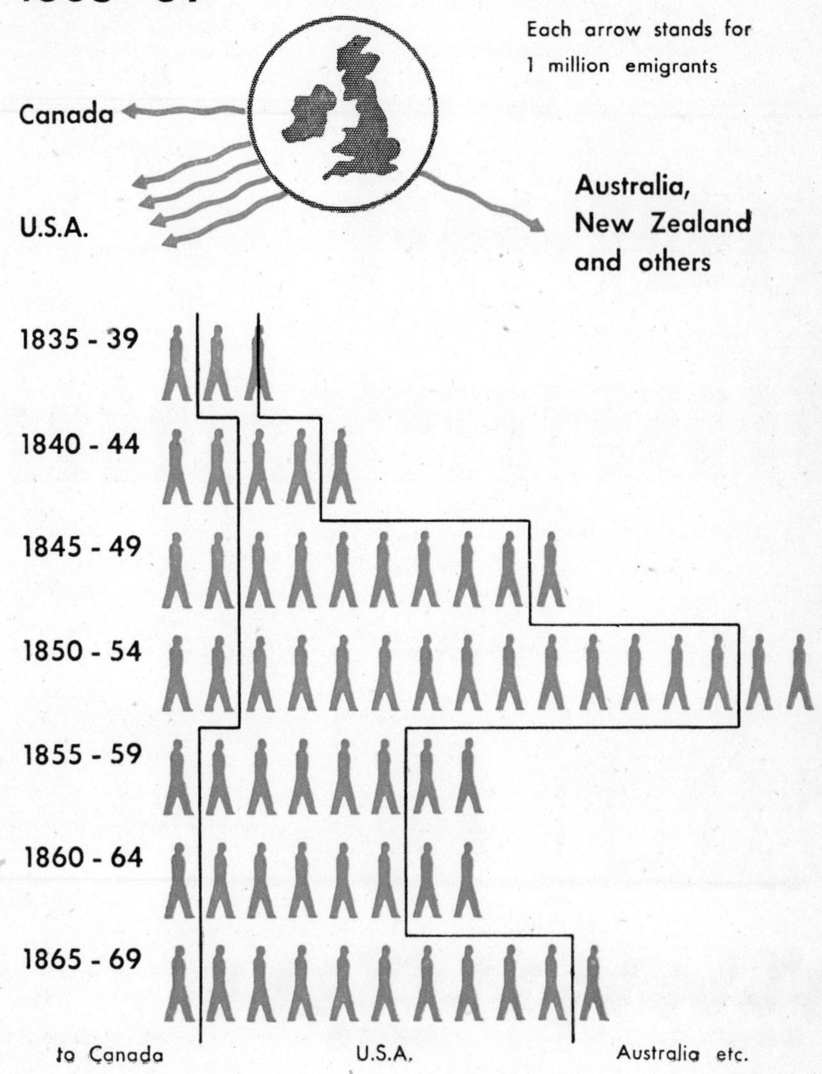

Each man symbol represents 100,000 emigrants from British ports

Public Revenue

Customs | Excise | other | Income tax

1841

1851

1861

1870

Each circle represents £2,500,000

Public Expenditure

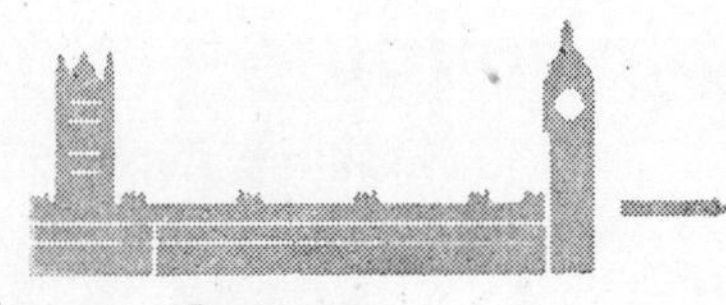

Coll. of Revenue | Service of Debt | Civil Charges | Forces (Army) (Navy)

1841

1851

1861

1870

Each circle represents £2,500,000

ISOTYPE INSTITUTE

CHART VII

Shipping

sailing ships steamships

1850

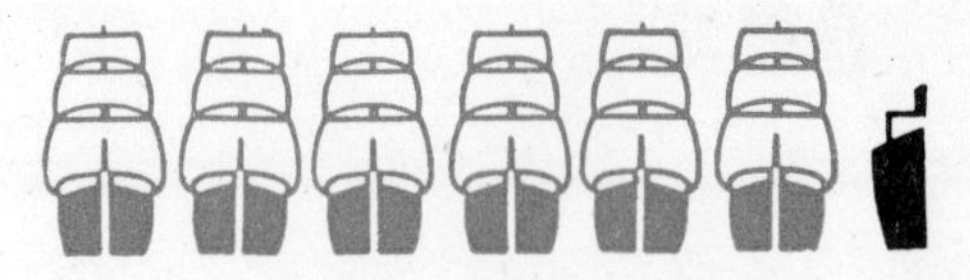

1860

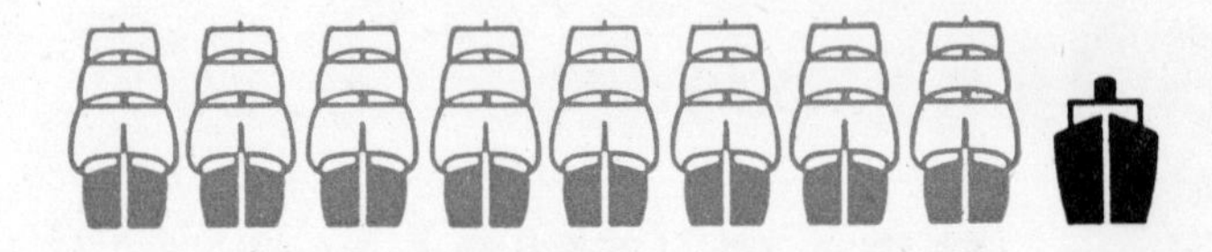

1870

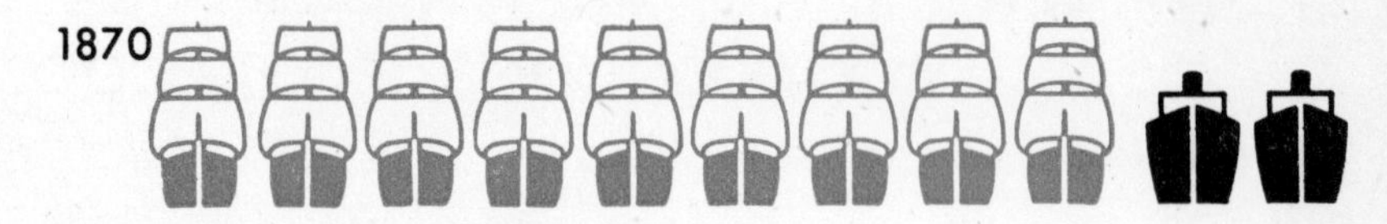

Each symbol represents 500,000 tons

Shipbuilding

sailing ships steamships

1840

1850

1860

1870

Each symbol represents 50,000 tons

ISOTYPE INSTITUTE

Imports of Wool

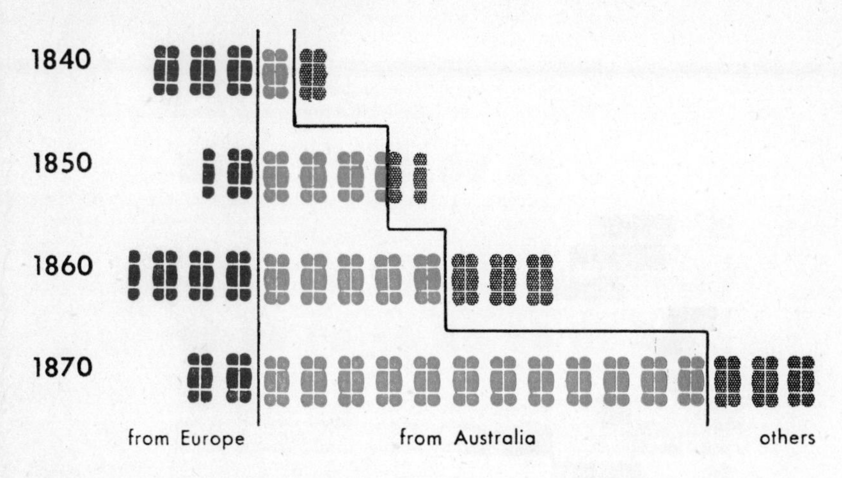

Each symbol represents 10 million lbs.

Exports of Woollen Goods

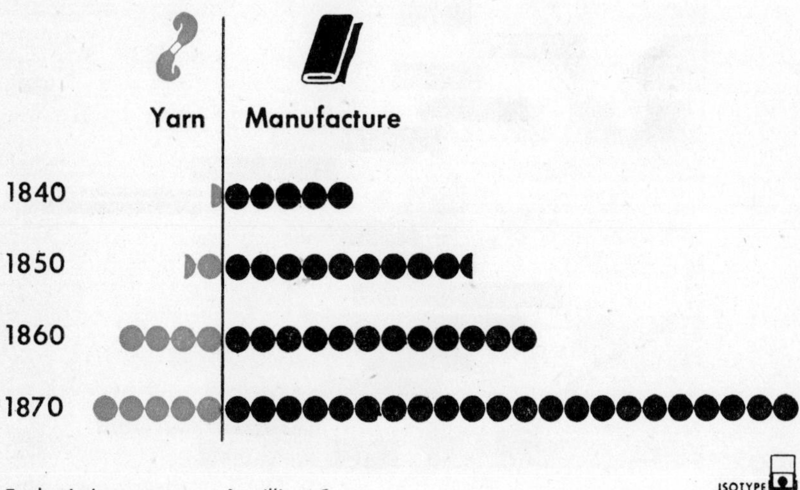

Each circle represents 1 million £

CHART IX

Fluctuations in Wheat Imports

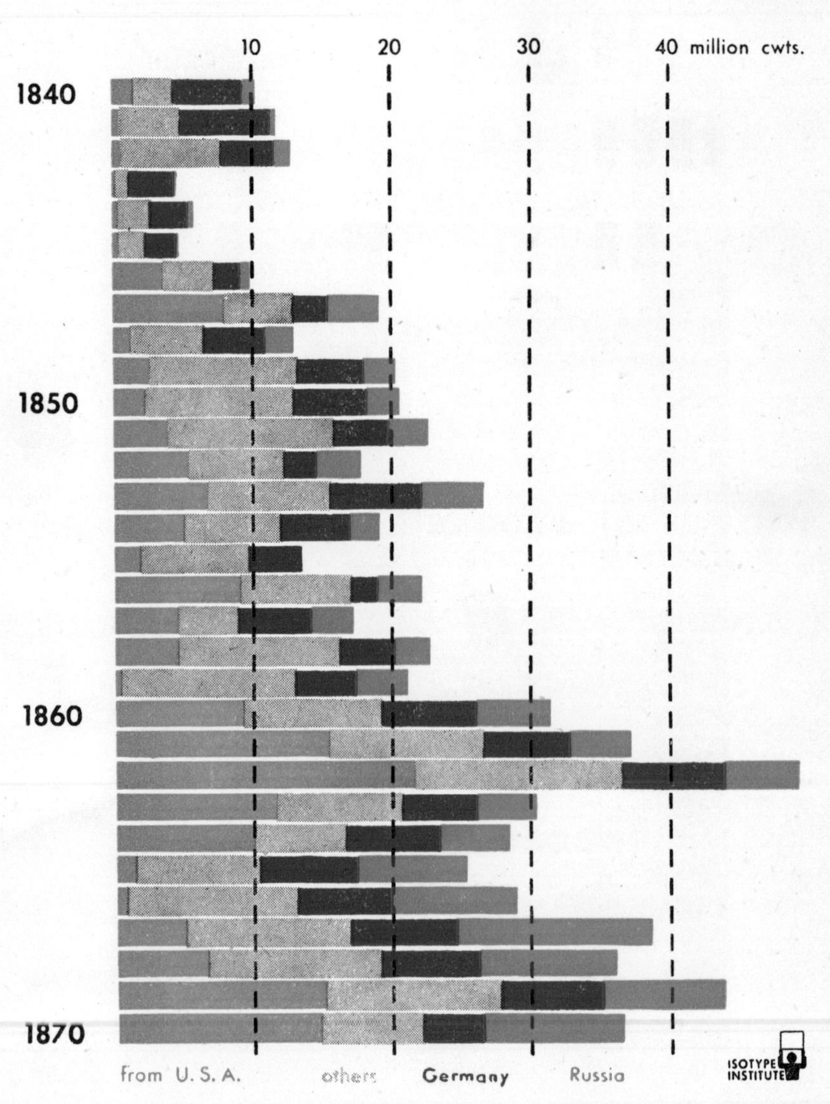

CHART X

Fluctuations in Cotton Imports

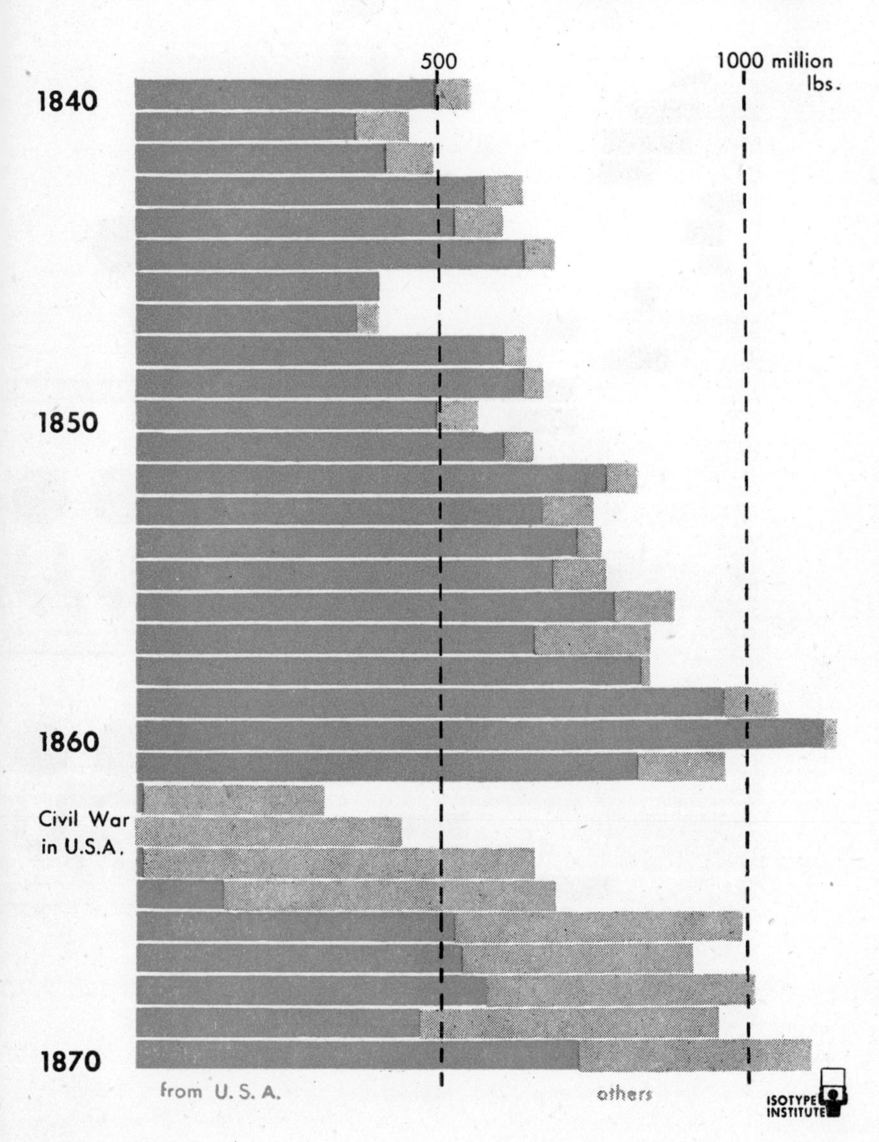

Railways in the United Kingdom

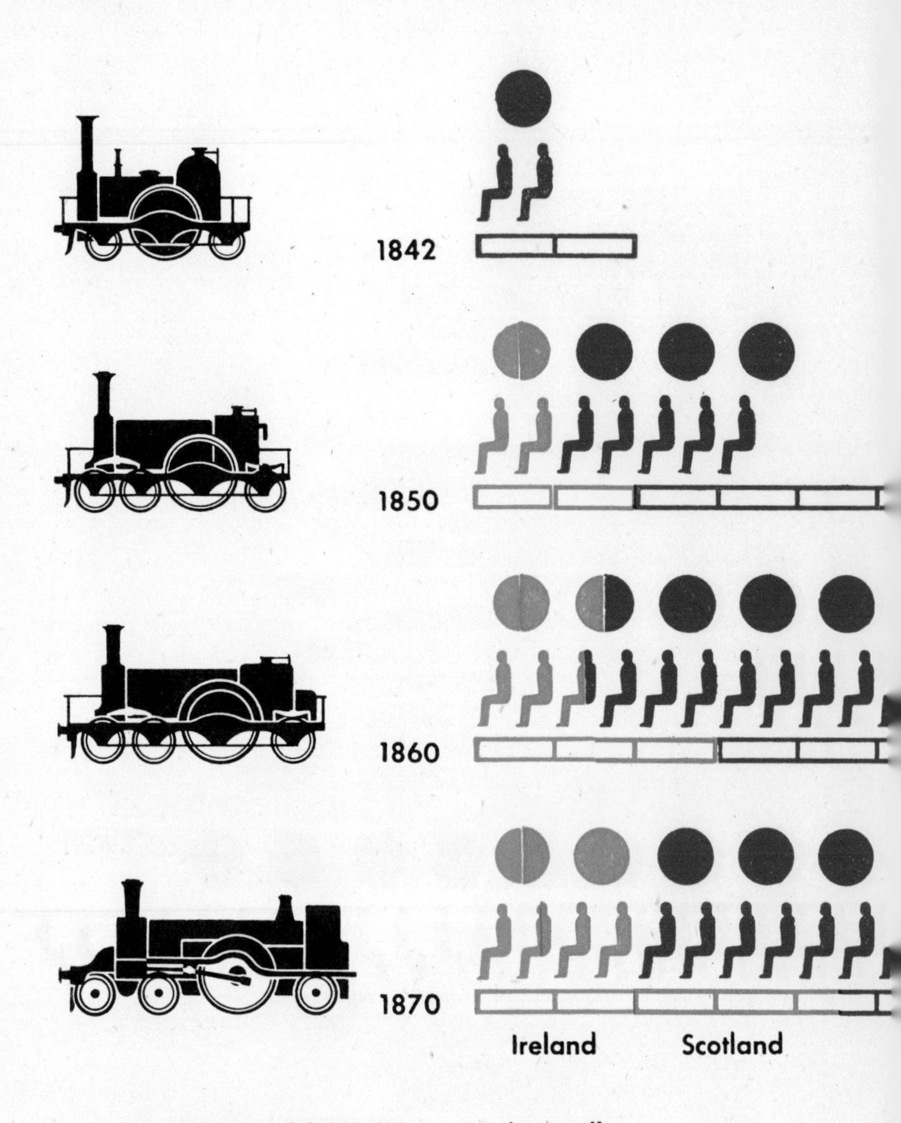

Each circle represents £ 3,000,000 receipts from traffic
Each man symbol represents 10 million passengers
Each unit of length represents 1000 miles of line

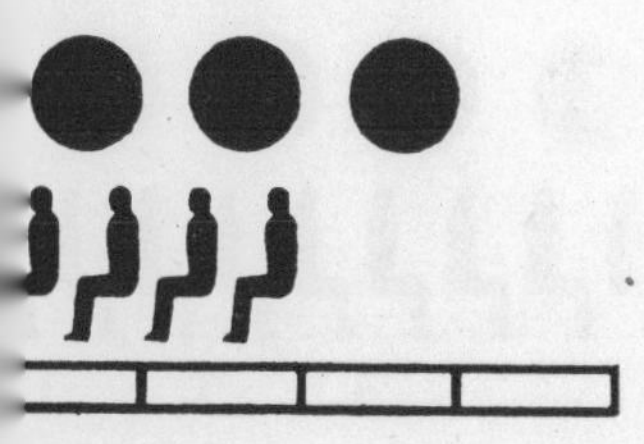

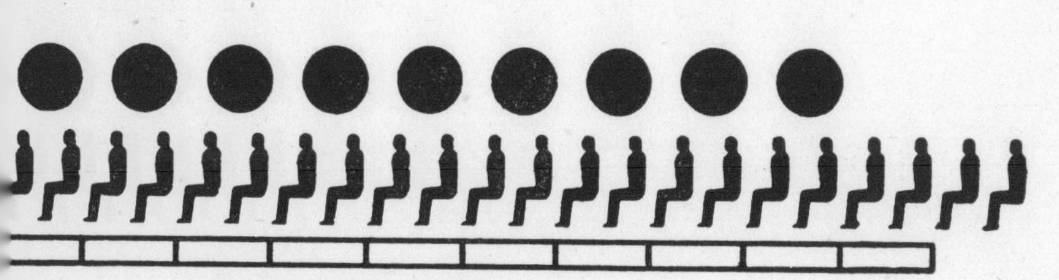

England and Wales

green: Ireland
blue: Scotland
red: England and Wales

CHART XII

Value of U.K. Imports and Exports

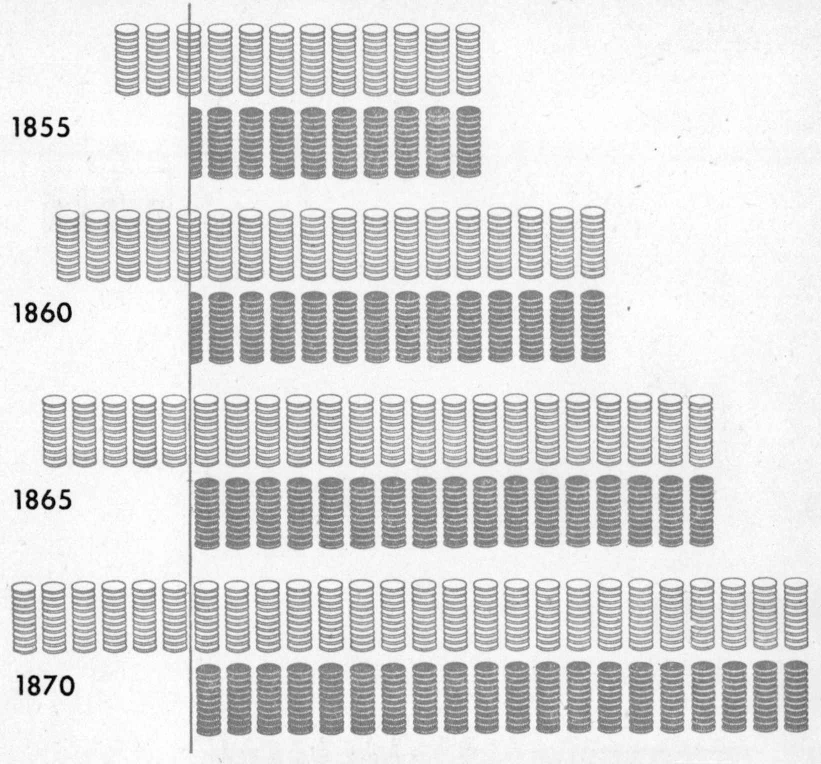

Each group of outline coins represents £10 million of Imports
Each group of full coins represents £10 million of Exports

U. K. Coal Exports

1840
1850
1860
1870

U. K. Iron and Steel Exports

1840
1850
1860
1870

Each circle represents £1 million

Home and Factory Weaving in England

1830

1845

1860

1880

Each blue symbol represents 50 million lbs. total production
Each black man symbol represents 10,000 home weavers
Each red man symbol represents 10,000 factory weavers

CHART XIV

Coffee, Tea, Sugar Consumption per head of the population

The symbols represent : 1 lb. for Coffee and Tea
5 lbs. for Sugar

Wine, Spirits, Tobacco Consumption per head of the population

The symbols represent : 1 pint for Wine and Spirits
2 ozs. for Tobacco